A HISTORY OF
THE ICONOCLASTIC
CONTROVERSY

AMS PRESS
NEW YORK

A HISTORY OF THE ICONOCLASTIC CONTROVERSY

BY

EDWARD JAMES MARTIN, D.D.

SOMETIME SCHOLAR OF ORIEL COLLEGE, OXFORD

Published for the Church Historical Society

LONDON

SOCIETY FOR PROMOTING CHRISTIAN KNOWLEDGE

NEW YORK AND TORONTO: THE MACMILLAN CO.

Library of Congress Cataloging in Publication Data

Martin, Edward James.
   A history of the iconoclastic controversy.

   Reprint of the 1930 ed. published by the Society
for Promoting Christian Knowledge, London, which
was issued as new series 2 of the Church Historical
Society's publications.
   Includes index.
   1. Iconoclasm. I. Title. II. Series: The
Church Historical Society (Gt. Brit.). Publica-
tions; new ser. 2.
BR238.M3   1978   248   77-84711
ISBN 0-404-16117-0

Reprinted from an original in the collections of
the University of Michigan Library.

Reprinted from the edition of 1930, London.
First AMS edition published in 1978.

Manufactured in the United States of America.

AMS PRESS, INC.
NEW YORK, N.Y.

PREFACE

FOR the English reader the Iconoclastic Controversy is illuminating in more ways than one. It reveals the Orthodox Eastern Church in its complete development, its sense of theology by the side of its taste for superstition, its tenacious loyalty to Christ co-existent with its judicious respect for Cæsar. It reveals also in that Church's sphere of influence an Oriental ferocity, shared alike by orthodox, heretic, and unbeliever, shocking to the Western mind. The West could reconcile itself even to the Inquisition, but only by concealing the torture-chamber and the stake behind an elaborate and impersonal legal system. How far this picture of the Eastern Church is still true is a question that of necessity must be faced if Christendom seeks either co-operation or Reunion between East and West.

The reader will, it is hoped, make allowance for the inordinate fullness of reference given in the footnotes. The excuse is that this is a field into which few English students have ventured. Even Bury was content to look at the Second Council of Nicæa from a distance and pass on, while hardly any one has appreciated the philosophic realism of the *Caroline Books* or the very Anglican temper of Claudius of Turin.

My thanks are due to the *Church Historical Society*, which has made the publication of this book possible, and to the Librarians of the London Library, and of Dr. Williams' Library, who have made it easy to consult some of the less accessible material.

CONTENTS

BIBLIOGRAPHY

This Bibliography gives only (i) for the original authorities the texts used, and (ii) for modern writers a general list. The authorities are discussed fully and the more important modern articles on special points are described at the beginning of each chapter.

AUTHORITIES

(a) GREEK

Adversus Constantinum Caballinum. M.P.G. 95.
Cedrenus. Historiarum Compendium. Vol. I. M.P.G. 121.
Conciliorum Amplissima Collectio. ed. J. D. Mansi. Vols. XII, XIII. 1759-1798.
Epistola ad Theophilum. M.P.G. 95.
Genesios, Joseph. Reges. M.P.G. 109.
Georgius Monachus. ed. de Boor. 2 vols. Leipzig, 1904.
Joannes Damascenus. Πρὸς τούς διαβάλλοντας. M.P.G. 94.
Nicephorus. Opera. M.P.G. 100.
Simeon Magister :
    Leo Grammaticus. M.P.G. 108.
    Additions to Georg. Mon. M.P.G. 109.
ps-Simeon. M.P.G. 109.
Scriptor Ignotus de Leone Bardæ f. M.P.G. 108.
Theodorus Studites :
    Opera. M.P.G. 99.
    Epistolæ. ed. Mai. Nov. Bib. Patrum, vol. 8. Rome, 1871.
Theophanes, Chronographia. M.P.G. 100. Also ed. de Boor. 2 vols. Leipzig, 1883/5.
Theophanes Continuatus. M.P.G. 109.
Acta Sanctorum. Bollandist.
For hagiological writings see authorities for each chapter.

(b) LATIN

Liber Pontificalis. ed. Duchesne. Vol. I. Paris, 1886.
Libri Carolini. ed. Heumann. Hanover, 1731.
Codex Carolinus. ed. Gundlach. M.G.H. Ep. III.
Hadriani, Pap. Epistola ad Carolum. Mansi, vol. XIII.
Dungal. M.P.L. 105.
Claudius Tauronensis. M.P.L. 105.
Agobard. M.P.L. 104.

ix

Jonas Epis. Aurelianensis. M.P.L. 106.
Walafrid Strabo. M.G.H. Leg. II, Cap. Reg. Franc. II. ed. Krause.
Monuments Germ. Hist. Concilia. Leg. sect. III, vol. II, part 2,
ed. Werminghoff.

MODERN WORKS.

(a) GENERAL HISTORIES

Of the general Histories the most useful are :

Cambridge Medieval History. Vol. IV. Cambridge, 1923.
DIEHL, C. Histoire de l'Empire byzantine. Paris, 1919.
   „   Byzance, grandeur et décadence. Paris, 1919.
FINLAY, G. History of Greece. Vol. III. Oxford, 1877. Reprinted
   in Everyman Lib. as The Byzantine Empire. Finlay is very
   valuable for the Isaurian Emperors.
GIBBON, E. The Decline and Fall of the Roman Empire. ed. Bury,
   J. B. 7 vols. London, 1896. The only value of Gibbon for this
   period is in Bury's notes.
GIESELER, J. C. L. Compendium of Ecclesiastical History. 5 vols.
   Eng. trans. Edinburgh, 1846.
HARNACK, A. History of Dogma. Eng. trans. Vols. IV and V.
   London, 1899. For the Iconoclastic period Harnack depends on
   Schwarzlose.
HEFELE, C. J. VON. History of the Councils. Eng. trans. Vol. V.
   Edinburgh, 1896. French trans. ed. Leclerq. Vols. III (2) and
   IV (1). Paris, 1910. Leclerq's notes are valuable but unduly
   prolix.
KRUGER, G. Handbuch der Kirchengeschichte. Zweiter Teil. Ficker
   u. Hermenlink. Tübingen, 1912.
NEANDER, A. General History of the Christian Religion and Church.
   9 vols. Eng. trans. London, 1876. Full and good on this period.
OMAN, C. W. C. Byzantine Empire. 2nd ed. London, 1897.
PARGOIRE, J. L'Empire byzantine. 3ème ed. Paris, 1923.
SCHAFF, P. History of the Christian Church. Mediæval Christianity.
   2 vols. Edinburgh, 1885.
WALCH, C. W. F. Historie der Ketzereien. Vols. X and XI. Leipzig,
   1782. Very full and sound. Not yet superseded.

(b) SPECIAL WORKS ON THE ICONOCLASTIC PERIOD

BRÉHIER, L. La querelle des Images. Paris, 1904.
BURY, J. B. History of the Later Roman Empire. 2 vols. London,
   1889.
BURY, J. B. History of the Eastern Roman Empire. London, 1912.
GARDNER, A. Theodore of Studium. London, 1905.
HIRSCH, F. Byz. Studien. Leipzig, 1876.
HODGKIN, T. Italy and her Invaders. Vols. VI, VII, VIII. Oxford, 1898.
LOMBARD, A. Constantin V. Paris, 1902.
MANN, II. K. Lives of the Popes. Vols. I (2) and II. London, 1903.
MARIN, E. Les Moines de Constantinople. Paris, 1897.
SCHWARZLOSE, K. Der Bilderstreit. Gotha, 1890. This supersedes
   all the older works.

(c) ART AND ARCHÆOLOGY

BEYLIÉ, C. L'Habitation byzantine. Paris, 1912.
BRÉHIER, L. L'Art chrétien. Paris, 1918.
BRITISH MUSEUM. Guide to Early Christian and Byzantine Antiquities. 2nd ed. London, 1921.
DALTON, O. M. Byzantine Art and Archæology. Oxford, 1911.
DIEHL, C. Manuel d'Art byzantin. Paris, 1910.
LOWRIE, W. Christian Art and Archæology. New York, 1901.

(d) WORKS OF REFERENCE

COBHAM, C. D. The Patriarchs of Constantinople. Cambridge, 1911.
GINZEL, F. K. Handbuch der mathematischen u. technischen Chronologie. Vol. III. Leipzig, 1914.
FABRICIUS, J. A. Bibliotheca Græca. 14 vols. Hamburg, 1708.
HERZOG, J. J., u. HAUCK, A. Realencyclopädie für prot. Theologie u. Kirche. Gotha, 1896-1909.
MAS LATRIE, J. M. J. L. DE. Trésor de Chronologie, d'Histoire et de Géographie. Paris, 1889.
SMITH, W., and WACE, H. Dictionary of Christian Biography. 4 vols. London, 1877-87.
SMITH, W., and CHEETHAM, S. Dictionary of Christian Antiquities. 2 vols. London, 1875-80. Both the latter are largely superseded by Hauck, but many articles remain of permanent value. Hastings, J. Encyclopædia of Religion and Ethics, Edinburgh, 1908-1921, has nothing of any great importance relating to our subject.
SPRUNER-MENKE. Handatlas für die Geschichte des Mittelalters u. der neueren Zeit. Gotha, 1880.
WROTH, W. Cat. of Imp. Byzantine Coins in Brit. Mus. 2 vols. London, 1908.

For magazine articles, see authorities for the separate chapters.

ABBREVIATIONS

The following abbreviations are used :

Bury-Gibbon = Gibbon's Decline and Fall. ed. Bury.
D.C.A. = Smith and Cheetham, Dict. of Christian Antiquities.
D.C.B. = Smith and Wace, Dict. of Christian Biography.
Hefele-Leclerq = Hefele's History of the Councils. French trans.
    ed. H. Leclerq.
M.G.H. = Monumenta Germanicæ Historiæ.
M.P.G. = Migne, Patrologia Græca.
M.P.L. = Migne, Patrologia Latina.
R.E. = Hauck, Realencyclopädie f. prot. Theologie.

A HISTORY OF THE ICONOCLASTIC CONTROVERSY

CHAPTER I

INTRODUCTION

THE Iconoclastic Controversy is in some ways the beginning of the vague period called the Middle Ages. It is quite clear that the capture of Constantinople by the Turks in 1453 and the uneasy ferment of ideas fifty years earlier when Huss carried further the tradition of Wyclif marked the end of an age. With the Renaissance and Reformation a new Europe is shaped. The essential character of the change is an assault on the body of thought which was enshrined in the mediæval Church, and displayed visibly in the Papacy. It is the Papacy as the embodiment of Christian thought that gives homogeneity to the Middle Ages. The Papacy, it is true, does not stand unchallenged during that period ; it meets with some of its most ignominious encounters and reaches some of its most contemptible levels. But it is the fixed element in a constantly changing Europe. And it is the standard of thought to which new ideas must be related. The Papacy dominates the intellectual world. That does not imply that the Papacy itself was a great intellectual machine. But it was the responsible head of Christendom, with which all thought during those centuries must come to terms. The period in which the Papacy made for itself this position may therefore be considered the beginning of the Middle Ages. The Iconoclastic Controversy is the chief ecclesiastical event of that period and was a strong contributing cause of the development of the unique sovereignty which the Papacy exercised in mediæval Europe.

The Iconoclastic Controversy also helps to explain the

comparative futility of the Roman Empire, and the decadence of the Church in Eastern Europe. In a sense the Papacy was the real heir of the Empire, but throughout the Middle Ages the Empire itself continued to live, with its seat at Constantinople, and orthodoxy as one of its main supports. It maintained a level of culture and refinement to which no part of Western Europe approached. But it was almost entirely barren. The seeds of all new thought continued to come from the East, but it was within the range of the Papacy that they germinated. Western Christianity, though in its theory as rigid as that of the Empire, was a more fertile soil for the development of ideas.

Progress of thought was no easier in the West than in the East. The policy of authority in both quarters was suppression. In the eyes of the dominant Christian authority new thought was heterodox thought, and as such was wrong, because it implied thinking outside of the fixed limits. So that the term " heresy " covers every kind of original thinking ; progress in idea has for that reason to be sought first among heretical thinkers. The reason that Western Europe got further than the thinkers of the East was partly the stronger creative faculty of the West, partly a larger reasonableness in the ultimate ecclesiastical authority.

The general result, however, was to throw into one confusing heap the good and the bad, the rational inquiry and the eccentric speculation. The natural reaction of man is to see in consequence profound wisdom in every speculation that bears the seductive stigma of heresy and barren obscurantism in every authoritative declaration of the orthodox. So that Gibbon finds in the Paulicians a delightful idyll of primitive Christianity, and Protestants like Spanheim credit Iconoclasm with a noble anticipation of the principles of the Reformation.

What we can say with reason is that mediæval heresy is usually an effort towards intellectual liberty, that the immediate result of every effective heretical outbreak was a temporary mental and moral improvement, and that all the sporadic outbursts from Iconoclasm to Wyclif are related to each other. In some dim fashion they represent an identical spirit, continuous throughout Christian history, seeking to express and supply the demands made by reason upon an authority the ultimate rational foundation of which its upholders have at the moment failed to understand.

Iconoclasm was a mixture of religion and politics, for in Constantinople the two were inseparable. The political effects present no obscurity. Western Europe, with its trick of turning the speculation of the East to active ends, found in Iconoclasm a means to immense social and political progress. It is true that in the West some disputations took place about images, but they caused no violence and comparatively little interest. What did happen as a direct result of the controversy was that a succession of able bishops occupied the Papal See, created the temporal power of the Papacy, greatly increased its spiritual ascendancy, turned their backs upon the Roman Emperor in Constantinople, and set up the empire of Charles. The fruit of an eastern idea was gathered once again in Western Europe. Its own harvest was a barren one. Thanks to the Iconoclastic Emperors the Empire rose to one of its most brilliant periods. But the actual effects of the struggle in secular politics were almost entirely negative. Constantinople was alienated further from Western Europe ; her conservative tradition was deepened. Moreover, the controversy made explicit the exact nature of the fatal ecclesiastical outlook of Constantinople. This consists in the idea that the Church will always express the ideals of the dynasty. It is common to orthodox and heterodox. It might be called Erastianism if such an idea had then come into being. The view finds few opponents. One or two do stand out, Theodore Studites, and the Emperor Michael the Amorian, the latter of whom seems to have failed to realise his ideal more fully because of his dislike of the clergy. Ultimately for these reasons Iconoclasm was the true cause of the breach with the West and of the paralysis of the Orthodox Church.

In the realm of thought, however, Iconoclasm counted probably for less than any of the heterodox movements that invaded the Church. It was in itself of little importance intellectually. It did not command the allegiance of a single intellectual leader at its birth. It broke out in a barbarous age when the seventh century closed on what Bury calls " perhaps the darkest age of Europe within historical times." [1] Within the Empire literature was practically dead. Iconoclasm did revive the stagnant intellect of the Empire. But the revival was not in the ranks of its supporters but in the ranks of its opponents. The two chief literary names of the eighth century are Theophanes and Nicephorus,[2] the outstanding champions of orthodoxy. Theophanes, if no great writer, is a respectable chronicler, and Nicephorus is the equal of all but the greatest of the Fathers. Intellectual curiosity was practically dead. On the orthodox side there is scarcely a sign of it. Glimpses are shown by a few of the Iconoclasts, the Emperors Constantine V and Theophilus, and the Patriarch John the Grammarian, but all three awake the suspicion that they are not so much Iconoclasts as independent thinkers, outside the mass of their party. The genius of Iconoclasm, being entirely negative and destructive, and being concerned primarily with visible objects and not with ideas, could hardly achieve great intellectual successes. It scarcely went beyond a measure of common-sense interpretation of Scripture and a common-sense rejection of the more extravagant eccentricities of popular devotion. It had not intellectual support strong enough even to bring its own case down to first principles. It was really a Philistine movement preferring Force to Reason. The best that can be said of Iconoclasm intellectually is that it failed to make the rational appeal it might have done, but it may have failed deliberately, because there was no audience that an appeal to Reason could touch.

[1] *The Later Roman Empire*, I, 337.
[2] I omit St. John Damascene as living outside the Empire.

CHAPTER II

THE END OF THE SEVENTH CENTURY

ACCORDING to the view of Gibbon, the Roman Empire, after existing not more than four centuries,[1] spent 1200 years over the process of decay. It would be a more truthful paradox to say that the Roman Empire only entered on its inheritance when Rome was abandoned and the Latin language ignored. After the line of Western Emperors closed with the apposite name of Romulus Augustulus, all that the Empire stood for burst into fullest life.

It is unnecessary to vindicate the later Empire from Gibbon's casual summary as " a tedious and uniform tale of weakness and misery." The defence of the Empire has been successfully made by a lengthening line of historians, conspicuous among whom are Diehl and Bury. But there is still an element of truth in Gibbon's view. For a thousand years Constantinople maintained a tradition of dignity and culture, at times of magnificence. But often its culture and its magnificence were barren. Like Constantinople itself, the Roman Empire of this period was a thing neither of nationality nor race. It was Greek only in language. It kept alive a literary tradition, but it had no originality and little inspiration. It performed acts of great military prowess, but they were almost entirely operations carried out in self-defence, too often in the desperation of the last ditch. It upheld the old Roman law and it lived in the prestige of the Roman name, but it developed steadily into an Oriental power, turned away from Europe towards Asia. As the centre of the world shifted towards North-West Europe, the Empire became more and more of a fabulous fairyland. It was a remarkable monument of

---

[1] *I.e.* from the battle of Zama, 202 B.C., to the death of Marcus Aurelius A.D. 180.

5

civilisation, but it was a monument rather than a thing of life. And the Orthodox Eastern Church, which has outlived the Empire, still bears the mark of the Empire, magnificent but Oriental, and still breathing the atmosphere of the fifth century.

Gibbon's indictment is thus partly true. The Empire was not uniformly futile, but it had little dynamic or creative force, and after Justinian it almost ceased to have any influence on the life of Europe. It could draw individuals into itself and civilise them into its life ; it could not radiate its life outside. Frederic Harrison claims that during " the eighth, ninth, and tenth centuries the Roman Empire on the Bosphorus was far the most stable, and cultured power in the world." This is true, but it would be more difficult to justify his inference that " on its existence hung the future of civilisation." [1]

There is, however, little doubt that with the eighth century began one of the greatest periods of the Empire. The seventh century had been a catastrophe. The evolution of the Empire as a purely Oriental state, which began with the foundation of Constantinople, was temporarily checked by Justinian (518–565), who desired to be, and actually was, the last of the great Roman emperors. In the next hundred years the original tendency continued with increasing rapidity. " The Empire paid dearly for the lofty ambitions of Justinian. After his death, his work was wound up with disastrous effects. Internally the Imperial exchequer and the Imperial army were exhausted. Outside the Persian menace became critical, and was only checked by Heraclius after a threat of disaster so grave that the Emperor seriously contemplated removing his capital to Carthage. Before long the still more terrible flood of the Saracen invasion broke upon the Empire. Religious disunion, following the controversies on the Person of Christ, aggravated the political anarchy. In Byzantine history the seventh century (610–717) is one of the darkest periods, a gravely critical epoch, a decisive moment when it seemed that the very existence of the Empire was at stake." [2]

Heraclius (610–641), by a strong military and religious

[1] *Byzantine History in the Early Middle Ages* (London, 1900), p. 11.
[2] Diehl, C., *Byzance*, p. 8.

policy, succeeded in saving the situation for the time. But the Empire was forced to draw in its borders in the face of the Saracens in the East and the Lombards in the West. " Its territory was reduced to Asia Minor, the Balkan Peninsula, and the exarchate of Ravenna, and even that restricted dominion was threatened in every quarter, by Lombards, by Slavs, by Saracens, and by Bulgars. Hitherto the monarchy had preserved its œcumenical character as the Roman Empire ; now it became literally the Byzantine Empire, with all its powers concentrated on Constantinople." [1]

In the seventy years following Heraclius twelve emperors reigned, for the most part in anarchy. The whole moral tone degenerated. Superstition increased. The Iconoclastic struggle will reveal something of this, not merely among the ignorant but among the more intelligent classes. In 717 a horrible example of superstitious credulity is recorded. The inhabitants of Pergamus, besieged by the Saracens, cut open a pregnant girl and boiled the pieces of the unborn child ; the soldiers then dipped their gauntlets in the mixture as a means of strengthening their hands to fight. [2] Further, in Bury's phrase, " Credulity was generally accompanied by moral obliquity."[3] Legislation occurs during this period against clerks bathing with women, keeping brothels, attending race-meetings and the theatre, and following the trade of usurer, as well as against the practice of anchorites taking periodical holidays in the world. [4] The Ecloga of the Isaurian Emperors seems to be partly an attempt to meet the moral decay by revising the law of persons in a Christian direction, notably on such matters as marriage and fornication. [5] Manners had become more savage. The frequent military revolts of the last quarter of the seventh century point to a serious diminution of loyalty.

Learning had all but ceased. There is practically not a single writer in the latter part of the century. The old tradition revives in the eighth with George the Syncellus, Theophanes, who is at least a lucid and competent chronicler,

[1] Diehl, *op. cit.*, p. 9.
[2] Nicephorus, *Brev.*, 957b.
[3] *Op. cit.*, II, p. 387.
[4] Quinisext Council, Canons 9, 10, 24, 51, 77, 86.
[5] Bury, *op. cit.*, II, pp. 416 *sqq.*

Nicephorus the Patriarch, who aims at writing correct Greek, and Theodore Studites, a writer of vigorous mind and expression; and by the ninth century the highest standards are recovered in Photius, a scholar who would have been remarkable in any period.

It seems quite clear that the schools with which the Isaurian Emperors interfered were barren institutions, producing nothing, while, on the other hand, it was the energy of the Iconoclastic period that led to a revival both of literature and science. The ninth century is notable for the enthusiasm for science shown by such figures as Leo the Mathematician and the Patriarch John the Grammarian. The common bond which drew together the Emperor Theophilus and his opponent, the future patriarch Methodius, was probably an interest in natural science.[1]

Out of the trough in which the Empire laboured at the end of the seventh century it rose, in some ways having undergone permanent changes. New settlers appeared within its borders. The Slavs took up their quarters in the Balkans, Serbs and Croats in the north-west, Bulgars in the north-east. The Slavs soon gave conspicuous figures to Imperial history, the earliest of whom were Nicetas the Patriarch and Basil the founder of a dynasty. In the administration of the Empire the exigencies of defence in the troubles with which the seventh century closed made it necessary to concentrate all power upon the high officers of the army. The consequence of this was that the system of Themes became the permanent organisation of the Empire.

In the social sphere we have noticed some of the temporary changes. More permanent was the increase of a Greek element, which, if effecting nothing else, made the literary use of Latin entirely obsolete. In the Christian Church monasticism advanced and became the dominant force.[2]

Politically the greatest change was a steady widening of the breach with Rome, in consequence - of which the

---

[1] ἀπόκρυφα ζητήματα, " the occult," is the phrase of Genesios, 1088b.
[2] The advance of monasticism is seen in the increase of hagiography. The period of Iconoclasm and Photius gives 60 lives of Saints compared with 13 for the seventh century and 11 for the tenth.

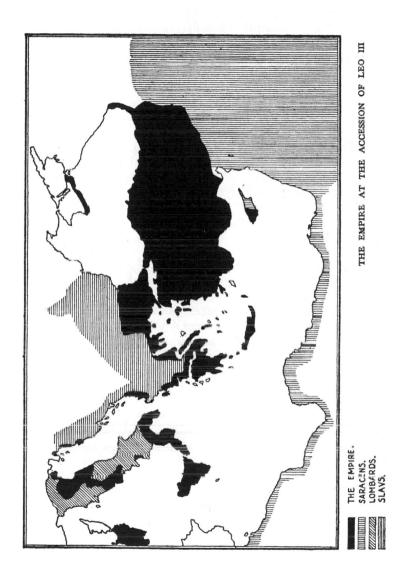

THE EMPIRE AT THE ACCESSION OF LEO III

THE EMPIRE.
SARACENS.
LOMBARDS.
SLAVS.

Empire became more and more Oriental in character and the Emperor more and more of an Oriental despot.

Thus what actually rises from the chaos of the seventh century is the Byzantine Empire, a cosmopolitan Power, Oriental in outlook, greatly reduced in size, but more compact, and when relieved of the dead weight of the West and the separatist tendencies of the East, a power well suited to the guidance of a capable hand. That capable hand it found in Leo, the founder of the Isaurian dynasty.[1]

The map of the Empire provides the clearest elucidation of the position. The dominion to which the Isaurian succeeded was entirely Oriental. Britain, Germany, Gaul, and Spain had long ceased to be part of the Empire. Italy which Justinian recovered from the Ostrogoths, within three years of his death (565) fell to the Lombards. The Empire retained only small parts of the country, in the north-east the territory on the Adriatic, Venetia, the Ravenna district, and the Pentapolis, in Central Italy the Ducatus of Rome, and in the south the toe and heel (Calabria and Brutii) with a strip in the neighbourhood of Naples, and the islands of Sicily and Sardinia. In the tragic seventh century Syria, Egypt, and Africa fell to the Saracens ; Asia Minor remained intact as far as Armenia in the east and the mountains of Cilicia in the south-east, but on the European side the Bulgarians had crossed the Danube and were steadily pressing the frontier nearer to Macedonia, while other Slavs were eating the heart out of the Adriatic side of the peninsula.

No little religious disunion helped to increase the chaos. Monophysitism had already weakened the three ancient Patriarchates of Antioch, Alexandria, and Jerusalem, and when they fell under Mohammedan rule they were all but completely cut off from intercourse with their fellow-Christians of the Empire. So jealously indeed were they watched, that the messengers of the Emperors failed to reach any one of the three Patriarchs with the letters inviting them to assent to the summoning of the Council of Nicæa.[2] The ultimate effect was that the Patriarch of Constantinople, whose relationship to the Emperor gave a peculiar character to the Church over which he presided, lost the corrective

---

[1] Diehl, *op. cit.*, pp. 9, 10.   [2] Mansi, XII, 1127.

of association with his equals, became entirely an Imperial official,[1] and eventually gave the whole Eastern Church that quality of immobility, mixed with opportunism, which became its fixed characteristic. The one hope for the Church of Constantinople was close co-operation with Rome. That hope the events of the eighth century destroyed. The breach of East and West was not really the result of heresy or misunderstanding. It was the result of Imperial policy, blindly accepted by the Church. After the event the Church of Constantinople appealed to questions of doctrine to explain a position which was created not by religion but by politics.

[1] The Patriarchate of Constantinople always had that character, and even justified its claim to the title of Patriarchate by quoting Constantine I as the founder of the Church in the city and giving him the title Ἰσαπόστολος.

CHAPTER III

THE OUTBREAK OF ICONOCLASM

The Authorities for Chapters III and IV may be taken together :

(a) PRIMARY AUTHORITIES

1. Theophanes, *Chronographia*.[1] For Texts, see Bibliography. This is our chief authority. It is the continuation of the Chronicle of George, syncellus of the Patriarch Tarasius. On the death of George, Theophanes continued his work from the accession of Diocletian to the reign of Leo the Armenian. The date at which Theophanes wrote was 811/815. He died in 817, a confessor for the cause of Images. He is thus a first-hand witness for the orthodox revival under Irene and the subsequent history. For the period of Leo III and Constantine V he followed the same sources as Nicephorus, probably official records. Theophanes seems to have had access to more material, for he records facts omitted by Nicephorus and at times shows traces of more than one source for the same event. Thus 880b, 881b, and 893b appear to give two accounts of the conspiracy of Constantine Podopagouros, not completely harmonised. Theophanes, apart from his obvious bias against the Iconoclasts, gives the impression of a cautious and honest chronicler. Up to the reign of Leo the Armenian he takes first place.

Theophanes uses a very complicated system of chronology. The basis is the Alexandrian world Era in which A.M. 5501 = A.D. 9. Occasionally he adds the Indiction, which is a cycle of fifteen years related to no chronological event, used by the Imperial government for purposes of taxation. The Indiction runs from Sept. 1st, the Alexandrian A.M. from March 25th, but Theophanes probably dates the latter for Calendar purposes from Sept. 1st,[2] to correspond with the Indiction. In addition he sometimes equates his date to a year of the Incarnation which corresponds with A.D. 9. Regnal years of Emperors and Caliphs together with subsidiary records of the years of office of the principal bishops complicate his system still further. In two periods (607–714 and 726–774) the A.M. and the Indictions do not correspond.[3] It was formerly supposed that the Indictions

---

[1] The Latin version by Anastasius Bibliothecarus (circa 886) is sometimes useful.

[2] Bury implies that Theophanes always counts the A.M. from March 25th (Bury-Gibbon, V, 500), but Ginzel, *op. cit.* p. 290, says Sept. 1st.

[3] To find the Indiction add one to the A.M. and divide by fifteen. The remainder is the Indiction number.

were most likely to be correct, and therefore they must be made the foundation for a true chronology. But a suggestion was made by Bury (*Later Roman Empire*, II, p. 425), and worked out by Hubert (*Byzant. Zeitschrift*, VI, pp. 491 *sqq.*), that in 726 Leo III raised double taxes and put two indictions in one year, while in 774 or 775, Constantine remitted a year's taxation and spread one indiction over two years. This suggestion has been generally accepted. On the other hand, it is purely conjectural. Ginis (*Das Promulgationsjahr d. Isaur. Ecloge. Byz. Zeitsch.*, XXIV, pp. 346 *sqq.*) would trace the error to Theophanes having confused the April of Indiction 10 (Sept. 1st, 726, to Aug. 31st, 727), with April of the 10th regnal year of Leo (March 25th, 725, to March 24th, 726). E. W. Brooks (*Byz. Zeitsch.*, VIII, pp. 82 *sqq.*) explains the error by differences in the chronological systems of the sources used by Theophanes. An indisputable date is the death of the Patriarch Nicetas, Feb. 6th, 780. He was consecrated on Nov. 16th, in a year of which Theophanes gives the Indiction as 5 and the A.M. as 6258. He held the see for fourteen years. The year then of his consecration according to Brooks would be 766, and Theophanes' Indiction is right. But the exact period of his episcopate is unknown. From Nov. 16th, 766, to Feb. 6th, 780, might be described as fourteen (incomplete) years. But from Nov. 16th, 765, might also be counted as fourteen years.[1] As Constantine held the see for twelve years and Anastasius for twenty-four, the other leading dates would be fixed according to Brooks' reckoning as 754 for the Iconoclastic Council, and 730 for the deposition of Germanus. Unfortunately Bury is inclined for other reasons to accept 730 (see p. 33, *infra*), thus introducing an inconsistency into his chronology. A certain amount of contributory weight in fixing the date of these episcopal consecrations is to be allowed in favour of the year in which the alleged month date fell on a Sunday. Brooks uses this in establishing the consecration of Nicetas and Bury in establishing that of Anastasius. But all that can be said is that Sunday was a customary but not invariable day for consecrations ; the Iconoclastic Emperors after making uncanonical appointments might ignore the customary day. The argument from the day of the week presents one strong support for Bury's dating of the Iconoclastic Council, *i.e.* 753, which does not seem to have been noticed. The Council opened on Feb. 10th. In 754, the old date which Brooks supports, Feb. 10th fell on a Sunday, an unlikely day for the opening of a Council. On the whole the soundest line seems to be to follow Bury's theory consistently (whether the explanation of it be the doubling of the Indiction or not). This has been done by Paigoire, who has a consistent if at times improbable chronology.

2. Nicephorus.—Nicephorus was the great champion of orthodoxy of a moderate cast. He had been present at the Council of Nicæa in 787, and became Patriarch of Constantinople in 806. In 815 he was deposed for his resistance to Leo the Armenian, and died in exile in 829. (1) Two short historical works of his exist. (*a*) Χρονογραφικὸν σύντομον, which is simply a list of dates. (*b*) Ἱστορία σύντομος, a brief

---

[1] And as a matter of fact Nicephorus gives the exact period as fourteen years and four months, though there is a doubt about the reading (*Chron.*, 1049a).

narrative of events from the death of Maurice to A.D. 769. It is usually styled the Breviarium. It is exceedingly dry and bare, but is free from the moralising tendency of Theophanes, and gives a stronger impression of impartiality. Nicephorus uses the same sources as Theophanes, though possibly not all. (2) The theological writings of Nicephorus consist of three *Antirrhetici against the Iconoclasts*, an *Apologeticus Major*, and an *Apologeticus Minor*, both in defence of the Images. These works were written in exile and reflect the atmosphere of the second Iconoclastic period, under Leo the Armenian ; the material, however, is largely drawn from the first period. The two first Antirrhetici quote from an Iconoclastic pamphlet, attributed to Mammon, who may be identified with the Emperor Constantine V. At least one unpublished work of Nicephorus against the Iconoclasts exists. It is in MS. in the Bibliothèque Nationale, Paris, MSS. grecs Fonds Coislin, 93 folio 215. In spite of highly-coloured invective, Nicephorus represents a moderate position in the struggle. Less learned than St. John Damascene and less able than Theodore Studites, he is a more careful and sounder theologian than either.

3. St. John Damascene.—St John Damascene, known also by his Arab name of Mansur, was a Greek living in Damascus, and therefore not a subject of the Empire. The three Orations on the Images (πρὸς τοὺς διαβάλλοντας τὰς ἁγίας εἰκόνας, M.P.G. 94) give the earliest and most learned orthodox reply to Iconoclasm. Many of his arguments became permanent features of the controversy. The Orations were written between 726 and 736.

Two spurious works included in the writings of St. John are important :

(i) *Adversus Constantinum Caballinum* (M.P.G. 95). This is an anonymous work, but important because on internal evidence it appears to be the oldest document of the Iconoclastic period, except the writings of St. John. The seventh general Council had not been held (320d, 333a, 344b). Constantine the Patriarch was dead (333a), and so apparently was the Emperor Constantine, for he is described as " now choking in the abyss of impiety " (341b), *i.e.* in another world. It may be dated between 775 and 787. It uses phrases like ἐπίσκοτοι and φατριάρχης, characteristic of the *Vita Stephani* (circa 808), and probably comes from a similar monastic source. Like the *Vita Stephani* its chronology of events is untrustworthy, but it appears to reproduce the spirit of the time of Constantine V.

(ii) *Epistola ad Theophilum* (M.P.G. 95) is a much less valuable work. It is addressed to the Emperor Theophilus and dates itself circa 847 (see 356c). Its historical knowledge is confused. It sends Leo III, before succeeding to the throne, on an expedition to Campania and Neapolis (357c). It describes the Emperor Nicephorus as orthodox (365c). It has a marked hostility to the Patriarch Antony (372, 373). It bears traces of the phraseology of the circle of Theodore Studites, *e.g.* a comparison of the arguments of Iconoclasm to spiders' webs (372b). It has some curious lore such as the famous description of Christ's appearance (349c), and it solemnly collects the most fantastic legends (*e.g.* 352, 353). It may be of Palestinian origin, certainly it seems to come from outside the Empire. Its historical value is small.

4. Hagiology.—A considerable number of Lives of Saints are concerned with Iconoclasm. Hagiography is marked by two tendencies : (*a*) the introduction of a miraculous element ; (*b*) an artificial handling of chronology to give greater scope for the activities of the hero of the biography. The Lives of Saints are designed primarily not for information but for edification. Their facts are not necessarily fraudulent, but they must be accepted with reserve. The following lives fall within the period of Leo III and Constantine V.

I. *Vita Stephani Junoris*, compiled by Stephen the Deacon in 808 (M.P.G. 100). Literature : Diehl, C., Une Vie de Saint de l'époque des empereurs iconoclastes in *Comptes rendues de l'Academie des Inscr.*, Paris, 1915. Pargoire, J., and Clugnet, C., *Vie de St. Auxence et Mont Auxence*, Paris, 1904.

This is the most important of the hagiological writings. It is also the oldest document of the period except the Acta of Nicæa and the pamphlet *adv. Const. Caball.* It should, however, be regarded as a historical novel rather than history (though still authoritative), for the following reasons :

(1) Its chronology, especially in the details of Stephen's trial, cannot be reconciled with that of the chroniclers. Time is artificially extended to admit more incidents ; even the atrocities of Lachanodrakon in Asia (770–772) are introduced. The order of events at the beginning of the movement under Leo III is reversed. The destruction of the image on the Chalce Gate follows the Silentium which deposed Germanus, and would therefore be dated 729 instead of 726. Pargoire (*op. cit.*) accepts this, but he is always inclined to set too high a value on hagiological literature.

(2) All the principal characters of the Iconoclastic history are introduced, including Constantine of Nacolia, who must long have been dead, and probably Beser.

(3) Constantine the Emperor is made to show a regard for Stephen and a hesitation, almost a fear, that corresponds to nothing in his record. The inference to be drawn is that the biographer magnifies the hero and exaggerates the reluctance of Constantine. The atmosphere and spirit of the narrative are of the highest historical value.

II. The only other important life is *Vita Nicetæ* by Theosteriktos, Acta Sanct. Ap. I, app. 23. Written 820/830.

III. The following touch on the history of the time more or less remotely :

Vit. S. Andreæ in Crisi. Acta Sanct. Oct. VIII, 135. Described by Loparev as a rhetorical exercise of the ninth century, based probably on an earlier life. (See Bréhier, L., L'Hagiographie byz. des viii et ix siècles, in *Journal des Savants*, 1916, pp. 358 *sqq.* and 450 *sqq.*)

Vit. Pauli Junioris. Acta Sanct. June II.

Vit. Joann. ep. Gotthiæ. Act. Sanct. June VII, p. 167.

Passio X Martyr. Cpltanorum. Act. Sanct. Aug. II. Another version of the same is *Encomium Theodosiæ.* Act. Sanct. May VII. Cf. Leclerq, H., *Les Martyres.* Paris, 1905, vol. iv, pp. 292 *sqq.* and 300 *sqq.*

Vit. Leonis Thaumaturgi. Act. Sanct. Feb. III. The interest of this life is that it was written before the Council of Nicæa, and deals with the middle of the eighth century, when Leo was bishop of Catana in Sicily. There is not a single allusion to Iconoclasm in the life, a remarkable testimony to the general indifference of the West.

5. Acta of the Second Council of Nicæa, Mansi, vols. XII and XIII. With the Acta are preserved several letters including (in Mansi) the spurious letters of Pope Gregory to Léo III. See below, p. 36. The Acta are of course contemporary. The Latin version is by the Papal librarian, Anastasius. Another Latin version is printed in Mansi, XIII, 497–758. This was first circulated in 1540 by Gybertus Langolius at Cologne. Fragments of the original Latin translation survive in the Caroline books. This was so literal and inaccurate as in places to be meaningless.

(b) SECONDARY

Of the secondary authorities none are of much importance.

1. Georgius Monachus. George wrote 842/867. He is easily the worst of all the chroniclers, much of his writing being empty abuse. For this period he depends on Nicephorus, Theophanes, and the lives of Stephen and Nicetas.

2. The later compilations of Cedrenus (twelfth century), Zonaras (twelfth century), and Glycas (twelfth century), have nothing to add to our knowledge. They repeat Theophanes, often in the second-hand version of George.

(c) MODERN

For general works, see Bibliography.

Schenke, H., Kaiser Leons III Walten in Innern, *Byz. Zeitschr.*, vol. V, 1896, pp. 256 *sqq.*

Lombard, A., *Constantin V*, Paris, 1902.

Diehl, C., *Leo III and the Isaurian Dynasty*, in Camb. Med. Hist., vol. IV, 1923.

THE steady decline of the Empire was stayed by the Isaurian, Leo. Raised to the throne in 716 by the Eastern armies which refused to support Theodosius III, he is, as Freeman says, " the highest type of conservative politician." [1] He and his son " stopped the progress of degradation at home and abroad ; they drove back the irresistible Saracen ; they reformed the administrative machine, and strove to re-establish a purer faith and worship. They gave, indeed, three centuries of greatness to an Empire which they found on the brink of ruin ; but even they did but preserve, restore, wake into new life ; the mission of original creation was denied even to them." [2] The fatal

[1] Freeman, E. A., *Hist. Essays*, 3rd series (London, 1892), p. 240.
[2] *Ib.*, p. 241.

lack of creative power is like a doom written against the later Empire. Thanks first to Finlay and then to Zachariä von Lingenthal's publication of the Ecloga[1] in 1852, the greatness of the Isaurian dynasty has been established. A striking panegyric on the achievements of Leo and Constantine had long been overlooked. Their bitterest enemies, the Fathers of the Second Nicene Council, declared that " they deserve the praise and honour of all their subjects for their care for the preservation of their people, their victories, their reforms in government and law,[2] the improvement they brought into their cities ; the monuments which commemorate their achievements are a perpetual reminder of their courage and success, making the beholder regret their loss and strive to emulate their example." [3]

Leo, who was known as the Isaurian, was born about the year 675 in Germanicia in Commagene, on the borders of Syria and Cilicia, though the title *Isaurian* suggests that Germanicia may be a chronicler's error for Germanicopolis, a town to the north-west of the Isaurian mountains.[4] In the reign of Justinian II the family removed to Thrace (685–692), and came under that Emperor's notice by sending him a present of five hundred sheep for army supplies, when he was advancing on Constantinople to recover his throne in 704. Leo in consequence advanced rapidly in the Imperial army, and after holding a command in the Caucasus,[5] became under Anastasius II strategus of the Anatolic theme, the position from which he mounted the throne. The early years of his reign were employed in defending the Empire against the Saracens. In 718 he drove them from the walls of Constantinople, gaining a victory which was almost as important as the battle of Poitiers.[6]

It was not until 725 that Leo took the first measures against the Images, after ten years first of military operations,

---

[1] The Ecloga was a revised code of law. See Bury-Gibbon, V, app. 11.
[2] τὰς κοσμικὰς συστάσεις, τὰς πολιτικὰς καταστάσεις.
[3] Mansi, XIII, p. 355.
[4] But Bury (Bury-Gibbon, V, p. 185, n.) gives good grounds for supporting the emendation ἐκ τῆς Συρίας instead of ἐκ τῆς Ἰσαυρίας in Theophanes. If this is the correct reading, then the traditional title *Isaurian* is simply built on a misunderstanding.
[5] The *Ep. ad Theoph.*, with a startling ignorance of geography, says Campania, Amalphis, and Neapolis, 357c.
[6] Placé aux avant-postes du monde chrétien vers l'Orient le nouvel Empereur dévancait Charles Martel. Bayet in Lavisse et Rambaud, *Hist. générale du iv siècle*, I, p. 626, Paris, 1893.

and then of careful administrative and financial reform, had brought a period of settlement, favourable to the development of social activities. In A.M. 6217, says Theophanes, the impious Emperor issued orders for the destruction of images.[1]

The use of sacred pictures and images in the Christian Church was by this period widespread. It had not always been so. Two lines of approach made the primitive Christians hostile to the representation of human or even animal forms in connection with their religion. They inherited the Jewish abhorrence of such representation, which from the time probably of the Hellenic propaganda of Antiochus Epiphanes was so strong that Josephus condemns Solomon for making the twelve oxen which supported the molten sea in the Temple,[2] and Origen declares that neither painter nor sculptor existed in the Jewish state.[3] Converts from paganism brought into their new religion a hatred even more intense for what had formed so large a part of the cults they had forsaken.

In the second century Tertullian holds it a deadly sin in Hermogenes that he was a painter,[4] and Clement of Alexandria lays down definitely that the second commandment is a prohibition of pictorial art. " It has been plainly forbidden us to practise deceptive art ; for the prophet says, Thou shalt not make the likeness of anything that is in heaven, or in the earth beneath."[5]

A symbolic art alone is found among the Christians

---

[1] Theophanes, A.M. 6217, 816a. The phrase λόγον ποιεῖσθαι is possibly to be interpreted as " issue a decree," as the Pope is said in the same passage of Theophanes to have warned the Emperor that it was outside his sphere λόγον ποιεῖσθαι on matters of Faith. The *Vita Stephani* says that Leo held an open meeting (in the Hippodrome or the Tribunal of Magnaura) and himself in a speech made his intentions public, τὸν ὑπ' αὐτοῦ λαὸν ἐκκλησιάσας, *Vit. Steph.*, 1084c. The phrase is copied in *Ep. ad Theoph.*, 360b, and Bury understands it to refer to the Silentium of 730 (Bury-Gibbon, V, p. 536, n.). The chronology of the *Vit. Steph.* is in any case unreliable. Theophanes' A.M. 6217 is 725, while the other sources agree that the Iconoclastic policy of Leo dates from the tenth year of his reign, *i.e.* 726 ; *Adv. Const. Cab.*, 336d ; John at the Coun. of Nic, Mansi, XIII, 197 ; *Vit. Steph.*, 1084b (*Ep. Theo.*, 360b, and the spurious letter of Gregory, Mansi, XII, 959, also agree, but are probably derived from *Vit. Steph.*). Probably we should with Bréhier, *La Querelle des Images*, p. 14, n., interpret λόγον ποιεῖσθαι=make a public statement, and place the actual decree in the following year, when Theophanes chronicles the first definite action against the Images.

[2] *Antiq.*, VIII, 7 : 5.   [3] *contra Celsum*, IV, 31.
[4] *Adv. Herm.*, I. Cf. *de Spect.*, 23.   [5] *Diss. ad gent.*, IV, 62.

of the first two centuries. There is the dove, the fish, the ship, the anchor, the lyre, the fisherman, and the shepherd, the last being found even on the chalice.[1] In the catacombs, besides conventional decoration, flowers, fruit, animals, and birds, there are Old Testament characters, all probably bearing the symbolic meaning of deliverance, Noah's ark, Moses and the rock, Jonah. New Testament figures are much more rare. In all cases the representations are paintings or drawings. Sculpture hardly exists in the Church before the fourth century.

At the end of the second century Gnosticism had undoubtedly made itself felt here as in other spheres of Christian practice. As Gnosticism aimed at producing a synthesis of Christianity and paganism, it approached such a matter as pictures with less hostile prepossessions than the ordinary Jewish or pagan convert. Irenæus records that some Gnostic sects had pictures of Christ, which they placed with those of Pythagoras, Plato, and Aristotle.[2] No doubt it was from such eclectic coteries that the Emperor Alexander Severus in the third century got the effigy of Christ which he placed in his chapel with those of Apollonius, Abraham, and Orpheus.[3] To the less rigid attitude that Gnosticism developed in the Church may be traced in the third century a great increase of pictorial representation, a development responsible Christians viewed with misgiving. The 36th Canon of the Synod of Elvira in Spain laid down about 305 that there should be no pictures in churches, lest what is worshipped and venerated should be depicted on the walls.[4] By the end of the century pictures and even statues [5] must both have grown common,

[1] Clem. Alex., *Paed.*, III, 11 : 59 ; *Tert*, *de Pudic*, 7, 10.

[2] Quasdam quidem (sc. imagines) quasi depictas quasdam autem de reliqua materia fabricatas habent dicentes formam Christi factam a Pilato illo in tempore qua fuit Jesus cum hominibus. Et has coronant et propinunt eas cum imaginibus mundi philosophorum, videlicet cum imagine Pythagorae et Platonis et Aristotelis (Iren., *Contra. Haer.*, I, 25).

[3] Lampridius, *Vita Alex. Sev.*, 29. These were probably plaques in low relief.

[4] Mansi, XII, 264. Placuit picturas in ecclesia esse non debere ne quod colitur et adoratur in parietibus depingatur. But no great weight can be attached to this, the exact bearing of the Canon being unknown.

[5] Statues were still rare. Before the time of Constantine the only figure represented as a statue was that of the Good Shepherd, a fine example of which (late third century) is in the Lateran Museum (illustrated in Baum-Geyer, *Kircheng.*, p. 128). Examples like the Paneas group were probably of pagan origin.

for Eusebius mentions the celebrated statue at Cæsarea-Philippi (Paneas) reputed to be a figure of Christ, set up by the woman healed of the issue of blood, as well as ancient paintings of St. Peter and St. Paul.[1] At the same time Eusebius was alive to the evils of the development, for a letter of his to the wife of the Cæsar Callus is quoted in which he refuses her request for a picture of Christ, as unlawful and idolatrous.[2]

By the end of the fourth century historical pictures of incidents both of the Old Testament and of the lives of the saints, including the Apostles, and even of the life of Christ, were common, though representations of Christ alone were still rare. Pictures formed part of the new influx of wealth into Christianity which came with the conversion of Constantine ; they represented the aspirations of fashion rather than of piety. The *Epistle to Theophilus* preserves the tradition that Constantine depicted the sign of the cross with a figure of Christ and set up pictures of Christ in mosaic.[3] Asterius, bishop of Amasea (circa 400), rebukes the habit of wearing clothes decorated with embroidered pictures of the gospel stories.[4] But while Asterius criticises the display of these arrogant Christians, pictures in themselves he approves as means of stimulating the emotion of the ideal.[5]

From the middle of the fifth century a rapid development took place. The figure of Christ became more and more frequent, doubtless as a result of the Christological controversies. There seems no doubt that the picture of Christ was felt to be a defence of the Incarnation against heretical teaching. This is definitely shown by the 82nd Canon of the Quinisext Council in 692, which required that Christ should always be depicted in human form and not symbolically as a lamb, as had been the more orthodox custom, " so that all may understand by means of it the depths of the humiliation of the Word of God, and that we may recall to our memory his conversation in the flesh, his passion and salutary death, and his redemption which was wrought in the whole world." In consequence, crucifixion

---

[1] Eus., *H. E.*, VII, 18.
[2] Mansi, XIII, 176e, 313a ; Pitra, *Spicil. Solesm.*, I, 363–386.
[3] *Ep. ad Theoph.*, 348c.
[4] *Hom. in Div. et Laz.*, *passim.*
[5] *De Martyr. Euphem.*, M.P.G. 40, p. 337. Cited Mansi, XIII, 16b.

pictures and the crucifix, which had been almost unknown before the fifth century, became increasingly common.[1]

Simultaneously with the development of pictures many of the worst fears of the older generations were realised. All kinds of superstition began to flourish. Virtue is found to reside in the picture. Theodoret records that images of Simeon Stylites were set up in the workshops of Rome, and were a protection to the workers.[2] The figure of Christ on the Chalce Gate of the Imperial Palace at Constantinople, which played an important part in the Iconoclastic struggle, was known as Antiphonetes (the Surety). The significance of the title is lost, but later legend points to a superstitious use. According to the story, in the reign of Honorius the statue stood surety to a sailor named Theodore for a series of loans he had contracted with a Jewish moneylender named Adam. Though the legend is without historical value and appears only after the end of the Iconoclastic period, it represents the superstitious spirit of the seventh century.[3]

Perhaps the most characteristic pagan revival was that of the picture not made with hands, created in the heavens (ἀχειροποίητα), which cannot but recall the image which fell down from Jupiter at Ephesus,[4] and the like. By the time of the Iconoclastic struggle Christian superstition had accumulated a small collection of these monstrous objects, the authenticity and virtues of which were passionately upheld by the image-worshippers. In an interesting list compiled by George the Monk,[5] the principle is discovered in the golden cherubim over the Mercy Seat, and in the brazen oxen in the court of Solomon's Temple, these figures having been made by divine order and after the divine plan. Then come two pictures that meet us at every turn in the Iconoclastic controversy. The first is the portrait of

[1] The earliest literary reference belongs to the latter part of the sixth century (575–594), Gregory of Tours, *de Glor. Martyr.*, I, 23.

[2] Cited Mansi, XIII, 73a.

[3] The legend is told at length in an anonymous sermon preached in St. Sophia, probably in the tenth century, on the feast of Orthodoxy (the annual thanksgiving for the restoration of the images). This was printed by Combefis, *Hist. Monothel.*, II, Paris, 1648. A compressed English version is given by S. Baring Gould under the title *Adam the Usurer* in *Historical Oddities* (London, 1899), vol. I, pp. 103 *sqq.*

[4] Acts xix. 35.

[5] Georg. Mon., II, p. 784.

Christ alleged to have been sent by our Lord Himself to Abgar, king of Edessa. The whole story of relations between Jesus and Abgar is an early legend, but the portrait is first heard of in the historian Evagrius (circa 590).[1] St. John of Damascus embroiders the simple statement still further. According to his account, the painter sent by Abgar found that he could not reproduce the brightness of the Lord's face ; Christ therefore took his outer garment and pressing it against his face, left upon the linen the famous portrait.[2] The second of the two pictures is one of the Blessed Virgin, the work of St. Luke, preserved at Rome. It first appears, like Abgar's picture, in the sixth century.[3] Another miraculous picture of the Virgin was made by unseen hands on the pillar of a church in Lydda in answer to the prayers of the apostles Peter and John. It resisted all the efforts made by Julian the Apostate to obliterate it.[4] The last two effigies in George's list are the familiar statue of Christ and the woman with the issue, a group preserved at Paneas-Cæsarea, and a picture of Christ transfigured, from the hands of Peter and Paul, presented by them to the Church of Rome. By all of these, some of which unquestionably existed, miracles were performed. The picture of Edessa was reputed to have saved the city from fire when carried round the walls by the bishop.[5] Cures were wrought by the Virgin of Lydda and the Christ of Paneas. Of St. Luke's picture of the Virgin, she was understood to have said herself, " My grace shall go with it." [6]

From time to time protests were made. As early as 488 Xenais, Monophysite bishop of Hierapolis (reputed by the orthodox to be a Manichæan probably because of this action), forbade throughout his diocese pictures of the Virgin, saints, and angels.[7] The case of Serenus of Marseilles (599) became a kind of authoritative precedent

---

[1] It is mentioned in the Syriac *Doctrina Addæi* (middle of the fourth century), but is absent from the earlier version, the *Acts of Thaddæus*, which circulated in the Empire and was used by Eusebius.

[2] The better known legend of Veronica is a doublet, of much later date. It was unknown at the Iconoclastic period.

[3] First recorded by Theodore Lector, frag. in M.P.G. 86.

[4] *Ep. ad Theoph.*, 352.

[5] *Ib.*

[6] *Ib.* 349d.

[7] Theoph., 325c.

in the later controversies. Serenus, finding in his diocese
pictures being used as objects of worship, unceremoniously
went into one or more of the churches and with his own
hands tore the pictures down, and threw them outside.
The affair reached the ears of the Pope, Gregory I, who
diplomatically supported and rebuked Serenus. Pictures,
said the Pope, are the books of the illiterate, and you should
not therefore forbid them, while you should certainly
forbid the worship of them.[1]

The old dislike of pictures was by no means dead.
The Nestorians remained hostile to the new fashion, which
they connected with their enemy Cyril. Bréhier gives some
reason to believe that the native Syrian and Coptic
Christians never did use pictorial representations of the
human figure. He attributes the Mohammedan practice
to the influence of these Christians, pointing out that
Persian Moslems have no dislike of portraiture. In 699
it is noticeable that the caliph Abd-el-Malek, who had
previously had his head on the coinage, replaced it with
verses of the Koran, an example regularly followed by his
successors.[2] At the same time Mohammed himself strongly
reprobated the art of representation, and the Koran lays
down in the 92nd verse of the Fifth Sura : " Surely wine
and games of chance and statues and the divining arrow
are an abomination of Satan's work. Avoid them that ye
may prosper."

That the Mohammedans disliked pictures and images
of the human figure was known to all Christians ; they
looked to Mohammedanism and to Judaism for an explanation of the Iconoclastic policy of Leo. All the
authorities agree that the caliph Iezid II (720–724)
ordered the destruction of all pictures[3] in Christian churches
within his dominions. The incident was described in a

---

[1] Greg., *Magn. Epp.*, IX, 105 ; XI, 44 (M.P.L. 77).
[2] Bréhier, *op. cit.*, p. 11.
[3] Theoph., 812b ; *Ep. ad Theoph.*, 356c ; Mansi, XIII, 197a. Theophanes'
date 6215 (*i.e.* 722) is probably the correct one. The *Ep. ad Theoph.* (356c)
says it was 130 years before, in the reign of Theodosius and Iezid the
caliph. But Iezid reigned 720–724, and Theodosius III 715–717. The
historical value of the *Ep.* is not sufficient to justify the view, *e.g.* of Leclerq,
that it was Omar II and not Iezid who attacked the pictures (Hefele-Leclerq,
vol. 3 (ii), p. 627, n. 3). Omar's date is 717–720, which would correspond in
717 with Theodosius. Finlay is astray in supposing that Iezid I (679–683)
is meant (*Byz. Empire*, p. 25).

carefully written statement submitted to the Second Council
of Nicæa by John the priest who represented the Eastern
patriarchs. " The caliph Omar II was succeeded by Iezid,
a man of unstable character. At Tiberias a Jewish diviner
and ally of demons, named Sarantapechys,[1] promised him
a reign of thirty years if he would order the destruction
of all pictures in Christian churches and of all ornamental
representations in public places in the cities, naming all
to avoid appearing to attack only the Christians. Iezid
carried out this advice and the pictures were destroyed.[2]
The bishop of Nacolia and his associates heard of what was
done and imitated it. But Iezid died after two and a half
years, and departed into eternal fire. The pictures were
restored, and the unhappy soothsayer was executed by
Walid, the son of Iezid." [3]

Later historians like George the Monk represent the
soothsayer as handing to Leo the task and the promise,
before which Iezid had succumbed.[4] The simple fact
is as stated by Theophanes that Leo adopted the heresy
of Iezid.[5] There is no reason to question the story about
Iezid apart from the decorative incident of the soothsayer.
The bishop of Messana stated at the Council of Nicæa that
as a small boy he was himself living in Syria when Iezid
carried out his attack.[6] The connection between Iezid
and Leo is not, however, direct. There is evidence of a
strong Iconoclastic influence coming out of Asia by other
routes, with which Leo's various Asiatic connections must
have made him familiar. The Nestorians as a factor may
be dismissed. They were Iconoclasts, but were subjects
of the caliph, shut off from contact with the Empire. But
in the very region of South-Eastern Asia Minor from which
Leo's family sprung, there flourished the vigorous sect of
the Paulicians. They were strong Iconoclasts.[7] The head
of this sect, Gegnæsius, was brought to Constantinople in

[1] Others give the name a form even more reminiscent of the nursery,
Tessarakontapechys, Forty-Ells-Long.
[2] Theophanes (*loc. cit.*) says that he died before the diabolical decree was
known to the majority of his subjects.
[3] Mansi, *loc. cit.*
[4] George, II, p. 736.
[5] Theoph., 812a. μεταλαβὼν ταύτης τῆς ἀθεμίστου καὶ πικρᾶς κακοδοξίας.
[6] Mansi, XIII, 200b.
[7] Conybeare, F. C., *Key of Truth* (Oxford, 1898), pp. 86 and 115. See
appended note on the Paulicians.

720, examined before the Patriarch, and sent home with a safe conduct.[1] Leo may well have been sympathetic to this sect, a feeling also entertained by his son Constantine. Some of the Asiatic bishops were already suspected of similar ideas. Before the Emperor took any Iconoclastic action at least two bishops had given the Patriarch anxiety. These were Constantine of Nacolia in Phrygia,[2] and Thomas, bishop of Claudiopolis, the metropolitan see of Honorias on the Black Sea. A letter from the Patriarch Germanus to John, bishop of Synnada, was read at the Council of Nicæa.[3] In this letter the Patriarch relates that he has had a conversation with the bishop of Nacolia, in which the latter had expressed his fear that the use of images implied idolatry. The Patriarch explained that a different honour was paid to images from the honour paid to God, and added his theory of the use of pictures of the Virgin and the saints. The bishop of Nacolia accepted the explanation, and the letter was entrusted to him to deliver to his metropolitan. Constantine went home, but never delivered the letter. The Patriarch then wrote to Constantine himself,[4] suspending him from office until he had fulfilled his commission. Thomas of Claudiopolis had been more reticent and the Patriarch only heard of his views after he had left Constantinople. The tone of the Patriarch's letter to Thomas [5] shows great agitation. He admits that there is considerable unrest in every country about the question of images. He warns Thomas against a passion for novelty, in particular against Jews and Saracens, the latter of whom are idolaters themselves in the honour they pay to the Kaaba. He then enters into a full defence of

---

[1] Photius, *contra Manich.*, I, 54, 56.

[2] Mansi, XIII, 100.

[3] Schwarzlose is probably right in emphasising the significance of Phrygia, always a centre of strong religious feeling, *op. cit.*, p. 42. Ramsay, *Studies in the Eastern Roman Provinces* (Aberdeen, 1906), pp. 285, 286, remarks on the strong monotheism of the Semitic or Eastern element in contrast with the paganising tendency of the Greek and European Christians after the year 300. He notices that the Nestorians, the Paulicians, and the Iconoclasts, all of whom showed this feature, were mainly Oriental in origin and character. He might have added the Monophysites.

[4] Mansi, XIII, 105b.

[5] *Ib.* 108. The reference to the image of Christ before the palace shows that the outbreak of 727 had not yet taken place, but the agitated tone suggests that the Patriarch was more anxious than when he wrote to Constantine. Probably the letter may be dated early in 725, that to John of Synnada a year or two earlier.

images as unspoken sermons and a vindication of the
humanity of Christ against heretics. In Christ idolatry
is done away and there can in consequence be none among
Christians. Reverence to the saints paid by lights and
incense is glorifying God through His creatures. Honour
is paid to the saints only because they are His saints. He
quotes several authorities, Gregory of Nyssa on the sacrifice
of Isaac, Eusebius who saw pictures of Peter and Paul, the
statue at Paneas-Cæsarea—all of which recur more than
once in the subsequent controversy, and commits himself
definitely to the opinion that " by images miracles are
worked and difficulties resolved."[1]

The admission of the Patriarch that there is considerable
disturbance about this matter in every country, allows us
to see behind the reticence of our authorities, all of whom
are defenders of the images, an Iconoclastic movement of
some strength and duration. It also explains the abrupt
introduction of the subject in Theophanes. What the
Emperor did in 725 was to make a public declaration of
policy on a question which had long been agitated.[2]

The policy of a simplification of religion to which Leo
declared himself favourable by ranging himself with the
enemies of images was consistent with what he had done
already. In 722 he attempted to force Jews and Montanists into the Church by a compulsory baptism. The
Jews submitted without conviction ; they purified themselves from the baptismal water, and mocked the Eucharist
by taking food before they received it. The Montanists
with a greater devotion burnt themselves alive in their
churches.[3] It was probably such liberal tendencies as
these that brought the Emperor in 718 a dogmatic
epistle from the caliph Omar inviting his conversion to
Islam.[4]

The motives which led Leo to adopt the policy of

[1] *Loc. cit.*, 125a.
[2] That would seem to be the interpretation to be given to Theophanes'
words, λόγον ποιεῖσθαι, discussed above.
[3] Theoph., 812a. From the beginning of his reign Leo had never
used the image of Christ on his coinage. But nothing explicit could be de-
duced from that, for the figure had only been introduced by Justinian II,
and his example had not been followed by the Emperors between him and
Leo. Wroth, Vol. II, Plates xli and xlii. In 739 the Ecloga (XVII, 52)
enacted penalties against the Montanists.
[4] Theoph., 808a.

Iconoclasm need, however, further analysis. In interpreting the mind of heterodox thinkers, the Church authorities upon whom alone we depend give us little help. One motive alone explains for them the action of Leo, obedience to the orders of the devil, and if details are wanted, the devil's natural emissaries, the Jew and the Moslem, are enough.[1]

It becomes thus a nice historical riddle to define Leo's motive and aim. In any movement in which men try to translate ideas into a practical policy, it is unlikely that an exact plan of advance is prepared at the start. The historian of Iconoclasm is in danger of attributing to Leo definite aims, which only revealed themselves as the controversy developed. Even Schwarzlose, who is the most careful of the modern historians of the subject, exaggerates the motives of Leo, in the sense that he defines them too exactly. Experience shows that the policy and aims of any movement only reveal themselves as the movement takes shape.

That Leo's motives were partly religious seems indisputable. The Asiatic environment in which he lived so long was, as we have seen, permeated with Iconoclastic ideas. All the traditions of the Christian Emperors involved them in theology. The connection of Church and State in Constantinople was of such a character that the Emperor was by his office a church official. Conflict of Church and State in the Western sense for that very reason could not exist. It did arise in the course of the Iconoclastic controversy, because a new theory of Church policy was imported into Constantinople by Theodore Studites. But Leo's position cannot be explained by the later situation which Theodore created.

At the same time Leo's motive cannot have been purely religious. A religious fanatic on the throne is the rarest of phenomena and only fanaticism can make religion an instrument of violence. The mild rationalism of Leo could hardly alone inspire the bold policy that followed. The two statesmen with whom Leo can be compared are Philip the Fair of France, the destroyer of the Templars, and Henry VIII of England. Not one of the three was devoid of religion, but not even Henry (over whom of the three religion had most influence) followed the impulse

[1] Mansi, XIII, 373c.

of religious motives alone. When Iconoclasm was brought to an end, we shall see that the political factor can still be discovered underneath the chronicler's explanation of Theodora's motives. A political and social aim is to be sought in Leo also. Schwarzlose defines it as the necessity that faced Leo of consolidating his position by strengthening the army and weakening the monasteries. But the attack on the monasteries did not come until some thirty-five years after the movement had started. A generation had passed away, and the Isaurian dynasty must long before that have either failed or justified itself. The monks became a primary object of attack only when they showed themselves the real centre of opposition.

Leo's political ideal seems to have been simply to make use of his religious point of view to support his general scheme of purifying and raising the low tone of society. It was not the preliminary plan of Leo but the reactions that met it that moulded the form and the theology of Iconoclasm. For that reason Constantine V is a much larger figure in the controversy than his father. Time had revealed the orthodox theological reply and the orthodox centre of resistance so that Constantine was able both to systematise the theology of Iconoclasm and to make his attack fall directly upon the monasteries.

With these qualifications the motive of Leo is to be explained as a combination of Asiatic monotheism with a strong reformative social policy, working on conservative lines. In the later stages a new theory of Church polity developed, represented by the party of Theodore. This introduced the idea of opposition between Church and State, a feature entirely foreign to Oriental Christianity, which saw in the Christian ruler part of the divine scheme of the Church. In the same degree the theology of the movement changed in the course of time and the charge of idolatry which was the main indictment against image-worship at the beginning of the struggle had nearly disappeared in the later stages, and was definitely repudiated by the Iconoclastic Council of 815.[1] Corresponding stages in the line of orthodox resistance may be traced in the writings of St. John Damascene, Nicephorus, and Theodore Studites.

[1] Hefele-Leclerq, III (ii), p. 1218.

There can be no doubt that at least within the Empire Christianity was full of superstition and that it was in the sacred pictures and images that superstition found a stronghold. Germanus the Patriarch definitely accepted the view that images worked miracles.[1] Many examples in support of that view were brought as evidence at the Council of Nicæa. Manzon, bishop of Pracana, declared that only a year before he had been cured of an illness through appealing to the image of Christ.[2] Two grotesque stories from the *Life of Simeon Stylites the Second* were cited by one of the abbots attending the Council. A woman whom the saint had delivered from a demon lover set up an image of her deliverer which worked miracles. A second image of the same saint struck to the ground evil-disposed persons who tried to overthrow it.[3] This evidence was received with great satisfaction by one of the principal figures of the Council, Constantine, bishop of Constantia in Cyprus. He added some anecdotes from his own personal experience. He knew a man in Constantia who knocked out the eye of an effigy of the Virgin with his ox-goad; subsequently when he struck the oxen, the goad broke and a fragment of it knocked out his own eye. Another man in Citium fixed a nail in the head of an image of St. Peter to fasten a rope; he was immediately struck with a severe pain in the head, which was only relieved when he removed the nail from the image. Worst of all was the fate of a Saracen. He knocked the eye out of an image, when forthwith his own eye fell out and he was laid low with a fever.[4] The most grotesque powers were attributed to images and solemnly accepted by the Council. A woman in Apamea having no water was bidden in a dream to lay the picture of the Abbot Theodosius on the well. She did this and the well filled. An old man was in the habit of lighting a candle before a picture of the Virgin whenever he left home, asking the Virgin to take care of it. Whether he came back after a month, two months, or even six months he found the candle burning and unimpaired.[5] All this gives strong support to the picture of image-

---

[1] *Ep. to Thomas of Claudiopolis*, Mansi, XIII, 108.
[2] Mansi, XIII, 65e.
[3] *Ib.* 73c.
[4] *Ib.* 77c.
[5] *Ib.* 193–195.

worship drawn a hundred years after the first Iconoclastic attack by the Emperor Michael II in a letter to Lewis the Pious (824).[1] The people, says Michael, sang psalms before the images, worshipped them, and prayed to them for help. Many dressed the images in clothes and made them god-parents to their children. When they tonsured their children,[2] they laid the hair upon the images. Some priests scraped the colours off images and mixed it with the offering of bread and wine, and after the Mass gave communion from this mixture. Others placed the Lord's Body in the image's hands, whence those who communicated had to take it. Some ignored the church and celebrated the Eucharist in private houses, using tables of images for altars. There is no reason to doubt the accuracy of Michael's description. Theodore Studites writes to the spatharius John in terms of the highest commendation for making the image of the martyr Demetrius sponsor to his child.[3]

It is true that the description given by Michael refers to the period of reaction under Irene, after the severe Iconoclastic measures of Constantine V, when the orthodox were carried away by something like a fanatical joy at their success. But it differs only in degrees from the superstitions cited as ancient precedent by the Council of Nicæa and even by St. John Damascene.

There is not the least doubt that pictures were objects of superstitious misuse. It is also clear that a party of religious reformers had been active for some time. This was led by some of the bishops, and in the bishops rather than in the Emperor must be sought the origin of Iconoclasm. Nicephorus says that the persons responsible for introducing the new doctrine into the Empire were the chiefs of the hierarchy.[4] These included Constantine of Nacolia, Thomas of Claudiopolis, and possibly Theodosius of Ephesus,[5] a son of the Emperor Apsimar (Tiberius III).

---

[1] M.G.H. Leges Sec., III, vol. ii (2), p. 479.
[2] In preparation for holy orders.
[3] *Ep.*, I, 17 (961b).
[4] Niceph., *Antirrh.*, III, 529c.
[5] He presided at the Iconoclastic Council in 753, a fact which suggests that he was an Iconoclast of long standing. The unsupported statement of the spurious letter of Pope Gregory (Mansi, XII, 968) that he was one of the original leaders of the movement may be only an inference from this.

The party also numbered some prominent laymen such as Beser, who may or may not merit the contempt with which Theophanes dismisses him as a Christian who had become a Moslem and had then returned to Christianity and won the Emperor's favour by his immense size and Iconoclastic ideas.[1] This group may well have been directly influenced by Islam, or more exactly by the Semitic monotheism which gave Islam its chief strength, and is the ultimate basis of all the Asiatic heresies like Paulicianism and Nestorianism. Witnessing the success which the Moslem had gained over the Christian, they would be attracted to his religion as at a later time were many of the Crusaders. There are too many references to Mohammedanism to be overlooked.[2] The Mohammedan influence, though it cannot be accurately traced, was probably the significant one in this group, and this group was the real centre of Iconoclastic activity.

In 725, the Emperor declared himself an adherent of their views. It is unknown whether an edict was issued or not. The statement frequently made [3] that the Emperor ordered all images and pictures to be moved to a higher position to be out of reach of grosser acts of veneration is certainly a mistake as the incident of the removal of the Antiphonetes shows.[4] In the following years volcanic disturbances in the Ægæan caused widespread fear, and the Emperor saw in the occurrence a manifestation of the Divine anger against continued toleration of image-worship.[5] Under the leadership of Beser an active onslaught was made. The first object of attack was the ancient figure of Christ on the Chalce Gate (the south-west entrance) of the Imperial Palace.[6] A soldier [7] climbed a ladder to remove

---

[1] Theoph., 812ab.

[2] Cf. Mansi, XIII, 108 ; Theoph., 808a, 812ab.

[3] *E.g.* by Finlay.

[4] It is founded on an old Latin translation of the *Vit. Steph.* published by Billius in 1603, differing widely from the original Greek. The policy of placing pictures higher belongs to the second Iconoclastic period, the reign of Leo the Armenian.

[5] Nic., *Brev.*, 963b.

[6] See above, p. 21.

[7] The name of the soldier is given in the spurious letter of Gregory as Jovinus, where also the site of the image is called the Chalcoprateia, a confusion most writers, including Hefele, have failed to notice. The Chalcoprateia was not near the Royal Palace. It was a bazaar on the north side of St. Sophia.

the figure ; the mob, most of them women, rushed at the ladder ; the soldier fell and was so severely handled that he died. In consequence of this episode many persons were arrested and punished with mutilation, flogging, exile, or fines, but none were executed.[1] Images in public places were probably the object of a general attack. Theophanes records one example at Nicæa, where an army officer named Constantine knocked down an image of the Virgin. Theophanes only records this case to point a moral ; for, according to his story, the Virgin appeared in person and warned the Iconoclast that his crime would fall on his own head, and next day he was struck down with a stone fired from a catapult. It may be inferred that unless some sequel of the kind could be introduced, Theophanes had no occasion to catalogue the images destroyed.

The organised attack provoked resistance. An outbreak occurred in Greece and the Cyclades, for which taxation probably shared the responsibility with the images. Greece remained strongly loyal to the images throughout the period.[2] The rising was led by Agallianus, turmarch of the Greek forces,[3] and Stephanus, a certain Cosmas being cast for the part of Emperor. The conspiracy failed badly. It is an indication of the moderation of Leo's policy that no one suffered the death-penalty but the two ringleaders.

Meanwhile, nothing is heard of the Patriarch Germanus. His sympathy with image worship was well known to the leading Iconoclasts, the bishops of Nacolia and Claudiopolis. He was an old man of about ninety years. The Emperor

[1] Theophanes, who collected everything adverse to the Iconoclasts, records no capital punishments. The hagiologists, on the other hand, give to the woman leading the attack the name of Theodosia, and she appears in the Calendar on May 7th (Act. Sanct. May VII, 69. Leclerq, H., *Les Martyres* (Paris, 1905), vol. iv, pp. 292 *sqq*.). She is a good example of the historical worthlessness of hagiology. Obviously her existence is built round the episode of the attack on the Antiphonetes. Even Pargoire, who is no enemy of hagiology, qualifies her with a " peut-être " (*L'Eglise Byzantine* (Paris, 3ième ed. 1923), p. 363). Her fictional character is further illustrated by the fact that she appears again in the Calendar under the name of Mary (Act. Sanct. Aug. II, 428–434 ; Leclerq., *op. cit.*, pp. 300 *sqq*.). Here her fellow-sufferers are named, Gregory the spatharius, nine other men, and two children. These are the only martyrs the Act. Sanct. place in the reign of Leo III.

[2] Theoph., 817bc.

[3] τῶν Ἑλλαδικῶν, not as Finlay supposed a diminutive of contempt, but the correct title of the Greeks of the military district (Bury, *Later Roman Empire*, II, p. 437).

perhaps ignored him.[1] At least it is not until 728 that Theophanes brings him into the struggle. In that year the Emperor made overtures to the Patriarch. The Patriarch said that he had heard that one day the holy images would be destroyed, but that it was to be in the reign of Conon. " But," said Leo, " my baptismal name was Conon." " God forbid," answered the Patriarch, " that the evil thing should happen in your reign. For he who will do this is the forerunner of Antichrist, the destroyer of the dispensation of the Holy Incarnation." [2] The Patriarch then reminded the Emperor of his coronation oath to observe and maintain the rules of the Church. It seems likely that the conversation describes the attitude of Germanus at the beginning of the Emperor's attack, for it implies that no action had yet been taken. As the years went by and Germanus proved unyielding, the Emperor made another attempt. He accused Germanus of conspiracy, which probably means that, according to the view of the Emperor's position in the Church accepted in Constantinople, the Patriarch by failing to support his Emperor was guilty of sedition.[3] The supporters of the images were at this moment rallying their forces, for in 727/728, St. John of Damascus had issued his first *Oration against the Slanderers of the Images*, a powerful statement of their side of the case.

In the following January a Silentium was held by the Emperor.[4] Germanus attended and definitely refused to accept any doctrinal alteration without an Œcumenical Council. " If I am Jonah," he said, " cast me into the sea." He was forthwith deposed by the Emperor and lived the rest of his life in quiet retirement on his ancestral estate.[5]

---

[1] The statement of George the Monk (II, 741) that he was expelled and then recalled to the Silentium of 729/730 is due to one of George's usual misinterpretations of his authorities, *Vit. Steph.*, 1085b.

[2] *Vit. Steph.*, 1085a, summarises the Patriarch correctly : " Attacks on the image of Christ are attacks on Christ himself."

[3] Theoph., 821bc.

[4] A Silentium would in the more loquacious West be called a Parliament. It was a mixed lay and clerical Imperial council. There is great difficulty about its date, which Theophanes gives as A.M. 6222, 7th Jan., Tuesday. In 729, Jan. 7th was really Friday. A slight emendation suggested by Hefele, ιζ' for ζ' would make it 17th Jan. 730 (accepted by Bury, Bury-Gibbon, V, p. 536), or 17th Jan. 729 (Pargoire), neither of which is quite consistent, for the year, according to Bury's revised chronology, ought to be 729, in which 17th Jan. was Monday.

[5] So Niceph., *Brev.* 965a. *Vit. Steph.* says he was sent to a monastery, 1085b.

To the see of the deposed Patriarch Leo appointed Anastasius, the ex-Patriarch's own syncellus or chaplain, whose subsequent career shows him to have been the time-server that the image-worshippers declared him to be.[1] The orthodox party was still strong, and no sooner was he enthroned on the 22nd January than a mob of angry women rushed to the Patriarchate and attempted to stone Anastasius, who fled to the Emperor for protection.[2] The Emperor then took vigorous action against images, and in the resistance that was provoked " many clerics, monks, and pious lay-people were in great peril of putting on the martyr's crown for the true word of the Faith." [3] Many of the orthodox fled from Constantinople,[4] where the Imperial policy was prosecuted with most vigour, among them the parents of Stephen, who becomes a notable figure in the Iconoclastic struggle during the next reign.[5] For the remaining nine years of the reign of Leo III no incident of the Iconoclastic movement is recorded by the chroniclers. The inference must be drawn that the Emperor had broken

[1] τὰ τῆς ἐκκλησίας πάντα τοῖς βασιλείοις παρέδωκεν. *Vit. Steph.*, 1085c. He miscalculated the situation when the rebel Artavasdus occupied Constantinople on the accession of Constantine V, and suffered at the hands of Constantine.

[2] Such is the story told in *Vit. Steph.*, 1085d, with the further addition that at the request of the Patriarch the women were executed, and were the first martyrs in the cause of the Images. But the *Vit. Steph.* connects the incident with the destruction of the image on the Chalce Gate which Theophanes places three years earlier, before the Greek rebellion. As Theophanes carefully dates his events and on general grounds, his authority must be preferred to that of the *Vit. Steph.* even though the *Vita* is the earlier. George the Monk, who used both Theophanes and the *Vita*, though not a reliable authority, follows Theophanes. George, II, p. 743.

[3] ὑπερεκινδύνευσαν . . . τὸν μαρτυρικὸν ἀναδησάμενοι στέφανον. Theoph., 825b. The phrase must mean that they were not actually put to death. Nicephorus agrees that they only suffered violence : τιμωρίας πλείστας καὶ αἰκισμοὺς ὑπέμεναν. Nic., *Brev.*, 965a. It is only George who substitutes θάνατον for αἰκισμοὺς, II, p. 744. *Adv. Const. Cab.* also makes no mention of executions, 337a. In addition to the names given above from the Act. Sanct. Pargoire hesitatingly adds the improbable case of Theophanes the apocrisarius, the envoy of Pope Gregory III (*op. cit.*, p. 363), on the authority of the life of Germanus in Act. Sanct.

[4] Iconoclasm was an Asiatic movement, supported by Asiatic emperors, Asiatic bishops and the Asiatic army. This is seen many times in the course of the struggle. It was particularly repugnant to pure Greeks like the Empress Irene. But Schwarzlose, pp. 49 and 50, is inclined to over-emphasise the Moslem character of this Asiatic influence. The epithet σαρακηνόφρων (*e.g.* Theoph., 817), as applied by the chroniclers to Leo, is a generic term of abuse. Theodore Studites uses ἰουδαιόφρων (*e.g.*, 1272c) in the same way.

[5] *Vit. Steph.*, 1088a.

the direct opposition and was satisfied to let his ideas take root. There are other indications that after the first burst Leo acted with great restraint. In 732 he married Constantine to the daughter of the Khazar chief, Chaganus. She was baptized and took the name of Irene and apparently developed into a supporter of images.[1] Most significant of all is the fact that the Ecloga or revised Civil Code of Laws, which was published in 740, contains no penalty for image-worship. During this period there was maturing the theological polemic on both sides which emerged in the next stage. The orthodox position had already been stated by St. John of Damascus so effectively that every subsequent writer repeated his arguments and authorities. The three Orations of St. John in defence of the images belong approximately to the years 726, 730, and 732. St. John was, however, a subject of the Caliph, and could take no direct part beyond the literary one. Another significant member of the orthodox party at this time was George, a bishop in Cyprus. Little is known of him, but he was considered important enough to deserve a special anathema with St. John of Damascus and the Patriarch Germanus at the Iconoclastic Council of 753.[2] A work entitled Νουθεσία γέροντος περὶ τῶν ἁγίων εἰκόνων is attributed to him by its Russian editor Melioranski.[3] The line of defence which John and perhaps George set out, and the evidence they collected, must have been assimilated by both sides during the last years of Leo's reign. For when Constantine V succeeded, the theology of the subject becomes a prominent feature. On Leo's own speculative interests the historians are silent. They must have been small. Theophanes says that he was opposed to intercession to the Theotokos and the saints, and despised relics "like the Arabs his teachers."[4] But there is no other evidence of these views, and they are so peculiar to Constantine V that it is fair to assume that Theophanes has transferred them to Leo in error.

One point of Leo's policy, however, did touch the sphere of thought. He closed the schools and suppressed

[1] διέπρεψεν ἐν εὐσεβείᾳ (i.e. image-worship), ἐλεγχούσα τὴν τούτων δυσσεβείαν. Theoph., 825c.
[2] Mansi, XIII, 356a.
[3] Melioranski, B., *George of Cyprus and John of Jerusalem*, Petrograd, 1901.
[4] Theoph., 820c.

their teaching—that is, the teaching given by existing masters who would be supporters of the images. A preposterous story is told in this connection by George the Monk. He says that the school of Imperial foundation near the Chalcoprateia, which maintained an Œcumenical doctor and twelve fellows, was burnt down with all its books and the thirteen scholars, because they refused to assent to the Emperor's doctrine. The burning of the men may be rejected on the ground that Theophanes and Nicephorus could not have failed to notice an atrocity so damaging to the Iconoclasts. That the books and the building were burnt is probable. Theophanes notices the attacks on the schools, and in the time of Leo the Armenian books were rare, a fact for which the Iconoclasts may share the responsibility with the civil disorders of the previous century and with the Council of Nicæa.[1]

On the 8th June, 740, Leo III died, leaving the kingdom to his son Constantine, a man his equal in administrative ability, his superior in culture and intelligence, and at one with him in policy and outlook.

NOTE I

THE SPURIOUS LETTERS OF POPE GREGORY II

Two epistles in Greek purporting to be addressed by Pope Gregory II to Leo III are prefixed to the Acta of the Second Council of Nicæa in Mansi, XII, pp. 959 *sqq.* They were first unearthed in the sixteenth century by Fronton le Duc ; MSS. as early as the tenth century exist. The authenticity of the letters was long unquestioned, but now finds few supporters, thanks to the investigations of Duchesne (*Liber Pontificalis*), Guerard (in *Mélanges d'Archéologie*, 1890, pp. 44 *sqq.*), Hodgkin, and Bury. The evidence of the last-named is important, for he originally accepted the letters (*Later Roman Empire*). See Bury-Gibbon, V, app. 14. The main points against the letters are :

(1) The absence of the letters from the Acta of Nicæa, and the absence of any trace of the original Latin.

(2) Misrepresentation of minor facts of Italian geography and history.

---

[1] Theoph., 817abc. ; Georg. Mon., II, p. 742. Cedrenus, I, 872d, who practically reproduces the text of Theophanes, has interpolated George's story at this point, showing that he realised that it was George's version of the simpler notice of Theophanes. The question is discussed fully by E. Rein, Kaiser Leon III und die ökumenische Akademie, *Ann. Acad. Scient. Fennicæ*, XI, pp. 1–43.

(3) The Antiphonetes is said to have stood not on the Chalce Gate but in the Chalcoprateia.

(4) The insolence of tone, which is quite unlike the pacific attitude characteristic of Gregory.

Mann (*op. cit.*, I (ii), pp. 488 *sqq.*) has attempted to defend the letters. His starting-point (though he does not state it) is a reluctance to depart from what has been accepted by Hefele. His main arguments are :

(1) That the arguments of the letters correspond with the arguments against Iconoclasm used by Pope Gregory in the Roman Council of 727. This argument is Hefele's, and loses most of its value in face of the contention (discussed in Chap. V) that the alleged council was really held in 731 by Gregory III.

(2) That the supposed insolence of tone is an exaggeration of English translators. This is sufficiently answered by the citations themselves, viewed in the light of the unfailing courtesy which was Gregory's most conspicuous characteristic. The crudity of such expressions as the following are typical, not of Gregory, nor indeed of Rome, but of Constantinople :

ἀνάγκην ἔχομεν γράψαι σοι παχέα καὶ ἀπαίδευτα ὥσπερ εἶ ἀπαίδευτος καὶ παχὺς διὰ τὴν πόλλην σοῦ ἀναισθησίαν, 963E. γύρωσον εἰς τὰς διατριβὰς τῶν στοιχείων . . . καὶ εὐθὺς τὰς πινακίδας αὐτῶν εἰς τὴν κεφάλην σοῦ ῥίψουσι, 966C. καὶ ὅπερ οὐκ ἐπαιδεύθης ὑπὸ τῶν φρονίμων παιδευθήσῃ ὑπὸ τῶν ἀφρόνων, *ib.* σοῦ τοῦ βασίλεως ἀστατοῦντος καὶ βαρβαρίζοντος, 970B. τὸ ἐγχείρημα ὅπερ εἰργάσω . . . ἀκαταστασίας καὶ ἀλαζωνείας καὶ ὑπερηφανείας ἐστί, 970D. εἰς τὰς διοικήσεις τοῦ κόσμου τὸν πολεμικὸν καὶ σκαιὸν νοῦν ὃν ἔχεις καὶ παχύν. 978C.

If a date for the composition of the letters were to be hazarded, it might be fixed after the Council of Nicæa, perhaps in the second Iconoclastic period when so much polemical writing was coming from the hands of Nicephorus and Theodore. The appeal to authorities was characteristic of that time. Cf. 962A, ἠκολουθήσας διεστραμμένοις καὶ πλήρης τῶν δογμάτων τῆς ἀληθείας σφαλλομένοις. The phrase attributed to the Emperor, βασιλεὺς καὶ ἱερεύς εἰμι (975), is also reminiscent of the age of Theodore.

CHAPTER IV

THE REIGN OF CONSTANTINE V

AUTHORITIES

As for Chapter III.

IN Constantine Iconoclasm found its greatest figure. He possessed all his father's skill as a soldier and administrator. But while Leo was never more than an able soldier, with no culture beyond that which comes from the natural endowments of an active mind, Constantine had been educated and trained in the traditions of Constantinople. He was a vigorous thinker with a natural theological bent. Under his direction Iconoclasm took a new line of development. It found its place in the theology of Christianity and entered into the sphere in which violence is tempered or supplemented by a warfare of pamphlet and debate. The chroniclers being all opponents of Iconoclasm have recognised the great importance of Constantine and have exhausted over him their vocabulary of abuse. He is the " inheritor of a double portion of his father's wickedness." [1] To George the Monk, whose power of invective balances his weakness as a historian, Constantine is the Antichrist of the tribe of Dan. [2] He has the faith of a Saracen and the heart of a Jew. " He is not a Christian (God forbid), but a Paulician, or to speak more truly and fitly, an idolater, a worshipper of devils and a devotee of human sacrifice." [3] Nicephorus the patriarch describes him as " wallowing in dung and unspeakable vices, with bloodstained hands, unbridled tongue, and a corrupt mind." [4] He surpassed the beasts in foulness.[5] His arguments are " the belchings

[1] adv. Const. Cab., 337a.
[2] Georg. Mon., II, p. 750.
[3] Ib., p. 751.
[4] Niceph., Antirrh., I, 229d.
[5] Ib. III, 504d.

of a disordered digestion, the spreading of the manure which is his chief delight, the fruits of unceasing vomits, of a life lived with dogs and swine, imitating the habits of wild beasts ; his acts are the acts of hunters of the brute creation, men who dip their hands in Christian blood and arm themselves against Christ, the inventions of ravishers of human flesh." [1]

His private life and his personal morality are held up to condemnation. On this matter it will be wisest to accept no more than the more cautious of the statements of Theophanes. [2] " The Emperor was devoted to flute-playing and banquetting, training his associates in unseemly jesting and dancing." [3] This means that under Constantine life was more luxurious than in the days of Leo III. But the general statement that punishment was inflicted on any who observed vigils or frequented churches or lived piously or refrained from profane oaths, [4] because such were enemies of the Emperor, may be interpreted as a rhetorical description of the discouragement of monasticism. There is a still more inconclusive hint of the Emperor's addiction to unnatural vice in the statement that he sentenced to death " any member of the army or civil service, who attempted to enter the religious life, especially if he were one of his own entourage, sharer in his lascivious secrets." But the motive suggested, " as though in fear of the disgrace their confessions would bring on himself," [5] reads more like an insinuation than an attested fact. Theophanes more than once describes Constantine as stained with " the invocation of demons and the offering of pagan sacrifices," [6] an accusation which is not only unsupported by any evidence but is inconsistent with the whole tenour of his theology. For Constantine is consistently cast for the part of religious enthusiast and not for that of notorious evil-liver. Theophanes summarises his private life : " He reigned, devoted to magic arts, lasciviousness, bloody sacrifices, horse-dung, and urine, taking pleasure in

---

[1] Niceph., *Antirrh.*, II, 289ab.
[2] Our earliest authority; *adv. Const. Cab.*, says nothing against the Emperor's private character.
[3] Theoph., 892c.
[4] *Ib.* 892d.
[5] *Ib.* 893ab.
[6] *Ib.* 905a. Cf. 883c.

unnatural vice (μαλακίαις) and the invocation of demons." [1]
Where no other evidence and no fact are brought forward
in support, little significance can be attached to general
accusations of immorality. We do know some indisputable facts about Constantine's personal tastes. He was
inordinately fond of horses, as is indicated by the original
title of abuse applied to him, Caballinus, [2] and he spent much
of his time in the stables and in the stableyard, a hobby
which his chroniclers regarded as beneath an Emperor's
dignity. This explains the contemptuous connection of
his name with manure, [3] which eventually developed into
the title Copronymus. He married three times, a breach
of propriety upon which the Eastern Church looked
askance. [4] Further, he cannot be completely acquitted
of the accusation of sodomy. The charges are vague and
they may be no more than evil rumour, but they are
consistently made by all the authorities, and they have not
the inherent improbability of such accusations as pagan
and Jewish sacrifices or magic. [5] But to see how the
Constantine legend grew, it is only necessary to read the
later chroniclers like George or even Cedrenus, or the
survivals of popular credulity preserved in the *Life of
Stephen*. George reproduces from the *Life* a passage
in which Constantine is described as the new Julian. " He
worshipped Aphrodite whom the Greeks honoured and
Dionysus, and offered human sacrifices to them outside
the city in the place where had stood the church of the
martyr Maura, which the hater of the saints razed to the
ground and turned into a slaughter-house, calling the place
Maura. [6] There celebrating at night the rites of demons, [7]

---

[1] Theoph., 883c.
[2] By the author of *adv. Const. Cab.*, and by Nicephorus.
[3] Especially by Nicephorus, *Antirrh.*, I, 289a, τῆς φίλης καὶ ἡδίστης κοπρίας. *Antirrh.*, III, 493d, κοπρῶνας. *Antirrh.*, I, 229d, ἐν κοπρίᾳ . . . ἐμμολυνόμενον. *Apol. pro S. Imag.*, 579, κοπροσύνοδον, applied to the Iconoclastic Council, διὰ τὸ τοῦ συναγάγοντος φιλόκοπρον. Cf. Theoph., 833c, Constantine devoted to καβαλλίαις κόπροις. 888a, The church of St. Euphemia made into κοπροθέσιον.
[4] See J. M. Ludlow in D.C.A., s.v. Digamy. Theophanes refers to Con-
stantine evidently in reproach as ὁ τρίγαμος, 896a.
[5] The author of *Vit. Steph.* implies that the Emperor's orders that members of the Court circle should be clean-shaven were of vicious intention. He compares the clean-shaven to ἵπποι θηλυμανεῖς, 1133c.
[6] *I.e.* without the epithet " Saint."
[7] *I.e.* the pagan gods.

he slaughtered a child. To this witness is borne by the child of Sufflamius thus slaughtered for sacrifice. The sacrifice the devil-worshipper offered in a corner God revealed to many." [1] The last clause is George's own conclusion of what ought to have happened. His source dismisses the sacrifice of the child as a matter upon which " it is not the time to enlarge." [2] This piece of popular gossip looks like an expansion of the phrase " the new Julian." The sacrifice is invented out of the improbable incident recorded by Theodoret to the effect that at Carrhæ Julian offered a living woman in sacrifice. [3]

The enemies of Constantine have so greatly exaggerated their case against him that any accusation they bring can only be treated with scepticism. So malignant is Nicephorus that he does not hesitate to belittle even the military achievements of Constantine. As Nicephorus has himself recorded many of the facts in his *Short History*, it is only theological animus that allows him to attribute the Emperor's successful campaigns against the Bulgarians to treachery and disaffection in the enemy ranks, and to throw all the emphasis on the Roman losses in the war. He disparages what was done in the East, though Constantine made more progress against the Saracens than any general up to the time Nicephorus was writing. Out of the welter of disparagement, insinuation, abuse, and actual misrepresentation, the temptation is to draw a picture of Constantine in which no black remains and very little grey. [4]

Constantine V, the son of the Emperor Leo and his wife Maria, was born in 718, probably in October, for on the 25th of that month he was brought by his mother to baptism at the church of St. Sophia. The ceremony was being performed by the Patriarch Germanus when an accident occurred which afterwards was read as a grave omen of misfortune. " As soon as the Patriarch said, M. or N. is baptised in the name, etc., immediately the ill-omened enemy of the Church befouled the basin and filled all who stood by with the evil odour of his foul evacuation, so that

---

[1] Georg. Mon., II, p. 752, cited from *Vit. Steph.*, 1169c.
[2] περὶ οὗ οὐκ ἔστι καιρὸς διηγήσασθαι, *Vit. Steph.*, loc. cit.
[3] Theod., III, 26.
[4] This has been done by Lombard, *op. cit.* For Nicephorus' disparagement, see *Antirrh.*, III, 508.

E

the hierophant Germanus said, This child is like to bring an evil odour upon the Church." [1] In the following year the child was proclaimed Augustus, and from infancy was trained to be his father's colleague. He was twenty-two when he succeeded to the throne on June 18th, 740, and entered on his long reign of thirty-four years.[2] No sooner had he mounted the throne than his brother-in-law Artavasdus broke into rebellion and seized Constantinople. Part of the appeal of Artavasdus was the restoration of Images, and among those who acquiesced in the rebellion was the Patriarch Anastasius. His contribution to the usurper's propaganda was to make a public statement " with his hand on the Cross." He said, " By him who was fixed to this wood, I swear that Constantine the Emperor said to me, Regard not as son of God him whom Mary bore, called Christ, but as bare man. For Mary bore him as my mother Mary bore me." This was evidently good propaganda among the pious population. They indignantly declared that Constantine was deposed.[3] We need not doubt that the Patriarch told the story. But is it probable that the Emperor said what he was alleged to have said? A position of pure Arianism such as this saying implies is inconsistent with the whole Iconoclastic metaphysic and with that of Constantine in particular. Iconoclasm was in tendency Monophysite, the very antithesis of Arianism. Nicephorus quotes Mammon, who is certainly Constantine, as arguing against pictures on the very ground that a picture represents the person of a bare man, which is equivalent to turning Christ into a creature with no divine nature in him.[4] George the Monk, followed by Cedrenus, garbles the story still further, and makes the Patriarch report that

[1] *adv. Const. Cab.*, 337b. Cf. Theoph., 808b. The incident may well be historical, the Patriarch's comment being an addition made in the light of subsequent events. No one earlier than Zonaras connects this mishap with the title Copronymus (Zon., 1320), and we can definitely reject this explanation of the name. See above. Conybeare suggests that the incident symbolically states Constantine's dislike of the practice of Infant baptism under Paulician influence (*Key of Truth*, p. cxvii). But there is no support of fact for this theory, and it is so ingenious as to be incredible.

[2] Theoph., 833a. On the year see note on the chronology of Theophanes above, p. 13.

[3] Theoph., 837c.

[4] Niceph., *Antirrh.*, I, 252c, 253a. Cf. Theod. Stud., *Antirrh.*, III, 409a, where the Iconoclast accuses the Orthodox of Arianism in depicting Christ as ψιλὸν ἄνθρωπον. The subject is treated more fully below, Ch. VII.

Constantine said, " Christ is not God and therefore I do not hold Mary to be Theotokos." [1] As Constantine is represented by the theologians, his Christology is consistent. It is Monophysite, sublimating Christ, and not humanitarian, either in an Arian or Nestorian sense. The Patriarch who must be credited with originating this inappropriate but effective story soon found that he had miscalculated the chances. In 742 Constantine crushed the rebel and recovered Constantinople. Anastasius was not deposed but underwent public humiliation. He was flogged [2] and exposed in the circus, mounted backwards on an ass. It may be conjectured from his readiness to associate himself with the rebels that he was a man of feeble character, and so escaped deposition, Constantine considering him incapable of hindering or helping any cause. During the time that Artavasdus held Constantinople, papal ambassadors were in the city with a letter for the Emperor. They also apparently put little faith in the Patriarch's judgment, for they waited until Constantine had recovered the city before they delivered their letter to the Emperor and the Papal enthronistica to the Patriarch. [3]

For ten years (744–753) Constantine took no recorded action in religious affairs. For three of these years (744–747) Constantinople was devastated by plague, according to the chroniclers a punishment from God for Iconoclasm. [4] It is possible that the Emperor was aware of superstitious feelings of this character and was content to wait. It was otherwise a period of comparative calm, free from war or internal dispute. Iconoclasm must have been making steady progress A generation was growing up in the Iconoclastic tradition. The hierarchy was almost without exception Iconoclastic, for when the Council of 753 assembled, there was no opposition and no less than 338

---

[1] Georg. Mon., II, p. 756 ; Cedr., I, 893b. George has combined two unrelated passages of Theophanes, the one before us and 877a, in which the Emperor is represented as asking the Patriarch Constantine, If we called the Mother of God (Theotokos) Mother of Christ, what harm would be done ?

[2] Τυφλωθέντι (was blinded) in the text of Theophanes, 848b, should be corrected to τυφθέντι. It is so transcribed by Cedrenus, I, 885b, and is translated by Anastasius percussus publice.

[3] Lib. Pont. (ed. Duchesne), I, 432. Hubert (see authorities for Chap. V), *op. cit.*, p. 33.

[4] Theoph., 852b ; Niceph., *Brev.*, 972c.

bishops[1] were present. At the Œcumenical Council of Constantinople in 381 there had been only 150 bishops. At the second Council of Nicæa which overthrew Iconoclasm the minutes record about 260 bishops or delegates for episcopal sees, the other members of the Council being monks. The years of peaceful propaganda were successful, and Theosteriktus is probably right at least in fact when he says : " The poison of heresy had spread everywhere." [2] The *Life of Stephen* in a catalogue of the districts which had refused Iconoclasm can only point to the three most distant outposts of the Empire, where the Imperial authority was least stable, the settlements in the Crimea,[3] Imperial Italy, and the south-east coast of Asia between Lycia and Joppa, with the island of Cyprus.[4]

By 752 twenty years had passed since Leo's more drastic policy had done its work. Progress had been made and the line of opposition must have revealed itself as well as the quarter from which opposition came. Except the work of St. John Damascene no apologetic writing of this period has survived. But the warfare of pamphlet and argument must have persisted. In that year Constantine decided to bring the question to an end by obtaining from a Council of the Church a definite pronouncement. " Looking forward to future impiety," says Theophanes, " the Emperor held synods and influenced his people to favour his policy." [5] We may connect with this propaganda the theological document which Nicephorus quotes in his first and second *Antirrhetici*, attributing it to Mammon—that is, Constantine writing either with his own pen or with that of his clerical advisers. Early in the following year the Patriarch Anastasius died of strangulated hernia, in which Theophanes sees a fit punishment for his outrages on God and his master.[6]

[1] Probably no monks were present in 753. The comment was made at Nicæa that the Iconoclasts boasted of the number at their Council. Mansi, XIII, 233a.
[2] *Vit. Nicet.*, xxiii.
[3] Where a vigorous anti-Iconoclast ruled as bishop (755–790), John of Gotthia. He sought consecration from the Iberian bishops of the Caucasus rather than hold communion with his own Patriarch at Constantinople. *Vit. Joann. ep. Gotth.* Act. Sanct. Jun. VII, 167–171.
[4] *Vit. Steph.*, 1117cd.
[5] 861a. The year is 6244, *i.e.* 752/753.
[6] *I.e.* Germanus, Theoph., 861a.

The vacancy in the see freed Constantine from the handicap of an invertebrate Patriarch. He summoned a Council which was intended to be œcumenical. The bishops met in the palace of Hieria below Chalcedon on the Asiatic side of the straits. They assembled on the 10th of February and continued their deliberations until the 8th of August. The length of time occupied is some indication of the care and honesty of the Council.[1] Of the Acts of the Council nothing survives but the "Ορος or Definition, preserved in the Acts of Nicæa II.[2] It is necessary by seeking every shred of evidence to clear this Council from the misrepresentation of which it has been the victim. Hefele, for example, speaks of "the dishonesty with which the Council went to work,"[3] as a self-evident fact. But the Council worked for seven months, an indication at least of the seriousness of its intention. The charge of dishonesty depends partly on the ready acquiescence of the Council in the Emperor's policy, partly on the evidence of certain of its members who afterwards attended the second Council of Nicæa and retracted their errors. These, notably Gregory, bishop of Neo-Cæsarea, and Theodore, bishop of Myra, stated that the extracts read from the Fathers in 753 had been garbled, were presented on slips, and the actual books from which the extracts were taken were not produced.[4] In other cases available evidence, it was alleged, was suppressed. The deacon Cosmas brought from the patriarchal Library an Old Testament MS. with scholia, in which the notes favourable to images were obliterated. On hearing this the ex-Iconoclast Theodore of Myra lamented (somewhat hypocritically, it would seem) that it was " the concealment of these treasuries of truth " that had done the harm.[5] That the members of the Council were pronounced Iconoclasts is undisputed. There was even a rumour current that at one session one of the bishops trampled under his feet a paten which bore pictures of Christ, his Mother, and St. John the Baptist.[6] But to be an Iconoclast was not in itself dishonest. The

---

[1] The second Council of Nicæa only sat from Sept. 24th to Oct. 13th.
[2] Mansi, XIII, 207 *sqq.*
[3] *Hist. of the Councils*, Eng. trans., V, p. 373.
[4] Mansi, XIII, 37b. Cf. 173d.
[5] *Ib.* 188cce.
[6] *Vit. Steph.*, 1144b.

seven converts who appeared at Nicæa were too deeply
implicated to be impartial witnesses.

On the œcumenical character of the Council there are
graver doubts. Its president was Theodosius, archbishop
of Ephesus, son of the Emperor Apsimar. He was supported
by Sisinnius, bishop of Perga, also known as Pastillas,[1]
and by Basil of Antioch in Pisidia, styled Tricaccabus.[2]
Not a single Patriarch was present. The see of Constantinople was vacant. Whether the Pope and the Patriarchs
of Alexandria, Antioch, and Jerusalem were invited or not
is unknown. They were not present either in person or
by deputy.[3] The Council of Nicæa considered this was
a serious flaw in the legitimacy of the Council. " It had
not the co-operation of the Roman Pope of the period nor
of his clergy, either by representative or by encyclical
letter, as the law of Councils requires." [4] The *Life of
Stephen* borrows this objection from the Acts and embroiders
it to suit the spirit of the age of Theodore. " It had not
the approval of the Pope of Rome, although there is a canon
that no ecclesiastical measures may be passed without the
Pope." [5] The absence of the other Patriarchs is then
noticed.[6]

[1] Theoph., 861b.
[2] *adv. Const. Cab.*, 332a ; *Vit. Steph.*, 1140b. His name signifies the Three-Legged Pot, probably in allusion to his appearance.
[3] There was ample opportunity to invite the Pope. In 752 and in 753 embassies passed between Constantinople and Rome, but the question of images does not seem to have been raised. Perhaps we may infer that less spiritual problems fully occupied the attention of the Pope. See below, Ch. V. *adv. Const. Cab.*, 333a, says that the Pope refused to attend, but this need only be a rhetorical flourish.
[4] Mansi, XIII, 207d. Lombard is inaccurate in saying : Les évêques de Nicée . . . n'ont pas cherché à invoquer la nullité du concile de 753 pour vice de forme. *Op. cit.*, p. 135.
[5] *Vit. Steph.*, 1144c. καίπερ κανόνος προκειμένου μὴ δεῖν τὰ ἐκκλησιαστικὰ δίχα τοῦ Πάπα Ρώμης κανονίζεσθαι. This is not strictly true. Nicephorus agrees in principle. " Without Rome no conciliar action would be approved because Rome has the primacy." *Apol. pro S. Imag.*, 597a. The last practically reproduces the official Papal view. Hadrian writing to Tarasius on the eve of the Council of Nicæa asks that one of the first acts of the Council should be to anathematise the pseudo-synod of 753, " it having been summoned without the apostolic see of Peter, the see which is conspicuously first in the world and the head of all the churches." Mansi, XII, 1083. The earliest reference to the imaginary canon is Socrates, *Eccles. Hist.*, II, 8, 17, and Sozomen, III, 10, who wrongly infer it from the letter of Pope Julius to the Eastern bishops (cited in Athanasius, *Apol. contra Arian.*). See Barnby, s.v. Julius, in D.C.B.
[6] Mansi, XIII, 207d ; *adv. Const. Cab.*, 333a ; *Vit. Steph.*, 1144c.

But clearly the technical objection was not felt to be decisive even by those who raised it. For they proceeded to refute the Council in detailed argument. In fact, this Council was evidently the greatest triumph the Iconoclastic party achieved in the whole history of the struggle. It never disappears from the discussion. The Council of Nicæa laboriously refutes every word of its Definition and the exegesis of its patristic citations. It is the great weapon in the Iconoclastic Revival under Leo the Armenian.[1] The Council of 815 simply restored its decisions.[2] In the same way every defender of the Images, from the anonymous author of *adv. Const. Caball.*[3] onwards, sooner or later comes to the Council. Fifty years after it sat, Theodore Studites was still discussing its orthodoxy as a vital question of the day,[4] while to his contemporary, the Frankish Emperor Charles, it was just as much (or as little) a General Council as the second of Nicæa.[5] The Council was what Constantine designed it to be, an authoritative pronouncement of the Church in support of his policy.

From the little that remains of its proceedings it appears that its exact purpose was " to make a scriptural examination into the deceitful colouring of the pictures, which draws down the spirit of man from the lofty adoration of God to the low and material adoration of the creature, and under divine guidance express their view of the matter."[6] The Council proceeded along two lines of argument ; (i) They related the question of the image of Christ to the doctrine of the person of Christ as defined in the six General Councils, and drew the conclusion that to make a representation of Christ either implied depicting the Godhead and mingling it with the manhood (which was Monophysite) or dividing Christ into two beings and showing the manhood separately (which was Nestorian).[7]

---

[1] Cf. *Script. Incert.*, 1036c.

[2] Ὅρος of 815 in Hefele-Leclerq, III (2), App. iv, pp. 1217–1221. Theod. Stud. calls it " the Council summoned to confirm that at Blachernæ " (*i.e.* that of 753), 465a. Cf. *Vit. Niceph.*, 136b.

[3] 333a. His is probably the earliest attack on the Council, being prior to the assembly of Nicæa II. " The Iconoclastic synod is without head and offensive to God. . . . We can call it best a Jewish sanhedrin."

[4] *Ep.*, II, 72.

[5] *Libr. Carol.*, passim.

[6] Mansi, XIII, 207. I quote the translation (corrected) of Perceval.

[7] See below on the theology of the controversy.

(ii) They examined Scripture and the Fathers and collected passages which told against images.[1] From the image of Christ they argued a fortiori that images of the Virgin and the saints were forbidden ; for such only recall the heathen use of idols and add nothing to the glory the saints enjoy with God.[2]

These two lines of argument correspond exactly to the two described by Nicephorus [3] as marking two distinct stages of the movement. " The writer, who was the inventor and father of the movement,[4] made his attack by applying to image-worship the passages of Scripture and the Fathers which dealt with idolatry." It is not difficult to give this anonymous protagonist a name—Constantine of Nacolia. Later a new line of argument developed, " derived from Arian and Manichæan sources," connecting the controversy with the doctrine of the person of Christ.[5] The other evidence supports this. The earliest defence of the pictures, by St. John of Damascus, by Pope Gregory II, and by the Patriarch Germanus, does not seem to enter into the Christological argument.[6] In his *Antirrhetici* Nicephorus answers, sentence by sentence, this Christological argument, the author of which he designates Mammon. Nicephorus certainly identifies Mammon with the Emperor Constantine.[7] From the statements of Nicephorus it is clear that the Christological controversy was first seriously used to solve the image-problem on the side of the Iconoclasts and in the entourage of Constantine, if not by Constantine himself. It was to this theological argument that the Council of 753 gave most attention. It receives the first place in the Definition and the longest treatment. It can hardly be a coincidence that the Council's decision on this point is almost verbally identical with what Nicephorus gives as the summary of the argument of Mammon. A

---

[1] Mansi, XIII, 280a *sqq.*   [2] *L.c.* 269.

[3] *Apol. pro S. Imag.*, 560c.

[4] τοῦ εὑρέτου καὶ πάτρος τῆς ἀποστασίας.

[5] Niceph., *l.c.*

[6] Greg. II to Germanus, Mansi, XIII, 92c. Germanus to John of Synnada, *ib.* 100a. Germanus to Thomas of Claudiopolis, *ib.* 108a.

[7] *E.g.* Antirrh., III, 493–496, where he describes the actions of Constantine by the name of Mammon. Cf. 504c. Mammon was credited with length of life, prosperity, and victory as a consequence of his Iconoclasm. Cf. the frequent appearance of the word κόπρος in connection with Mammon. *Antirrh.*, I, 229d, 289a, 296c.

picture of Christ either implies the representation of God-head (*i.e.* Monophysitism), or else it is the picture of a mere man and is Nestorianism.[1] The nature of Mammon's pamphlet can therefore be inferred. It was Constantine's theological argument used for preliminary propaganda, and eventually adopted by the Council as the framework of its decision.

One of the citations is of special interest, both because it contains phrases that indicate the audience to which it was addressed, and because of its subject. " If we can persuade you," said Mammon, " that in regard to this one representation [*i.e.* of Christ] we are right, then we purpose to bring before you views on the other images, for you to judge of them likewise. For we shall rejoice in your judgment when you agree with the other bishops and find the arguments for accepting the evidence sound." [2] This passage apparently led to the discussion of images of the Virgin and the saints.[3] On this subject it is commonly agreed that Constantine held a position far in advance of the Council. The Council condemned images of the Virgin and the saints, but it set out anathemas against those who did not confess the Theotokos, against those who did not admit her to be " higher than every creature, visible and invisible, and do not with sincere faith seek her intercessions as of one having confidence in her access to our God, since she bare him," and against those who denied the profit of the invocation of saints.[4] But Constantine himself denied the intercession of the Virgin and the invocation of saints. He abolished the word Theotokos,[5] prohibited prayers in her name and litanies

---

[1] Niceph., *Antirrh.*, I, 908a ; Mansi, XIII, 245b. There are other sentences in the citations from Mammon closely resembling the phraseology of the Definition, *e.g.* the relation of the Eucharist to Christ's body. *Antirrh.*, II, 337a ; Mansi, XIII, 264d. " The word Christ is understood to signify not only man but God." *Antirrh.*, I, 309a ; Mansi, XIII, 216a.

[2] ὡς ἐὰν εἰς τοῦτο τὸ ἐν εἰκόνισμα πληροφορήσομεν ὑμᾶς ὅτι καλῶς λέγομεν τότε καὶ περὶ τῶν ἄλλων εἰκόνων σκόπους προαγάγειν ἔχομεν ἐνώπιον ὑμῶν καὶ ὡς κρίνετε καὶ περὶ ἐκείνων. τῇ καὶ κρίσει ὑμῶν ἔχομεν ἀσμενίσαι ὅτε μέλλετε καὶ μετὰ τῶν ἄλλων ἐπισκόπων συμφωνεῖν. καὶ ἐξ εὐλόγων προφάσεων μαρτυρίας παριστᾶν. *Antirrh.*, II, 340d.

[3] The bishops addressed are probably those in one of the preliminary meetings to which Theophanes refers, 861a, the other bishops being those whose opinions Constantine had already collected.

[4] Mansi, *loc. cit.*, anathemas, 3, 15, and 17.

[5] Niceph., *Antirrh.*, II, 341c.

to her Son that introduced her name, precisely because orthodox teaching confessed her ready access to him. " He prohibited the invocation of Mary and of every saint, denying their power of intercession." [1] From these facts it has been inferred that the Council refused to listen to the full programme of the Emperor and preserved a moderate position. This is possible. But the relevant passage Nicephorus quotes from Mammon does not imply that anything was suggested by Constantine beyond the prohibition of figures of the Virgin and the saints. Nicephorus cites nothing further from Mammon,[2] and all the evidence confirms the statement made at Nicæa II in reference to the intercession of saints that " the Iconoclasts *subsequently* abandoned this themselves and obliterated the words in their books." [3] It was not that the Council was sufficiently independent to anathematise the Emperor's personal opinions, but that it anathematised them in ignorance.

The decision of the Council was that, " supported by the Holy Scriptures and the Fathers, we declare unani-

[1] Niceph., *Antirrh.*, II, 341c. Cf. *adv. Cons. Caball.*, 337d ; Theoph., 885b (under A.M. 6258, thirteen years after the Council). Theoph., 877a, himself represents the Emperor under A.M. 6255 as using the name Theotokos.

[2] He gives all the views of Constantine on the saints and intercession without quotation, which seems to imply that Mammon had not included the subject in his book. The only document stating explicitly that Constantine brought these violent opinions before the Council is the Synodicon Vetus, which says that at the Council Constantine denied the intercessions and burnt the relics. Mansi, XII, 758. This Synodicon is a 9/10-century compilation of little value. It must remain an open question whether or not the Council knowingly repudiated views openly held by the Emperor. Probably they did not. Besides the fact that no authority except the Synodicon mentions the Emperor's views on intercession until after the Council, it is hardly possible that the Emperor would have tolerated the deliberate rejection of his views that Lombard, *e.g.* assumes, provided he attached any significance to them. Lombard, *op. cit.*, pp. 114 *sqq.* On the other hand, there seems little indication that he did attach such significance to them. The whole series of views attributed to Constantine on the saints and the Virgin and their names may be nothing but an imaginary attack built on the Emperor's prohibition of pictures and images of the saints. The orthodox said, If he insults the picture of the Theotokos, he insults the Theotokos herself. Then the Emperor might say, That is not the Theotokos, it is an image. Rumour would represent this as a denial of the Theotokos, or might even put it that the Emperor had said that Mary was not the Theotokos. The summary of this purely personal and subjective criticism is (i) the Council did not anathematise Constantine's views on the Virgin and the saints, because (ii) he had not divulged those views in 753, and (iii) he never held these views at all in the peculiarly nihilistic form reported by the chroniclers.

[3] Mansi, XIII, 348c.

mously in the name of the Holy Trinity that there shall be rejected and removed and anathematised out of the Christian Church every likeness which is made out of any material and colour whatsoever by the evil art of painters." In future not only to venerate a picture or image, but to make one, to set one up in public or private, or even to possess one secretly, would be punished by degradation from orders for a clerk. For a monk or layman the penalty was even more serious ; the offender, after the anathema was passed on him, would be liable to trial in the secular court as an adversary of God and an enemy of the doctrine of the Fathers.[1] It was in this clause that the Emperor found his most powerful weapon, as subsequent events show. It may well be that this discloses the chief demand the Emperor made from the Council.

The Council gave special warning against indiscriminate destruction of sacred vessels and vestments decorated with figures. No alteration was to be made without the assent of the Patriarch or the command of the Emperor. Secular officials were warned against robbing churches on pretext of destroying images. Many such acts of Vandalism must have occurred. At the Council of Nicæa, Demetrius, a deacon and sacristan, stated that in the archives of Constantinople he found that two MSS. described in the catalogue as having pictures in silver had been burnt. He also showed a volume of Constantine the Chartophylax mutilated inside to destroy passages supporting images, but as the Imperial secretary pointed out, still bearing pictures of saints intact on its binding.[2] The preservation of the binding may be due to the Council's ruling on this point.[3] The Council then anathematised all divergences from orthodox belief " in the Father, the Son, and the Holy Ghost, one Godhead, nature and substance, will and operation, virtue and dominion, kingdom and power in three subsistences, that is in their most glorious Persons." Besides

[1] Mansi, XIII, 328.

[2] *Ib.* 184de.

[3] *Vit. Steph.*, which has used the Acta, perverts the facts by describing the Council as having excommunicated the faithful, torn up the sacred vestments, expunged the title Saint from the names of those who bear it, 1144b. This contains one true statement, one direct contradiction of the actual ruling of the Council, that on the sacred vestments, while the Council did not touch the question of the title Saint at all. It shows how little value can be set on the more lurid statements of the *Vit. Steph.*

52 *A History of the Iconoclastic Controversy*

those who failed to accept the Chalcedonian formulæ they anathematised "any who ventured to represent with material colours or by human figure the divine image of the Word after the Incarnation, the hypostatic union of the two natures, or Christ the man separately." Lastly, they anathematised those who attempt to represent the saints, those who deny their intercession or who deny the resurrection of the dead,[1] and the judgment, and those who refuse to accept this Holy and Œcumenical Seventh Council.[2]

On 8th August the Council was brought by the Emperor from Hieria to the church of St. Mary of Blachernæ, the extreme northern suburb of Constantinople, when the Emperor, holding by the hand Constantine, bishop of Sylæum in Pamphylia, announced, that this was the new Patriarch. The uncanonical action of the Emperor is strongly reprobated in the *Life of Stephen* (followed by George the Monk). It is equivalent to the Emperor making himself a priest and ordaining to the ministry, and the enormity of it is increased by the military career of the Emperor and by the scandal of his triple marriage.[3] From an early date the new Patriarch was marked as the Emperor's table companion and designated the Phatriarch or Mess-President.[4] His subsequent career shows him to be a nonentity of the type of Patriarch usual between Germanus and Nicephorus.

The Council having reported their conclusions, on the 17th August the Emperor, accompanied by his young son Leo, and by the members of the Council, took part in the public proclamation of the conciliar decrees. The usual orthodox and loyal acclamations followed. "The divine Emperors Constantine and Leo said : ' Let the Holy and Œcumenical Council say if with the assent of all the most holy bishops the definition just read has been set forth.' The holy synod cried : ' This we all believe, we all are of the same mind. This is the faith of the apostles. Many

---

[1] This is especially interesting because Nicephorus describes the Iconoclasts contemporary with himself as " never mentioning death, resurrection, or judgment." *Antirrh.*, III, 489b.
[2] Mansi, XIII, 340 *sqq.*.
[3] *Vit. Steph.*, 1112c ; Georg. Mon., II, 755.
[4] By the earliest source, *adv. Const. Cab.*, 332a. The φρατρία from which φατριάρχης is derived signifies in late Greek the military mess.

years to the Emperors. They are the light of orthodoxy. God preserve your Empire. You have banished all idolatry. You have destroyed the heresies of Germanus, George,[1] and Mansur.[2] Anathema to Germanus the double-minded, the wood-worshipper. Anathema to George his associate, the falsifier of the doctrine of the Fathers. Anathema to Mansur of the evil name and the Saracen opinions, the betrayer of Christ and enemy of the Empire, the teacher of impiety and perverter of Scripture, to Mansur be anathema. The Trinity has deposed the three.'[3] The Council congratulated the Emperor : ' To-day salvation is come to the world because thou hast delivered us from idols.' "[4]

The weapon put into the Emperor's hand by the Council was not brought into use at once. Trouble with the Bulgarians and Slavs diverted attention from religious problems. But one small act of policy in the year after the Council shows the tenacity with which Constantine held to his position. The suppression of the Slav revolt in Thrace gave him the opportunity of settling more loyal subjects in some of the depopulated districts. He chose Syrians and Armenians from Theodosiopolis and Melitene, a district recently recovered from the Saracens, and he chose them because they were Paulicians or Monophysites and therefore no friends to orthodoxy.[5] In 761 occurs a martyrdom in the cause of images, the first certainly in the reign of Constantine, possibly the first in the history of the controversy. The victim was a monk of Blachernæ named Calybites (the Hermit of the Cell). His first name was either Andrew[6] or Peter.[7] He came to the royal

---

[1] George of Cyprus. See above.

[2] *I.e.* St. John of Damascus, who, this passage implies, was now dead.

[3] Mansi, XIII, 351.

[4] *Vit. Steph.*, 1121b.

[5] Theoph., 865a ; Georg. Mon., II, 752. Nicephorus in order to depreciate Constantine attributes the removal of these people to Constantine's inability to protect them against the Saracen. *Antirrh.*, III, 508. Many of the immigrants were not Paulicians but Monophysites (Jacobites) from the district of Germanicia recovered in 745, and the more probable tradition is that preserved by George, who calls them " the Emperor's kindred," θεοπασχῖται κατὰ Πέτρον τὸν δείλαιον (*i.e.* Peter the Fuller). Georg. Mon., II, 752. Constantine was himself probably a Monophysite.

[6] Theoph., 872b.

[7] *Vit. Steph.*, 1165c. The editors of Act. Sanct. accept the name Peter and suppose that Theophanes confused him with Andrew in Crisi. A.S. Oct. VIII, 128, May III, 625.

palace, denounced Constantine as a new Julian and another Valens,[1] was flogged, and died under the lash. His body was rescued by his sisters from being thrown into the sea.

It was evident by now that the whole opposition to Iconoclasm centred in the monasteries. The reason that the monasteries filled this rôle is an entirely creditable one. The monasteries were the sources of culture ; since Leo had attacked the schools, the monasteries were the only intellectual centres. Theophanes, Nicephorus, and Theodore Studites, all of whom were monks, are sufficient evidence that the monasteries contained nearly all the learning of the day. It was the monasteries also that provided the only schools of art. So that even making allowance for vested interests and conservative traditions, we are compelled to admit more than obscurantism behind the attitude of the monks. From the monastcries resistance to the Imperial policy was organised. Some indication of this is given in the *Life of Stephen*, in the statement that Stephen was consulted by monks from Europe, Byzantium, Thynia, and Bithynia, and by hermits from Pisidia.[2] After settling the Bulgarian war, the Emperor took direct measures against the monks,[3] " the idolaters worthy to be forgotten for ever," as he called them.[4] The year was 764/5.[5] Thus it is only forty years after the first Iconoclastic action that the objective of the attack is narrowed down to the monks. " The attack fell most severely on the holy order of monks," says Nicephorus.[6] This fact should be sufficient to dispose of the theory that Iconoclasm was originally conceived as an instrument for establishing a state supremacy or for repressing the anti-military tendencies of monasticism. The monks came to be the chief

---

[1] Theoph., 872b. The atrocities of the Arian Valens against the orthodox are notorious. *Vit. Steph.*, 1165c, says less pointedly a Dacian and a transgressor (παραβάτης). Dacian no doubt is Valens, who was of Pannonian descent. παραβάτης was applied to Julian with the significance of Apostate.

[2] *Vit. Steph.*, 1113c.

[3] ἀντανακρουσθεὶς δὲ ὑπὸ τῶν τῆς εὐσεβείας μυστῶν τῶν τοῦ μοναρχικοῦ σχήματος κατ' αὐτῶν συγκροτεῖ τὸν πόλεμον. *Vit. Steph.*, 1112a.

[4] *Ib.* ἀμνημόνευτοι was his usual name for monks, parodying the word μόνευτοι. Niceph., *Antirrh.*, III, 517a.

[5] Niceph., *Brev.*, 981b, says after the Bulgarian defeat in the 3rd Indiction, Theophanes (888b) fixes this date as November A.M. 6257, 4th Indiction. The November of 6257 would be 764, which the Indiction of Nicephorus confirms. This is one of the cases where Theophanes' Indiction is clearly wrong.

[6] Niceph., *Brev.*, 981b.

victims after forty years because, as the movement advanced, the monks revealed themselves as the centre of opposition.

Theophanes introduces the campaign against the monks with an anecdote damaging to the Emperor's orthodoxy. The Emperor sent for the Patriarch and said : " If we called the Mother of God Mother of Christ what harm would be done ? " The Patriarch embraced him and answered, " Have mercy, sir, and let no thought of this kind enter your mind. Do you not see how Nestorius is held up to rebuke and dishonour throughout the world ? " The Emperor replied, " I but asked to learn. Let the matter go no further." [1] Whether the Emperor was indulging his speculative inclinations, or whether he was showing his hostility to the name Theotokos, the expression was understood by the orthodox to have a sinister meaning, indicating further action against them.

The leading figure in the monastic resistance was Stephen of Mount Auxentius, distinguished from the Protomartyr by the title " The Younger." He takes the first place in Theophanes' narrative as the new Protomartyr, while his biography by his namesake, deacon of St. Sophia, is much the longest and most valuable of the hagiological writings of the Iconoclastic period. [2] Stephen was born about 715. His parents were among the orthodox refugees who left Constantinople at the first Iconoclastic outbreak. They retired to Chalcedon, where Stephen was placed in the care of John, head of the monastery of Mount Auxentius. By the time of Constantine's attack Stephen had himself risen to the headship of the house. At the beginning of the attack (763/4) [3] Callistus, a patrician, was sent to get Stephen's assent to the decrees of the Iconoclastic Council. The request was sternly rejected. Callistus refrained from using his guards to arrest the monk,[4] but a member of the

---

[1] Theoph., 877a.

[2] On the chronology and historical value of *Vit. Steph.*, see on Authorities, p. 15.

[3] Theoph., 830b, fixes the date of Stephen's martyrdom as Nov. 20th in the 25th year of the Emperor's reign, Indiction 4, *i.e.* 764, the indiction being wrong. Nicephorus, *Brev.*, 984a, puts the general attack first. The *Vit. Steph.* represents Stephen as a witness of the whole persecution. But the chronology of the *Vit. Steph.* is not related to anything, nor can it be really authoritative. See above, p. 15.

[4] *Vit. Steph.*, 1124. That Callistus handled the situation cautiously and kindly, though not stated, is to be gathered from the text.

community, named Sergius, was induced to bring a series
of charges against his head, that he had made treasonable
accusations of heresy against the Emperor, had plotted
against him, and had seduced a noble lady whom he kept
as a nun. A local director of taxes named Anticalamus,
and a maid of the lady, helped Sergius with his charges.[1]
Stephen's alleged victim (her name was Anna) was brought
before the Emperor, then on campaign against " the
Scythians." [2] She was asked if her motive in entering
a monastery was lust. Her reply was that Stephen was a
holy man, a teacher who helped the soul, and her spiritual
guide.[3] The true meaning of the charge against Anna
was that Stephen was a powerful influence in inducing
noble women not to live a life of immorality but to enter
convents. Anna was flogged by two men simultaneously
on the back and the breast, and then confronted with her
treacherous maid. She still denied any misconduct with
Stephen.[4]

As this plot came to nothing a member of the Emperor's
staff, George the Syncletus, was used as an agent pro-
vocateur. He came to Stephen and asked to be admitted
to the monastic life. This request Stephen granted very
unwillingly, for he recognised the postulant for one of the
Emperor's men by his shaven face.[5] The Emperor then
declared publicly that George had been enticed into the
religious life, and stirred up public indignation.[6] Three
days later George escaped. A silentium was called in the
theatre of the hippodrome, where George was exposed
to the people, who shouted, Punish him, kill him, burn him
for breaking thy law.[7] George was dressed in military
garb and placed by the Emperor among the strators.

After the enactment of this comedy a large force of
soldiers crossed to Mount Auxentius, fired the church and
monastery and dragged Stephen from his cell. He was
brought to the monastery of Philippicus at the village of

---

[1] *Vit. Steph.*, 1125d.
[2] *I.e.* Bulgarians. It would be the campaign of Anchialos (762).
[3] *Vit. Steph.* 1129b.
[4] *Ib.* 1132c.
[5] *Ib.* 1136a. The Emperor required all his personal staff to be clean shaven, which was in the eyes of the author of the *Vit. Steph.* a blasphemous attack on the law of Moses. 1133c.
[6] *Ib.* 1136b.
[7] *I.e.* Stephen. *Ib.* 1137a.

Chrysopolis,[1] where a commission of Iconoclastic bishops [2] and officials were sent to interview him. They included Theodosius " falsely styled " bishop of Ephesus, Constantine " the Revolutionary," [3] Sisinnius Pastillas, Basil Tricaccabus, with the patrician Callistus already mentioned, Comboconon the Antigrapheus (Audit Clerk), and Masara " the Saracen-minded." [4] The Patriarch Constantine refused to accompany the Commission, alleging Stephen's power of eloquence in the Spirit,[5] from which it would not be rash to infer that the patriarch was an Iconoclast but not an ardent supporter of the campaign against the monks. The Commission met in the church of Chrysopolis. Stephen was brought before them, so weak that he had to be supported on each side. The Commissioners began by remonstrating with him mildly for classing them as heretics, to which Stephen sternly replied in the words of Elijah, " It is not I that trouble Israel but thou and thy father's house " (1 Kings xviii. 17). Constantine, bishop of Nicomedia, who was a young and vigorous man of thirty, made as though to stamp upon Stephen who had fallen on the ground, and a soldier kicked him in the stomach.[6] Callistus and Comboconon restrained the violence of Constantine and offered Stephen the choice of submission to the decrees of the Iconoclastic Council or death as a rebel to the law of the Emperor. Stephen boldly chose death, but asked first to hear the decree of the Council. Constantine read the title, " The Definition of the Seventh Holy Œcumenical Council," whereupon Stephen gave a long harangue which is a close but garbled version of the refutation of the Iconoclastic Council's Definition read at Nicæa.[7] He con-

---

[1] *Vit. Steph.*, 1137c, 1140b.

[2] ἐπίσκοτοι, " men of darkness " they are called. In 1120a the *Vit. Steph.* attributes the word to St. John of Damascus, but it does not occur in his extant works. See M.P.G. 94, pp. 1229–1230.

[3] ὁ νεωτερίζων. The word is used much in the spirit of the modern use of the term Bolshevik.

[4] The list is interesting as representing the author's idea of the leading personnel of Iconoclasm. He includes Constantine of Nacolia, the adviser of Leo III nearly forty years before. But he must have been dead or more would have been heard of him. Masara may be a doublet of Beser. *Vid., supra.*

[5] *Vit. Steph.*, 1140b.   [6] *Ib.* 1141b.

[7] *Ib.* 1144. Cf. Mansi, XIII, 207d *sqq.* This is obviously unhistorical. The whole of this interview is suspiciously like a scene constructed to refute the Iconoclastic Council. Definite misstatements are inserted, *e.g.* that the Council expunged the title Saint from all saints, apostles, and martyrs, and tore up the sacred vestments. *Vit. Steph.*, 1144b. Cf. *supra*, p. 51.

F

cluded by crying, "Anathema to those who worship not
our Lord Jesus Christ represented in a picture as concerning
his manhood."[1] The Commission reported to Constantine,
Callistus even speaking favourably of Stephen's courage
and conviction. The threatened sentence of death was not
carried out, and Stephen was banished to Proconesus.[2]

Two years later Stephen was recalled on a charge of
teaching idolatry, and was incarcerated in the prison
of Phiale.[3] He was examined by the Emperor, and demonstrated the justice of his attitude to images by throwing
on the ground a coin bearing the Emperor's effigy and
trampling on it.[4] The destruction of the monks was now
at its height. The prison was filled with them, and stories
of suffering and martyrdom came from all quarters.[5] In
the early winter,[6] Constantine, learning that the prison
had become a rallying-place for all the orthodox, removed
Stephen to the place called Maura.[7] The Emperor held
a public assembly and bitterly denounced the monks.
One of his party suggested that Stephen should be put to
death. "That is only what he wishes," said the Emperor.
"Besides, the Empress would not wish the Broumalia to
be defiled with bloodshed." Stephen was therefore kept
in the prætorium.[8] There another effort was made to win
him. Two of the younger members of the Imperial staff
were sent to remonstrate with him. They fell victims to
his arguments, but reported falsely that they had beaten
him nearly to death. Next morning the Emperor learnt

[1] *Vit. Steph.*, 1145a.
[2] *Ib.* It is very difficult to believe that the case of Stephen was prolonged
as the *Life* represents. The *Life* constructs artificial situations to bring into
the story the whole of Constantine's persecution of the monks and all the
actors in the drama. The whole of the Chrysopolis incident seems unhistorical.
[3] *Ib.* 1156d. It would be 764, if the dates of the Life were anything but
imaginary.
[4] *Ib.* 1160a.
[5] On the details see below. They are introduced into the *Life of Stephen*,
apparently to make the picture complete.
[6] *I.e.* 764. Constantine was celebrating the Broumalia (a kind of Harvest
Festival in honour of Demeter and Dionysus), which was held between
Nov. 24th and Dec. 17th. It had been prohibited by the 62nd Canon of the
Quinisext Council, but survived at intervals up to the time of Constantine
Porphyrogenitus in the tenth century. Its observance was popular, and cannot
be taken as indicating any anti-Catholic tendency in Constantine. See
Crawford, J. R., de Bruma et Brumalibus Festis., *B.Z.*, vol. xxiii, 1920, pp.
364–396.
[7] Said to be a dismantled church of St. Maura. *Vit. Steph.*, 1169c.
[8] *Ib.* 1172c.

what had happened. " Will no one aid me ? " he cried.
" I am not even Emperor. He is Emperor at whose feet
ye fell." " But, sir," they answered, " who is above you
in all the world ? " " Stephen of Auxentius, the leader
of the monks," replied Constantine.[1] A rush was made
to the prison by a crowd of Imperial servants, soldiers, and
idlers. Stephen was brought out, a rope was tied to his feet,
and he was dragged into the public highway. He was
kicked and beaten. As he was being dragged past the image
of the martyr Theodore he saluted the image. Immediately
a man in the mob, Philomates by name, took a lump of
wood from a fire-extinguishing apparatus, and dispatched
him with it.[2] He had been sadly mishandled, but his dead
body was subjected to further ill-usage, and eventually
after a fish-cook had split the skull and scattered the brains,
the corpse was thrown into the hole where the bodies of
pagans and criminals were buried. This had once been the
church of the martyr Pelagius and was now known as the
place of Pelagius.[3] The chronology and the evidence
of the chroniclers make it difficult to believe that Stephen's
trial and execution were so prolonged as this narrative
requires. It does, however, reproduce with great verisimilitude the verbal and physical violence and the Oriental
ferocity with which theological problems were so often
debated in Constantinople.

If we place the martyrdom of Stephen in November
764,[4] it will mark the beginning of a persecution of the monks
which lasted for ten years, and only ceased with the death
of Constantine. At times other classes were involved as

---

[1] There is little verisimilitude in these dramatic scenes. Constantine
laid his plans and carried them out unhesitatingly. He was not a Henry II.

[2] *Vit. Steph.*, 1176c. Theodore (martyr of the persecution of Galerius) was
extremely popular in Constantinople. Three churches were named after him.
The salute to the effigy of the martyr is probably unhistorical, for it is unlikely
that a conspicuous statue should have been permitted to survive to this date.
The rest of the martyrdom is confirmed by Theophanes (880b) and by
Nicephorus (*Brev.*, 984b). Nicephorus gives the scene as the Forum Bovis, some
halfway across the city. Theophanes confuses the scene of the martyrdom with
the place where the body was buried.

[3] *Vit. Steph.*, 1177cd ; Theoph., *loc. cit.* ; Niceph., *Brev.*, *loc. cit.* The place
is called τὰ Πελαγίου. The explanation that it was once a church is probably
a guess of the *Vita*. Theophanes does not appear to know the origin of the
name. Possibly Pelagius was a former owner of the property.

[4] So Clugnet and Pargoire, *Mont St. Auxence*, Paris, 1904, pp. 50–53,
accepting the *Vita* as completely historical. If its detail is not accepted as
historical, the chronology of course is no more than a piece of realistic fiction.

supporters. The fall of Stephen is alleged to have led to
the punishment of certain army officers, ostensibly for
treason, and probably for close association with Stephen.[1]
The Emperor devised as a test an oath against images,
which was imposed universally, at least as far as the
Imperial authority was active.[2] The Patriarch Constantine,
evidently already evoking suspicion, was required to take
the oath publicly. He was also required to dissociate
himself entirely from monasticism by taking a wife, eating
flesh meat, and listening to orchestral music at the royal
table.[3] The active measures which began in the winter
of 764 were probably interrupted by the Bulgarian war
and resumed in August 765.[4] Monks were seized in large
numbers and publicly made to parade the circus, each
leading a woman by the hand.[5] They were spit upon,
and ridiculed by the populace now all attached to the new
party. Many monks joined their persecutors, yielding,
some to force, others to bribery, and others to hope of gain.
They put on lay dress and married.[6] The parade of monks
took place on 24th August. On the 25th a conspiracy
against the Emperor was unmasked, the details of which
are obscure. Nineteen highly placed officials were concerned, including among others Constantine Podopagouros,
patrician and logothete of the cursus, Strategius, patrician
and domesticus of the excubiti, Antiochus, dux of Sicily
and logothete of the cursus, David, spatharius and count of

[1] ὥσπερ ἐπὶ καθοσιώσει ἁλόντας. Niceph., *Brev.*, 984b. Nicephorus adds
that some were executed and others expatriated. Theophanes says only
that they were punished, 880c. Theophanes makes this a separate incident
from the conspiracy of Podopagouros, 884a, but they look like the same
incident drawn from two sources.
[2] Both Theoph., *loc. cit.*, and Nicephorus, *loc. cit.*, agree that it was applied
universally. Nicephorus describes those who were subjected to it as ἅπαν αὐτοῦ τὸ
ὑπήκοον, Theophanes as πάντας τοὺς ὑπὸ τὴν αὐτοῦ βασιλείαν. adv. Const. Cab.,
misdating it at the beginning of Constantine's reign, says that the edict requiring
the oath was sent to all provinces of the Empire, 337c. *Vit. Steph.*, 1112a,
states that the oath was imposed in Constantinople, but says nothing of other
parts. No doubt its extension depended on the zeal of local administration.
Plato, the uncle of Theodore Studites, was left unmolested as head of the
monastery of Symboli at Olympus in Bithynia. Theod. Stud., 820c.
[3] Constantine had been a monk. Monks were prohibited from operatic
performances by Canon 24 of Quinisext. Nicephorus is silent about this
humiliation of Constantine.
[4] Theoph., 881b.
[5] *Ib.* According to Nicephorus the women were nuns. *Brev.*, 985a;
Antirrh., III, 524a.
[6] Niceph., *Brev.*, 981d.

Opsikion. Theophanes offers the partly improbable explanation that the Emperor was jealous of their physical attractions and of their communications with Stephen.[1] It may well have been a plot against the Emperor, perhaps encouraged by Stephen before his death and brought to a head during the Emperor's absence in the early months of 765. Moreover, the already suspected patriarch Constantine was implicated in it. He was banished first across the strait to Hieria, and then to Prince's island. The ring-leaders, Constantine Podopagouros and Strategius, were executed, the other principals blinded.[2]

At the end of the year the Emperor again appointed a Patriarch himself.[3] He chose Nicetas, a priest of the church of the Holy Apostles, one of the secular clergy, who presents some unusual features. He was a eunuch and a Slav, who, tradition said, never learned to pronounce Greek correctly.[4] Further, with the intention of pushing his measures against the monks, the Emperor carefully selected administrative officials definitely in sympathy with his views. Thus Michael Melissenus was appointed to the command of the Anatolic theme, Michael Lachanodrakon to the Thracesian and Manes (a sinister name says Theophanes) to the Bucellarian.[5]

The Emperor's severity increased, no doubt as a sequel to the abortive plot of Podopagouros. In the year following the plot occurs the first mention of a prohibition of prayers, written or unwritten, to the Virgin or the saints.[6] Such a prohibition is characteristic of the Monophysite zeal for safeguarding the unity and majesty of God which is

---

[1] Theoph., 881b, 884a. If they were among those who consulted Stephen, their activities had begun in the preceding year. Stephen is not named, but he must be τὸν προρρηθέντα ἐγκλείστον of Theoph., *loc. cit.* Evidently from another source, Theoph., 893b, repeats the statement that Strategius (here called the son—Anastasius says, the brother—of Podopagouros) had renounced the passions of the Emperor and confessed to the sainted monk of Mount Auxentius, and in revenge was charged with conspiracy.

[2] Theoph., 884abc.

[3] ἀθέσμως, uncanonically. Theoph., 888b.

[4] The tradition is preserved by the twelfth-century chronicler Glycas, p. 539.

[5] τὸν τῆς κακίας ἐπώνυμον. Theoph., 888c.

[6] Theoph., 885b. *Vit. Nicet.*, xxiv, notices the absence of invocations in the sermons (λογίδρια) of Constantine he had read. Cf. Niceph., *Antirrh.*, II, 341d. It is more likely that Constantine discouraged than prohibited the practice. He hardly had the means of prohibiting it. Cf. *adv. Const. Cab.*, 337c.

the foundation of the Iconoclastic position. It reappears in the later period, but it never aroused the popular interest as did the destruction of pictures, just because it affected only the inner unseen things and could, therefore, make no popular appeal. Indeed, it revolted the common sense of the day to think that Christ was inaccessible to the prayers of his mother. The writer of *adv. Const. Cab.* quite naively asks : " If the Theotokos cannot help us after death, what protection or ally or helper can the whole body of Christians give us ? For who is a son more likely to hear than a mother ? " [1] Nicephorus accepts the same position in more sophisticated language. " She is a mediator because she has a mother's access." [2] The support to the practice of such intercession given by the Iconoclastic Council of 753 is a strong reason for supposing that Constantine himself was responsible for the new development. There was no decree on the matter. It was therefore rather an expression of the Emperor's views than an official regulation. The pamphlet *adv. Const. Cab.* says : " He abolished the use of the title Saint and said the Theotokos could help no one after death, and that the saints had no power of intercession, their martyrdom helping only themselves and saving their own souls from punishment." [3] The cult of the Virgin gave the Emperor the greatest offence. It meant punishment even to use the common exclamation, " Mother of God, help me." [4] An anecdote told by Theosteriktos and reproduced by the later chroniclers bears the mark of truth.[5] " Taking in his hand a purse full of gold and showing it to all he asked, What is it worth ? They replied that it had a great value. He then emptied out the gold and asked, What is it worth now ? They said, Nothing. So, said he, Mary (for the atheist would not call her Theotokos), while she carried Christ within was to be honoured, but after she was delivered she differed in no way from other women."

The Emperor attempted in other directions also to stem the tide of superstition. He destroyed relics whenever

[1] *Op. cit.* 340a.
[2] Niceph., *Antirrh.*, II, 341d.
[3] *Op. cit.* 337cd. Cf. Niceph., *Antirrh.*, II, 341. *Vit. Steph.* alone is silent on this topic.
[4] θεοτόκε βοήθει. Theoph., 892d.
[5] Theost., *Vit. Nicet.*, xxviii ; Georg. Mon., II, 751.

he could find them. He refused to permit relics to be inserted in altars and dedicated churches with no relics, which Nicephorus observes is uncanonical.[1] But, as Theophanes notices with some satisfaction, he was not very successful with relics. The relic of the martyr Euphemia, for example, which sweated perfume was thrown into the sea with its casket, but it floated to Lemnos and was restored by the pious finder in the reign of Irene.[2]

The monks with their houses and churches were now more systematically suppressed. It was forbidden to receive communion from a monk, and instead of greeting a monk with a χαῖρε, it was suggested that the fitting salute would be a stone.[3] A number of churches were destroyed, but they must have been the churches of the monasteries, for there is no indication that Constantine was hostile to churches as such.[4] In part the idea that he did destroy churches is due to a rhetorical flourish in the *Life of Stephen*. It is stated there that Constantine destroyed the church of St. Mary of Blachernæ, the walls of which bore frescoes of the Nativity and events of the life of Christ. But the author then explains that " destroyed " means that the Emperor " made the church a storehouse of fruit [5] and an aviary," that is to say, that he replaced the sacred pictures by a scheme of decoration consisting of " trees, birds, and beasts of various sorts, leaves of ivy, cranes, jackdaws, and peacocks, in festoons." [6] He makes it quite clear that he so explains " destroyed " by adding that it was in the church so defiled that the Emperor held his Iconoclastic Council.

Large numbers of monks fled from the monasteries,[7] and it was the buildings they had deserted that the Emperor appropriated. He made some of them barracks for the

---

[1] Niceph., *Antirrh.*, II, 344a. For the canons on relics in churches see Can. Carthag., 83, and II Nic. 7.

[2] Theoph., 888a.

[3] *Vit. Steph.*, 1112b. Both the *Vit. Steph.* and *ep. ad. Theoph.*, 361c (following the *Vit.*), suppose that these two acts were included in the Iconoclastic oath, which is improbable.

[4] Can. 13 of II Nic. refers to the monastic buildings which had been confiscated, and among these must be included the churches, which the canons do not otherwise mention. Niceph., *Antirrh.*, II, 344b, writes as though it were churches in which pictures were still preserved.

[5] Citing LXX of Ps. lxxviii. 1, where the word ὀπωροφυλάκιον occurs.

[6] *Vit. Steph.*, 1120cd.

[7] *Ib.* 1120b, says that all monks fled from Constantinople.

army—for example, the monastery of Dalmatus.[1] Other religious houses were destroyed. Those of Callistratus, of Dius, and of Maximin are mentioned. The chapel of St. Euphemia (where her relics were kept) was made an arsenal and a manure-tip.[2] It is of monastic buildings that we are most probably to understand the general charges laid to the Emperor's score. Thus Nicephorus says that "Mammon dared to spoil churches and raze them to the ground ; he made monasteries habitations of demons ; he turned churches of God into stables and manure-yards, the effects being still visible. Some consecrated places, such as the monasteries of Florus and Callistratus, were sold." [3] The *Life of Stephen* (followed in one place by Nicephorus) attributes the destruction of churches to the pictures they contained,[4] but it is difficult to accept that. At the stage of the controversy now reached, it was the monks and their property that were the objects of attack. It could scarcely have been necessary to destroy a church in order to obliterate its pictures. As a matter of fact, the *Life* itself tells us of the fate of pictures. Sculptures in relief were broken. Actual pictures were whitewashed over.[5] "But where there were trees or birds or beasts or Satanic riding scenes, pictures of hunting or horse-racing, they were treated with honour and improved." In this way Iconoclasm was not actually destructive of Art. Indeed, Diehl has shown that so far from destroying even religious art it produced a temporary renaissance from the decadence into which Byzantine art had been falling. To Iconoclasm he traces the second golden age of Byzantine art.[6] It is an interesting testimony to the patience with which the policy was carried out to find in 766 pictures still survived in the Patriarch's official residence. For

[1] Theoph., 893a. Nicephorus, *Antirrh.*, III, 493d, says that of Callistratus was sold.

[2] Theoph., 888a. The last phrase is probably not intended to be understood literally, but as meaning that Constantine turned it to purposes of his own.

[3] Niceph., *Antirrh.*, III, 493d. Such cases were dealt with by Canon 13 of Nicæa II, which required monastic property to be restored on pain of degradation for ecclesiastics and excommunication for others. Mansi, XIII, 432.

[4] *Ib.* ; *Antirrh.*, II, 344b ; *Vit. Steph.*, 1113a.

[5] *Vit. Steph.*, 1113a ; Mansi, XIII, 401.

[6] Diehl, C., *Manuel d'Art byz.*, Paris, 1910, pp. 352, 359 *sqq.* Diehl quotes as an example of the reinvigoration due to Iconoclasm the popular illustrations in the Chloudof Psalter, recently in the monastery of St. Nicholas in Moscow.

only then did the new Patriarch Nicetas erase the mosaics
in the lesser secretariat, plastering up those in the larger
halls which were in relief, and whitewashing the others.[1]
The Emperor himself had the mosaics representing the six
Œcumenical Councils which stood by the Milestone in
the Forum replaced by scenes drawn from the circus.[2]
For one class of representation—the coinage—the evidence
is still extant. As long ago as the seventh century Justinian II had introduced the head of Christ on the coinage.
His successors Philippicus, Anastasius II, and Theodosius III
dropped this usage and were followed by Leo III, who,
however, retained the cross. Constantine abandoned even
the cross. On his coins Imperial personages appeared on
both sides. Nor did the orthodox revival restore the former
custom. It was not until the reign of Theophilus that the
cross reappeared, and then only occasionally, while the head
of Christ was only restored by Michael III, after which
all kinds of variations of Christ, the Virgin, and the Saints
are to be found.[3]

The martyrs to the cause of images under Constantine
are with a single exception to be found among the monks.
The exception is the Patriarch Constantine, and, as we have
seen before, the cause of his fall, while remaining obscure,
seems ultimately due to his failure to fill the rôle allotted
to him by the Emperor. In 766 he was brought from his
retreat in Prince's Island to Constantinople, and flogged
until he was unable to walk. At a public meeting of the
citizens in the church of St. Sophia the charges against
the Patriarch were read, the secretary punctuating each
accusation with a blow at the accused. The anathema
was pronounced against him, he was stripped of his pallium
(ὠμοφόριον), and amid shouts of " Skotiopsis "[4] he was made
to walk out backwards. The next day at the games in the
circus, with beard, eyebrows, and head shaved, dressed in
a short sleeveless coat, he was mounted backwards on an ass
and publicly exhibited. The ass was led by the Patriarch's

[1] Theoph., 896a. He did the same in the monastery of the Abraamites,
which stood outside the city near the Golden Gate. It possessed one of the
celebrated pictures " not made with hands."

[2] *Vit. Steph.*, 1172a.

[3] Wroth, I, xxxvi–xliv.

[4] Cf. *Ep. ad. Theoph.*, 361b, where Constantine calls the monastic habit
σκοτίας σχῆμα.

nephew Constantine, with his nose slit. The Patriarch was spit at, pelted with mud, thrown off the ass, trampled underfoot, and finally placed in a public seat, an object of gibes until the end of the games.[1] On the 5th August, a deputation from the Emperor asked him his opinion of the Faith of the Iconoclasts and of the Council of 753. " You are right both in Faith and in holding the synod," said the Patriarch. The deputation replied that they had only wished to hear this from his own evil lips, and he might now betake himself to perdition. He was forthwith beheaded at the Kynegion. His head was exposed for three days at the Milestone, suspended by the ears. His body was dragged by a rope and thrown into the place of Pelagius, whither three days later the head followed.[2] The temporising policy which marked the Patriarch's career would seem to indicate that the brutal treatment he received was due to his unwillingness to support the Emperor's policy, and that the conspiracy in which he was concerned was promoted by sympathisers, not so much with the images as with the monks. For Theophanes connects the execution of the Patriarch with another violent outbreak against the monks. In the same year, 766, Theophanes records the death of the venerable Peter the Stylite,[3] who was dragged from his pillar, and, refusing the Emperor's doctrine (*i.e.* the oath against images), was thrown into the place of Pelagius.[4] Theophanes then makes a general statement that " others the Emperor ordered to be fastened in sacks weighted with stones and thrown into the sea." A single example of such a victim is given in the *Life of Stephen*, John, abbot of Monagria, who met with that end after refusing to trample on an image of the Virgin.[5] These are the only authentic cases of the death penalty recorded

---

[1] Theoph., 889abc.   [2] *Ib.* 892ab.
[3] *Ib.* 892b.
[4] I have entirely failed to follow the identification of Peter with Andrew in Crisi, Act. Sanct., Oct. VIII. Andrew Calybites may well be an error for Peter (see above), but it is difficult to make the complementary identification here. Andrew was called in Crisi from the place of his burial which does not accord with the end of Peter in the place of Pelagius. Andrew came from Crete and was not a Stylite. It is alleged that he was dragged through the streets and eventually killed by a fisherman cutting off his foot. For lack of further evidence Andrew must remain an improbable shadow of the more celebrated St. Andrew of Crete. He is not mentioned in the *Vit. Steph.*, a fact which strongly supports a disbelief in his existence.
[5] Theoph., 892b ; *Vit. Steph.*, 1165d ; Act. Sanct. Jun. I.

in Constantinople. Other cases occurred in such provinces as were administered by officers in close sympathy with the Emperor. In Crete the abbot Paul was seized by the prefect Theophanes Lardotyrus and bidden to trample on an image of Christ. Instead he adored it and was in consequence tortured on the Catapeltai and burnt alive.[1]

The prefect of the Thracesian Theme, Michael Lachanodracon, carried out the policy of the Emperor with complete fidelity. He summoned all the monks and nuns within his theme to Ephesus, and addressed them in a mass meeting at the Tzucanisterium or Polo-ground. He urged them to show their acceptance of the Emperor's wishes by marrying, threatening them as an alternative with blinding and deportation to Cyprus. Many chose to suffer and many fell in with the Prefect's advice.[2] The Prefect proceeded, with the help of his bastard son Leo Culuces and an ex-abbot named Leo Cutzodactylus, to sell by auction the whole of the monastic property, buildings, books, live stock, and sacred equipment, sending the proceeds to the Imperial treasury.[3] The patristic works belonging to the monasteries he burnt as well as any relics he could find. Many of the monks were flogged, some executed, and a large number blinded. He had the beards of some of them covered with a mixture of wax and oil and then set on fire.[4] The incident is related in greater detail in the *Life of Stephen* on the authority of Theocteristus of the monastery of Peleketc, the scene of the atrocity. After the burning of beards and slitting of nostrils, thirty-eight of the principal monks were chosen and removed to the outhouse of a disused bath on the outskirts of Ephesus. The entrance was blocked and the men were buried alive by means of a mine driven through an adjacent hill.[5] Lachanodracon did not leave a single man in his theme in the monastic habit. He received the personal congratulations of the Emperor as a man after his own heart.[6]

---

[1] *Vit. Steph.*, 1164c ; Act. Sanct. Mar. II.
[2] Theoph., 897bc.
[3] *Ib.* 900b. Cf. *Ep. ad Theoph.*, 361a, τὰ τῆς ἐκκλησίας πάντα τοῖς βασιλείοις παραδέδωκεν.
[4] Theoph., 900c.
[5] *Vit. Steph.*, 1165b.
[6] Theoph., 900c. The date given by Theophanes is 770–772. He mistakenly identifies 770 with the first year of Pope Hadrian I.

Less atrocious actions were being carried out systematically. The number of actual martyrs was small. But many had their beards burnt or pulled out, some had their heads broken with the bas-reliefs of the sacred pictures. Eyes were gouged out, ears mutilated, and limbs torn off,[1] no doubt in mob attacks on the monks. Wanton destruction of property accompanied these personal attacks. Books in particular were destroyed wholesale. Leo, bishop of Phocæa, reported to the Council of Nicæa that in his city (which was in Lachanodracon's theme) thirty books had been burnt.[2]

It is uncertain how far the persecution aroused public sympathy. A modern reader is likely to be revolted by the atrocities perpetrated by Christian men in the name of Christ. This, however, is beside the point. Atrocities are of the very substance of mediæval life, and of Oriental life even to-day. Integrity of purpose and even moral idealism were compatible with the practice of savage brutalities. If the monks found sympathisers, it was not a sentimental sympathy because they were the victims of atrocities. It would be a sympathy with the principles for which the monks stood. Among the secular clergy Iconoclasm was firmly established. The unanimity of the Council of 753 shows that, especially when it is contrasted with the difficulty of securing similar unanimity in 787. It is not improbable that the bishops represented the best moderate opinion of their day. They are therefore denounced by the orthodox as materialists, occupied chiefly with trade and business, their first interests sport and a good table.[3] A violently abusive attack is made by Nicephorus on the Iconocalastic leaders, who are most probably the bishops. It includes a series of 150 epithets like " blasphemers," " drunkards," " lewd in intercourse," " litigious." They are said "to ridicule the priesthood and belittle the apostolic habit, ignore the reading of the Scripture, observe neither prayer nor fasting, honour not

---

[1] Niceph., *Brev.*, 981b. The Brev. ends about the year 770. *Vit. Steph.*, 1160c.

[2] Mansi, XIII, 185a. Cf. *Ep. ad Theoph.*, 361b.

[3] *adv. Const. Cab.*, 329d ; *Vit. Steph.*, 1120a. " Those frequenters of the racecourse, the ring, and the theatre, Pastillas and Tricaccabus, Nicolaitas and Atzypius the friend of demons."

virginity nor love temperance." [1]   But reduced to its lowest terms it all means that they were opposed to monasticism.

They carried with them the army and the official classes, the latter only in part. [2] A large section of the population of Constantinople showed their support by their readiness to join in attacks on monks. But Nicephorus accuses them of being gangs of loafers looking for a drink, [3] many of them ex-soldiers, either cashiered for crime, or too old for the service. [4] Certainly there were marked survivals of orthodoxy. When Stephen lay in prison in Constantinople, the wife of one of the gaolers secretly brought him three images, [5] an indication of the popular affection for the cult, while Irene, the Emperor's daughter-in-law, was probably all her life a secret image-worshipper. [6] The Iconoclastic convictions of a large body of respectable clergy cannot be seriously doubted, but it was the dominating influence of the Emperor that made it possible for these opinions to make progress. " I consider it [*i.e.* Iconoclasm] a terrible heresy," says Theosterictus, " for earlier heresies have been promoted by priests, but this has behind it the authority of the Emperor himself." [7]

The closing years of Constantine's reign were occupied with a new Bulgarian war. On 14th September, 775, Constantine died on shipboard from a fever and eruptions on the legs. [8] The chroniclers find a certain satisfaction in giving him a painful death. To it they add a death-bed repentance. " In the agonies of his death-bed he sought the consolations of our faith," [9] begging that hymns and praises should be sung " to the Holy Virgin, the Theotokos." [10] But the probability of this change is reduced by the persistence with which the chroniclers continue to attack him. He is never treated as the penitent sinner. All agree with the author of *adv. Const. Cab.* that his doom is to " choke

---

[1] *Antirrh.*, III, 489a.
[2] The plot of Podopagouros shows that many were not convinced.
[3] περισκοποῦσι συχνῶς ἔνθα τε πότοι καὶ συσσίτια γίνονται. *Antirrh.*, III, 492c.
[4] The Roman army was now a professional one. At this period it was recruited mainly on the Syrian and Armenian frontier.
[5] *Vit. Steph.*, 1164a.
[6] Cedrenus, I, 901a.
[7] *Vit. Nicet.*, Act. Sanct. Ap. I, xxiii.
[8] ἄνθρακες; Possibly small-pox.
[9] Niceph., *Antirrh.*, III, 505c.
[10] Theoph., 905a.

in the abyss of impiety,"[1] while Nicephorus is of the opinion
that had he lived longer he would have proceeded to further
Iconoclastic developments.[2]

This would indicate that Iconoclasm was not completely
successful. The end of Constantine's reign probably is
the high-water mark of the movement. It left a momentum
behind it, sufficiently strong to retain considerable vigour,
when after thirty years' reaction Leo the Armenian inaugurated the second Iconoclastic epoch. It was Constantine who saw that Iconoclastic supremacy could only
be obtained by a strong policy against the monasteries.
It was Constantine who developed the philosophical basis
of Iconoclasm and gave it what intellectual appeal it had.[3]
It was Constantine who left behind a name which continued
to provoke a respect that scandalised Nicephorus,[4] and
proved fatal to the pious incompetence of Michael I.[5]
But even so Iconoclasm depended for its success on the
personal will of the Emperor. Its common-sense simplicity
was more than outweighed by its philosophical weakness
and its disproportionate emphasis on the trivial.[6] Leo and
Constantine undoubtedly raised the prestige of the Empire
and the prosperity and comfort of its inhabitants. It
cannot honestly be said that much of their success can be
attributed to their religious policy. The most that can
be allowed is that the religious ideas of a man of the
vigorous temper and political ability of Constantine
demand respect. Much as we might wish to trace the
revival of the Empire under the Isaurians to Iconoclasm,
the evidence would seem to indicate that, apart from the
personality of the Emperors, it made no difference.

It remains to conclude with some notice of the effect
of the new religious policy in the other Patriarchates.
With the West we shall deal separately. In the three
Eastern Patriarchates the tradition with which St. John of
Damascus met the movement at the beginning appears

[1] *adv. Const. Cab.*, 341b. Cf. Niceph., *Antirrh.*, III, 508a, πικροτέρας αὐτῷ
καὶ μακροτέρας ἅμα τῷ πατρὶ καὶ συγκληρονόμῳ αὐτοῦ θεοκρίτως ἐν τῇ γεέννῃ τῆς
τιμωρίας ἑτοιμασθείσης.
[2] Niceph,. *Antirrh.*, II, 345b.
[3] The weakness of the intellectual side of Iconoclasm was very marked.
[4] οἱ ἐκεῖνον μακαρίζειν ἀνοήτως οὐκ αἰσχυνόμενοι. *Antirrh.*, III, 505d.
[5] Theoph., 1005a.
[6] See below on the theology of the Controversy.

to have been steadily maintained. By the time of the Council of Nicæa, though not one of the Patriarchs was able to be present, the most loquacious and bigoted person present was the priest John, who in default of official delegates was accepted as a representative of the three Patriarchs. As all three Patriarchs only existed by favour of the Moslems it is no matter for surprise that they had no inclination to enter into new experiments in the Faith which they held in the face of such difficulty. They took what opportunities they could of protesting against Iconoclasm. The Patriarchs of Antioch and Alexandria wrote letters in which they designated Constantine apostate and heresiarch. They joined the Pope and probably the Patriarch of Jerusalem in anathematising the Emperor.[1] It is probable that it was because of these letters that Theodore, Patriarch of Antioch, was expelled from his see by the caliph [2] (754–755). More than once the Patriarchs communicated to the Pope their abhorrence of the Iconoclasts.[3] Theodore of Jerusalem at an unknown date (circa 754) is credited with a synod which anathematised Iconoclasm.[4] The three Patriarchs acted together and took immediate steps against any innovation. In 763 Cosmas, bishop of Ephiphaneia, near Apameia in Syria, was accused before Theodore of Antioch of misappropriating the sacred vessels. On being accused he declared himself an Iconoclast. The three Patriarchs, Theodore of Jerusalem, Theodore of Antioch, and Cosmas of Alexandria, simultaneously anathematised him.[5] Possibly the same cause may explain the anathema directed in 754 against Nicetas, bishop of Heliopolis in Palestine, by the whole Church.[6] Iconoclasm found no support in partibus infidelium.

[1] *Vit. Steph.*, 1117d.
[2] Theoph., 865c.
[3] One such letter arrived during the reign of the anti-Pope Constantine in 767. It showed, says Constantine to Pippin, qualis fervor sanctarum imaginum orientalibus partibus cunctis Christianis imminet, *Cod. Car.*, 99.
[4] τῶν ἁγιοκαύστων αἵρεσιν. The statement of the Synodicum Vetus (Fabricius, XI, 249) is probably only an inference from the synodical letter of Theodore cited at Nicæa. Mansi, XII, 1135.
[5] Theoph., 873c.
[6] *Ib.* 865a.

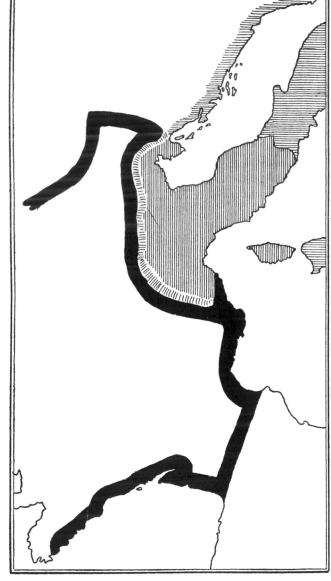

IMPERIAL ITALY AND THE DOMINION OF CHARLES

ORIGINAL FRANKISH FRONTIER.
ADDED BY CHARLES.
LEFT TO EMPIRE.

CHAPTER V

ICONOCLASM IN THE WEST TO THE DEATH OF CONSTANTINE V

AUTHORITIES

1. Theophanes. As before.
2. Liber Pontificalis, Text ed. Duchesne, Vol. i, Paris, 1886. The Lives of Gregory II and Zacharias are full and contemporary, that of Gregory III is mainly a list of church repairs and furnishings. With Stephen II, Paul, and Stephen III the previous level is resumed. The Lives of Hadrian I, Leo III, and Paschal I are made bulky by architectural information, but are otherwise meagre. After Hadrian I the bearing of the Papacy on the question of Iconoclasm is small.
3. Codex Carolinus. Letters of the Popes (Gregory III to Hadrian I) to the Frankish princes, Text ed. W. Gundlach in M.G.H., Epp. iii. The numbering of this edition is followed. Unfortunately the dating of the letters can only be determined by their contents.

MODERN WRITERS

Of modern writers Gibbon is so misleading as to be valueless. An important study is Hubert, C., Études sur la Formation des États de l'Église (Revue Hist., 1899, Vol. lxix, pp. 1–40, 241–272).
The best guide is Hodgkin, T., Italy and her Invaders, Vols. vi and vii, Oxford. Second edition, 1916.
Also useful is Mann, H. K., The Lives of the Popes, Vols. i (part 2) and ii, London, 1903. It is written from a definitely Papal standpoint and is unsympathetic to Constantinople. Mann follows Hefele uncritically and often lapses into moralising.

THE development of the Iconoclastic struggle produced in the West far less controversy but infinitely more extensive results. It was the principal, though not the only, factor in three great events : (i) the loss of the Imperial dominions in North Italy ; (ii) the establishment of the temporal power of the Papacy ; (iii) the separation of the Eastern and Western Churches.

At the accession of Leo III, Italy had long been overrun by Lombards, but a strong Imperial dominion still remained. This embraced the Exarchate of Ravenna, the

Duchies of Rome and Naples, cities on the coast of Liguria, the extreme South of Italy, and the islands of Sicily and Sardinia. The Greek chroniclers make the new religious policy directly responsible for the loss of the bulk of these dominions. Theophanes believed that the first declaration by the Emperor of an Iconoclastic intention was met by Pope Gregory II with a refusal of the Italian tribute and a warning that it was outside the sphere of legitimate Imperial action to interfere with matters of faith or to introduce innovations on the doctrines of the Fathers.[1] Nicephorus agrees that the West was lost to the Empire through the new religious policy.[2] But the Western information at their disposal must at best have been small. In the local evidence the situation is seen differently and more correctly.

The state of Italy was turbulent. Before news of Leo's Iconoclasm had arrived in the year 725[3] an incursion of Lombards into the Imperial domains seized Narni and Classis.[4] Elsewhere difficulties presented themselves over the collection of the Imperial taxes, presumably new taxation. The Pope, according to the Liber Pontificalis, hindered the Emperor's levy and his plan of robbing the churches.[5] Obscure but violent measures were attempted against the Pope. A band of Imperial officials, the Duke Basil, Jordanes the Chartularius, with John Lurion, a sub-deacon, and the Imperial spatharius Marinus had already for unknown motives conspired to murder the Pope. The patrician Paul, arriving as Exarch, encouraged them in their plot. But they were discovered. Lurion and Jordanes were killed and Basil escaped to a monastery.

---

[1] Theoph., 816ab. Cf. 824b, 825b.

[2] διὰ τὴν τῶν σῶν διδασκάλων ἀπιστίαν καὶ τὴν εἰς Χρίστον καὶ τὴν ἐκκλησίαν ὕβριν πλεῖσται ὅσαι χῶραι . . . καὶ τούτων μάλιστα τὰ πρὸς ἥλιον καταδυόμενον πρόσοικα γένη πρὸς ἀπόστασιν εἶδον. Niceph., Antirrh., III, 525c. Vit. Steph., 1117c; records the failure of Iconoclasm in Italy but not the loss of the West.

[3] So Hodgkin, op. cit., vi, p. 444.

[4] Lib. Pont., i, 403.

[5] Eo quod censum in provincia ponere præpediebat ex suis opibus ecclesiam denudari sicut ceteris actum est locis. Liber. Pont., i, 403. The spoliation of churches Döllinger explains to mean the removal of pictures and vessels ornamented with figures of saints (Fables respecting the Popes, E. Tr., London, 1871, pp. 253 sqq.). But this must be incorrect, for nothing had yet been heard of Iconoclasm. The attractive suggestion that it means making Church property liable to taxation is denied by Hubert (op. cit., p. 7) on the ground that it was always liable. We shall, therefore, best explain it as being an increase of taxation which the Church authorities refused to pay. Cf. Theoph., 816b.

The Exarch then tried to effect the murder himself, supported by the Emperor's orders. The exact situation and the correct facts behind this account remain undiscovered. Possibly the alleged attempt at murder represents a real request of the Emperor that the Pope should be deposed and brought to Constantinople. That Leo should at any time, much less at this early stage, have resorted to murder is unlikely. As Hodgkin says, Leo was a patient enemy. The Exarch set about his purpose by collecting troops, a proceeding which throws further doubt on the project of murder, while the Pope in his turn was protected by the Lombards, who welcomed a chance of checkmating the Imperial power in the Exarchate.

At this point [1] (circa 727) the Imperial decree against images reached Italy, and the Pope was informed that if he opposed this decree as well as the other he would be deposed.[2] The Pope's reply was to warn Christians against the new impiety and prepare to defend himself.[3] Some writers have assumed that the Pope's defence was to summon a council and anathematise the Emperor. But not only is such a course incompatible with the very pacific policy Gregory followed, it is unsupported by any evidence.[4]

---

[1] *Iussionibus postmodum missis* (*i.e.* after the trouble over the taxes). Lib. Pont., *loc. cit.*

[2] Si *et hoc* fieri præpediebat a suo gradu decideret. Lib. Pont., *loc. cit.*

[3] Contra Inperatorem quasi contra hostem se armavivit renuens hæresim eius. Lib. Pont., *loc. cit.* It looks as if force of arms were meant, but the word "armavivit" may be used in a general and not in a military sense.

[4] The evidence alleged is the spurious letters of Gregory, relying on which Dury says that in a Council in 727 the Pope anathematised the exarch, Paul, but not the Emperor. All other references to a Roman council under Gregory II (*e.g.* Hadrian, Ep. in Mansi, XIII, Vetus Synodicon in Fabricius) are to be referred to the council under Gregory III in 731. That anathemas were far from the mind of Gregory II is borne out by Lib. Pont., i, 400, inperatori quoque mandavit suadens salutaria ut a tali execrabili miseria declinaret. The evidence of Hadrian, Ep. Mansi, XIII, 709a, seems decisive against the alleged council. There the list of Popes defending the images is given, Gregory (II), Gregory (III), Zacharias, Stephen, Paul, and Stephen. Two councils only are mentioned, that under Gregorius papa secundus iunior una cum lxxix sanctissimis episcopis, which is the council of 731, secundus iunior = the *third* of the name. The other council is Stephen's in 769. There is not a single reference in the many occurring in Hadrian's letter that can be shown to refer to any council earlier than that of 731. Cf. Mansi, XIII, 792d. If any further evidence is needed the statement of Walafrid Strabo is decisive against a Roman council on images earlier than 731. Sub Gregorio papa iuniore Constantinus inperator apud Constantinopolim omnes imagines deposuerit et sub Gregorio tertio Romæ synodus sit facta contra supradictam ut dixerunt heresim. *De Exord.*, p. 482 (ed. Krause).

The Pope did all he could to maintain peace. The people of Pentapolis and the army of Venice (that is, probably in both places, the local militia) declared against the Emperor and anathematised the Exarch, while the Italians (probably of Rome and Naples) decided to elect a new Emperor in Leo's place. The Pope did his best to dissuade them from their project, still hoping for Leo's conversion.[1] The Imperial governor of Naples, Exhilaratus,[2] made matters worse by persuading the Campanians to attempt the Pope's life. Riots took place all over the Imperial dominions. Exhilaratus was killed by Romans, probably the Roman civic guard.[3] Peter, the dux of Rome, was blinded and expelled, while Paul the Exarch was killed in the fighting at Ravenna. To add to the confusion Lombard armies again invaded Imperial territory. At the end of the year (727) Eutychius, the last bearer of the title of Exarch, was sent to Naples to finish the business. He attempted unsuccessfully to conciliate the Lombards, who had declared their intention of standing by the Pope. The Pope still struggled for peace, and urged on the Italians the duty of loyalty to the Emperor. By January, 729, Eutychius succeeded in securing an alliance with the Lombard king Luitprand. The Pope then made a personal appeal to Luitprand, and eventually a reconciliation between all three, Eutychius, Luitprand, and the Pope, took place.[4] Luitprand marked his sense of the Pope's service by surrendering Sutri to him, the first recorded instance of a city given to the Church. The Pope on his side signalised his determination to remain loyal to Constantinople by repudiating Tiberius Petasius, who had proclaimed himself Emperor in Southern Italy, a rebellion that was quickly smothered. But the Pope's loyalty failed to advance the cause of orthodoxy in Constantinople. Anastasius replaced Germanus in the Patriarchate, and to his enthronistical letter the Pope replied that he disowned the election unless the Patriarch returned to the Faith.

[1] Lib. Pont., *loc. cit.*
[2] Exhilaratus had an old grievance against the Pope. In 721 his son Hadrian had been excommunicated for marrying a deaconess.
[3] Hodgkin, *op. cit.*, p. 453.
[4] Hubert suspects that the Lib. Pont. has exaggerated the personal influence of the Pope. But there can be little doubt that the Pope was the one person working for peace.

It would seem that Gregory II played a difficult part with credit and dignity. He upheld the rights of the Italians without encouraging rebellion. He upheld the claims of orthodoxy without proceeding to extremes, and with a consistent courtesy and forbearance. But he failed to make any progress, and it fell to his successor to accept a more hostile rôle.

Gregory III, a Syrian by birth, succeeded on 18th March, 731. Almost from the first he adopted a less conciliatory tone. A Roman council was held on 1st November, 731,[1] attended by the Archbishops of Grado and Ravenna, and by ninety-three [2] other Italian bishops. The proceedings of the council are not extant, but the Liber Pontificalis records that it decreed that any one who should stand forth as destroyer, profaner, or blasphemer against the veneration of the sacred images should be excommunicated. Four attempts were made to send the Papal letters embodying this decision to Constantinople. All failed through the misadventures of the messengers.[3] Eventually the Pope's warning did reach the Patriarch and the Emperor. The Emperor's reply was in the following year to send a fleet against the Italians. It was wrecked in the Adriatic, but even so, the purpose for which it was sent seems to have been mainly spectacular. For Northern Italy, including Ravenna, was in its immediate state of disorder, beyond recovery. The Emperor contented himself with stringent economic measures in the parts in which his authority could be enforced. He confiscated the Papal patrimonies in Sicily, Calabria, and probably Naples,[4] the total valuation of which was $3\frac{1}{2}$ talents (£16,000). He increased the taxation in Sicily and Calabria, and ordered the registration of births, in order to ensure a complete record for levying the capitation tax. And he dealt the final stroke of severance from the bishop of Rome by

---

[1] The date is given in a letter of the Pope to Antony, archbishop of Grado. Mansi, XII, 301c.

[2] The number is given as seventy-nine in Hadrian, Ep. Mansi, XIII, 789a.

[3] The first envoy returned in a fright, the others were arrested by the prefect of Sicily.

[4] The story that the dux of Naples, Theodore, refused to obey the Imperial orders, and saved the Neapolitan patrimonies for the Pope is due to a forged document inserted by the eighteenth-century scholar, Pratilli, in Peregrini's *Historia principum Langobard.*, III, p. 31. Cf. Mann., *op. cit.*, I (ii), p. 208.

detaching Calabria, Sicily, and Illyria from the Roman
Patriarchate and joining them to Constantinople.[1] All
Greek-speaking districts were thus removed from the
Roman jurisdiction. The Exarchate, which remained
under the Pope's spiritual authority, was practically lost
to the Empire. Gregory III signalised his temporal
independence by issuing his own coinage.[2] He was the
first of the Popes to do so, a fact marking a definite period
in the growth of the Temporal Power, and in the widening
of the breach between East and West. On the image
question the Western Church had given its final decision,
for later Councils only re-affirmed the canons of 731.
The question appeared again, but· it was as a political
weapon rather than a debatable problem.

   In 741, Gregory III was succeeded by Zacharias, a
Greek of mild and unambitious character. He continued
the policy of politeness to the Emperor, sending his letters
of enthronement to the church of Constantinople, to which
he added a personal letter to the Emperor urging him to
restore the images. The Papal ambassadors found the city
in the hands of the pretender Artavasdus and waited until
Constantine had recovered it, but it is doubtful whether
their motive was loyalty to Constantine or mere indecision.[3]
Constantine, at all events, gave them credit for the higher
motive. For he tactfully avoided any reference to subjects
of disagreement, and presented to the Pope the two estates
of Ninfa and Norma, possibly as some return for the con-
fiscation of the patrimonies of Sicily and Calabria.[4]
Relations with Constantinople after that all but ceased.
In 751, Ravenna fell for the second time to the Lombards,
and the Exarchate came to an end. The ducatus of Rome

   [1] Theoph., 825 ; Mansi, XIII, 808, XV, 167. The Lib. Pont. fails at
this point. The preponderating Greek element in these districts had been
re-enforced by orthodox exiles flying from Constantinople.
   [2] They are of bronze and square in shape, bearing on the obverse no
device but a very small cross above the inscription GRE II PAPE in two lines,
and on the reverse a similar cross above SCI PTR also in two lines. It is doubtful, however, whether these were actual coins, or tokens, entitling the holder to
a food-dole. The earliest Papal coins, if these bronze tesseræ are something
else, will be the silver denarii of Hadrian I, some of which bear the Pope's
head, and clearly mark independence of the Empire. These early Papal
coins are described and depicted in Serafini, C., *Le Monete et le Bolle plumbee
pontificie del Medaghiere Vaticano* (Milan, 1910), pp. 3 *sqq.* and Plate I.
   [3] Lib. Pont., i, 432.
   [4] *Ib.* i, 433.

remained. Its government was virtually in the hands of the Pope. The aggression of the Lombards and the involuntary retirement of the Empire out of Northern Italy left the Pope great political opportunities as the upholder of Italian freedom. This is the period when the foundation of the Pope's temporal power was laid, and the Papacy definitely accepted the rôle of heir to the Imperial dominions of Italy. To enter into details of the events of the next fifty years is outside our scope. But we cannot entirely ignore the political development because the image question appears from time to time on the horizon of the political sky. Just before his death Pope Zacharias determined the course of events by accepting the deposition of the Frankish *roi fainéant*, and the succession of the family of the Mayors of the Palace in the person of Pippin. The recognition of Pippin by the Pope is one of the great critical points in history. The king of the Franks is henceforth to be the Christian champion of Western Europe. These eighth-century Popes who turned their backs on the setting sun of Constantinople to hail the new day in the West must be credited with something greater than territorial ambition or disgust with an unsound theology. They had the inspiration to see that " Westward the course of Empire takes its way."

Zacharias did not live to advance the alliance with the Franks. But his successor Stephen II (752–757) [1] brought the vigour of an aggressive personality to the new policy. For the moment Stephen temporised with Constantinople. Embassies passed from Constantinople to Rome, from Rome to the Lombards, or from Rome to Pippin. Constantinople sought the restoration of the Exarchate. The Pope was concerned most about the threatening progress of the Lombards. At the end of 752 Stephen asked Constantine to come and drive off the Lombards. [2] In Constantinople the Iconoclastic Council was about to assemble. What passed between the Emperor and the embassy is unknown. Stephen is next found paying a personal visit to Pippin, the outcome of which was a promise from the latter that

[1] Confusion in the numbering of the Stephens is explained by the fact that a Stephen who was elected to succeed Zacharias died before his consecration. He is therefore omitted and his actual successor is here called Stephen II. Some historians count the other as an actual Pope, numbering the Stephen with whom we are concerned, Stephen III.

[2] Lib. Pont., i, 441.

he would restore to the Pope the Exarchate and the rights and territories of the republic. It is not too much to conjecture that the decision of the Iconoclastic Council finally determined the Pope's action.[1] Constantinople had failed to do anything, and now showed itself to be rooted in error. Henceforth Constantinople is regarded by the Pope with indifference or fear. His ally is the Frank. Constantinople awoke to the situation and approached the Frank with studied politeness. In 757 Pippin received from Constantine an organ, and from the Pope almost simultaneously a request that he will defend the faith against the Greeks.[2]   In the latter part of the same year Paul was elected to the Papal chair (757–767), and for the first time his election was formally announced not to the Emperor but to Pippin.[3] Rome and Constantinople are finally separated.

Paul was not without some tremors for the wisdom of the policy he had adopted. The Codex Carolinus shows him obsessed with reports of attacks on himself, planned by the " ineffable Greeks, the enemies of God's holy church and fighting foes of the orthodox faith." [4] Direct references to Iconoclasm are rare. The misadventures of an Italian priest named Marinus seem the only case recorded. He fell under the influence of the Imperial secretary George, who was conducting negotiations with the Lombards, and in consequence became involved " in evil doing against the holy Church of God and the orthodox faith." [5] This may have been Iconoclasm. The punishment devised by the Pope is ingenious. He asked the Emperor to get the erring priest consecrated to the episcopate by Wilchar, then bishop of Sitten (Sedunum), and sent to some Frankish diocese, where he might have opportunity to recall his sins and repent.

The interest of the Pope is henceforward centred on the political problem. He is concerned primarily for the fulfilment of Pippin's promise that he would restore to the

---

[1] This ingenious suggestion is due to Hubert, *op. cit.*, p. 247.

[2] Ut . . . ita disponere iubeas de parte Gæecorum ut fides sancta Dei ecclesia sicut ab aliis et ab eorum pestifera malitia liberetur. Cod. Car., Ep. 11.

[3] Cod. Car., Ep. 12.

[4] Cod. Car., Ep. 30. Cf. *ib.* 17, 20, 31, 32.

[5] Cod. Car., Ep. 25. Cf. Epp. 29 and 99. In the latter the anti-Pope Constantine prays that Marinus may be restored to his sorrowing relatives.

Roman republic the territory seized by the Lombards. Constantinople also was exercised about the same matter from a different standpoint. About 766 an embassy was trying to persuade Pippin to support the Imperial claims. At the same time theological questions were brought to Pippin's notice by the Greeks, first the doctrine of the procession of the Holy Spirit, and secondly the image question.[1] It is possible that the Greek envoys tried to seduce Pippin into Iconoclasm with the object of setting him at variance with the Pope, who in turn tried to prejudice Pippin against Constantinople by accusing the Emperor of heresy. For in one letter the Pope mentions the fact that the Imperial embassy indignantly accused the Papal chamberlain Christopher of inserting in the Emperor's letters "a spurious statement on the establishment of the holy images and the integrity of the orthodox faith."[2] Early in the following year (767) a council of Frankish bishops met at Gentilly, near Paris, to consider the two theological problems that had been raised.[3] No record exists of the decision of the Council, nor is there any subsequent reference to it, and the only safe conclusion to draw is that no definite decision was reached.[4] But momentarily the image question had become again a live issue in the West.[5] Pope Paul died in

---

[1] That the discussion of these points was due to the Greek envoys may be inferred from the description of the Council of Gentilly given in *Annal. Lauriss.* ad ann. 767 (MGH I). Habuit D. Pippinus . . . synodum magnum inter Romanos *et Græcos* de s. Trinitate vel de ss. imaginibus. Cf. *Cod. Car.*, Ep. 36.

[2] *Cod. Car.*, Ep. 36.

[3] Mansi, XII, 677.

[4] So Hodgkin, *op. cit.*, VII, p. 274. Hefele thought the Council reached a decision favourable to images (Hefele-Leclerq, III, p. 726). He founded his opinion on *Cod. Car.*, Ep. 36. In that letter Pope Paul congratulates Pippin on the orthodoxy of his response to the Emperor, de observatione fidei orthodoxe, and on his promise that nothing will move him from his engagement to Pope Stephen. Similar vague language is used in Ep. 37 : de vestra . . . integritate quam pro spe cuncta Dei ecclesie et fidei orthodoxe habere videmini. But in that epistle he explains what he means : quæ beato Petro pollicita . . . permanenda conservare satagitis. It is improbable that either of these letters was written after the Council of Gentilly, or has any reference to it. It is the donation of the Pentapolis that the Pope has in mind. Nor does there seem enough evidence to support Neander's opinion (V, p. 323) that the Frankish king supported the Papal claims and opposed images. If this Frankish Council had reached any conclusion it could hardly have failed to reappear in the later controversial discussions of Charles and Lewis the Pious.

[5] The great Iconoclastic persecution had just taken place in Constantinople and Italy was probably full of refugees.

June, 767. For one year and a month there was an inter-
regnum while the anti-pope Constantine claimed the see.
During the year a synodical letter in support of the images
arrived in Rome from Theodore, Patriarch of Jerusalem,
with the assent of the Patriarchs of Alexandria and Antioch
and most of the Oriental bishops. Constantine sent it
on to Pippin with a covering letter in which he commented
favourably on the enthusiasm for the holy images displayed
by all Christians in the East.[1]

Pippin died 28th September, 768. In the August of
the same year the Papal succession had been restored by
the election of Stephen III. A Lateran Council was summoned in 769 to deal with the affairs of the anti-pope Constantine. The opportunity was taken of reaffirming the
orthodox position on the image question. Though on this
subject the Council probably did no more than repeat the
Canons of the Council of 731,[2] it gains in importance
because much fuller information is available, and part of
its proceedings have survived.[3]

Fifty-two bishops or episcopal representatives were
present, including twelve from Frankish sees.[4] The image
question came up in the fourth session. Divers testimonies
of the Fathers were produced. After examining them the
Council decided that images were venerated [5] with a great
sentiment of honour by all Christians. The images are
those of the Lord, his Mother, and all the saints, prophets,
martyrs, and confessors. The character of the honour is
defined by the introduction of a passage of Athanasius [6] :
" We do not venerate images as God in the way the heathen
do. We only use the delineation of the images to stimulate
our affections." [7] With images the Council included
relics of the saints, either of their person or dress, churches

---

[1] Qualis fervor sanctarum imaginum orientalibus partibus cunctis Christianis imminct. Cod. Car., Ep. 99.
[2] Dominus Stephanus papa . . . prædecessoris sui venerabile concilium
confirmans atque amplectans. Hadr. Ep. Mansi, XIII, 789a.
[3] Mansi, XII, 701 *sqq.* Lib. Pont., i, 473 *sqq.*
[4] The others were two representatives of the Archbishop of Ravenna,
three bishops from North Italy, five from Lombard Tuscany, eight from the
Pentapolis, and twenty-two from the Ducatus Romæ.
[5] The word used is venerari and not adorari.
[6] *Quæst. ad Antioch.*, 39.
[7] Tantummodo affectum et caritatem animæ nostræ ad vultum faciei
imaginis aptamus. Mansi, XII, 720. Cf. Lib. Pont., i, 477.

dedicated to their memory, considering the great danger of the controversy to be the possibility of discrediting these. Accordingly " they overturned and anathematised the ill-omened synod which has recently been held in Greece with the object of abolishing the holy images." [1] The actual details of the arguments and discussions have not been preserved except in a few references contained in Hadrian's letter to Charles. We learn that among the evidence was read a Latin translation of the epistle of the Eastern patriarchs which had reached Rome in the previous year. [2] The analogy between an image and the brazen serpent, and between images and the Mercy Seat, Cherubim, and Ark, was among the arguments investigated. [3] Other Old Testament evidence discussed and accepted as providing precedents for images were : the fringes worn on the robe as a reminder of the commandments, [4] the bulls in Solomon's Temple, and the cherubim described by Ezekiel. [5] On other points the Council heard and accepted as valid the evidence adduced from Dionysius the Areopagite, [6] from Gennadius of Marseilles, [7] from Gregory, *Epistle to Secundinus,* [8] from ps-Ambrose, [9] from John Chrysostom on the honour paid to the Emperor's image, [10] and from Gregory of Nyssa and Cyril on the picture of Abraham's sacrifice. [11]

The Council evidently went over old ground, no doubt examining new evidence, but it added nothing to the definite position taken up in 731. The Franks apparently accepted the Roman view. The two Frankish kings, Charles and Carlomann, assented to the meeting of the Council, twelve Frankish bishops took part, and one of them, Herulphus of Langres, was active in bringing evidence to support the images. [12] Western Europe at this stage seems unanimous.

After the Lateran Council the affairs of the West do not enter into the Iconoclastic controversy again until Charles adopts the rôle of hostility to Nicæa. The Empire retained

[1] Lib. Pont., *loc. cit.*   [2] Mansi, XIII, 764.
[3] *Ib.* 772c, 781a.   [4] *Ib.* 797c.
[5] *Ib.* 805e.   [6] *Ib.* 777c.
[7] *Ib.* 785e.   [8] *Ib.* 792d.
[9] *Ib.* 793e.   *Expos. sanct. martyr. Gervasii et Protasii.* Act. Sanct. Jul. VI.
[10] Mansi, XIII, 798d.   [11] *Ib.* 777c.   [12] *Ib.* 792d.

its hold on Istria and the Venetian islands,[1] and made sporadic and futile bids for its old dominions. But the Pope had abandoned all but the most formal recognition of Constantinople, and after 772 no longer even dated his documents by the years of the Eastern Emperor.[2]

[1] Cod. Car., Ep. 63.
[2] Hodgkin, *op. cit.*, VIII, p. 55, n.

CHAPTER VI

THE END OF THE FIRST ICONOCLASTIC PERIOD AND THE RESTORATION OF ORTHODOXY

AUTHORITIES

1. Theophanes. As before.
2. Acta of the Second Council of Nicæa. As before. Translations and notes on parts of the proceedings are to be found in :
Mendham, J., *The Seventh General Council*. London, n.d.
The Seven Œcumenical Councils, tr. Perceval, H. R. (Nicene and Post-Nicene Fathers, vol. xiv.) Oxford, 1900.
Neither is satisfactory.
See also Hefele, *op. cit.*
Haddan, A. W. (?), *The Seventh Œcumenical Council. Ch. Quart. Review*, July 1896, is of little value. It contains many inaccuracies on points of fact.
3. *Vita Tarasii*, ed. Heikel. Act. Soc. Fennicæ, XVII, 1889. Latin version in Act. Sanct. 25 Feb. III. and M.P.G. 98.

CONSTANTINE V was succeeded in 775 by his son Leo IV, called the Chazar, after his mother, who was a daughter of the chief of that people. He abandoned his father's anti-monastic policy, and when he reverted to the custom of appointing bishops from among the heads of monasteries it was assumed that he was orthodox.[1] At least he took no active measures affecting religion.[2] In 780 the Patriarch Nicetas died. His place was filled by the appointment of Paul of Cyprus, described by Theophanes as tolerant and no Iconoclast, and for that reason only with difficulty induced to accept the office.[3] What is represented as an attack on image-worshippers followed, but if Theophanes' view of the character of Paul is correct, and from the names of those concerned, it would appear rather that a political plot was unmasked. The victims included some highly-placed officials, James, a protospatharius,

[1] Theoph., 905c.
[2] γαληνικωτάτῃ καὶ εἰρηναίᾳ διαγωγῇ τὸν πολυτάραχον κλύδωνα τῆς ἐκκλησίας μετήνεγκεν. *Ep. ad Theoph.*, 364a.
[3] Theoph., 913a.

Theophanes, chamberlain and accubitor, with Leo and Thomas, chamberlains. They were beaten and tonsured,[1] conducted through the city on exhibition, and confined in the Prætorium. Theophanes died.[2] The Empress Irene, a Greek, known to be a friend of image-worship, cannot be acquitted of complicity in this affair. For a story was current to the effect that two images were found in her room and the Emperor refused after this to live with her.[3] The Emperor did not long survive this affair. He died later in the same year of the same disease as his father (8th Sept. 780).[4]

The only point upon which Leo had diverged from his father's policy was in his view of monasticism, and that had not been part of the original Iconoclastic faith. In all other respects Leo made no concessions to orthodoxy, even continuing Constantine's Monophysite policy. For in 778 he settled a group of Syrian Jacobites in Thrace. With the death of Leo the first and greatest period of Iconoclasm ended. Irene the Empress as guardian of the infant Constantine VI was a devout image-worshipper. Her accession was hailed with enthusiasm by the orthodox and no compliment was too extravagant to pay her. She is " the lion-hearted godfearing woman, if woman is the right name for one who surpassed men in the piety of her character." [5] She is the new Helena with her son Constantine " like a rose and a lily set in the midst of thorns," [6] " Irene the queen of the happy name, the bearer of Christ." [7]

In the first year of her regency she restored the images and the monks.[8] A favourable omen was reported from Thrace. An inscription was unearthed reading : " Christ was born of Mary the Virgin and in him I believe. Under Constantine and Irene, o Sun, you will see me once more." [9]

[1] Tonsuring was a penalty never inflicted by Constantine V on account of his hostility to the monastic life. The revival of the punishment is an indication of the moderate position of Leo.
[2] Theoph., 913a.
[3] Cedrenus, I, 901a. But as no evidence earlier than Cedrenus exists it can only be regarded with suspicion.
[4] Theoph., 916a.
[5] Vit. Niceph., 52c. Cf. Niceph., Antirrh., III, 502b.
[6] Ep. ad Theoph., 364d.
[7] ἡ χριστόφορος Εἰρήνη ἡ φερωνύμως βασιλεύσασα. Theod. Stud., 824b.
[8] Theoph., 917b. Leo's attitude had been probably negative. He took no measures against the monks, but did not officially recall them from exile.
[9] Ib.

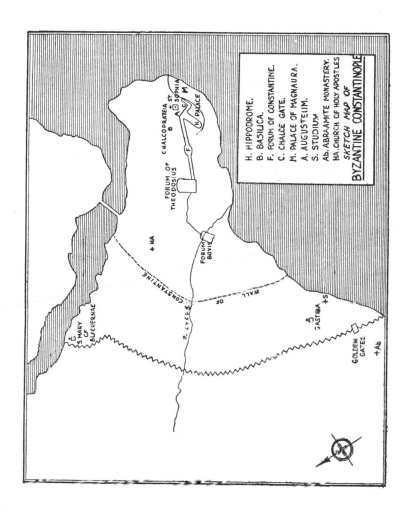

SKETCH MAP OF
BYZANTINE CONSTANTINOPLE

H. HIPPODROME.
B. BASILICA.
F. FORUM OF CONSTANTINE.
C. CHALCE GATE.
M. PALACE OF MAGNAURA.
A. AUGUSTEUM.
S. STUDIUM
Ab. ABRAAMITE MONASTERY.
HA. CHURCH OF HOLY APOSTLES

A year or two went by. Iconoclasm must still have been strong. In 784 the Patriarch Paul displayed that sensi-tiveness to the Imperial temper which Patriarchs of Con-stantinople developed. He announced that he must abdicate, for it had been borne upon him that the church of Con-stantinople was in schism with the rest of the world. In reply to a deputation of patricians and notables he suggested that only an Œcumenical Council could purge the Church. The members of the deputation had evidently been icono-clastic in sympathy. For when they proceeded to ask pertinently, Why, if he held such convictions, he had taken the Iconoclastic oath at his election? he replied that he had been afraid of them, and now his conscience troubled him. Paul did not long survive his abdication (31st Aug. 784).[1]

Four years had passed since the death of Leo IV. The strength of Iconoclasm was evidently by this time declining sufficiently to allow the orthodox but cautious Regent to go forward. Free discussion of the image question again became common.[2] And at this point without waiting for the appointment of a Patriarch the Empress wrote to the Pope requesting a General Council.[3] Having prepared the way, she proceeded to seek a suitable successor for the Patriarchate. The ranks of the clergy apparently were unable to offer any one sufficiently clear of the Iconoclastic stigma. That alone can explain the uncanonical action of one so orthodox as Irene in selecting a layman. The choice fell on the chief Imperial secretary Tarasius. The election was well staged. It was reported that the late Patriarch had designated Tarasius as his successor. Tarasius refused the personal request of the Empress. She then called a popular assembly at Magnaura where Tarasius was proclaimed Patriarch. He came forward and haran-gued the people in a speech which must have been of great value in re-establishing the images.[4] He said that he feared

[1] Theoph., 921cd ; Niceph., *Apol. Min.*, 840a.   [2] Theoph., 924a.
[3] Mansi, XII, 984.   The letter is dated a. d. iv Kal. Sept. 7th Indiction, *i.e.* 29th Aug. 784.   It contains no reference to a Patriarch.   Conference with " our most learned divines " is mentioned, and Constantine, bishop of Leontine in Sicily, is mentioned as one whom the Empress had interviewed. A reference to the bishop of Naples implies that he is another.   All this confirms the impression that Paul was forced to abdicate and the bishops of the neighbourhood of Constantinople were distrusted.
[4] It is reported at length by Theoph., 925, and in the Acta of Nicæa, Mansi, XII, 986. Cf. Niceph., *Apol. Min.*, 840b.

to undertake the office to which he was called. When St. Paul who had heard unutterable words in heaven itself and had borne the name of God to Gentiles and kings could say, "Lest when I have preached to others I myself should be a castaway," how could one aspire to the episcopate, who was a layman, his whole life spent in the world, in the experience of secular service alone ? He saw the Church itself in schism and division, the Christians of the East in disagreement with those of the West, and those of Constantinople alienated from all and daily objects of anathema. God wanted nothing so much as the unity of the One Catholic Church, confessed in the creed, and sought in prayer. His own personal view was that the people of Constantinople ought to appeal to their orthodox princes for an Œcumenical Council which would restore Christian unity. If their rulers assented to that wish, he would on his part accept the office to which he had been called. Otherwise he could not do so lest he should find condemnation on the day of the Lord Jesus Christ when no king, priest, noble, or multitude could avail to save him.

The assembled people assented with few exceptions, there being still some with Iconoclastic sympathies.[1] Tarasius added that Leo had destroyed the pictures and when the Council met the work was already done. A discussion of principles was very much to be desired.[2] On Christmas Day 787, Tarasius was consecrated bishop *per saltum* and became Patriarch. He is hailed in extravagant terms in the orthodox records, "a second Sylvester," "the holy morning-star of orthodoxy."[3] He was really a man of moderate temper and stood for a position between the subservience of the Church to the State which was sought by Justinian, Leo III, and Constantine V and the complete ecclesiastical independence for which Theodore Studites fought.[4] Accordingly, he at once opened up overtures with the Pope in a letter announcing his appoint-

---

[1] ἀφρονες, Mansi, XII, 990. Theophanes suppresses the fact that there were dissenters.

[2] Theoph., 928a.

[3] *Ep. ad Theoph.*, 364d. Sylvester was bishop of Rome at the time of Constantine's conversion. *Vit. Theoph.*, ap. Theoph., ed. de Boor, vol. ii, p. 9.

[4] See Gelzer, Der Verhältnis von Staat in Kirche in Byzanz., *Hist. Zeit.*, N.F. I, pp. 193 *sqq.*, 1901.

H

ment.[1] The Pope must have waited to investigate the Patriarch's credentials, for some time elapsed before his replies came. To the Empress he wrote at great length and not too cordially.[2] He commended her wish to restore the images,[3] upon the legitimacy of which he made a statement. He laid still greater emphasis on the necessity of submitting to the judgment of the Church of St. Peter. The primacy of Peter and the authority of the keys form the main theme of the letter. The Pope expressed surprise at finding the Empress applying the title " Universal " to the Patriarch of Constantinople. " If he is named Universal above the holy Roman Church, which has a prior rank as head of all the churches of God, it is plain that he shows himself a rebel against the holy Councils and a heretic." He expressed further surprise and disapproval at the irregularity of the appointment of a layman to the episcopate, but was prepared to condone it if the new Patriarch restored the images. In his letter to the Patriarch himself [4] Hadrian stated the same objection, again waiving it in view of the Patriarch's promised orthodoxy. He accepted the proposed Council and appointed as his representatives his steward (οἰκονόμος), the priest Peter, and the abbot of St. Sabas, who also was named Peter. The first task of the council would be to anathematise the pseudo-synod of the Iconoclasts because it had been called without the authority of the see of Peter, " the see that is conspicuously first in the whole world and the Head of all the churches of God." He closed ungraciously with a warning that if the Empress did not restore the images, he would be unable to accept the Patriarch's consecration.

The Patriarch wrote also to the three Eastern Patriarchs, of Antioch, Alexandria, and Jerusalem.[5] This letter followed the usual model of the enthronisation epistle. A confession of faith led to the question of images and the disunion which had ensued. Tarasius stated his intention

---

[1] The letter is not extant.

[2] Mansi, XII, 1055 *sqq.*

[3] It hardly represents the facts to say as Mann does (*op. cit.*, I (ii), p. 446) that " in compliance with the exhortations of the Pope Hadrian she decided to take measures for the restoration of the images and of communion with the West." The first move came from her side.

[4] Mansi, XII, 1078 *sqq.*

[5] *Ib.* 1122 *sqq.*

of holding a council and invited the Patriarchs to co-operate by sending each two representatives who should bring with them if possible letters stating the faith of the Patriarchates. Access to the Eastern Patriarchs, however, was impossible owing to the Moslem occupation. The bearers of the letters were entertained at an unknown place, probably in Egypt,[1] and there concealed by the monks. " Knowing, reverend sirs," wrote the monks to the Council of Nicæa, " the hostility of that ill-omened race (the Saracens), we decided to keep the messengers and restrain them from approaching those to whom they had been sent (the Patriarchs). We brought them before ourselves and advised them to avoid causing disturbance, or, to speak more accurately, destruction in the churches, which then by the grace of God were enjoying quiet peace. . . . They resented this advice, and declared that they were appointed to hazard their lives unto death for the Church and carry to a conclusion the commission of the most holy Patriarch and the orthodox Emperors." It was explained to them that it was not the risk of their own lives that gave concern, but the safety of all Christians in the Moslem dominions. As the messengers still hesitated to return with their mission unfulfilled, it was suggested that two monks, John and Thomas, syncelli respectively of the Patriarchs of Antioch and Alexandria, might go to Constantinople and explain the situation. Communication with the Patriarch of Jerusalem had been completely cut off, he having been exiled on a trivial charge. The two might be accepted as representatives of the three Patriarchal sees, being perfectly conversant with their orthodoxy. The monastic letter accepted the legitimacy of a General Council under the circumstances without the three Patriarchs. The Sixth Council was not invalidated by a similar compulsory absence, and the presence of the Pope was sufficient guarantee.[2]

The two Eastern monks and the two delegates from the Pope accordingly arrived in Constantinople, authorising the Emperors to summon the Council.[3] The two from the

---

[1] Thomas, one of the Eastern monks who came to the Council, gave evidence of a picture still standing (ἕως τοῦ νῦν) in Alexandria (Mansi, XIII, 60c) which might imply that he had recently come from there.

[2] Mansi, XII, 1127 *sqq.*   [3] *Ib.* 990c.

East had obviously no authority behind them and cannot technically be designated delegates. Their views, however, fairly represented the very orthodox opinions of the three Patriarchates, now greatly reduced in numbers by Monophysitism.

In Constantinople intrigues were set on foot by the Iconoclastic bishops and laity to prevent the meeting of the Council and to injure the Patriarch. This was countered by the Patriarch forbidding meetings without his consent as contrary to Canon law.[1] On Thursday August 17th, 786, the Council opened in the church of the Holy Apostles at Constantinople, the Empress and the Emperor watching from the seats of the catechumens.[2] But the Iconoclastic party was still active. Soldiers of the Imperial Guard (Scholarii and Excubitors) burst in, and violence was only prevented by the Iconoclastic bishops present in the Council calming the storm by crying out, " We have won." The Empress was helpless. The Council had to close.[3] During the winter Irene got the actively Iconoclastic units of the army sent on field service on a pretext of a Saracen attack.[4] But it was deemed impolitic for the Council to meet in Constantinople, an indirect witness to the strength of Iconoclasm. The meeting was called for May of the following year, and for place Nicæa on the Asiatic side of the water was chosen. There the foreign bishops were kept during the summer, and not until September did the first session open. The attendance was small, about 300 bishops[5] or their representatives and a number of monks. The order of the first names is always the same. The first place is given to " Peter, archpriest of the Holy Church of the Apostle Peter in Rome, and Peter, priest and abbot of St. Sabas, representing the Apostolic see of the pious

---

[1] Mansi, XII, 990d.
[2] Theoph., 928c.
[3] *Ib.* 929a ; Mansi, XII, 990e–991b.
[4] Theoph., 929c ; Mansi, XII, 991c.
[5] The names catalogued in the Acta vary from 258 at the opening to 335 at the close. The signatories to the Definition number 309. Mansi, XII, 999b ; XIII, 364e, 398. Nicephorus, *Ep. ad Leo.* 194b, apparently says that only 150 bishops were present, a number accepted by Lombard without discussion (*op. cit.*, p. 133). But this number is plainly contradicted by the Acta. Cedrenus (I, 905a) gives 350, which may be the correct reading in Nicephorus. With this agrees *Vit. II Theod. Stud.*, 240c. 350 would be approximately correct for the total number of bishops, episcopal representatives, and heads of monasteries.

and most holy archbishop of old Rome, Hadrian." Then follow in order, Tarasius, " the pious and most holy archbishop of the famous New Rome, Constantinople," then John and Thomas, " most reverend priests and monks, deputies of the apostolic sees of the Eastern dioceses," and after that the rest of the bishops or diocesan representatives, beginning with Agapius, bishop of Cæsarea in Cappadocia, John, bishop of Ephesus, and Constantine, bishop of Constantia in Cyprus. The bishops were almost entirely from the Asiatic provinces. Twenty-one came from the dioceses of Thrace and Illyria, including Theophanes, bishop of Sugdæ on the Danube, and a monk representing the distant Gotthia in the Crimea ; there were eight from Sicily, a ninth, a deacon of Catana, representing Thomas, archbishop of Sardinia, and six from Calabria.[1] The rest of the Council came from Asia and the islands, including Crete and Cyprus, the immense majority of them being votes rather than voices. A considerable number of abbots and monks also attended. They played an inconspicuous but decisive part, for it was they who supplied the bishops with brains. Such was Plato, the uncle of Theodore Studites, then head of the monastery of Saccudion in Constantinople. He was the Patriarch's chief adviser at the Council.[2] Other conspicuous monks present were Sabas, abbot of Studium, Gregory, abbot of St. Sergius, John, abbot of Pagurion,[3] and Nicetas and Nicephorus, monks from the monastery of Medicios.[4] Among the delegates arriving on horses and mules, in litters and post-carts, there was another remarkable figure, " a father journeying like a father, in a coat of hair with his shepherd's staff in his hand." It was the historian Theophanes, brought there by compulsion, for " he hated meetings and always sought quiet." He was haled to the Council from his monastery because of his learning.[5] The other great champion of

---

[1] The Sicilian dioceses represented were Catana, Leontine, Lilybæum, Messana, Panormus, Syracuse, Tauromenia, and Triocala. There were fourteen sees in Sicily at this period. The Calabrian dioceses represented were Cyriaca (*i.e.* Gieraci), Croton, Nicoteria, Rhegium, Taurianæ, and Tropæum. These figures are based on the attendance when the Council opened.

[2] σύμβουλος αὐτῷ τὰ πάντα καὶ συλλήπτωρ δεξιὸς καθίσταται, *Vit. II Theod. Stud.*, 240c. Cf. Theod. Stud., *Or.*, XI, 828b.

[3] Mansi, XII, 1111.

[4] *Vit. Theoph.*, p. 9.   [5] *Ib.* pp. 9 and 10.

94   A History of the Iconoclastic Controversy

orthodoxy, Nicephorus, was also present in a different capacity. He was still a secular official, and attended as one of the Imperial secretaries,[1] on the staff of the officers who sat to represent the Emperor, Petrona, ex-consul, patrician, and count of the Opsician theme, and John, Imperial ostiarius, and Logothete of the military chancery.[2]

On Monday, the 24th September, 787, the Council assembled in the church of the Holy Wisdom in Nicæa.[3] The Sicilian bishops proposed that Tarasius should open the proceedings. This cannot, however, mean that he was to preside in the modern sense. Instead of an actual chairman, the book of Gospels was, as usually in church assemblies, laid in the chief place, to·signify the presidency of Christ.[4] The bishops voted or signed their names in order of rank. There is no doubt that the first place in rank was assigned to the two Papal delegates. Nicephorus who was present says definitely that the Council was presided over by Rome, for without Rome no conciliar action would be approved, because Rome has the primacy,[5] and in every list recorded in the Acta their names are the first.

Tarasius opened the meeting by asking for the admission of the Iconoclastic bishops who had disturbed the Council when it had attempted to meet in Constantinople. He was supported by Constantine of Cyprus and, the Council agreeing, the offenders were admitted.[6] The Imperial Sacra constituting the Council and defining its object was read by the secretary Leontius.[7] It is a verbose document, mainly describing the abdication of Paul and the appointment of Tarasius, and only obliquely indicating the business of the Council : (i) to investigate the Iconoclastic Synod and (ii) to restore union with Rome and the Christians of the East. The usual hypocritical exhortation was given that every one might speak his mind boldly and discuss the subject freely. The Iconoclastic bishops

[1] Vit. Niceph., 53a.
[2] στρατιωτικοῦ λογοθεσίου. Mansi, XII, 994–999.
[3] Ib. 999b. Theoph. gives 11th Oct. as the date of the first session, 932b.
[4] Tarasius in his letter to Hadrian describing the Council says that, the Gospel-book being on the throne, κεφαλὴν ἐποιησάμεθα Χριστόν, Mansi, XIII, 459c, but he is careful to tell the Pope that the Papal letters were read first and then those of the Eastern Patriarchs.
[5] ὡς δὴ λαχόντων κατὰ τὴν ἱερωσύνην ἐξάρχειν καὶ τῶν κορυφαίων ἐν ἀποστόλοις ἐγκεχειρισμένων τὸ ἀξίωμα. Niceph., Apol., 597a.
[6] Mansi, XIII, 1002c.   [7] Ib. 1002.

may well have assumed that this permission applied particularly to them. They did not, however, avail themselves of it, but, led by Basil, bishop of Ancyra, they came asking the Council to receive their recantation.[1] They repudiated absolutely and utterly the Iconoclastic Council, "a synod gathered together out of stubbornness and madness, which styled itself the Seventh Council, but which by those who think correctly was lawfully and canonically designated a pseudo-council, being contrary to all truth and piety, and audaciously and temerariously subversive of the traditional law of the Church by its yelping and scoffing at the holy and venerable images."[2] Several bishops followed Basil, making their plea for readmission, Theodore of Myra, Theodosius of Amorium, Hypatius of Nicæa, Leo of Rhodes, Gregory of Pessinus, Leo of Iconium, George of Hierapolis, and Leo of Carpathus.[3] A long discussion followed in which precedents for the readmission of heretics were discussed. The monks present showed themselves disinclined to accept the penitence of the converts. The patriarch tried hard to fill the rôle of peacemaker, but John the Oriental monk roundly declared : " This heresy is worse than all heresies . . . it is the worst of all sins, for it destroys the dispensation of the Saviour."[4] The Council continued to discuss the technical problem of the admission of those ordained by heretics, it being assumed without discussion that Iconoclasm was heresy. It was pointed out that authorities were favourable to heretics on both issues, and it was eventually agreed that at a later session the Iconoclasts should be admitted to the Council.[5]

On resembling after a day's interval on 26th September, Nicephorus the Imperial secretary announced that the Emperor's delegate[6] desired to introduce to the Council another ex-Iconoclast, Gregory, bishop of Neo-Cæsarea.[7] Tarasius very pointedly asked if his repentance were genuine.[8] Protesting his sincerity, Gregory was ordered to attend the next session with a written recantation.

[1] Mansi, XII, 1007–1015. [2] *Loc. cit.*
[3] Mansi, XII, 1015d. [4] *Ib.* 1034a. [5] *Ib.* 1050e.
[6] βασιλικὸς ἄνθρωπος, βασιλικὸς μανδάτωρ, *i.e.* the lay officer who watched proceedings for the Emperor.
[7] Mansi, XII, 1051d.
[8] μήπω ὡς παραπετάσματι πανούργῳ τὸ σὸν φρόνημα συσκιάσαι θέλων ῥήμασι σχηματίζῃ τὴν ἀλήθειαν. Mansi, XII, 1054b.

The actual business of the Council began with the reading of the Papal letters addressed to the Emperors and to Tarasius, the passage protesting against the title " Universal (Œcumenical) Patriarch " being omitted. The Roman delegates asked for the Patriarch's opinion of the doctrine set out by the Pope. Tarasius declared his complete assent, " receiving the images according to the ancient tradition of the holy fathers ; these we venerate with relative honour, made in the name of Christ our God and of our spotless Lady, the Holy Theotokes, and of the Holy Angels, and of all the Saints, while plainly giving our adoration and faith to the one only true God." [1] Two hundred and sixty-two other bishops or their representatives then gave this assent individually, usually in a few words, though John the Eastern monk, who voted first, seized the opportunity of making a speech, a practice he observed throughout the proceedings. After him followed in order Agapius of Cæsarea in Cappadocia, John of Ephesus, Constantine of Constantia, Basil of Ancyra, and the others. [2] The monks did the same. [3]

On the next day but one, 28th September, [4] the Council reassembled, and Gregory of Neo-Cæsarea read his recantation, in the same terms as the previous Iconoclastic petitioners. [5] Tarasius called attention to the fact that some Iconoclastic bishops had persecuted the faithful and were therefore liable to be deposed under the 26th Apostolic Canon. [6] It was agreed that definite charges must be brought, and Gregory declared that no such charge could be brought against him. [7] Sabas, abbot of Studium, said that Gregory was a leading Iconoclast (probably meaning that he had taken part in the Iconoclastic Council), but for himself he was willing that he should be pardoned according to the directions of Athanasius to Rufinianus. On the motion, therefore, of Peter, the Roman delegate, and of John and Thomas, the representatives of the East, all the

[1] Mansi, XI, 1086.
[2] *Ib.* 1086, *sqq.*
[3] *Ib.* 1111.
[4] The Latin version of the Acta says 29th Sept.
[5] Mansi, XII, 1114e.
[6] Really Canon 27. " If a bishop, presbyter, or deacon shall strike any of the faithful . . . with the intention of frightening them we command that he be deposed."
[7] Mansi, XII, 1115.

Iconoclastic bishops present were allowed to take their seats.[1]

The business of the Council then proceeded. The position of the Eastern Patriarchates was explained, and the two Eastern priests related how they came to be present, and though not possessing authority [2] they offered to read a Synodical letter of Theodore, late Patriarch of Jerusalem,[3] which would set out the doctrinal position of the three Patriarchates. The letter made the usual statement of faith in the Trinity and the Incarnation, and in the six Councils. It proceeded : " We . . . accept also with reverence the sacred images, namely that of the Incarnate Word, as representing not the divine nature which is uncircumscribed, but the humanity to which the godhead was completely united, as well as the images of the Virgin, apostles, prophets, and martyrs, not paying honour to the material of colours, but led by them through the eyes of understanding to the original." The charge of idolatry brought against image-worship is to be met with the cherubim, the mercy-seat, the ark, and the table.

The Roman delegates declared that these views were in agreement with those of the Pope and Tarasius, and again the bishops gave their assent in order.[4] Constantine of Constantia made a statement which subsequent misinterpretation made notorious : " I receive and salute with honour the holy and venerable images. But the worship of adoration I reserve alone for the supersubstantial and life-giving Trinity." [5]

The Council had now really done its work. It had, indeed, reached its decision before ever it assembled. But it was necessary to bring together the evidence upon which the orthodox case stood. On 1st October, citations from Scripture and the Fathers were read in support of the

[1] Mansi, XII, 1118–1119.

[2] It is unnecessary to comment on the grotesque misrepresentation of Gibbon on this point and indeed on nearly all he says about this Council. Bury-Gibbon, V, 277.

[3] Mansi, XII, 1135 *sqq.* It was apparently a synodical letter sent to Cosmas of Alexandria and Theodore of Antioch. Theodore became Patriarch circa 742. His views on images are indebted to St. John of Damascus.

[4] Mansi, XII, 1146c.

[5] δεχόμενος καὶ ἀσπαζόμενος τιμητικῶς τὰς ἁγίας εἰκόνας· καὶ τὴν κατὰ λατρείαν προσκύνησιν μόνῃ τῇ ὑπερουσίῳ καὶ ζωαρχικῇ Τριάδι ἀναπέμπω. *Ib.* 1147b. It was this passage that, owing to a mistranslation or misinterpretation, the Frankish king Charles used to attack the Council. See below, p. 231.

98   *A History of the Iconoclastic Controversy*

images.[1] All were received with naive approval, however irrelevant to the real issue they might be, and the voice of criticism was silent. Seldom can an episcopal assembly have displayed such vocal unanimity. When Gregory of Nyssa was produced as a witness to the emotional influence of a picture of the sacrifice of Isaac, the ex-Iconoclast Basil of Ancyra reflected that many times as the father read the story perchance he had never wept, but when once he saw it painted then his tears flowed.[2] When the legend was mentioned which said that the woman with the issue erected a statue of Christ, it was hailed as evidence that God accepted the dedication of images.[3] " A picture," said John the Eastern priest, " is more effective than a sermon ; it is God's provision for simple souls." [4] Excerpts from the *Miracles of Anastasius* seemed to the Roman and Eastern delegates to prove that images worked miracles.[5] A spurious sermon of Athanasius gave Constantine of Constantia confidence that Athanasius believed in the miraculous powers of images, but the more cautious Tarasius thought that such powers were only exerted to convert unbelievers.[6] Theodore of Myra offered the delightful statement that his archdeacon had recognised St. Nicholas in a vision from his resemblance to his picture.[7] Theodore had been at the Iconoclastic Council and perhaps was anxious to say something that would please. When an excerpt was read from the writings of Maximus, the orthodox champion against the Monothelites, in which it was said that both sides paid honour [8] to images of our Lord and the Virgin equally with the Cross and the Gospels, Constantine of Constantia was confident that the word " honour " meant that they made a motion of reverence.[9] Tarasius again with customary caution said that it was not the worship (λατρεία) which is paid to God alone, while Peter of Nicomedeia felt that there was great weight in the example of so high an authority as Maximus, a confessor and warrior for the truth.[10] When the Council came to the passage from Sophronius which aroused the contempt of Gibbon,[11]

[1] This is examined in detail in ch. vii below.
[2] Mansi, XIII, 9.   [3] *Ib.* 13e.
[4] *Ib.* 20c.   [5] *Ib.* 24d.
[6] *Ib.* 32ab.   [7] *Ib.* 33d.
[8] *Ib.* 40a. τὴν εἰκόνα . . . ἠσπάσαντο.   [9] ἐπὶ προσκυνήσεως ἔλαβον.
[10] *Ib.* 40c.   [11] Bury-Gibbon, V, 277.

John the Eastern representative said that this piece of evidence showed that perjury is preferable to refusing veneration to the images. He offered this as a solution of the difficulty felt by many who had taken the Iconoclastic oath. These comments may serve to show the quality of the debate.[1] It is significant that no attempt was made to discuss the subject on its merits by seeking a general basis for the use of pictures. The principle followed was the appeal to authority. But even that method was not pursued in any logical fashion. The most irrelevant references to pictures were accepted as authorising image-worship, with no consideration of the context. There is not the slightest indication in the proceedings of the Council that any one present had the least idea that there was a gradual development of the use of pictures in the church, or that one authority was older or better than another. The *Life of Holy Mary the Egyptian* was as good as St. Basil and a spurious sermon of St. Athanasius was as acceptable as a genuine one. After some half-dozen Scriptural texts and about thirty Patristic passages, the correspondence of Germanus at the outbreak of Iconoclasm was read.[2] The Council then solemnly anathematised those who did not pay reverence (ἀσπάζευθαι) to the holy images, those who did not assent to their use and the other ancient traditions of the Church, the accusers of the Christians [3] (*i.e.* the Iconoclasts), those who apply the Scripture warnings against idolatry to the images, those who say the orthodox regard images as gods, those who communicate with Iconoclasts, and those who dare to say that the Catholic Church has ever accepted idols.[4]

A formal summary of the Council's findings was then read by Euthymius of Sardis.[5] After recalling the rule of the Fathers to set the light of divine knowledge before all and the purpose of the Council to expel error from the Church, he proceeded to a formal recognition of the faith of the six Councils in the Trinity and the Incarnation. The incarnate God had delivered the faithful from idols by his coming. The Virgin, Apostles, Prophets, Martyrs, and Doctors are to be honoured and their intercession

---

[1] The patristic quotations are discussed in detail below.
[2] For these letters see above.   [3] Χριστιανοκατήγοροι.
[4] Mansi, XIII, 128c.   [5] *Ib.* 129a.

sought. "Moreover, we salute the image of the life-giving Cross and the holy relics of the saints, and we receive the holy and venerable images ; we salute them and embrace them according to the ancient tradition of the holy Catholic Church of God, that is to say, of our holy Fathers who also received these things and established them in all the most holy churches of God and in every place of his dominion. These honourable and venerable images, as has been said, we honour and salute and reverently venerate, to wit, the image of our great God and Saviour Jesus Christ, and that of our spotless Lady, the all-holy Mother of God, from whom he was pleased to take flesh, to save and deliver us from all impious idolatry, and also the images of the holy and incorporeal angels who in the form of men appeared to the just, likewise also the figures and effigies of the divine and all-lauded Apostles, and of the God-inspired prophets, and of the striving martyrs and of the saints, that through their representations we may be led back in memory and recollection to the prototype, and have some share in their holiness." To this declaration the members assented individually, beginning with Peter of Rome, who added that he received into communion all who were converted from Iconoclasm.[1]   His colleague, Peter abbot of St. Sabas, followed, then Tarasius, the two Eastern monks, Agapius of Cæsarea, John of Ephesus, Constantine of Constantia, Theophilus of Thessalonica (who apparently was not present in the earlier sessions), Basil of Ancyra, and 225 other bishops or their delegates, and 128 monks, most of them abbots, beginning with Sabas, abbot of Studium, and Gregory, abbot of Hormisdas.[2]

The fifth session was held on 4th October. Tarasius opened the proceedings by saying that the Iconoclasts had imitated Jews and Saracens, pagans and Samaritans, "above all Manichæans and Phantastiastæ, that is Theopaschites."[3]   Further patristic passages were then read. The comments as usual came from John the Eastern monk and from Constantine of Constantia. John offered the

[1] Mansi, XIII, 133b.
[2] *Ib.* 133c, 152a.
[3] The Phantastiastæ were Monophysites of the party of Julian of Halicarnassus : they were not identical with those who stood with Peter the Fuller for the formula that "one of the Trinity was crucified" (Theopaschites).

opinion that the Samaritans were the worst of all heretics, but the Iconoclasts were a match for them. They were worse, said Constantine, for the Samaritans were ignorant of what they did.[1]

The collection of evidence was brought to a close with some items of a miscellaneous character. A pseudonymous Περιοδοὶ τῶν ἀγίων ἀποστόλων was condemned as apocryphal in origin and docetic in teaching. The historian Eusebius was also written down an Arian, and passages were read to show that the early opponent of images, Xenaias, was a notorious heretic.[2] This was intended to dispose of the evidence that might be brought forward against the use of images. A record was made of acts of vandalism perpetrated by the Iconoclasts. Books in Constantinople and Phocia had been burnt or mutilated.[3] A few more quotations were read in support of the contention that miracles were wrought by images, including the story of the picture of Christ sent to Abgar, king of Edessa. This was read from the sixth-century historian Evagrius, who is the earliest known authority for the legend,[4] and Leo, lector of the imperial church at Constantinople, testified that he had actually seen the picture in Edessa.[5] Fifteen further passages of the Fathers were taken as read, the Council agreeing with Tarasius that the evidence was already more than enough,[6] and John the Eastern representative read a written statement of the origin of Iconoclasm.[7] It was agreed in general terms that images should be restored, and on the motion of the Papal delegate that a picture should be set up in the Council and honour paid to it,[8] and another session should be held at which all writings against images should be burnt. The session closed with a thanksgiving pronounced by John and anathemas on the opponents of images delivered by the Council.[9]

The sixth session was held on 6th Oct.[10] The secretary Leontius announced that the Definition (ὅρος) of the Iconoclastic Council of 753 was ready for presentation together with a refutation of it. The Council agreed to

---

[1] Mansi, XIII, 164ab.
[2] *Ib.* 168–181.
[3] *Ib.* 184–188.
[4] *Ib.* 189e.
[5] *Ib.* 192c.
[6] *Ib.* 195d.
[7] *Ib.* 197a.
[8] ταύτην ἀσπασώμεθα. *Ib.* 200d.
[9] *Ib.* 200e–201b.
[10] So the Greek text. The Latin says Oct. 5th. *Ib.* 204a.

hear these. The Iconoclast, Gregory of Neo-Cæsarea, was appropriately appointed to read the Iconoclastic Definition, while he was answered, section by section, from the other document, read by John the deacon (with another deacon, Epiphanius, to relieve him), each reading alternately. " The other document opposes the ὅρος from sentence to sentence and in this way contains much that is certainly superfluous, and it is of unnecessary extent." [1] This is certainly not an overstatement. The refutation of the eight words of the title, " "Ορος of the Holy, Mighty, and Œcumenical Seventh Council " takes nearly a column.

The ὅρος itself has been examined elsewhere. The refutation, the authors of which are unknown, for all its verbosity is a very complete statement of the orthodox position. Beginning with a lie, it runs, and supporting the whole course of their revolutionary sophistry with that lie, the calumniators of Christianity closed with a lie. . . . They apply the term idol indiscriminately to the picture of the Incarnate Word, our Lord Jesus Christ, and to the picture of Satan. . . . How can it be the seventh Council when it is not in harmony with the six that preceded it ? . . . The charge of idolatry is self-contradictory. The acceptance by the Iconoclasts of Zech. xiii. 2, " I will cut off the idols out of their land," and of Ps. cxlv. 13, " His kingdom is an everlasting kingdom," admits the permanence of Christ's conquest. The acceptance of the six Councils implies the acceptance of the images, for the use of images went on through the whole period of the Councils, and after the sixth, Justinian, four or five years later, reassembled the members and passed the 82nd Canon, which definitely ordered that Christ should be depicted as a man and not as a lamb. [2] The picture represents Christ as he appeared on earth. The essential godhead is uncircumscribable, and no one attempts to circumscribe it. The human life of Christ was entirely circumscribed. The Iconoclasts show their affinities with Arians like Eusebius and Monophysites like Xenaias, both of whom they quote. No one supposes that a picture of Christ is actually Christ. The picture has

[1] Hefele, E. Tr., V, 373. It is given fully in Mansi, XIII, 205-364.
[2] This is a mistaken view of the Quinisext Council to which the Canons are due.

the name of the original but not the essence.[1] The authority upon which the use of images is based is tradition, as the evidence of the Fathers shows. The tradition of pictures stands with the tradition of the Gospel and both serve the same end. Pictures of the Virgin and the saints are legitimate a fortiori, and the Church has always recognised the right of asking their prayers and remembering them. The evidence of Scripture and the Fathers which the Iconoclastic Council had used is then examined. The practice of tearing sentences out of their context is severely reprehended. After summarising the new policy of Iconoclasm as annihilating the tradition of the Church, the refutation comments on the Anathemas of 753.[2]

On Oct. 13th, the Council reassembled for its seventh session, 347 bishops or their representatives attending, besides the monks and Petrona the Imperial officer.[3] The Definition (ὅρος) of the Council was read by Theodore, bishop of Tauriana in Sicily.[4]

" The Holy, Mighty, and Œcumenical Council . . . has defined as follows : . . . Some have fallen from the right faith . . . because certain priests, priests in name only, had dared to speak against the God-approved ornaments of the holy churches . . . and following profane men, led astray by their carnal sense, they have calumniated the Church of Christ our God . . . and have failed to distinguish between holy and profane, styling the images of our Lord and of his Saints by the same name as the statues of diabolical idols."

After assenting to the Creed and the doctrines enunciated in the Six Councils they proceeded :

" We therefore following the royal pathway and the divinely inspired traditions of the Catholic Church . . . define with all certitude and accuracy that, just as the figure of the precious and life-giving Cross, so also the venerable and holy images, as well in painting and mosaic

---

[1] But there was a tendency to attribute to the picture some of the reality of the original. This is seen in the theology of images in St. John Damascene and in popular superstition. The Council which represents a moderate position ignored this.

[2] Mansi, XIII, 207–356. This Council is merely summarised here. It is dealt with in detail above, Ch. IV.

[3] Mansi, XIII, 364e.

[4] *Ib.* 373c.

as of other fit materials, should be set forth in the holy
churches of God and on the sacred vessels and on the
vestments and on hangings and in pictures both in houses
and by the wayside, to wit, the figure of our Lord God and
Saviour, Jesus Christ, of our spotless Lady, the Theotokos,
of the honourable angels, of all saints, and of all pious people.
For by so much more frequently as they are seen in artistic
representation, by so much more readily are men lifted
up to the memory of their prototypes and to a longing
after them ; and to these should be given due salutation
and honourable reverence, not indeed the true worship
of faith which pertains only to the divine nature,[1] but to
these as to the figure of the precious and life-giving Cross
and to the book of the Gospels, and to the other holy objects
incense and lights may be offered according to ancient
pious custom.   For the honour which is paid to the image
passes to that which the image represents, and he who
reveres the image reveres in it the subject represented.
For thus the teaching of our holy Fathers, that is the tradition of the Catholic Church . . . is strengthened. . . .
Those therefore who dare to think or teach otherwise
or as wicked heretics to spurn the traditions of the Church
and to invent some novelty or else to reject some of those
things which the Church hath received (*e.g.* the book of
the Gospels or the image of the Cross or the pictured images
or the holy relics of a martyr) or evilly and craftily to devise
anything subversive of the lawful traditions of the Catholic
Church or to turn to common uses the sacred vessels or the
venerable monasteries, if they be bishops or clerics, we
command that they be deprived, if religious or laics that
they be excommunicated."

Three hundred and nine episcopal delegates then signed
this document in the usual order, beginning with Peter,
"protopresbyter of the see of the holy Apostle."[2]   The
session closed with the traditional applause.

" . . . This is the faith of the Apostles, this is the faith
of the orthodox. . . . Believing in one God in Trinity,
we salute the images.   Anathema to those who do not so

[1] καὶ ταύταις ἀσπασμὸν καὶ τιμητικὴν προσκύνησιν ἀπονέμειν, οὐ μὴν τὴν κατὰ
πίστιν ἡμῶν ἀληθινὴν λατρείαν ἣ πρέπει μόνῃ τῇ θείᾳ φύσει ἀλλ' ὃν τρόπον τῷ τύπῳ
τοῦ τιμίου καὶ ζωοποιοῦ σταυροῦ. . . . Mansi, XIII, 377.
[2] *Ib.* 380c.

believe. . . . Anathema to those who presume to apply to the holy images what Scripture says of idols. Anathema to those who do not salute the holy images. Anathema to those who call the sacred images idols. Anathema to those who say that Christians resort to the sacred images as to gods. . . . Anathema to those who dare to say that at any time the Catholic Church received idols. Long life to the Emperors."

The synodical letter to the Empress was then drawn up.[1] The Empress and the Emperor were hailed as those " who upheld the Church which was ready to fall, strengthening it with sound doctrine and bringing into the unity of a right judgment those who were at variance." The purpose and the decision of the Council are then recorded. " Certain men rose up, having the form of godliness, inasmuch as they were clothed with the dignity of the priesthood, but denying the power thereof . . . they banded themselves together in a sanhedrin (*i.e.* the Iconoclastic Council) . . . and proceeded to stigmatise as idolaters the royal priest-hood and the holy nation," and set about the destruction of pictures of our Lord and the saints. You ordered our Council to deal with this situation. The Council has traced the traditions of the Apostles and Fathers, and has reached a unanimous conclusion " that the sacred images of our Lord Jesus Christ are to be had and retained inasmuch as he was very man, as well as those which set forth what is narrated in the Gospels and those which represent our undefiled Lady, and those of the Holy Angels or saints," and such representations may also be depicted on walls, sacred vessels, or vestments. These images or pictures are to receive veneration (προσκυνεῖν). The word προσκυνεῖν is derived from κυνεῖν signifying either " to salute " or " to kiss," and the preposition πρὸς gives the additional idea of strong desire. Examples of the word occur fre-quently in the Bible : " David . . . bowed himself (προσεκύνησε) three times " (1 Sam. xx. 41). Jacob is said to have done reverence (προσεκύνησεν) to [or on] the top of his staff (Gen. xlvii. 31, LXX). This is not understood to be worship in spirit (ἐν πνεύματι λατρεία). It is parallel to the words used in honour of the Cross. " We venerate (προσκυνῶμεν) the Cross, o Lord, and we also venerate

[1] Mansi, XIII, 400d.

I

the spear which opened the life-giving side of thy goodness."
There are degrees of veneration, for veneration is an
ambiguous term, but the service of worship (λατρεία) is paid
to God only. " May the Saviour of us all, who reigns with
you [1] . . . preserve your kingdom for many years."

To the priests and clergy the Synod wrote in similar
terms but more briefly.[2] " On the principle of loyalty
to the fathers we honour and salute the images." [3] The
Council was summoned by the Empress to Constantinople
for its eighth and final session. On 23rd October [4] they
met in the palace of Magnaura, the Empress and her son
presiding. The session opened with a suitable address
from the Patriarch, which has not been reported. The
Empress delivered a careful speech of kindly feeling which
evoked applause from the Council but also was not recorded.
She then ordered that the ὅρος should be read and asked
if it were unanimously accepted. A hearty assent was
given, and the anathemas were repeated against Theodosius of Ephesus, Sisinnius Pastillas, Basil Tricaccabus,
and the others. The Patriarch asked the Empress to sign
the ὅρος. After she had signed, she made her son sign,
amid the applause of the gathering. The Patristic
authorities were read from the fourth session, and the
assembly dispersed with applause from the people, who had
attended in large numbers.[5]

Twenty-two canons were promulgated by the Council.[6]
The majority of them are concerned with minor matters of
Church and monastic discipline not immediately connected
with Iconoclasm. Four of them—numbers 7, 9, 13, and
16—have a direct connection.

7. In churches consecrated without any deposit of relics
of saints the defect shall be made good.

During the Iconoclastic triumph evidently new churches
were built without the observance of the former practice
of depositing relics in them. This is indirect evidence
that the Iconoclasts built churches.

9. That none of the books containing the heresy of the
traducers of the Christians are to be concealed.

---

[1] A curious phrase. συμβασιλεύων ὑμῖν.
[2] Mansi, XIII, 408d.
[3] τιμητικῶς προσκυνῶμεν καὶ ἀσπαζόμεθα.
[4] Mansi, XIII, 413b.   [5] Ib. 417b.   [6] Ib. 417c sqq.

All Iconoclastic writings were to be delivered at the Patriarch's office in Constantinople and to be kept under lock and key with the other heretical books. The retention of any such books in private hands will be punished in a cleric with degradation from orders, in a layman or monk with excommunication.

13. That those who turn monasteries into public houses are worthy of special condemnation.

" During the calamity . . . in the churches (*i.e.* iconoclasm) . . . some of the sacred houses, . . . bishops' palaces, and monasteries were seized . . . and became public inns. If those who now hold them choose to give them back so that they may be restored to their original use, well and good." Otherwise the usual penalty is ordered. Many such buildings had been deserted by the fugitive image-worshippers and were occupied by the government and probably by private adventurers.

16. That it is unbecoming that one in holy orders should be clad in costly apparel.

Such as were defiled by it (*i.e.* Iconoclasm) not only detested the pictured images, but also set at naught all decorum, being exceedingly mad against those who lived gravely and religiously." [1]

We may now inquire (i) What was the immediate effect of the Council? (ii) What was its permanent significance in the history of the Church? [2]

(i) The immediate effect of the Council was the official restoration of orthodoxy. The Church of God had peace, says Theophanes.[3] But it is probable that throughout

---

[1] It is assumed that the Iconoclastic bishops were worldly and ostentatious. But it would appear that it was rather the monastic habit that they attacked. Cf. Niceph., *Antirrh.*, III, 489a.

[2] The following supplementary matter contained in the Acta is of little importance :

(i) Encomium pronounced at the Council by Epiphanius, deacon of Catana, deputy for Thomas, archbishop of Sardinia. Mansi, XIII, 442a. This is a wordy and pointless panegyric on the Council. Probably it was composed, but no opportunity for its delivery was realised. Hence its place in the supplement to the Acta.

(ii) Letter of Tarasius to Pope Hadrian. *Ib.* 458c. It describes the Council without detail.

(iii) Two letters of Tarasius, one to Pope Hadrian, the other to the Eastern monk John, dealing with simony, the Patriarch having been accused of laxity in this matter. *Ib.* 462e, 471e.

(iv) An anonymous document on the interpretation of the Scripture passages which attack idolatry. *Ib.* 479c. [3] Theoph., 932b.

the East the actual restoration of pictures was ineffectual.[1] Twenty-five years later Iconoclasm was strong enough to make the name of Constantine a rallying-cry and to over-throw the reigning dynasty, and the significance of the hostility displayed by orthodox writers against the Emperor Nicephorus is probably that he made no attempt to enforce the decision of Nicæa for the wise reason that he saw that it could not be done. The Council was, however, effective in restoring an outward unity of the Church. At the same time outward communion with Rome was accompanied by spiritual alienation. The image question was not a living issue in Western Europe. Hadrian's whole attitude is not that the pictures do not matter, but that neither he nor his subjects have any real difficulty over them. But the patrimonies of Peter were a vital question, and Hadrian took good care to press it in his acceptance of the decision of the Council.[2] Nothing, however, came from Constantinople. Constantinople was thinking of orthodoxy, the Pope was thinking of system and order.

(ii) That introduces the answer to the larger question of the permanent meaning of the Council for Christendom. " A faithful version (*i.e.* of the Acta of the Council) with some critical notes," said Gibbon, " would provoke in different readers a smile or a sigh." " The Acts are . . . a curious monument of superstition and ignorance, of falsehood and folly." [3] It is true that the issue was trivial and the handling of it often foolish. But what Gibbon failed to see was that the Council is the logical sequel to Chalcedon. It completed the process of identifying Chris-tianity with the Græco-Latin civilisation. The Icono-clasts, like the Nestorians, Monophysites, Paulicians, and other Oriental sects, even like Mohammedanism, represent the more truly Oriental idea of religion trying to express itself in Christianity. Rooted in a different civilisation and seeing the Christian facts under a different philosophy, this Syro-Semitic Christianity fought a losing battle. The effect of the earlier councils of Constantinople and Chal-cedon was to cut adrift this school and reduce the Eastern Patriarchates to very small dimensions. Constantinople as

---

[1] Cf. Bréhier, *op. cit.*, p. 31.
[2] Hadr., *Ep. to Charles;* Mansi, XIII, 808.
[3] Bury-Gibbon, V, 276n, 277.

much as Rome stood for the Christianity of the Empire. The Second Council of Nicæa was the last gesture of refusal to the claims of the Asiatic ideal. For Constantinople itself the effects were disastrous. While growing more and more definitely Oriental in general outlook, she committed herself to the Christian theology of which Rome was the natural and actual leader. The consequence was that as Constantinople lost political touch with the West and had refused to meet the religious outlook of the East, she was isolated. The political jealousy which prevented her from moving side by side with Western Christendom left her stranded. Different spectators will see in Byzantine Christianity either the wonderful semper eadem of a deathless faith or a tragic monument of obstinate isolation. The Orthodox Church stands to-day where it stood in the ninth century. On one side of it the Christianity of the Roman Empire for which it declared itself has gone forward, developing for good or ill with the advance of civilisation. On the other side what was once the genuine Oriental Christianity lies sapped by Islam and submerged in Monophysites and Nestorians. The Council of Nicæa is one of those events, trivial in themselves, which are great crises in the history of Christianity.

CHAPTER VII

THE THEOLOGY OF THE FIRST ICONOCLASTIC PERIOD (725-802)

AUTHORITIES

St. John Damascene, Nicephorus, Acta of Second Council of Nicæa. All as in Chapters III and IV.
The work of Theodore Studites belongs 'to the second Iconoclastic period, with the exception of a small collection of epigrams in verse included with the writings of Theodore (M.P.G. 99, pp. 435 sqq.). They are attributed to four Iconoclasts named John, Ignatius, Sergius, and Stephen. They all celebrate the Cross or the Passion of Christ, and clearly relate to Leo III and Constantine V, who made a reverence for the Cross a prominent feature of Iconoclasm and are mentioned by name in one poem. One iambic line (476c) printed in the shape of a cross seems to refer to the military successes of the Isaurian Emperors :

ἐχθροὺς τροποῦμαι καὶ φονεύω βαρβάρους.

Miss Gardner considers the poems contemporary with Theodore, assuming John to be John the Grammarian, but the internal evidence makes this dating improbable. (Gardner, A., *Theodore of Studium* (London, 1905), p. 272.)
Modern literature : Schwarzlose, as above. Lupton, J. H. in in D.C.B. s.v. Joannes Damascenus.

ICONOCLASM was ultimately a movement in the realm of thought, and must therefore have a philosophy and a theology. It is that philosophy or theology that we now proceed to examine. It will simplify our examination if we approach the theology historically as it developed stage by stage.

The first period, that of the original outbreak under the Isaurians followed by the orthodox reaction under Irene, falls into two stages, each concerned with a different line of argument. The first stage is the original attack of Leo and his party. They saw image-worship simply as idolatry. The orthodox reply to their contention is given by St. John Damascene. In the second stage the Christological question is introduced and images are denounced as conflicting with the definition of Chalcedon.[1] The answer to this argument predominates in the apologetic writings of Nicephorus. In fact, this topic becomes more and more the point at issue, and in the second Iconoclastic period idolatry almost fades out of the discussion.

In a controversial subject of this kind both sides may be expected to supply us with information. But practically all the material comes from the orthodox party alone. Of the writings of the Iconoclasts we possess only (i) the Definition (ὅρος) of the Council of 753, preserved in the Acta of Nicæa ; (ii) fragments of a statement of the Iconoclasts' Christological argument, quoted in the first two *Antirrhetici* of Nicephorus, and attributed to Mammon, who may be identified with the Emperor Constantine V ; (iii) some half-dozen Iconoclastic epigrams on the Cross and Passion, preserved among the writings of Theodore Studites. To this may be added the imaginary interlocutor found in most of the orthodox controversial writers. He is always a man of straw, but in the earlier tracts like *adv. Const. Cab.*, he is allowed to put his case with some vigour. Lastly, the Acta of the Council of Nicæa reveal many of the ideas of the Iconoclastic position.

In contrast with the paucity of Iconoclastic writings, the orthodox statement of the case is very voluminous. So voluminous indeed is it, that it gives the impression of greater variety than it possesses. For a great part of it is repetition. St. John Damascene repeats in his second and third Discourses much of the argument of the first, while Nicephorus makes the same points over and over again. A large part of the material found in every writing from *adv. Const. Cab.* to Theodore Studites comes out of a common stock which must have been public property.

But philosophical discussion forms only a small part of the statement of the case. Rationalistic curiosity found a very inconsiderable place in Eastern theology [2] after the beginning of the fifth century. As early as 383 the Emperor Theodosius had fallen back on tradition (as

---

[1] The two stages described as προηγουμένη and ἐπομένη are clearly distinguished by Nicephorus, *Apol.*, 560c.

[2] A good example of the absence of such curiosity is seen in the shocked surprise with which the patriarch Constantine received the emperor's inquiry, What would happen if we called the mother of God the mother of Christ? Theoph., 877a.

opposed to new expression of thought) to settle disputes.[1] From the end of the fourth century there is scarcely a genuinely constructive theologian found in Eastern Christendom. The mysticism of Dionysius the Areopagite represents the scope of the future contribution that the Greek-speaking world can make to Christian thought. It is no matter of surprise, therefore, to find that a very large part of the Iconoclastic controversy is composed of the appeal to authorities. These authorities are of three types : (i) Biblical ; (ii) Patristic, *i.e.* in both cases written statements more or less applicable to the problem; while the third (iii) are the actual historical precedents preserved either in writing or in human memory. We may therefore consider the theological question under the three heads :

(i) The philosophical argument that an image is or is not an idol.

(ii) The philosophical argument that an image undermines or supports a true doctrine of the Person of Christ.

(iii) The use and abuse of authorities and precedents establishing or overthrowing both the preceding points.

I

The first problem, then, was to settle the question whether or not a picture or image was an idol. The direct inspiration of the Iconoclastic movement was the conviction that pictures or images as used in the Church were nothing but a return of idolatry. The movement starts with Constantine, bishop of Nacoliä, telling the Patriarch Germanus of his fear that images implied idolatry.[2] The conclusion of the Council of 753 was that images did imply idolatry. Germanus was anathematised with the epithet Woodworshipper.[3] The Council greeted the emperor with the words : " To-day salvation is come to the world because thou, o Emperor, hast delivered us from idols." [4] The ὅρος of the Council also stated it quite explicitly : " The before-mentioned demiurgos of wickedness . . . gradually brought back idolatry under the appearance of Christianity. As then Christ armed his Apostles against idolatry with the power of the Holy Spirit . . . so has he

---

[1] Soc., *Hist. Eccl.*, V, 10.   [2] Mansi, XIII, 100b.
[3] ξυλολάτρης. *Ib.* 356a.   [4] *Vit. Steph.*, 1121b.

awakened against the new idolatry his servants our faithful Emperors and endowed them with the same wisdom of the Holy Spirit." [1] To a simple mind the Christian use of images was finally settled by such words as : " Thou shalt not make to thyself a graven thing nor the likeness of anything that is in heaven above or in the earth beneath," or " Let them all be confounded that adore graven things." [2] It was apparently in such an ingenuous spirit that the original Iconoclastic attack was made. The Iconoclasts simply said that it was a heathen and not a Christian custom to make images. [3] They made little or no attempt to argue what seemed self-evident. And indeed the credulity behind the arguments used in defence of images by the bishops at Nicæa might appear to prove beyond dispute that images were little more than idols. The most grotesque anecdotes in popular hagiography were seriously read as evidence. From the *Life of Holy Mary the Egyptian* there was produced an extract showing that by praying to an image of the Virgin she was able to enter a church which had been closed to her. [4] From the *Passion of the Martyr Procopius* came a story of a cross which miraculously produced from itself three figures bearing the names Emmanuel, Michael, and Gabriel, [5] and from the *Life of St. Theodore*, archimandrite of Sicea, an account of an image of Christ which sent out a balm that healed the saint of an otherwise fatal tumour, and gave him power to memorise the psalter. [6] The belief that many images and pictures possessed miraculous powers was not confined to the illiterate. It was shared both by the very loquacious Constantine, bishop of Constantin, [7] and by Germanus the Patriarch. [8]

There was a strong conviction that images were not idols. The loose condemnation levelled by the Iconoclasts against the worship of images as a species of idolatry was easily countered by demanding a definition of terms. What was an image ? What was an idol ? and, What is meant by worship ?

The reply to the accusation is ably and completely

[1] Mansi, XIII, 233.
[2] Jo. Dam., *Or.*, I, 1235a. Cf. *adv. Const. Cab.*, 324b, 329b.
[3] Niceph., *Antirrh.*, III, 420a.
[4] Mansi, XIII, 85d. The Life is in Act. Sanct. Ap. II.
[5] Mansi, XIII, 89b. [6] *Ib.* 89e.
[7] *Ib.* 77c. [8] *Ib.* 125a.

put by St. John of Damascus. But a less convincing answer that is repeated in all the more popular controversial writings shows that the soundest argument is not necessarily the one that catches the ear. The popular answer was given at the very outset of the struggle by the Patriarch Germanus. The Old Testament command against idolatry, he said, meant that God was like no visible being or thing, and consequently any representation of a visible thing would involve a wrong conception of God's nature. But the coming of Christ has revealed the nature of God, con- sequently in Christ idolatry is finally done away. The Christian by the very fact that he is a Christian cannot be an idolater. He knows the true nature of God and in whatever form or by whatever channel he offers his worship, it is to God alone he gives it.[1]   A comment on the second commandment cited at Nicæa from a mutilated MS. in the Patriarchal library said that while the heathen regard their images as actual gods, the image of Christ was not honoured as a god but as a stimulus to higher effort through the thought of the Incarnation.[2] The argument is put in a particularly catchpenny form in a document appended to the Acts of Nicæa entitled, "An Encomium pronounced at the Council by Epiphanius, deacon of Catana in Sicily, deputy for Thomas, archbishop of Sardinia."[3]   "How can Christians be charged with idolatry when the coming of Christ has destroyed idolatry according to the prophecy of Zechariah, 'In that day the Lord will appear and will destroy the gods of the nations of the earth'?"[4]   Then follows the kind of inapposite illustration which is apt to gain assent from incoherent listeners. Christianity has adopted no idolatrous rites. The Bacchic ritual of Aphro- dite, the orgies of Demeter, and the slaughter rites of Artemis, all have disappeared before Christ.[5] The pamphlet *adversus Constantinum Caballinum* had already adopted this view, that a Christian cannot be an idolater, for Christ abolished idolatry,[6] and it is also accepted by Nicephorus.[7]

---

[1] Germanus, *Ep. to Thomas of Claudiopolis*. Mansi, XIII, 108b.
[2] *Ib.* 188c.
[3] *Ib.* 442a. It is a verbose and straggling panegyric sent to the Council but (as its place in the supplement to the proceedings indicates) never delivered.
[4] Inaccurately cited from Zech. xiii. 2.
[5] Mansi, XIII, 442a.
[6] *adv. Const. Cab.* 320a.   [7] *Apol. pro S. Imag.*, 560c, 600 *sqq.*

This argument reveals what the orthodox quite innocently understood by idolatry. It meant to him the crude belief that the block of wood or metal is a god, that the material object has become the habitation of a spiritual being.[1] Since, therefore, prophecy or apostolic teaching showed that Christ came to destroy idolatry, and actually did so, a priori there can be no idolatry among Christians. Idolatry as seen by the orthodox of the period is a concrete fact and not an idea in the mind. Idolatry is paganism. Therefore, to charge the Church with idolatry is equivalent to saying that Christ has failed. For if idolatry has broken out, Christ's work has been in vain. Both the saying of the Gospel is contradicted, " None shall pluck them out of my hand," and the forecast of the Psalmist, "His dominion endureth throughout all ages." [2]

The Iconoclasts certainly took a different view of idolatry. They saw the images drawing " the spirit of man from the lofty adoration of God to the low and material adoration of the creature." [3] That is to say, they conceived of idolatry as an attitude of mind which led a worshipper to substitute the created thing for its Creator. But the other conception of idolatry seems among the Christians of Constantinople to have been the normal one, unconvincing as it sounds in modern ears, and it eventually made the charge of idolatry obsolete.

This notion rests on the distinction between the non-existent gods of the heathen and the one true God. An idol is the vain representation of what never existed in fact. Such is the view of Pope Gregory II.[4] In the same spirit the author of *adv. Const. Cab.* dwells on the truth told by the Christian images in contrast with the falsehood represented in the images of the heathen.[5] The reason, says Nicephorus, that Christians destroyed pagan images was just because they did represent false gods (*i.e.* gods that had no existence).[6]

This question of idolatry was not discussed with much

---

[1] Niceph., *Antirrh.*, I, 277b.
[2] This summarises a long and lucid passage of Nicephorus, *Apol. pro S. Imag.*, 705–744, the substance of which occurs in the refutation of the Iconoclastic Council. Mansi, XIII, 216.
[3] *Ib.* 228.   [4] *Ib.* 92c.   [5] *adv. Const. Cab.*, 324b.
[6] *Antirrh.*, III, 417d. ἃ δὴ καὶ εἴδωλα καὶ φασματώδη πλάσματα καλεῖν θεμιτόν.

penetration by the Iconoclastic party. There is no record that they even examined the meaning of the equivocal word "προσκύνησις," usually rendered "worship." This word covers a wide range of meaning. It signifies broadly the Oriental prostration of reverence, the salaam, and it is not offered only to God. The word in one of its forms, προσκυνεῖν, προσκύνησις, occurs frequently in the Septuagint with no idea of the honour paid to God. Thus it is used of Lot receiving the angels,[1] of Abraham bowing to the children of Heth,[2] of Absalom bowing before king David,[3] of the sons of the prophets doing reverence to Elisha,[4] and many other times in the same sense. It is regularly represented in the Vulgate by some form of adoro. But in neither case is the idea accurately translated in English by "worship." Even the Latin "adoro imaginem" does not imply a religious act any more definitely than does προσκυνῶ τὴν εἰκόνα. Suetonius relates that when Nero was awarded the musical crown coronam . . . ad se delatam adoravit, that is to say, he bowed low as he took the crown.[5] In English there is no word that will exactly reproduce προσκυνῶ, because the idea itself is foreign to Northern Europe. We use the phrase "image-worship," but the words do not in themselves mean that the images were worshipped in any real sense. "Venerate" is an inadequate word, for though it suggests the idea of rational regard for the sacred pictures which might seem intelligible to an educated Western mind, it does not really represent the humility suggested both by προσκυνῶ and by "adoro." The Christian of Western Europe who has considerable difficulty in raising his hat to the wayside figure of Christ can never understand the violence of Oriental reverence which apparently means much less than it shows.

The whole question of idolatrous worship with the subsidiary problems of degrees of adoration and the exact nature of images, is examined by St. John of Damascus so thoroughly and so finally that the argument about idolatry was felt by the Iconoclasts themselves to lack conviction and was practically replaced by a new one based on Christology.

The life of St. John of Damascus is obscure. His family

[1] Gen. xix. 1.   [2] *Ib.* xxiii. 7.
[3] 2 Sam. xiv. 33.   [4] 2 Kings ii. 15.   [5] Suet., *Nero,* 12.

though Christian held important hereditary office under the Arab government in Damascus, and he bore the Arabic name of Mansur (the Ransomed). He probably held this civil office during the time he was writing against Iconoclasm his Three Discourses (λόγοι ἀπολογητικοὶ πρὸς τοὺς διαβάλλοντας τὰς ἁγίας εἰκόνας) (726–733). After this period he entered the monastery of St. Sabas near Jerusalem and was ordained to the priesthood (circa 735). His writings rank him for philosophic quality and range of knowledge with the first of the fathers. It is assumed that he had died before 753 when he was anathematised by the Iconoclastic Council. Legends of attacks on him by the Emperor Leo have no foundation.

The Christian's answer to the charge of idolatry, says St. John, is the Incarnation.

"These injunctions (*i.e.* against idols) were given to the Jews on account of their proneness to idolatry. We on the contrary are no longer in leading strings. Speaking theologically, it is given to us to avoid superstitious error, to be with God in the knowledge of the truth, to offer service to God alone, to enjoy the fulness of his knowledge . . . The Scripture says, ' Ye have not seen his likeness ' . . . How depict the invisible ? How picture the inconceivable ? How give expression to the limitless, the immeasurable, the invisible ? . . . It is clear that when you contemplate God who is pure spirit becoming man for your sake you will be able to clothe him with the human form. When the Invisible One becomes visible in flesh you may then draw a likeness of his visible form. When he who is without form or limitation, immeasurable in the boundlessness of his own nature, existing as God, takes upon himself the form of a servant in substance and stature and a body of flesh, then you may draw his likeness and show it to any one willing to contemplate it." [1] " Of old God the incorporeal and uncircumscribed was never depicted. Now, however, since God has been seen clothed in flesh and conversant with men I make an image of God as he was seen." [2] The mere fact that the heathen made idols does not discredit the Christian practice. " The pious practice of the Church is not to be rejected because of heathen abuse

---

[1] *Or.*, I, 1237d *sqq.* (trans. Allies corrected).
[2] *Ib.* 1245a. Cf. *Or.*, II, 1288ab.

any more than the exorcism practised by sorcerers invalidates Christian exorcism or pagan sacrifices make the Christian unbloody sacrifice wrong." [1] Such a misapplication of the Jewish law to Christianity ought to be followed by a demand for other Jewish customs, the Sabbath and circumcision. "You should observe the whole law and not celebrate the Lord's Passover out of Jerusalem. You are ordered to marry your brother's widow and so carry on his name and not sing the Lord's song in a strange land." [2] Behind this cry against idolatry St. John suspects an abnormal fear of matter which is nothing but Manichæanism. [3]

He then gets to the root of the problem by examining the character and nature of the image. It is here that he offers the most profound explanation of image-worship. The fact that it is a train of reasoning that leaves us cold should not be interpreted as an argument against its validity. The image is the representation of an original, serving various purposes.

(i) It may be recollection of past events, the picture then being a pictorial book or record.

(ii) It may be a type, foreshadowing something else, as " the bush and the fleece, the rod and the urn foreshadow the Virginal Mother of God." [4]

(iii) It may be an analogy. " We see in created things images which remind us faintly of divine tokens." The examples cited are the sun, its light and its beam, or the rose, the tree, the flower, and the scent, which are in this way images of the Holy Trinity. [5]

(iv) It may be what St. John calls κατὰ μίμησιν, by imitation, the example of which is man made in the image of God, where the created cannot be strictly an image of the uncreated. [6]

(v) It may be a plan of a future undertaking, like the foreknowledge in the mind of God.

(vi) It may be the image κατὰ φύσιν, [7] as contrasted with that κατὰ θέσιν καὶ μίμησιν. The example is Christ, who

---

[1] *Or.*, II, 1304b. Cf. *Or.*, I, 1257a.
[2] *Ib.* II, 1300d.
[3] *Ib.* I, 1245c. μὴ κάκιζε τὴν ὕλην· οὐ γὰρ ἄτιμος. οὐδὲν γὰρ ἄτιμον ὃ παρὰ θεοῦ γεγένηται, τῶν Μανιχαίων τοῦτο τὸ φρόνημα. Cf. *Or.*, II, 1297.
[4] *Ib.* III, 1341c.   [5] *Ib.*
[6] *Ib.* 1340d.   [7] *Ib.* 1337c.

is the actual self-existent image of God as man is the artificial or potential image κατὰ θέσιν.

The historical image, the picture or statue is by John put lowest in this list of six, and its exact significance is evidently to be sought in the others. Clearly St. John understands " image " in the light of a form of Platonism. He sees six stages evolving from God, namely :

(i) Christ the direct image of God ;

(ii) The Thought (ἔννοια) of God, his Creative Mind ;

(iii) Man actually created but having affinities with the uncreated ;

(iv) The visible world as a medium revealing God but in no way part of God's being ;

(v) Particular objects or particular incidents in that visible world, forecasting particular facts in the plan of God (the plan of God being the Incarnation) ; and

(vi) The historical picture or statue, recording good and evil, to promote virtue and shame.

St. John conceives of a ladder of revelation. God uses visible things as images of the invisible,[1] and the visible is in some measure endowed sacramentally with the virtue of the invisible it represents. In the shadow and handkerchiefs [2] of the apostle which wrought cures there is a parallel to the shadow and statues of the saints.[3] As the image of the king is the king, so the image of a saint is the saint, and the image of Christ is Christ, and " if power is not divided nor glory distributed, honouring the image becomes honouring the one who is depicted in the image. Devils have feared the saints and have fled from their shadow. The shadow is an image, and I make an image that I may scare demons. . . . Material things are endued with a divine power because they bear the names of those they represent.[4] . . . Material things in themselves demand no veneration, but if the person who is represented be full of grace, the material becomes partaker of grace metaphorically, by faith." [5] An image therefore in St. John's view is in some sense a sacrament or emanation

---

[1] *Or.*, I, 1240c *sqq.*, gives the same argument.
[2] Acts xv. 6. [3] *Or.*, I, 1256a.
[4] *Ib.* 1264b. χάρις δίδοται θεία ταῖς ὕλαις διὰ τῆς τῶν εἰκονιζομένων προσηγορίας.
[5] αἱ ὗλαι αὐταὶ μὲν καθ' ἑαυτὰς ἀπροσκύνητοι, ἂν δὲ χάριτος εἴη πλήρης ὁ εἰκονιζόμενος μέτοχοι χάριτος γίνονται κατ' ἀναλογίαν τῆς πίστεως. *Ib.*

of the thing represented, and from the image to God there is a graded ascent by a neo-Platonic ladder. St. John was greatly influenced by the Greek mystical writer known as Dionysius the Areopagite. Indeed, this theory of images owes much to the symbolism of Heavenly and Ecclesiastical Hierarchies in which Dionysius reproduced the neo-Platonist's chain between God and the individual. Is this conception of the nature of images a private view of St. John's own, or can it be seriously accepted as representing the position of the orthodox Byzantine image-worshipper? Certainly it cannot be supposed that the ordinary superstitious believer had assimilated the theology either of Dionysius or of St. John of Damascus. But this sacramental view does make explicit the nature of the inarticulate sentiment of the masses. Though no subsequent theologian exactly reproduces St. John's reasoning in the course of the struggle, Theodore Studites reverts to it,[1] and echoes of it occur more than once. To the author of the *Life of Stephen* a picture is " a door opening the God-created mind to the likeness of the original within. When we venerate the image it is not the material thing we have in mind." [2] This sacramental view of images which was apparently adopted by the most orthodox [3] was never really answered. The Iconoclastic Council appears to feel the difficulty. For it treats the point summarily by saying : " The evil

[1] See below, Ch. X.
[2] *Vit. Steph.*, 1113b. Cf. *ib.* 1085b.
[3] Nicephorus alone of the leaders seems not to notice it, a fact which emphasises the moderate position of Nicephorus. Cf. Hefele-Leclerq, III (ii), p. 612n. It hardly falls to us to decide how far the argument of St. John is a legitimate one. But for arriving at a true theology help may be found in C. W. Emmet, The Psychology of Grace, in *The Spirit*, ed. B. H. Streeter, London, 1921. Emmet argues that a genuine symbolism for mediating Christ depends on the extent to which the symbols are charged with associations of Christ's own personality. The Eucharist is clearly such a genuine symbol. Similarly, if a fragment of the Cross or a visit to Calvary is treated simply as a means of bringing vividly before the mind the love of Christ through its associations it is, to some at least, psychologically effective and legitimate ; it does really help to Communion with him. Relics, on the other hand, may be regarded as possessing a quasi-magical property or *mana* through their inherent sanctity, and are therefore illegitimate symbols. But to St. John and Theodore and the image-worshippers in general the image possessed the quasi-magical property in itself. It was this view that the Iconoclasts so deeply resented. Their own veneration for the Cross, illogical as it appears, shows that they could appreciate a legitimate symbolism. It was only their conviction that abuse destroyed use (and of course their violence) that really separated them from orthodox moderates like Nicephorus.

custom of assigning names to the images [1] does not come down from Christ and the Apostles and the holy Fathers." [2] The force of this reasoning probably demonstrated the weakness of the charge of idolatry and led the Iconoclasts to elaborate their Christological argument. That is to say, they realised that the picture of Christ bore a relation to God which a pagan idol did not, and that their argument would have to consider "the image" at closer range than could be reached by merely levelling a general charge of idolatry.

To St. John also it fell to define the nature of worship. The original Iconoclastic attack had apparently made no attempt to define precisely what was the nature of the veneration the images received. Germanus said distinctly that the honour paid to the images was not the same as that paid to God. [3] But nothing in the surviving writings indicates that the Iconoclasts entered into this point. As they had little inclination to investigate the real symbolism of images, they had none to differentiate nice distinctions of worship.

St. John, on the contrary, lays down at the beginning the distinction which was accepted by the Council of Nicæa and may be said still to hold good. He sees at once that προσκύνησις which the Iconoclasts regularly used to represent "worship," is a general word signifying respect. He quotes some of the many examples from the Old Testament in which the word stands for a gesture of reverence between one man and another. "Abraham did reverence (προσεκύνησε) to the son of Emmor (sic) . . . men without religion, living in ignorance of God . . . Joshua the son of Nave and Daniel did reverence to an angel of God, but they did not worship him." [4] "For the reverence of worship is different from the reverence of honour paid to eminence." [5] Worship (λατρεία) is paid to God alone. [6] This worship paid to God is capable of analysis into :

(i) Service (δουλεία, a word used in later theology but not adopted in this controversy) ;

---

[1] Cf. Jo. Dam., *Or.*, I, 1264a. ἡ εἰκὼν τοῦ Χριστοῦ Χριστὸς καὶ ἡ εἰκὼν τοῦ ἁγίου ἅγιος.　　[2] Mansi, XIII, 269.

[3] *Ep. to John of Synnada. Ib.* 100b. Cf. *Ep. to Thomas. Ib.* 108a.

[4] *Or.*, I, 1240b. προσεκύνησαν Ἰησοῦς ὁ τοῦ Ναυῆ καὶ Δανιὴλ ἀγγέλῳ θεοῦ ἀλλ' οὐκ ἐλάτρευσαν.

[5] *Ib.* ἕτερον γάρ ἐστιν ἡ τῆς λατρείας προσκύνησις καὶ ἕτερον ἡ ἐκ τιμῆς προσαγομένη τοῖς κατά τι ἀξίωμα ὑπερέχουσιν.　　[6] *Or.*, II, 1292b.

K

(ii) Wonder and desire ;

(iii) Thanksgiving ;

(iv) Expectation of favour ; and

(v) Contrition.[1]

He then develops the scale by which pure worship is modified into simple actions of respect. Next after God a reverence is paid :

(i) To those persons who were God's resting-place,[2] such as the Virgin and the Saints. They are named gods though they are so not by nature but by arrangement,[3] even as red-hot iron is described as fire.

(ii) Next, places and objects receive a reverence of honour because of associations with our Lord, such as Sinai, Nazareth, Golgotha, the wood of the Cross, the nails, the linen clothes, and so on.

(iii) There is a third kind of reverence directed to consecrated objects, the gospel-book, the altar vessels, and

(iv) A fourth to sacred types of the Old Testament like Aaron's rod which prefigured the virginity of Mary.

Then we reverence

(v) Each other as bearing the image of God, and

(vi) Those in authority, and

(vii) Lastly, there is a reverence shown by servants to their masters and by petitioners to benefactors, illustrated by the attitude of Abraham to the sons of Emmor (*sic*).[4]

St. John thus in detail makes good the claim that " reverence " is the symbol of respect and honour. " We must understand that there are different degrees of reverence." [5]

Here again was an argument substantially good, which the Iconoclasts never met successfully : it was the strongest point in the decisions of the Council of Nicæa when they laid down that the images received " due salutation and honourable reverence, but not the worship which pertains alone to the divine nature." [6]

---

[1] *Or.*, III, 1348d *sqq.*   [2] ἐφ' οἷς ἀναπέπαυται ὁ θεός.   *Ib.* 1352a.

[3] *Ib.* οὐ φύσει ἀλλὰ θέσει.   *i.e.* by custom, conventionally.   The antithesis recurs in Theodore Stud.   [4] *Or.*, III, 1353 *sqq.*

[5] *Ib.* I, 1244a. ἡ προσκύνησις ὑποπτώσεως καὶ τιμῆς ἐστι σύμβολον καὶ ταύτης διαφόρους ἔγνωμεν τρόπους.

[6] ἀσπασμὸν καὶ τιμητικὴν προσκύνησιν, but not λατρείαν. Mansi, XIII, 373. Cf. Niceph., *Antirrh.*, III, 392bc, where the reverence to images is called σχετικὴ (relative) καὶ ἀσπαστική. Apol. pro S. Imag., 589c. The distinction of a relative (σχετική) honour goes back as far as the patriarch Germanus (Mansi, XIII, 100b) and may have been semi-official.

The minor problem of the saints and the pictures of saints is solved in the larger question. The saints themselves are honoured as the army of the friends of Christ, heirs of God and joint-heirs with Christ, exactly on the principle that the officials of the sovereign are honoured for the sake of the sovereign.[1] In the early days of the struggle there were apparently some whose objections were confined to the representation of the saints. They said, Make an image of Christ or his Mother, and let that suffice. This was clearly an objection not to images but to the honour paid to saints.[2] It gives St. John the opportunity of putting his sacramental theory in its most explicit form. " The saints in their lifetime were filled with the Holy Spirit, and when they are no more his grace abides with their spirits and with their bodies in their tombs and also with their likenesses and holy images, not by nature but by grace and divine power." [3]

St. John completes his argument with the protest against imperial interference which was too rarely heard in Constantinople.

" Christ did not give to kings the power to bind and loose, but to the apostles and their successors and to pastors and teachers." [4] " Kings have no title to make laws for the Church. What says the Holy Apostle? And God hath set some in the Church, first apostles, secondarily prophets, thirdly pastors and teachers, for the perfecting of the Church.[5] He does not say kings. . . . The political commonwealth is the king's business ; the ecclesiastical organisation belongs to pastors and teachers. To invade it is an act of robbery. . . . And now holy Germanus . . . has been beaten and become an exile, and many more bishops and fathers whose names are unknown to me. Is not this a prosecution ? . . . We are obedient to you, o king, in the affairs of this world, tributes, taxes . . . but in the government of the church we have pastors who preach to us the word and order the constitution of the church. We do not change the boundaries marked out by our fathers." [6]

[1] *Or.*, I, 1252b ; II, 1301a ; III, 1348c, 1352d.
[2] *Ib.* I, 1249b.   [3] *Ib.* 1249d.   [4] *Ib.* 1281b.
[5] A combination of I Cor. xii. 28 and Eph. iv. 11.
[6] *Or.*, II, 1296c *sqq.* Cf. *ib.* 1304a. This is a *locus classicus* cited over and over again in the controversy. The reference to Germanus shows that *Or.*, II, is to be dated after 729 when Germanus was deposed and probably before his death in 732.

So far as the original Iconoclastic argument, idolatry, was concerned, the work of St. John was final. The Iconoclasts of the time of Constantine V tacitly admitted as much by throwing the whole emphasis on a fresh line of investigation. Of St. John's other points, he definitely established degrees of reverence, but his argument on the symbolism of images received little support ; it was probably too subtle. His claim that the Church had independent rights was warmly accepted by Theodore of Studium, but it was foreign to the Cæsaro-papism planted in Constantinople by the first Constantine, which had now taken firm root. The strengthening of this tendency was the chief permanent contribution of Iconoclasm to the history of the Church. When the author of the *Life of Stephen* hears Constantine V called the thirteenth apostle, he makes the ironical suggestion that the faithful will before long be baptized in the name of Pastillas, Tricaccabus, and Caballus.[1] The Fathers of Nicæa made timid protests against the flattery of emperors of which they accused the Iconoclastic Council.[2] But they lay their complaint tactfully as men whose own hands are not over-clean, and even the vigorous Stephen has forgotten that it was not Copronymus but Constantine the Great who was called apostolic, not by himself but by the Church.[3]

II

We come now to the new line of theological discussion which appears first with Constantine V and supersedes the original argument. This is concerned with the relation of images to Christology. It started from the doctrine that God is uncircumscribed ($\dot{a}\pi\epsilon\rho\dot{\iota}\gamma\rho\alpha\pi\tau\sigma s$, incircumscriptus, *i.e.* not limited by confining boundaries). The word is of late occurrence. It does not appear either in the Greek or Latin Bible and the idea is represented in the Quicunque vult by the less exact word " immensus." It is clearly part of the definition of the Divine Nature brought into discussion by the Monophysite controversy. The earliest

[1] *Vit. Steph.*, 1121c.
[2] Mansi, XIII, 228e, 229d.
[3] $\iota\sigma\alpha\pi\dot{o}\sigma\tau\sigma\lambda\sigma s$. Cf. *Ep. ad Theoph.*, 348c, " the apostle of Christ among Emperors."

theological use of the word would seem to be in the 4th
Canon of the Lateran Council of 649 as reported in Agatho's
instructions to the delegates sent to the Sixth General
Council.[1] St. John of Damascus several times uses the word
in discussing how far the representation of God is legitimate,
God being uncircumscribed (ἀπερίγραπτος).[2]

Constantine [3] seized on the linguistic relationship between " uncircumscribed " and " incapable of being
depicted " (ἀπερίγραπτος and ἄγραπτος), and argued thus :
God is unlimited and uncircumscribed (ἀπερίγραπτος) ;
but Christ is God ; therefore Christ is uncircumscribed.
But that which is uncircumscribed cannot be represented ;
God therefore cannot be represented. But Christ is God,
therefore Christ cannot be represented in a picture or
image.[4] We are now plunged into the Christological
controversy. Each side tries to prove the views of the
other to be Arian, Nestorian, or Monophysite in one of its
many varieties, or all simultaneously. The Definition
of the Iconoclastic Council and the arguments of " Mammon " cited by Nicephorus, in substance the same, may
be assumed to give a fair statement of Constantine's case.
" How is it possible," says Mammon, " that there can be
a drawing, that is an image, made of our Lord Jesus Christ,
when he is one person of two natures in a union of the
material and the immaterial which admits no confusion ?
Since he has another immaterial nature conjoined to the
flesh, and with those two natures he is one, and his person
(πρόσωπον) or substance (ὑπόστασις) is inseparable from
the two natures, we hold that he cannot be depicted. For
what is pictured is one person, and he who circumscribes
that person has plainly circumscribed the divine nature
which is incapable of being circumscribed." [5] Or else,
he continues, the image circumscribes the manhood of
Christ alone and so introduces a new fourth person into

---

[1] M.P.L., vol. 87, pp. 1215 *sqq.* Christ is said to be circumscriptum
corpore, incircumscriptum deitate.
[2] *Or.* I, 1244c ; II, 1288a ; III, 1344b, etc.
[3] That Constantine (perhaps through his advisers) was responsible is
shown by the arguments quoted from " Mammon " by Nicephorus, by the
preponderance of this argument at the Iconoclastic Council, and by the
absence of any discussion of it in the earlier period.
[4] Cf. Niceph., *Antirrh.*, I, 232a ; *adv. Const. Cab.*, 317c ; Mansi, XIII,
252.
[5] Niceph., *Antirrh.*, I, 232a, 236c. Cf. 332b.

the Godhead,[1] namely, Christ, a man as separate from Christ God-man. The picture or image of Christ, that is to say, either attempts to represent the godhead, confusing the natures like the Monophysites, or else it depicts a mere man and is Nestorianism.[2] The argument is stated in the same terms and in almost identical language in the Definition of the Iconoclastic Council.[3]

There can be little question that this Iconoclastic Christology was unsound. One writer alone, the author of the pamphlet *adversus Constantinum Cabillinum*, fails to appreciate the fallacy. He mistakenly thinks that Iconoclasm attacked Christ's divinity by ignoring all memory of his conquest of idols.[4] But he wrote probably before the orthodox had discovered the exact reply. The Council of Nicæa saw that the argument of Constantine was a peculiarly gross form of Monophysitism. They compared him with Severus, who also rejected images.[5] Nicephorus really settles this question beyond all dispute. He sees that because Christ was visible and circumscribed throughout the Gospel story he can be depicted. To deny this is to lapse into an open Monophysitism of an extreme docetic character, denying the reality of the manhood of Christ.[6] So extreme is this doctrine that it recalls that of the Aphthartodocetæ [7] and merits the name of Agraptodocetism. It was in fact a descent into a horror of matter, a Manichæan tendency of which St. John Damascene had already accused the Iconoclasts.[8] Nicephorus correctly judges that this Monophysite tendency is revealed in the unwillingness of Mammon to admit that Christ was in (ἐν) two natures.[9]

Constantine was plainly a Monophysite, not probably

---

[1] Niceph., *Antirrh.*, I, 249c, 252c, 253a.
[2] *Ib.* 308a.
[3] Mansi, XIII, 252.
[4] *Op. cit.*, 336b. Though he is later than the Iconoclastic Council, this writer is concerned mainly with the question of idolatry.
[5] Mansi, XIII, 252c.
[6] Niceph., *Antirrh.*, I, 308b.
[7] Extreme Monophysites who held that the body of Christ before the Resurrection was only corruptible κατ᾽ οἰκονομίαν. Agraptodocetæ by analogy would hold that his body could not really be depicted. Niceph., *Antirrh.*, I, 268a.
[8] *Ib.* II, 337a.
[9] *Ib.* I, 300d. Mammon only says of (ἐκ) two natures, which would imply that manhood was a temporary experience in the life of Christ, but not a permanent quality of God the Son.

in the regular Monophysite tradition, but having as an amateur theologian brought himself more or less unconsciously to that position. Of all Christologies Monophysitism is that to which ignorant piety is most prone ; at the same time it is of all Christologies the most irrational, for it destroys the human values and reduces Christ to an unreal phantom, masquerading as a man. We may, indeed, go so far as to trace the whole Iconoclastic movement at least indirectly to Monophysite influences. The position developed by Constantine only made explicit the ideas working perhaps subconsciously on his predecessors. Many facts point in this direction. Iconoclastic incidents occurred in the history of Monophysitism ; the cases of Severus and Xenaias have been noticed already. The Armenian Bardanes, who reigned under the name of Philippicus (712 713) and was a strong Monothelite, has been suspected of iconoclastic views.[1] He certainly abandoned his predecessor's practice of having an effigy of Christ on the coinage. The indifference of Western Europe to Iconoclasm in general and to its Christological aspect in particular is in keeping with the complete freedom from formal Monophysitism enjoyed by the West.

In support of his Monophysite view of Christ Constantine developed a curious doctrine of the Eucharist. It is curious because it shows the independence and even inconsistency of thought to which the Christology of Constantine led. Christ, he says, gave a perpetual memorial of the Incarnation. He bade his disciples give a type (τύπον) of his body, which by the priestly ministration we may receive really and truly as his body.[2] And though we may wish to make it an image (εἰκόνα) of his body, what we actually have is a figure (μόρφωσις) of his body.[3] For the bread we receive is an image of his body representing in a figure (μορφίζων) his flesh as being a type of his body. And it is only the

---

[1] By Pitra, cited D.C.B., s.v. Iconoclastæ.

[2] Niceph., *Antirrh.*, II, 333b.

[3] *Ib.* 336a. εἰς μόρφωσιν τοῦ σώματος αὐτοῦ. The meaning seems to be that whilst some would describe the Bread as an image, and possibly marked it with an image, Constantine would use the word μόρφωσις as more exactly describing the process which makes the Eucharist his body without involving the idolatrous notion of the word "image." It is explained by the more lucid statement in the Definition of the Iconoclastic Council. "He ordered bread to be brought but not a representation of the human form, that so idolatry might not arise." Mansi, XIII, 264.

offering made by the priest's hands that fulfils its purpose. All bread is not his body.[1] As summarised at the Council of 753 this theory is less obscure. It maintains two things, (i) that the true representation of Christ is not a pictorial image but the Eucharist, a symbolical form definitely associated with him, and (ii) it becomes the divine body of Christ by an unseen process in the spiritual world, for it becomes the divine body of Christ by the mediation of the priest and by the descent of the Holy Spirit.[2]

The orthodox reply both of Nicephorus and of Nicæa is concerned with showing that this position is inconsistent with the Christology already advanced. In calling the Eucharist the body of Christ, Constantine admits, what he has previously denied, that the body of Christ is circumscribed. Or else he calls it not the body but an image of the body, and by his own theory of images that means either that the divine must be sacrificed in the offering (*i.e.* that the spirit must be put to death), or else that the body is separated from the Word and the Eucharist is simply ordinary bread.[3]

Actually that reply is sound because the Christology of the Iconoclast could not logically admit of any visible representation of the divine. At the same time he was conscious of the belief that the image was related closely to the original, that it involved in some sense a taking of the material into the spiritual and infusing it with divinity, and that in consequence an image mediated the divine to man. He saw that the Eucharist was a legitimate symbol fulfilling these conditions. The material was raised to the spiritual, infused with divine power, and made an instrument of grace. The weakness does not lie in the doctrine itself but in its inconsistency with the Christological arguments Constantine had already used. Indeed, the weakness of the Iconoclastic position lay in the illogical attack on images alone of all religious symbols. Here, as indeed throughout the controversy, the Iconoclastic case was stronger in fact than in logic. It was on the images and pictures that superstitious abuse concentrated. But to ignore all other

[1] Niceph., *Antirrh.*, 337c.
[2] Mansi, *loc cit.* Cf. Niceph., *Antirrh.*, II, 333b. ἵνα διὰ τῆς ἱερατικῆς ἀναγωγῆς κἂν εἰ ἐκ μετοχῆς καὶ θέσει γίνηται λάβωμεν αὐτὸ ὡς κυρίως καὶ ἀληθῶς σῶμα αὐτοῦ.
[3] Niceph., *Antirrh.*, II, 336a, 373c; Mansi, XIII, 264.

kinds of symbolism left a weakness in their armour which was penetrated from the beginning. St. John of Damascus almost began his argument by asking why the pictures are separated from every other material object used in the Christian church, the cross, the holy places, the gospel-book, the altar, the holy vessels, the Eucharist itself.[1] The inconsistency of the Iconoclastic position was exaggerated by the special devotion to the Cross they displayed. The Christ on the Chalce Gate of the Imperial palace was replaced by a Cross, underneath which was set an inscription in iambic verses, the composition of one Stephen :

> The Emperor Leo and his son Constantine
> Thought it dishonour to the Christ divine
> That on the very Palace Gate he stood,
> A lifeless, speechless, effigy of wood.
> Thus what the Book forbids they did replace
> With the believers' blessed sign of grace.[2]

Another epigram celebrating Leo and Constantine has a pictorial superscription thus :

$$
\begin{array}{c}
E \\
X \\
\Theta \\
P \\
O \\
Y \\
KAI\ \Phi ONEY\Omega\ \Sigma\ BAPBAPOY\Sigma. \\
T \\
P \\
O \\
\Pi \\
O \\
Y \\
M \\
A \\
I
\end{array}
$$ [3]

---

[1] *Or.* I, 1245. St. John's argument is strengthened by the sacramental theory of matter he holds. καὶ τὸ βάπτισμα διπλοῦν, ἐξ ὕδατος καὶ πνεύματος καὶ ἡ κοινωνία καὶ ἡ προσευχὴ καὶ ἡ ψαλμωδία, πάντα διπλᾶ σωματικὰ καὶ πνευματικὰ καὶ φῶτα καὶ θυμιάματα. *Or.*, III, 1336b.

[2] Preserved among the works of Theodore Stud., 437c, with seven other poems (six of them acrostics). All but one deal with the Cross or the Passion of Christ. The authors are named John, Ignatius, Sergius, and Stephen, but they are otherwise unknown. Theodore upsets their position completely when he says, If Christ had not a nature that could be represented, he had not a nature that could suffer, and the Cross is more meaningless than the picture of Christ. *Op. cit.*, 456c. Additional evidence of the Iconoclasts regard for the Cross is seen in their coinage. Cf. above, pp. 26n, 65, and Wroth, vol. I, pp. xxxvi-xliv.
[3] Theod. Stud., 476b.

III

We have given considerable space to the examination of the philosophic case on both sides. But these discussions are largely a side issue. The primary method of argument was appeal to authority, the authority being the dogmatic statements of the Bible and the Fathers with the precedents to be collected from both sources. Both sides accept the same principles. The Definition of the Iconoclastic Council says : We can prove our view by Holy Scripture and the Fathers.[1]   The orthodox Council of Nicæa says : We follow the royal pathway and inspired authority of our Holy Fathers and the traditions of the Catholic Church.[2] The loss of the Acta of 753 leaves us ignorant of the extent of that Council's investigations, but the length of time they deliberated would suggest that they went deeply into the evidence. The much shorter orthodox Council, besides examining most of the relevant passages of Scripture, discussed in detail fifty extracts from patristic writings and left fifteen more unread because the evidence was thought sufficient.[3] Here again the classic method and matter come from St. John of Damascus. His collections of Scripture texts, of patristic evidence, and of actual historical precedents, were increased numerically by later additions, but the passages he brought together were the most significant and continued to be quoted.

The evidence adduced falls into those three classes, (i) Scripture, (ii) Patristic, (iii) Historical precedents and tradition.

(i) As in so many Christian controversies, it was the Old Testament that provided most of the ammunition. The second commandment was the obvious starting-point. " Thou shalt not make unto thee a graven image, nor the likeness of any form that is in heaven above or that is in the earth beneath " (Ex. xx. 4).[4] With this text went a variety of kindred passages on idolatrous worship. " Thou

[1] Mansi, XIII, 280.
[2] *Ib.* 373. Cf. Niceph., *Antirrh.*, I, 296c, where Mammon's argument is charged with seeking no scriptural or patristic support.
[3] Mansi, XIII, 195d.
[4] Jo. Dam., *Or.*, I, 1235a, 1235d ; II, 1288d ; Niceph., *Antirrh.*, III, 448a ; Mansi, XIII, 285a.

shalt worship the Lord thy God, and him only shalt thou serve " (Deut. vi. 13).[1] " Confounded be all they that worship carved images " (Ps. xcvii. 7 (xcvi. LXX.)).[2] Such passages as these the Iconoclasts supplemented with others in which the spiritual character of God is emphasised. " God is a spirit, and they that worship him must worship him in spirit and in truth " (John iv. 24). " No man hath seen God at any time " (John i. 18). " Ye have neither heard his voice at any time nor seen his shape " (John i. 37*b*). " Blessed are they which have not seen and yet have believed " (John xx. 29*b*).[3] " They changed the glory of the incorruptible God into an image made like to corruptible man, . . . who changed the truth of God into a lie and worshipped and served the creature rather than the Creator " (Rom. i. 23, 25). " Faith cometh by hearing " (*i.e.* not by seeing) (Rom. x. 17). " Though we have known Christ after the flesh, yet henceforth know we him no more " (2 Cor. v. 16).[4]

The image defenders' answer to the New Testament passages, especially those from St. John, is weak, and the strongest of them (John iv. 24) is ignored. The essence of the reply, as we have already seen, is the notion that idolatry is possible only in paganism. To fail to see that Christ has destroyed idolatry is to nullify his work.[5] Christ is God, not a creature, and so his image cannot be an idol.[6] All the other Biblical quotations are intended to show that there was a legitimate use of material things that did not imply idolatry, and an act of reverence which was not the worship paid to God. As an example of the latter the word προσκύνησις is used of Abraham bowing before the children of Heth (Gen. xxiii. 7),[7] of Jacob greeting Esau (Gen. xxxiii. 3),[8] of Jacob and Pharaoh (Gen. xlvii. 7).[9]

The legitimacy of the image made of material things is ultimately based on the fact that man was created in the

---

[1] Jo. Dam., *Or.*, I, 1235a, 1235d.
[2] *Ib.* I, 1235a ; II, 1288d.
[3] Mansi, XIII, 280b.
[4] *Ib.* 288. The last passage was first interpreted as a prohibition of images by Eusebius. *Ep. ad. Const.*
[5] Mansi, XIII, 285a, 288a.
[6] Niceph., *Antirrh.*, III, 448a.
[7] Jo. Dam., *Or.*, I, 1240b ; Hadr. Ep., Mansi, XIII, 770.
[8] Jo. Dam., *Or.*, I, 1244b.
[9] *Ib* ; Had. Ep., Mansi, XIII, 771.

image of God (Gen. i. 26).[1] The elaborate regulations
God Himself gave about the details of the tabernacle is
divine authority for worship through material things,
while the cherubim over the mercy seat are a particular
example of the representation of spiritual things (Ex. xxv.
18, 40 ; xxxi. 1–6 ; xxxv. 4–10 ; xxxvi. 37 *sqq.*).[2]

The cherubim are followed by the bulls in Solomon's
temple (2 Kings vi. 25, 29),[3] and the cherubim and palm
trees in Ezekiel's mystical temple (Ezek. xli. 18).[4]   To justify
the principle of representation apart from form reference is
made to Jacob's pillar of stone (Gen. xxviii. 18),[5] and to
the stones set up by Joshua in memory of the passage of
Jordan (Josh. iv. 8, 21).[6]   One example of popular
ignorance of the text of Scripture occurs in the pamphlet
adv. Const. Cab.   The Jews who offered Christ the coin
bearing the Emperor's image are there made to ask whether
the image was to be venerated.[7]

The conclusion to which St. John of Damascus believes
the evidence of Scripture points is that though it calls the
idols of the heathen the work of men's hands, what it
forbids is not the veneration of inanimate objects but the
veneration of the images of demons (*i.e.* of pagan gods).[8]
A large number of other incidental allusions to Scripture
occur.   At the Council of Nicæa scriptural phraseology
decorated most of the speeches, and all kinds of turns were
given to Biblical phrases which in themselves they could
not bear.   A typical example is : " So shalt thou make
their image to vanish out of the city " (Ps. lxxiii. 19).[9]   The
attack of the *Caroline Books* spends considerable trouble

[1] Niceph., *Antirrh.*, III, 484a ; Had. Ep., Mansi, XIII, 769.
[2] The cherubim, Jo. Dam., *Or.*, I, 1244c ; Niceph., *Antirrh.*, III, 449b ;
Mansi, XIII, 4; Had. Ep., Mansi, XIII, 781.   The tabernacle, Jo. Dam.,
Or., I, 1248a ; II, 1292c, 1300a, 1308d ; Had. Ep., Mansi, XIII, 792d.
[3] Jo. Dam., *Or.*, I, 1252a ; Niceph., *Antirrh.*, III, 456c.
[4] Niceph., *ib* ; Mansi, XIII, 5b.
[5] Niceph., *Antirrh.*, 456a ; Had. Ep., Mansi, XIII, 780.
[6] Jo. Dam., *Or.*, I, 1249a ; Had. Ep., Mansi, XIII, 797e.
[7] εἰ δεῖ αὐτὴν προσκυνεῖσθαι.   *adv. Cons. Cab.*, 321b.   The author owes his
error to misinterpreting a passage of Jo. Dam., *Or.*, III, 1333c. St. John
draws an analogy between the identification of Cæsar with the coin that bears
his image and the identification of Christ with his statue.
[8] Jo. Dam., *Or.*, I, 1257c. Cf. in the Definition of Nicæa, Mansi, XIII,
373 : " They have failed to distinguish sacred and profane, styling the images
of our Lord and of his saints by the same name as the statues of diabolical
idols."
[9] Mansi, XIII, 94, 299 ; *Lib. Car.*, II, 3.

investigating such misuses, but it is largely misapplied criticism, for such quotation is obviously only the kind of rhetorical decoration to be expected in an episcopal assembly.

(ii) Patristic authorities are far more numerous but, if possible, less convincing for these reasons : (1) They are extracts torn from their context. They were not written in view of the Iconoclastic controversy, and their meaning is consequently not exactly what the controversialists desire it to be. (2) No discrimination or criticism is exercised. The most incredible hagiology like the *Life of Simeon Thaumaturgus* is cited by the side of Gregory Nazianzen or St. Basil. Both these objections were clear to impartial observers like the Emperor Charles, who in his letter to Pope Hadrian as well as in the *Caroline Books* criticised severely the misapplication of ancient writings and the use of apocryphal and childish stories.[1] It was not that the age was incapable of discrimination or criticism. The quotations of the Iconoclasts were critically examined. As early as St. John Damascene a damaging passage attributed to Epiphanius the hereseologist was pronounced spurious.[2] In the Council of Nicæa the authorities of the Iconoclasts were ruled to be irrelevant, heretical, spurious, misinterpreted, or interpolated.[3] There were even examples of the scientific method of testing isolated passages of an author by comparison with other examples of his own expressed opinion.[4] We have only a small number of the quotations used by the Iconoclasts to set beside the very large numbers used by their opponents. Comparison, therefore, may be unjust, but if such comparison is legitimate the Iconoclasts have a certain superiority in intelligent and honest use of authorities. The following are a selection of typical citations made by the Iconoclasts, showing their best features and their worst : [5]

---

[1] See below for details. Cf. Mansi, XIII, 776d, 784d.

[2] Jo. Dam., *Or.*, I, 1258b ; II, 1304c. See a full discussion, K. Holl, Die Schrift d. Epiphanius gegen d. Bildeverehrung, in *Berlin Sitzungb.*, 1916, pp. 826–868.

[3] Mansi, XIII, 36e, 56d, 168e, 176e, 292d, 297b, 301e, 312b, etc.

[4] *Ib.* 300b.

[5] In addition to the usual Eastern sources, light is thrown on the patristic catena by Hadrian, *Ep. to Charles* (Mansi, XIII, 759 *sqq.*) ; *Libri Carolini*, and the Council of Paris in Nov. 825 (M.G.H. Leges, Sect. III, vol. II (ii)).

(i) Epiphanius [1] (c. 315–413). One actual passage is quoted :

" Remember this . . . bring no images into the churches nor into the resting places of the saints ; but always remember God in your hearts. Neither bring them into your common dwelling ; for it becomes not a Christian to be unsettled by the eye or the fancies of the mind."

The origin of this passage is unknown, and it must be regarded as spurious together with another passage quoted from an alleged epistle to the Emperor Theodosius. At the same time there are grounds for supposing that Epiphanius, who was an eccentric character, gave some public exhibition of hostility to images, and this is borne out by his own record, preserved among the letters of St. Jerome, [2] to the effect that with his own hands he destroyed a curtain in a church in Palestine because, contrary to scriptural teaching, it was painted with pictures. It is from this incident and the tradition that spread with it that the actual texts cited by the Iconoclasts were fabricated.

(ii) Eusebius (265–340). Letter to the Augusta, [3] wife of the Cæsar Gallus. She had asked permission to have an effigy of Christ. Eusebius sternly refuses her request. " Has the Scripture escaped you in which God by law forbids to make the likeness of anything in heaven or in the earth beneath ? Have you ever seen such a thing in a church or even heard of one ? Have not such been banished throughout the world and driven out of our churches ? " Pictures alleged to represent St. Peter and St. Paul he tells his correspondent he has confiscated from another person " lest the impression go abroad that we carry our God about like idolaters."

This evidence is perfectly explicit. But the Nicene

[1] Mansi, XIII, 292d. Cf. Jo. Dam., *ut sup.* Niceph., *Apol. Min.*, 837bc. Theod. Stud., 388d.

[2] *Hier. Ep.*, 51. This is the only Iconoclastic record of Epiphanius in the long list of authorities appended to the Paris Synod of 825. Had the other passages been authentic they could hardly have been overlooked in this catena. The absence of these texts from the catena of the Paris Synod seems decisive against their genuineness, at least coming on top of the other arguments against them, viz. (i) that they are otherwise unknown ; (ii) that so reasoned a plea against images is not compatible with the early date of Epiphanius ; (iii) that the practice of the Church of Cyprus showed neither tradition nor memory of any such ruling of Epiphanius.

[3] Mansi, XIII, 176e, 313a. The latter is extant only in fragments, collected in Pitra, *Spicileg. Solesm.*, I, 363–386.

Council was able to negative it by showing at great length and with references to authorities that Eusebius was an Arian and consequently unworthy of credence in the Church.[1] Reference was not therefore made to him, though St. John of Damascus had cited several passages from his writings in support of the principle of image-worship.

(iii) Nilus (d. circa 430), *Ep. to Olympiodorus.*[2] The correspondent had inquired whether he might decorate the monastery he was building with pictures of beasts and fishes, both in the church and in the house. The answer of Nilus was that " it would be childish folly to divert the eyes of the faithful with the pictures described ; common sense would place a single cross in the sanctuary at the East end and nothing else ; . . . you may fill the chapel dedicated to the saints with stories of the Old Testament and New Testament . . . that the illiterate who cannot read the holy scriptures, by contemplating the painting may call to mind the courage of the true servants of God and may be stirred to imitation : . . . for the house and cells a cross is sufficient." It was stated that this passage had been read at the Iconoclastic Council, but the words were altered [3] so that the advice to paint pictures on the chapel walls was made to read " whitewash the chapel walls." It was not found possible to check the text at the time, for the actual books were not produced. Such was the evidence given at Nicæa by three bishops who had taken part in the Iconoclastic Council, Gregory of Neo-Cæsarea, Theodore of Amorium, and Theodore of Myra.[4]

(iv) Amphilochius of Iconium [5] (circa 345–403).

" It is not, however, our task to represent the physical form of the saints on slabs with paints, for we have no need of such, but to imitate their manner of life in the way of virtue."

An extraordinarily verbose and pointless commentary on this passage was read at Nicæa, the purport of which was that the pictures of the saints were not made out of carnal love or to confer any benefit on them, but to be examples

---

[1] Mansi, XIII, 177c, 313d *sqq.*
[2] *Ib.* 36a ; Nilus, *Ep.*, IV, 61 (M.P.G. 79).
[3] ἐκεῖνοι γὰρ ἀντὶ τοῦ ἔνθεν καὶ ἔνθεν " ἱστορῆσον " τὸ " λούκανον " τεθείκασιν. Mansi, XIII, 36e.
[4] *Ib.* 37b.
[5] *Ib.* 301d. Source unknown.

of virtue and so benefit us. This may be true, but it does
not meet the point of Amphilochius's text.

(v) Pseudopigraphic περιοδοὶ τῶν ἁγίων ἀποστόλων.[1]
Two passages were noticed. In one the apostle John
was described as rebuking a disciple for making a picture
of him and doing reverence to it. The second was an
apocryphal story of the Passion in which Christ appearing
in a cross of light said the Cross was himself (apparently
to deprecate the use of pictures). This work was examined
at Nicæa and declared to be apocryphal and marred with
docetism, and was unanimously condemned.[2]

These are representative of the patristic evidence used
by the Iconoclasts, both in its strength and its weakness.
They show a simple common-sense rationalism in the
passages from Eusebius and Amphilochius, the unscrupu-
lousness that doctored the text of Nilus and manufactured
that of Epiphanius, and the uncritical welcome that could
be given to such trash as the last cited work.[3]

The passages used by the orthodox are more numerous,
but no more apposite. They enjoy an advantage in that
the expositions of most of them also survive. The following
is a fair and typical selection of the good and the bad :

(i) Clement of Alexandria [4] (circa 200).

". . . That he may reach the summit of knowledge he
strives to adorn all his powers, and equip his person, using
all the advantages of the true Gnostic ; he contemplates
beautiful images, thinking of the many patriarchs who
before his time have reached perfection, the numberless
prophets and the countless messengers [5] and the Lord of
them all who taught and made attainable the life of those
leaders."

The images which the true Gnostic is to contemplate
are not pictures but mental reflections. The passage will

[1] Mansi, XIII, 168e.
[2] *Ib.* 172c–176a.
[3] Other passages cited by the Iconoclasts were, Anastasius of Theophilus,
Ep. to a scholasticus (Mansi, XIII, 56a), and some not very relevant passages
from Gregory Nazianzen, John Chrysostom, Basil, Athanasius, and Theodotus
of Ancyra. *Ib.* 297 *sqq.* Some of the authorities of the iconoclastic side have
probably been suppressed, but their stock was never large. In the reign of
Leo the Armenian iconoclastic evidence was difficult to find (Script. Incert,
1025b), and the reason is that the image-question was not a real issue in the
time of the great fathers and does not appear in their writings.
[4] *Stromata*, bk. vii, cited by Jn. Dam., *Or.*, III, 1404a.
[5] ἀγγέλους, probably not angels but apostles.

not support the claim of the image-worshippers any more than a short extract quoted by Nicephorus from Clement's lost work, *de legali paschale :* [1]

" As an image when the original is not present sheds a glory like the original, but when the reality is there the image itself is outshone, the likeness remaining acceptable because it reveals the truth." [2]

The meaning of this passage is obscure and its interpretation out of the context impossible. Nicephorus understands it to mean that a portrait is a substitute for an absent original, and therefore justifies the representation of Christ. These two passages from Clement are important solely because they are the only third-century authorities used. Their value for the purpose intended is small because Clement was not thinking of pictures and their veneration but using a common figure of speech.

(ii) Basil [3] (330–379).

" The image of the king is also called the king, and there are not two kings in consequence. Neither is power divided nor is glory distributed. Just as the power reigning over us is one, so is our homage one, not many, and the honour given to the image passes to the original. What the image is in the one case as a representation, that the Son is in his nature, and as in art likeness is according to form, so in the divine and incommensurable nature there is union in the fellowship of godhead." [4]

This passage is the *locus classicus* of the orthodox side. Reference is made to it in every orthodox writer.[5] It exposes the characteristic weakness of the orthodox party's citations. They use analogies to establish facts. In this

---

[1] Cited Niceph., *Antirrh.*, III, 416b.

[2] ὡς εἴ τινος εἰκὼν μὴ παρόντος μὲν τοῦ ἀρχετύπου τὴν ἴσην ἐκείνῳ δόξαν ἀποφέρεται καὶ παρούσης τῆς ἀληθείας καταλάμπεται ἡ εἰκὼν πρὸς αὐτῆς τῆς ὁμοιώσεως ἐκείνης ἀποδέκτης μενούσης διὰ τὸ σημαίνειν τὴν ἀλήθειαν.

[3] *de Spir. sanct.*, xviii, 45. Cited Jo. Dam., *Or.*, I, 1253a, 1261d, III, 1361a; Niceph., *Antirrh.*, III, 404a; Mansi, XIII, 69d, 72a.

[4] ὅτι βασιλεὺς λέγεται καὶ ἡ τοῦ βασιλέως εἰκὼν καὶ οὐ δύο βασιλεῖς. οὔτε γὰρ τὸ κράτος σχίζεται οὔτε ἡ δόξα διαμερίζεται, ὡς γὰρ ἡ κρατοῦσα ἡμῶν ἀρχὴ καὶ ἐξουσία μία οὕτω καὶ ἡ παρ' ἡμῶν δοξολογία μία καὶ οὐ πολλαὶ διότι ἡ τῆς εἰκόνος τιμὴ ἐπὶ τὸ πρωτότυπον διαβαίνει. ὁ οὖν ἐστιν ἐνταῦθα μιμητικῶς ἡ εἰκὼν, τοῦτο ἐκεῖ φυσικῶς ὁ υἱός· καὶ ὥσπερ ἐπὶ τῶν τεχνητῶν κατὰ τὴν μόρφην ἡ ὁμοίωσις οὕτω καὶ ἐπὶ τῆς θείας καὶ ἀσυνθέτου φύσεως ἐν τῇ κοινωνίᾳ θεότητός ἐστιν ἕνωσις. Basil, *loc. cit.*

[5] Add to the reff. above : Mansi. XII, 1146a (Synod. Letter of Theodore) ; Had. Ep., Mansi, XIII, 790d ; *Lib. Car.*, III, 16 ; Theod. Stud., *Antirrh.*, II. 369a ; Paris Synod, p. 510 ; and see note in Hefele-Leclerq, III (2), p. 1215.

L

passage St. Basil is not concerned with the problem of an image. He uses the analogy of the image and its original to illustrate the relation of the Son to the Father. The image he has in mind is the Emperor's image used in the official cult of Rome and Augustus. Leclerq is of the opinion that the argument can legitimately be transferred to the image-worshippers' problem. But he does not face a serious fallacy. By established rule the Emperor's image was admitted to be symbolically the Emperor. It was a symbol invested with its meaning by authority and association. That is, by consent and actually it was the very thing that the picture of Christ was not admitted to be. The Emperor's image was the Emperor by the Emperor's own authority. But it is a complete *non sequitur* that the image of Christ was Christ without Christ's authority. The argument thus built on verbal analogy breaks down.

(iii) Athanasius [1] (328–373).

" The godhead of the Father is seen in the Son. This will be easier to understand from the example of the king's image which displays his form and likeness. The king is the likeness of his image. The likeness of the king is indelibly impressed upon the image so that any one looking at the image sees the king, and again any one looking at the king recognises that the image is his likeness. . . . He who worships the image worships the king in it. The image is his form and likeness."

This passage is parallel to that quoted from St. Basil. The argument is founded on the same analogy of the worship of Rome and Augustus and involves the same fallacy.

(iv) Gregory of Nyssa [2] (335–394).

" The father proceeds to bind his son. I have often seen a painting of this touching scene and could not look at it with dry eyes, so vividly did art set it forth. . . ."

This is a good quotation, the object of it being to illustrate the genuine emotional effect of pictures.

[1] *Or.,* III, *contra Arian.* 1 and 5. Cited Jo. Dam., *Or.,* III, 1404c; Mansi, XIII, 69b; Theod. Stud., *Antirrh.,* II, 369b; Paris Synod, p. 516.

[2] *Sermon at Constantinople on the godhead of the Son and of the Holy Spirit.* It is not in the extant works of Gregory. Cited Jo. Dam., *Or.,* I, 1269c; III, 1361c; Mansi, XII, 9c; *ib.* 108a; *ib.* 1065; *adv. Const. Cab.,* 321d.

(v) St. John Chrysostom (d. 407). From the treatise, *Quod veteris et novi Test.*[1]

" I was particularly fond of a picture in relief that was marked by its piety. In it I noticed represented an angel putting the hosts of the barbarians to flight, and David prophesying truly : Lord, thou shalt make their image to vanish out of the city."

The saint's approval is quoted to justify the representation of purely spiritual beings like angels.

(vi) Severianus of Gabala (early fifth century).[2]

" . . . Tell me, devout servant of God, will you do what you have forbidden, and disregard what you have ordered ? Having said, Thou shalt not make to thyself a graven image, you condemned the golden calf, and yet do you make a brazen serpent ? And this do you do not secretly but openly so that it is known to all ? Moses answers, I laid down that commandment in order to root out impiety and to withdraw the people from all apostasy and idolatry. Now I have had the serpent cast for a good purpose—as a figure of the truth. And as I have set up a tabernacle and all that is in it with cherubim . . . over the Holy of Holies for a sign and figure of the future, so I have set up a serpent for the salvation of the people, to serve as a preparation for the image of the sign of the Cross. . . ."

This passage gives reasonable and sound support to the contention that abuse does not destroy use, and that there is a legitimate place for images in the scheme of Christianity.

(vii) Dionysius the Areopagite (circa 530).

From several extracts of similar purport the following are typical :

(a) " On the one side, through the veiled language of Scripture and the help of oral tradition, intellectual things are understood through sensible ones, and the super-existent things by the things that exist. Forms are given to what is intangible and without shape and immaterial perfection is clothed and multiplied in a variety of different symbols."[3]

<hr>

[1] Cited Jo. Dam., *Or.*, II, 1313b; III, 1400c; Mansi, XIII, 9a; *adv. Const. Cab.*, 321d.
[2] *Hom. de Serp.*, 2, in works of John Chrysostom (ed. Montfaucon), VI, 513. Cited Jo. Dam., *Or.*, I, 1275b; III, 1364a; Paris Synod, p. 515.
[3] Dionys. Areop., *de divin. Nomin.*, 1. Cited Jo. Dam., *Or.*, I, 1260b.

(*b*) "Sensible images do indeed show forth invisible things." [1]

As we have had occasion to notice already, the philosophy of the image which St. John of Damascus works out is based on the mystical Platonism of Dionysius the Aeropagite, and such passages as those quoted are real contributions to the orthodox case. Less scholarly disputants than St. John, however, were apt to miss the point, supposing, like Pope Hadrian, that the value of Dionysius was less what he had to say than his name which seemed to bring the evidence back to apostolic times. They never trouble to inquire whether the pseudonymous Dionysius could be identified with the Dionysius of the Acts of the Apostles. [2]

(viii) Sophronius (circa 580). [3]

The summary of this passage is that a certain hermit was greatly troubled by a demon of unchastity ; the demon eventually told him that he would be freed from his evil desires if he would take an oath to cease to pay reverence to an image of the Virgin and Child. The Abbot Theodore Æliotes who absolved him from his oath said that it was better to visit every brothel in the city than refuse veneration to the image of the Lord and his mother. This is the story which Gibbon uses to illustrate what he calls " the judgement of the bishops [*i.e.* at Nicæa] on the comparative merit of image-worship and morality." [4] In no way can it be construed into that, [5] but it is typical of a great deal of the evidence that was put forward in support of orthodoxy.

(ix) Acts of Fifth General Council (553). [6]

The twelfth anathema, which condemned Theodore of Mopsuestia, is quoted. Theodore is described as holding the worship paid to the Son to be parallel to that paid to the Emperor's image, [7] implying a quasi-adoptianist Christology. The passage is introduced for the sake of the words " after the manner of the Emperor's image." [7] But the

---

[1] ἀληθῶς ἐμφανεῖς εἰκόνες εἰσὶ τὰ ὁρατὰ τῶν ἀοράτων. Dionys. Areop., *Ep. X ad Johan.* Cited Jo. Dam., *Or.*, III, 1360a. Cf. Paris Synod, p. 512 ; Had. Ep., Mansi, XIII, 777c.

[2] Had. Ep., Mansi, XIII, 777c.

[3] *Pratum spirituale*, 45. Cited Jo. Dam., *Or.*, I, 1280a ; III, 1336b ; Mansi, XIII, 60d ; Had. Ep., *ib.* XIII, 794c.

[4] Bury-Gibbon, V, 277.

[5] It was submitted as evidence at Nicæa, but was not necessarily endorsed by the Council.

[6] Cited Jo. Dam., *Or.*, III, 1412c.   [7] κατ' ἰσότητα βασιλικῆς εἰκόνος.

sense of the analogy is here quite different from the use made of the same analogy by Basil and Athanasius, who see in the Emperor's image a true figure of the relation of the Son to the Father. The inconsistency sufficiently demonstrates the weakness of the argument from analogy.

(x) Leontius of Neapolis (582–602).

A long series of passages [1] from this author, evidently from the frequency with which they recur, considered convincing, may be summarised as follows : The Jew had accused the Christian of idolatry in his use of images of the saints. The Christian replies by quoting the Cherubim of the Old Testament. Those, said the Jew, were not worshipped. Neither are our pictures, replied the Christian. Christians indeed have no hesitation in burning wood which has once been painted with sacred pictures or formed a cross. These things are emblems, serving to stimulate memory, respect, or affection, exactly like the Emperor's seal, or the belongings of an absent member of a family. The kind of respect paid is illustrated by incidents of the Old Testament, Abraham and the sons of Heth, Joseph and Pharaoh. Pictures, like relics, are vehicles of God. Honour paid to the saints passes to God, for the saints were a habitation of the Holy Ghost. Mere wood is often used in the Old Testament as an instrument of God, Aaron's rod, the wood thrown into the water by Elisha (2 Kings vi.). Miracles were performed by the dead body of Elisha, and may well be performed also by pictures or any other relic. Jacob honoured God with a stone. In face of such facts Jews cannot charge Christians with an idolatrous use of symbols. Our ultimate justification is the contrast between a legitimate symbol like the Ark and an improper one like the golden calves of Samaria. Objects like the cross and pictures of Christ and the saints are not our gods, but means of decorating our churches and promoting feelings of reverence.

The views attributed here to Leontius of Neapolis in the first half of the seventh century are so complete an anticipation of the Iconoclastic struggle and its very

---

[1] From bk. V of a work entitled *Contra Judæos*. These fragments alone survive, and their authenticity is not above question. Cited Jo. Dam., *Or.*, I, 1272a ; III, 1391 ; Mansi, XIII, 44a ; *ib.* 92c (Ep. of Pope Gregory) ; Paris Synod, p. 513.

arguments that the authenticity of all the passages attributed to Leontius must be gravely suspect. Coming at least in name from Cyprus like the spurious quotations of Epiphanius, it may be that one is the counterblast to the other. It is attractive to conjecture that Leontius is really the champion of orthodoxy, George of Cyprus.

(xi) Simeon Stylites Junior (d. 596).[1]

" Possibly a contentious unbeliever will maintain that in venerating images in our churches we are convicted of praying to lifeless idols. Far be it from us to do this. . . . With the material picture before our eyes, we see the invisible God through the visible representation, and glorify him as if present, not as a God without reality but as God who is the essence of being. . . ."

(xii) Ecclesiastical History of Theodore[2] (early sixth century).

A certain Olympius blasphemed the Trinity by pointing to his private parts and saying, I too have a trinity. On entering the baths he was stricken and died in great agony. The Emperor Anastasius ordered a painting to be made recording the incident. The Arians had the picture removed ; in consequence the principal delinquent in the removal was miraculously afflicted and died.

(xiii) Anastasius Sinaita[3] (630–700).

An anecdote is related of some Saracens shooting an arrow through an image of St. Theodore in a church. Blood dripped from the place, and a plague attacked the sacrilegious persons who had occupied the church.

(xiv) Canon 82 of Quinisext Council[4] (692).

" . . . In order that ' that which is perfect ' may be delineated to the eyes of all at least in coloured expression, we desire that the figure in human form of the Lamb who taketh away the sin of the world Christ our God be henceforth exhibited in images instead of the ancient lamb, so that all may understand by means of it the depths of the humiliation of the Word of God, and that we may recall

---

[1] Possibly from a letter to the Emperor Justin. Cited Jo. Dam., *Or.*, III, 1409c.

[2] Probably Theodore Lector. The reference is given to the fourth book, but the work is not extant. Cited Jo. Dam., *Or.*, III, 1388d.

[3] Cited from an unknown work. Jo. Dam., *Or.*, III, 1393a.

[4] Cited Niceph., *Antirrh.*, III, 421a ; *Apol. Min.*, 836b ; Tarasius, Ep., Mansi, XII, 1119e ; XIII, 40e ; *adv. Const. Cab.*, 320b ; Paris Synod, p. 513.

to our memory his conversation in the flesh, his passion and salutary death, and his redemption which was wrought for the whole world."

The purpose of the Canon was to safeguard the doctrine of the Incarnation, against Monophysitism. It is thus the strongest of all the evidence against Iconoclasm.

(xv) Theodore of Pentapolis.[1]

An anecdote is told of one Dion whose slave ran away, whereupon he made a wax image of St. Theodore and the slave returned, and this method of recovering runaway slaves was adopted in the district.

(xvi) Isidore the Deacon.[2]

An anecdote relates how Theophilus after calumniating St. John Chrysostom was miraculously restored to health on doing reverence to the effigy of the man he had wronged.

(xvii) Ps.-Athanasius. Sermon on a miracle at Berytus.[3]

This is an eighth-century contribution, prepared specially for the Iconoclastic controversy. It relates how a life-size picture of Christ left behind in a house was stabbed by Jews. Blood and water came from the spear thrust. All infirm persons touched with this matter were healed and all Jews in the city were converted.

Clearly from authorities[4] so ill-arranged and so uncritically accepted no conclusions could justly be drawn. The weakness of the appeal to authority is emphasised in the list of alleged historical precedents collected. It was a common objection of Iconoclasm that images had no ancient church authority, especially no authority from Christ himself.[5] The reply to that was tradition. " The eye-witnesses and ministers of the Word handed down the teaching of the Church not only by writing but also in unwritten tradition."[6] Tradition is the only church authority for many of its chief ordinances, for fasting communion, worshipping towards the East, doing reverence

---

[1] Cited Jo. Dam., *Or.*, III, 1404b. Theodore of Pentapolis in Libia occurs in Act. Sanct., 26 Mar., III. Otherwise he is unknown.

[2] The work is cited as *Chronographia* in Jo. Dam., *Or.*, III, 1409a. Isidore is not otherwise known. Fabricius (*Bib. Gr.*, IX, p. 257) designates him nugivendulus. Le Quien is probably right in thinking the excerpt a pure fabrication.

[3] Cited at Nicæa. Mansi, XIII, 24e.

[4] For list of authorities, see Appendix to this chapter.

[5] *adv. Const. Cab.*, 320b ; Had. Ep., Mansi, XIII, 800a.

[6] Jo. Dam., *Or.*, II, 1301c.

to the gospel-book, the crowning ceremony at weddings.[1] Tradition alone is the authority for the creed, fast days, and festivals, and rites of worship.[2]   To tradition the Church owes its knowledge of the holy sites.[3]   " It must be remembered that Scripture does not teach us all " (John xxi. 25).[4]

The range and antiquity of the tradition of images is demonstrated by a catalogue of celebrated examples :

(i) A picture of Christ sent to Abgar, king of Edessa.

(ii) The statue of Christ and the woman with the issue of blood at Paneas-Cæsarea.

(iii) A portrait of the Virgin by St. Luke.

(iv) A portrait of the Virgin and Child made for a king of Persia.

(v) Portraits of St. Peter and St. Paul at Rome.

(vi) A miraculous portrait of the Virgin in a church at Lydda.[5]

These were all alleged to go back to apostolic times, and therefore carried great weight. They were undoubtedly accepted. But none of them will stand investigation. No record of any of them can be traced earlier than the fourth century, and the sixth century is the period in which they really became significant. The attempt to establish an apostolic tradition by such a list of pictures definitely breaks down. The earliest authentic examples of distinctive Christian pictures are those described by fourth-century writers like Gregory of Nyssa and St. John Chrysostom. Pictures of Christ are very rare among them. By far the majority still represented stories of the saints and symbolical Old Testament scenes like the sacrifice of Isaac.[6] The appeal to authority does not help the orthodox case much, while the appeal to tradition only carries it to the fourth century. The image-worshippers could reflect, however, with some

[1] *adv. Cons. Cab.*, 320b.
[2] Niceph., *Antirrh.*, III, 388a.
[3] Jo. Dam., *loc. cit.*
[4] Niceph., *Antirrh.*, III, 461b.
[5] The following are a few of the references to some or all of the six : Jo. Dam, *Or.*, I, 1261b ; III, 1369b ; *adv. Cons. Cab.*, 320a, 321c ; *Vit. Steph.*, 1085 ; Mansi, XIII, 108a, 189e ; Niceph., *Antirrh.*, I, 260a ; *Antirrh.*, III, 461b ; *Ep. Theoph.*, 349d, 352c ; Had. Ep., Mansi, XIII, 768 ; Georg. Mon., II, 740, 784. These pictures have been discussed in Chap. III, with the exception of that of St. Peter and St. Paul at Rome. This is first heard of in Eusebius (H.E., VII, 18), and is condemned by him in his *Ep. to the Augusta*.
[6] A catalogue of the pictures cited in the Iconoclastic controversy is given by Schwarzlose, pp. 31 *sqq.*

satisfaction that among the earlier opponents of images were notorious heretics. Eusebius was discredited as an Arian, and it was fitting that a conspicuous Monophysite Xenaias should hold strange views on images. He denied that angels could be depicted in human form, and forbade pictures of Christ, and attacked the custom of representing the Holy Spirit as a dove.[1]

Neither St. John Damascene with his instructive sacramental argument nor the fathers of Nicæa with their appeal to authority were really doing much beyond beating the bush. Iconoclasm was a controversy which could be decided by the ordinary man. The vital use and the vital abuse of images were in the hands of all. Their vital abuse was superstition. Their vital use was that they taught the ignorant. The sure instinct of Western Europe saw that from the first and had no need for further discussion. In the East this was appreciated only as one among many more irrelevant facts. The author of the popular pamphlet *adversus Constantinum Caballinum* saw and stated his case far more clearly than the Council of Nicæa. He argued that to teach the unbeliever your method will not be to tell him that you worship the invisible ; you will bring him into the church, rouse his curiosity to ask who is the figure on the cross, and so lead him to the spiritual. Similarly with the other objects seen in church.[2] He admits the abuses of ignorant minds. But, he says, you should teach the ignorant better. " If an ignorant rustic greeted a courtier as the Emperor, would you send the rustic and the courtier both to the gallows ? Would you not teach him better ? "[3] This man and the Iconoclast who appealed steadily to the second commandment are at real grips. It was they rather than the theologians who settled the controversy. There is much truth in the view Theosteriktos records of some who considered Iconoclasm not a vital doctrinal struggle, but a simple dispute over matters of practice,[4] which would imply that it was to be settled pragmatically rather than doctrinally.

---

[1] *Eccl. Hist. of John Diacrinomenos*, quoted at Nicæa, Mansi, XIII, 180e.
[2] *adv. Const. Cab.*, 325d.
[3] *Ib.* 329b.
[4] Theos., *Vit. Nicet.*, xxiii. ἔνιοι δὲ οὐδὲ αἵρεσιν ταύτην ἡγοῦνται ἀλλὰ φιλονεικίαν.

APPENDIX TO CHAPTER VII

List of Patristic Citations

The following is a synopsis of the patristic quotations (including those examined in the text) used by the orthodox party. It is significant that there is nothing earlier than the fourth century, except the two inappropriate passages from Clement of Alexandria. The list should be compared with the much wiser selection of the Paris Synod (see below). (*a*) prefixed to a passage signifies that it is a fragment not preserved elsewhere.

Third Century

Clement of Alexandria (circa 200).
Stromata, bk. 17 . . . Jo. Dam., 1404a.
(a) de legal. Pasch. . . . Niceph., 416b.

Fourth Century

Ambrose (333–397).
(a) Ep. ad univ. Ital. . . Jo. Dam., 1316b.
de Incarn. sacr.7 : 75 . . ib., 1405b; Mansi, XII, 1068.
Athanasius (328–373).
Cent. Capit., 38 . . . Jo. Dam., 1365c; Had. Ep., Mansi, XIII, 776d.
Or. III, contr. Ar. 1 and 5 . Jo. Dam., 1404c; Mansi, XIII, 69b.
Pseudo-Athanasius.
(a) Serm. on miracle at Berytus . Mansi, XIII, 24e.
Basil (330–379).
de Spir. Sanct., 18 : 45 . . Jo. Dam., 1253a; ib. 1261d; ib. 1361a; Mansi, XIII, 69d, 72a; Niceph., 404a.
ib. 27 . . . . . Jo. Dam., 1256a.
in S. Gord. (2 passages) . . ib., 1264d, 1265b.
Serm. XL, Martyr (2 passages) . ib., 1265c; ib. 1361a; Mansi, XII, 1067.
enarr. in Is. . . . . Jo. Dam., 1365.
ad sanct. Flav. . . . . ib. 1405d.
Ps.-Basil.
serm. in Balaam . . . ib., 1261c; ib. 1360c; Mansi, XIII, 80c.
Ep. 360 ad Julian . . . Mansi, XII, 1065; XIII, 72e.
Cyril of Jerusalem (313–386).
Catech., 12 . . . . Jo. Dam., 1405c.
Eusebius (265–339).
Evang. Dem., bk. 5 . . . ib., 1369a.
Hist. Eccl., 7 : 15 and 9 . . ib. 1373bcd.

Gregory *Nazianzen* (328–390).
Or. 2, de theol. . . . Jo. Dam., 1241c.
Or. 2, de fil. . . . . *ib.* 1367c.
Duo carmina . . . . *ib.* 1400b; Mansi, XIII, 13bc,
297b; Niceph., 401a.
Invect. I, p. 93 . . . Jo. Dam., 1377a.
de bapt. . . . . . *ib.* 1408a.
Gregory *of Nyssa* (335–394).
de struct. Hom. 4 and 15 . . *ib.*, 1268d, 1269a.
(*a*) serm. on Godhead of son . *ib.* 1269c; *ib.* 1361c; *adv. Const.
Cab.*, 321d; Mansi, XII, 1065;
XIII, 9c, 108a.
Jerome of Jerusalem (4th cent. ?).
(*a*) Frag. . . . . Jo. Dam. 1409b.
John Chrysostom (344–407).
enarr. Ep. Hcb. (2 passages
one (*a*)) . . . . *ib.*, 1269d, 1361c.
quod vet. et nov. Test . . *ib.* 1369a.
serm. I dc div. utrius Test. . *ib.* 1313b, 1400c; *adv. Const.
Cab.*, 321d; Mansi, XIII, 9a.
cnarr. in par. scm. . . . Jo. Dam., 1313c.
serm. in Melet. . . . *ib.* 1313d; Mansi, XIII, 8d.
serm. de prod. Jud. . . . Jo. Dam., 1316a.
enarr. in Ps. III . . . *ib.* 1368b.
Hom. III in Ep. Col. . . *ib.* 1367d.
enarr. in Job . . . . *ib.* 1377a.
Or. 15 de statuis . . . *ib.* 1396c.
Hom. in Ep. Tim. VIII . . *ib.* 1401d.
In Maccab. . . . . *ib.* 1488b.
contr. Julian, bk. 1 . . . *ib.* 1408b.
(*a*) serm. on washing . . Mansi, XIII, 68b.
Ps.-Chrysostom.
In Sanct. Flav. . . . . Jo. Dam., 1400b.
Vit. Jo. Chrys. . . . . *ib.* 1276c, 1364d.
Methodius of Patara (d. 311).
Or. II dc rcsurr. . . . *ib.* 1420b.

Fifth Century

Antipater *of Bostra* (5th cent.).
(*a*) Frag. of serm. on Woman with
issue . . . . . Mansi, XIII, 13e, 177e.
Asterius *of Amasea* (circa 400).
Martyr. Euphem. . . . *ib.*, 16b.
Cyril *of Alexandria* (370–444).
Alloc. ad Theod. . . . Jo. Dam., 1368c.
Thesaurus . . . . *ib.*
de Abr. et Mel. 6 . . . *ib.*
(*a*) Frag. Comm. in Rom. . . Niceph., 421d.
(*a*) Ep. ad Acac. . . . Mansi, XIII, 12b; Had. Ep., *ib.*
777e.

Nilus (d. circa 430).
  Epp. ad Heliodor. et Olympiod. .   Mansi, XIII, 32c, 36a.
Polychromios (d. circa 430).
  (a) enarr. in Ezek. . . . Jo. Dam., 1380b.
Severianus of Gabala (5th cent.).
  (a) Or. 4 in sanct. cruc. . . *ib.* 1408c.
  Hom. de Serp. (ap. Jo. Chrys. VI,
  523) . . . . . *ib.* 1275b, 1364a.
Socrates (circa 450).
  Hist. Eccl. I, 18 . . . *ib.* 1376a.
Theodoret (393–453).
  Relig. Hist. . . . . *ib.* 13865b ; Mansi ; XIII, 73a.
  Relig. Hist. (3 passages) . . Jo. Dam., 1397a.
  Hist. Eccl. (3 passages) . . *ib.* 1397c.

Sixth Century

Acta 5th Council (553).
  anathema 12 . . . . Jo. Dam., 1412c.
Constantine Chartophylax (6th cent.).
  (a) on all the martyrs . . Mansi, XIII, 185b.
Dionysius the Areopagite (circa 530).
  de div. nom. 5 . . . . Jo. Dam., 1240d, 1260b ; Had.
                     Ep., Mansi, XIII, 777c.
  de coel. hier. 1 . . . Jo. Dam., 1241a.
  de eccles. hier. (2 passages) . *ib.* 1360b, 1260d ; Niceph., 413d.
  ep. 10 ad Joann. . . . Jo. Dam., 1360a.
  ep. ad Tit. . . . . *ib.* 1260b.
John of Antioch (Malalas) (6th cent.).
  chronographia . . . *ib.* 1369b.
Leontius of Neapolis (6th cent. end).
  (a) contra Judæos. (sev. frag). . *ib.* 1272a, 1381d ; Mansi, XIII,
                     44a, 92c.
Simeon Stylites Junior (d. 596).
  (a) Ep. Justin. . . . *ib.*, 160d.
  (a) ep. de imag. . . . Jo. Dam., 1409c.
  Vit. Sim. . . . . *ib.*, 1393c ; Mansi, XIII, 73c.
Theodore Lector.
  (a) Hist. Eccl. IV . . . Jo. Dam., 1308 ; Mansi, XIII,
                     180e.
  (a) *ib.* another passage . . Jo. Dam., 1413a.

Seventh Century

  Acta 6th Council (680) . . *ib.* 1401d.
  Acta Quinisext. (miscalled 6th)   adv. Const. Cab., 320b ; Mansi,
    (692).   XII, 1119 ; XIII, 40e ; Niceph.,
                     421a, 836b.

Anastasius of Theopolis (7th cent.).
(*a*) de sabbato . . . . Jo. Dam., 1316c, 1412b ; Mansi,
XIII, 56e.
(*a*) unknown source . . . Jo. Dam., 1393a.
(*a*) in nov. Dom. . . . *ib.* 1416c.
(*a*) ad schol. . . . . Mansi, XIII, 56a.
John of Thessalonica (7th cent.).
(*a*) source unknown . . . *ib.* 164c.
Sophronius (d. 638).
Prat. spirit. 45 . . . . Jo. Dam., 1336b, 1280a ; Mansi,
XIII, 60d ; *ib.* (Had. Ep.),
794c.
de mir. Cyr. et Joann . . Jo. Dam., 1413c ; Mansi, XIII,
58c.
Vit. Mariæ Ægypt. (written 7th Jo. Dam., 1416d ; Mansi, XIII,
cent.). 85d ; Niceph., 399c.
Acta Maximi (580–662) . . Jo. Dam., 1316b, 1413b ; Mansi,
XIII, 40a.

Uncertain Date, but not Earlier than Fifth Century
Isidore :
(*a*) chronographia (spurious) . Jo. Dam., 1409a.
(*a*) Jew and a Christian, disputa-
tion between . . . . Mansi, XIII, 165d.
(*a*) περιοδοὶ τῶν ἁγίων ἀποστόλων
(spurious) . . . . *ib.* 168e.
Stephen of Bostra :
(*a*) contra Jud. 4 . . . Jo. Dam., 1376b.
(*a*) Theodore of Pentapolis . . *ib.* 1404b.
Anastasius, Martyrd. . . . Mansi, XIII, 21a.
Cosmas and Damian, Miracles of *ib.* 64b.
Daniel, Life of . . . . Jo. Dam., 1416d.
Eupraxia, Life of . . . *ib.* 1417c.
Martyrd. of Eustathius . . *ib.* 1381a.
John the Faster, an interpolation
in the Acta . . . . Mansi, XIII, 80c.
Procopius, Life of . . . *ib.* 89b.
Theodore of Siceon, Life of . . *ib.* 89e.

CHAPTER VIII
AFTER THE COUNCIL OF NICÆA

(a) Authorities

1. Theophanes. As before.
2. Theodore Studites (759–826) now appears, a first-hand authority, entering the scene of active politics in the matter of the marriage of Constantine VI. He represents the extreme church position which would subordinate the State to the Church in all matters in which the Church was directly concerned. The writings of primary importance are :

(i) *Antirrhetici tres adversus Iconomachos.* These are recapitulations and developments of the arguments against Iconoclasm. To these are appended two minor treatises covering the same ground : (*a*) *Seven chapters against the Iconoclasts*, a summary of the same and cognate arguments. (*b*) *Letter to his Father Plato on the veneration of the Images.*

(ii) *Oration, XI.* Funeral oration on Plato the Hegumenos. Plato was the leader of the extreme party whom Theodore succeeded.

(iii) Letters. Two collections (*a*) in Migne, (*b*) ed. Mai in *Nov. patr. Biblioth.*, VIII (1871), in all 550 letters, covering the whole of Theodore's active life and every matter of public concern into which he entered.

3. *Vita Tarasii*, as before.

Vita Nicephori, by Ignatius the deacon, his pupil. M.P.G. 100.

Vita Theodori Stud. Two versions in M.P.G. 99. The second is by Michael the monk, a younger contemporary of Theodore and is the original upon which the first and longer life is based.

(b) Modern Writers

Bury, J. B., *The Eastern Roman Empire from the Fall of Irene.* London, 1912.

Diehl, C., From Nicephorus I to the Fall of the Phrygian Dynasty, ch. II of *Camb. Med. Hist.*, vol. IV. Cambridge, 1923.

Gardner, Alice, *Theodore of Studium.* London, 1905.

Diehl, C., Une bourgeoise de Byzance, in *Figures byzantines*, vol. I, pp. 111 *sqq.* Paris, 1906. The life of Theoctista, mother of Theodore.

THE period immediately following the Council of Nicæa was one of moderation and neutrality. Even in Constantinople orthodoxy was far from dominating the situation. The prevalent atmosphere of toleration owed much to the tactful handling of two successive

Patriarchs of moderate opinion, Tarasius and Nicephorus, and not a little to the namesake of the last, the Emperor Nicephorus. These three represent a policy unusual in the religious life of Constantinople, and receive in consequence only a luke-warm appraisement from the more rigid partisans like Theodore Studites. Iconoclasm was by no means dead. Echoes of it were still to be heard. Irene had continued to hold the reins of government in her own hands, keeping her son in the background, and forcing him to marry a lady of the court named Maria. But the army could not endure her sex and her misgovernment. In 780 she was forced to withdraw, leaving Constantine VI sole Emperor. He determined to divorce the wife his mother had provided and marry Theodota, one of his mother's maids of honour. In this project he was encouraged by his mother herself, who expected to gain her own ends by his folly. But the triumphant party of orthodoxy proved an obstacle. The Patriarch Tarasius refused the divorce. Behind the Patriarch was a group which henceforth was to dominate the ecclesiastical scene. This was the monastic party which had already been the only force bold enough to resist the throne, but now had increased its power not merely by the favour which the Court showed to monasticism, but by the leadership and organisation of men of outstanding ability, Plato of Saccudion and his nephew Theodore. Plato had been the Patriarch's principal adviser at Nicæa.[1] It is no violent inference to suppose that he filled the same role still from his monastery in Constantinople.[2] The exasperated Emperor at last turned to threats. If the Patriarch would not facilitate his divorce and re-marriage, he would become an Iconoclast.[3] Iconoclasm must still have been a serious menace, for Tarasius yielded and permitted the re-marriage to be celebrated by Joseph, the Patriarch's œconomos. A controversy then began, in which the monks [4] found themselves at variance not only

[1] *Vit.*, II, Theod. Stud., 240c.
[2] He was now at Saccudion within the walls of Constantinople.
[3] *Vit.*, II, Theod. Stud., 257a ; *Vit.*, I, 143a. διαπειλοῦντα ἤδη ἔξαρνον καὶ αὐτὸν κατὰ τοὺς προλαβόντας τῶν θείων γένεσθαι εἰκόνων εἰ μὴ τὸ ἐφετὸν καταπράξοιτο. Cedrenus, I, 908c, gives the same apparently from an independent source : εἰ μὴ τοῦτο γένηται τοὺς ναοὺς τῶν εἰδώλων ἀνοίγω. The idol temples must mean the churches defaced by Iconoclasm. With this interpretation agrees Walch, *Ketzerhistorie*, vol. X, p. 544.
[4] Not all, for some supported the Emperor. Theod. Stud., *Or.*, XI, 832b.

with the Emperor but with a man so moderate as the
Patriarch. This incident, which did not close for many
years, has no further direct bearing on iconoclasm except
that it indicated the courage and determination of the
monks, and revealed an organised body with a clear policy
upon which any revival of Iconoclasm would be severely
tested. It also enabled the monks to lay down the lines
upon which they would work in any conflict. Theodore
declared himself out of communion with the Emperor,[1]
and at a later date appealed to the Pope.[2] That is to say,
he appealed from the separatist tendencies of Constantinople
to the voice of Christendom. And this, as we have already
seen, was the only fruitful policy Constantinople could have
followed. The controversy on the divorce and the subsequent atrocities perpetrated by Irene against her son fall
outside our subject. It must suffice to say that the am-
bitious Empress recovered her throne, caused her son to be
blinded, and was eventually deposed in favour of one of
the court officials. This man Nicephorus succeeded to
the throne in 802. He was of Semitic stock and had held
the post of General Logothete, providing the unusual
spectacle of one not a military officer overthrowing a
dynasty and taking its place. He proved himself a competent administrator faced with the task of making good
the extravagance of Irene's rule, while in religion he preserved an effective but not spectacular moderation. In
805 he lost a loyal supporter by the death of the patriarch
Tarasius. " By the will of the people, priests, and
Emperor " the vacant see was filled by the appointment
of Nicephorus the historian,[3] a man in many ways like his
predecessor. Behind the scenes, however, important events
had occurred before the Patriarch was chosen. We have
seen that a strong monastic party had grown up under the
leadership of Plato and his still more famous nephew
Theodore. Plato had been a power since the days of
Constantine Copronymus, when he was the head of the
monastery of Symboli near Olympus in Bithynia. Subsequently as head of Saccudion in Constantinople he had

---

[1] *Vit.*, II, 253a.
[2] *Vit.*, I, 141a ; *Ep.*, I, 33. πρὸς Πέτρον ἤτοι τὸν αὐτοῦ διάδοχον ὁτιοῦν
καινοτομούμενον ἐν τῇ καθολικῇ ἐκκλησίᾳ παρὰ τῶν ἀποσφαλλομένων τῆς ἀληθείας
ἀναγκαῖον ἀναφέρεσθαι.
[3] Theoph., 968a.

refused the bishopric of Nicomedia, and was the most influential ecclesiastic in Constantinople during the Patriarchate of Tarasius.[1] His sister's son Theodore had adopted the religious life at his uncle's suggestion, was ordained priest by Tarasius in 794, and immediately afterwards succeeded Plato as head of the house of Saccudion, which he subsequently exchanged for that of Studium (779). The two had been expelled as a consequence of their opposition to Constantine's divorce, but had been recalled on the fall of Constantine, whose memory Theodore pursued with a malignancy which is not really characteristic of him. Writing to the consul Demetrius, he described the blinding inflicted on the wretched Emperor as the fitting punishment sent by a just God for the imprisonment of the holy man Plato.[2] It was natural that so tolerant a ruler as the Emperor Nicephorus, seeing the influence of uncle and nephew, should try to conciliate them. Accordingly, at the death of Tarasius, he asked their advice on the appointment of a new Patriarch. It seems clear that both were agreed that Theodore was the fit person to nominate. "Plato," says Theodore, "sent his vote, though I refrain from saying for whom it was given."[3] The suggestion was supported by other bishops but promptly rejected by the Emperor.[4] Theodore's own letter to the Emperor is extant.[5] He names no one, but indicates the right candidate as one who has duly passed through the steps of holy orders, who has learnt experience by suffering, and who recognises that the rights of civil authority belong to the Emperor while the ecclesiastical dominion is exclusively the right of the Church. A more definite nomination Theodore would not give, but he could hardly have pointed more plainly to himself. The choice of Nicephorus as patriarch was anything but acceptable to Plato and Theodore. Theodore described the Patriarch later as in the Emperor's pocket.[6] At the moment they made a protest on technical grounds. The new Patriarch had been formerly an Imperial

---

[1] Theod. Stud., *Or.*, XI, 820–825.
[2] *Ib.*, *Ep.*, II, 218.
[3] τὸ δὲ ἐφ' ὅτῳ παρῶ λέγειν. *Ib.*, *Or.*, XI, 837b.
[4] οἱ μὲν ἀσμένως ἐδέξαντο οὐκ οἶδ' ὁποίῳ τρόπῳ βεβαιώσαντες τὸ γράμμα. ὁ δὲ λαβὼν ἀπεσέσσατο μετακυλίσας ὡς ἐν κύβῳ τὰς ψήφους. *Ib.* 837c.
[5] *Ep.* I, 16.
[6] ταμιευόμενον πάντα καίσαρι. *Ep.*, I, 26.

M

secretary, and was now a lay monk. His direct promotion to the episcopate was irregular.[1] Behind the technical objection was the genuine one, that Nicephorus could not be looked upon as a supporter of the advanced ecclesiastical party. Plato did not hesitate to convey his views to the Emperor. He sought out a monk, a relative of the Emperor, and told him what he thought.[2] The Emperor was prepared to take the drastic step of expelling Theodore and his party immediately, but was dissuaded in view of their popularity.[3] But it was not long before the inevitable question of Constantine's divorce came to the surface. Joseph, who had performed the ceremony, had been put under discipline after the fall of Constantine. He was now restored by the new Patriarch. The reply of Theodore and the Studites was to break off communion with the Patriarch.[4] The Emperor then had a synod convoked which expelled Plato, Theodore, and his brother Joseph, and dispersed the Studite monks. The method the Emperor followed is the most significant point in his action. He carried out his purpose by ecclesiastical law, thus establishing the Emperor's supremacy over the Church.[5] It was the attitude illustrated by this fact that brought on the Emperor Nicephorus the unrelenting hostility of all the ecclesiastical writers. Though he was not an Iconoclast, his policy was in principle the same. The incidents of his reign have little direct bearing on Iconoclasm, but his lack of enthusiasm for orthodoxy and his definite opposition to the strong ecclesiasticism of Theodore's party made him a perpetual object of suspicion.[6] And though the patriarch Nicephorus addressed a synodical letter to Pope Leo III,[7] no communication was maintained with the West, and the Emperor went far towards dissolving such church unity as Irene had restored. When a renegade monk in the suburb of

---

[1] Theoph., 968a.
[2] φθεγξάμενος τὰ εἰκότα. Theod., *Or.*, XI, 840a.   [3] Theoph., 968a.
[4] *Vit. Theod.*, I, 156d ; Theod., *Epp.*, I, 25, 26 ; *Or.*, XI, 840a ; Theoph., 973b. They professed to be out of communion only with Joseph, but as he was in communion with the Patriarch, the Patriarch was involved in the action.
[5] Mansi, XIV, 14 ; Theoph., 973b ; Theod., *Ep.*, I, 33, 48.
[6] The Patriarch is alleged to have consented to the restoration of Joseph like Tarasius to avoid worse evil. *Vit. Theod.*, II, 268c. This was probably after the death of Nicephorus. Theoph., 992c.
[7] *Vit. Niceph.*, 73.

Exokionium " attacked the True Word and the holy Images, the Emperor supported him and gave pain to the Patriarch and the faithful," [1] apparently by a general toleration which protected heretics against the attacks of the orthodox. The same fact explains the friendship he was reported to have for Manichæans or Paulicians, and Athingani, permitting them to make converts within the Empire.[2] He refused preferential treatment to the clergy : " he ordered military officers to treat bishops and clerks as slaves and to abuse their goods," [3] which must mean that he curtailed their exemption from taxation. He censured the practice of giving gold and silver vessels to churches, and contemplated the possibility of confiscating them.[4] All this goes to show that Nicephorus was a laborious administrator, neither friendly nor unfriendly to the Church. To Theophanes he seems worthy of condemnation as strong as the Icono-clastic Emperors received. " Never did Christians endure more than in his reign. He surpassed all his predecessors in greed, lust, and savage cruelty ; to recount it all in detail would only move posterity to incredulity and would be a great labour." [5] The simple truth seems to be, as recorded by the biographer of the Patriarch Nicephorus, that the Church enjoyed complete peace.[6] Nicephorus had a difficult reign, in his efforts to restore the economic ravages caused by the mismanagement of Irene. His difficulties were increased during his last two years by a serious war with the Bulgarians, in which he fell in action in the year 811.[7] His son Stauracius, who was severely wounded in the same battle, was proclaimed Emperor. But the military failure of the late Emperor, coming after his rigid financial policy, had lost him what little popularity he ever had. The church party now found their opportunity. The Patriarch Nicephorus made a last attempt at an arrange-

---

[1] Theoph., 981b.
[2] *Ib.* 981a. This is apparently contradicted in *Vit. Niceph.*, 69c, where Nicephorus the Patriarch is said to have written a treatise against the Cataphrygians, Jews, and Manichæans, in consequence of which these sects could only exist in obscurity. This, however, probably belongs to the reign of Michael.
[3] Theoph., 981b.
[4] *Ib.* 981c.
[5] *Ib.* 988a. Cf. *Vit. Theod.*, I, 157d ; II, 265c.
[6] σαββατισμὸν τῇ τοῦ θεοῦ ἐκκλησίᾳ ὑπέγραψεν. *Vit. Niceph.*, 69d.
[7] Theoph., 985b.

ment. He asked Stauracius what restitution he was prepared to make for his father's exactions. The evasive
answer he returned convinced the Patriarch that compromise
was impossible.[1] He accepted, therefore, the candidate of
the reactionaries, the late Emperor's son-in-law Michael
Rhangabe the Curopalates, exacting from him first a written
statement attested with the sign of the cross, that " he would
keep his hand unstained from Christian blood, and as to
priests, monks, and the whole ecclesiastical body, he would
inflict no punishment on them." [2] Stauracius retired to a
monastery, where he did not long survive.

The new Emperor Michael was a European Greek, an
unusual nationality to occupy the throne. He was an amiable
and incompetent man, completely in the hands of the vigorous
ecclesiastics, as Theophanes' epithet εὐσεβέστατος shows.[3]
He reverted to the full reaction of Irene's days. Relations
with Rome were restored. The exiled monks, including
Plato and Theodore, were recalled. A policy of persecution
was inaugurated against dissenters. The death penalty
was, on the advice of Nicephorus the Patriarch, enacted
against the Manichæans (" now called the Paulicians ")
and against the Athingani of Phrygia and Lycaonia. Others
dissuaded the Emperor from putting this law into operation
on the ground that the heretics might repent, and in any
case priests might not inflict death, a view indignantly
repudiated by Theophanes as conflicting with the action
of St. Peter in the matter of Ananias, and the precept of
St. Paul that " they who do such things are worthy of
death." [4] On the evidence of the *Life of Nicephorus*,
Theophanes may be corrected. It was probably the
pacific Nicephorus who dissuaded the Emperor from
extreme measures, for he is said to have attacked the
heresies of the Cataphrygians, Jews, and Manichæans in
a book presented to the Emperor, with the result that these
sects could only exist in obscurity.[5] The pious Michael
nevertheless decapitated a few of the heretics,[6] but the
policy of violence proved disastrous. Iconoclasm raised
its head. In the summer of 813 the Bulgarians gained
successes and the persecution of heretics was dropped.

---

[1] Theoph., 988c.   [2] *Ib.* 989b.
[3] *Ib.* 989c.   [4] *Ib.* 992c–993c.
[5] *Vit. Niceph.*, 69c.   [6] Theoph., 993c.

" The two Iconoclastic heresies of the Paulicians and Athingani, and that of the Tetraditæ [1] were allowed to go unblamed, and voices were raised against the holy and sacred images and the monastic habit." [2] The name of Constantine V was spoken with reverence, and an abortive attempt was made to promote a revolution in favour of his exiled and blinded sons.[3] A vagabond monk cut and defaced an image of the Virgin and had his tongue cut out.[4] Everything pointed to the approach of a crisis of the first importance. The Bulgarian campaign was going badly and peace was desirable. The negotiations broke down on the question of restoring to the enemy refugees who had fled to Constantinople. Again the moderating influence of Nicephorus was overridden by the party of Theodore. Nicephorus appealed for the sacrifice of the few for the welfare of the many. Theodore declared that the question was settled by the saying of the Gospel, " Him that cometh to me I will in no wise cast out " (John vi. 37). Theodore's courageous but impolitic view prevailed. The war went on. A minor success against the Bulgarians was attributed to the late Patriarch Tarasius, who had recently been canonised, and the pious Emperor covered the Patriarch's tomb with silver plates.[5] But the army grew more and more dissatisfied.[6] In Constantinople the Iconoclasts openly assembled at the tomb of Constantine V and called on him to rise and help the state in the day of its destruction. They played on popular superstition with stories of Constantine leaving the grave and riding against the Bulgarians. The old cry revived that orthodoxy and the monks were bringing God's curse upon the country. The instigators were "Paulicians disguised as Christians ;[7] they called

[1] The word implies belief in a quaternity ($\tau\epsilon\tau\rho\dot{\alpha}s$) instead of the Trinity ($\tau\rho\iota\dot{\alpha}s$). It was applied to the followers of the Monophysite Damianus, patriarch of Alexandria (578–605), who held so realistic a view of the ONE Substance that he was accused of making it a fourth Person added to the Trinity.

[2] Theoph., 996b.

[3] *Ib.* 996c.

[4] *Ib.*

[5] *Ib.*, 1004a.

[6] *Ib.*

[7] $\sigma\chi\dot{\eta}\mu\alpha\tau\iota$ $\mu\dot{o}\nu o\nu$ $\dot{\eta}\sigma\alpha\nu$ $X\rho\iota\sigma\tau\iota\alpha\nu o\dot{\iota}$ $\tau\hat{\eta}$ $\delta\dot{\epsilon}$ $\dot{\alpha}\lambda\eta\theta\epsilon\dot{\iota}\alpha$ $\Pi\alpha\upsilon\lambda\iota\kappa\iota\alpha\nu o\dot{\iota}$. *Ib.* 1005a. *I.e.* they were Iconoclasts. Lombard implies that they actually were Paulicians, which is a misinterpretation of the words of Theophanes, who regularly uses Paulician as a term of contumely.

Constantine blessed and embraced his heterodoxy to over-throw the dispensation of the Incarnation." The situation was ripe for an Iconoclastic revival when Michael defeated in battle abdicated in favour of Leo, strategus of the Anatolic theme,[1] himself retiring to a monastery on the island of Plate, where hidden under the name of Athanasius he survived for thirty-two years.[2]

Reversion to orthodoxy had proved disastrous, not as the effect of orthodoxy itself, but because the two rulers who had supported it, Irene and Michael, were of Greek nationality, and Greek nationality combined correct religious opinion with administrative incompetence. In the popular mind the triumphant reigns of the Isaurian Emperors were definitely associated with Iconoclasm. Although the combination must have been fortuitous, it was inevitable that a successful Emperor must definitely revert to the religious policy of Leo and Constantine. The consequence was that a second Iconoclastic period began, but in it Iconoclasm was with the Emperors a policy and with the people a prejudice rather than a conviction. A qualification must, however, be allowed. Large numbers both of laity and clergy in this age had grown up in the Iconoclastic tradition. There is no indication that the population of Constantinople held very tenaciously to any of their religious opinions. But at least the weight of inertia which had under the Isaurians been on the side of orthodoxy was now on the side of Iconoclasm. The orthodox party had, however, what they never possessed before in the same degree, a front line of educated men, and in Theodore a determined leader who was easily the foremost figure in the Church of the day.

[1] Theoph., 1005c.   [2] Cont. Theoph., 33a.

CHAPTER IX

THE SECOND ICONOCLASTIC PERIOD. THE REIGN OF LEO V THE ARMENIAN

AUTHORITIES

(a) PRIMARY

(i) *Contemporary*

(i) Theodore Studites. As before.

(ii) *Scriptor Incertus de Leone Bardæ F.* A fragment of a contemporary chronicle by an unknown hand. In spite of its marked bias against Leo, it is of the highest value and may well take precedence of all other authorities.

(iii) Georgius Monachus becomes a primary authority for the period 813–842, with which he was contemporary. He is singularly slight and valueless.

(iv) *Epistoa ad Theophilum.* See Ch. III.

(ii) *Not Contemporary, but based on Contemporary Records*

(i) Simeon Magister. See Bury, *East. Rom. Emp.*, App. III. This chronicle is found as the following :

(a) *Leo Grammaticus* (written 1013), M.P.G., 108.
(b) *Theodosius of Melitene* (? eleventh cent.), ed. Tafel, Munich, 1859.
(c) *Chron. in Cod. Par.* 854 (unpub.).
(d) *Additions to Georg. Mon.*, M.P.G. 109.

Simeon's date in the tenth century. He probably used a lost chronicle on the Amorians. The *Chronicle of Cod. Par.*, 1712, printed in M.P.G., 109, as Simeon Magister, is by an unknown hand. It should be designated Pseudo-Simeon. It is not a valuable chronicle. It displays many obvious errors, *e.g.* the significance of the name Chameleon applied to Leo V, the statement that Leo at his coronation signed a document promising to defend religion, the name Euphrosyne given to the mother of Theophilus. Its main source seems to be the same as one of those used by the Continuators of Theophanes. See *e.g.* the story of Theodore Graptos. Hirsch (*Byz. Studien*, pp. 318 *sqq.*) gives its sources as George, Simeon, Genesios, Cont. Theophanes, *Script. Incert. de Leone*, Nicetas, *Vit. Ignatii.* Its chronology is valueless (Hirsch, *op. cit.*, p. 342). It preserves some anecdotes otherwise unknown.

(ii) Joseph Genesios (written 944–948).
Continuators of Theophanes (949–950).
Both these chronicles were written at the suggestion of Constantine VII. The Continuators of Theophanes used Genesios and probably also the

sources of Genesios. Genesios has much less ecclesiastical interest than the Continuators, but for that reason whenever a political question is involved with a religious one, as in the matter of the final restoration of the images under Theodora, it is Genesios who is likely to be the more reliable.

(iii) The following lives of saints bear on the period :

Vita Nicephori Patr. .	. .	M.P.G. 100.
—— Theophanis Conf.	. .	in de Boor's ed., vol. II.
—— Theodori Stud. .	. .	M.P.G. 99.
—— Methodii .	. .	M.P.G. 100.
—— Nicetæ	. . .	Act. Sanct. Ap. I.

The above are practically contemporary. The *Life of Nicephorus* is of less value than the others.

Vita Nicolai Stud.	. .	M.P.G. 105.
—— Theodori Grapti	. .	M.P.G. 116.
—— Joannicii .	. .	(i) A.S. Nov. II ; (ii) M.P.G. 116.
Acta David	. . .	Analect. Boll., XVIII, 1899.
Vita Michael. Syncelli	. .	in Ἑλληνικὸς φιλολογικὸς σύλλογος. Archæol. Suppl. to vols. XXIV–XXVI, 1896.
—— Macarii Pelecetæ	. .	Anal. Boll, XVI.
—— Joannis Psichaitæ	. .	A.S. May VI.
—— Hilarionis heg. Dalmat.	.	*ib.* June I.
—— Ignatii	. . .	M.P.G. 105.
de S. Theophylact Nicomed.	.	A.S. March I.
Synaxarium Eccles. Cplæ. .	.	ed. Deleheye. Propylæum ad A.S. Nov., Brussels, 1902.

(*b*) Of the secondary sources the only one of any importance is Cedrenus, who for the period from 811 onwards reproduces the otherwise unpublished chronicle of Scylitzes. Scylitzes lived in the eleventh century, and used Theoph. Cont. and other (unknown) sources and shows considerable judgment in his selections.

(*c*) MODERN

Bury and Gardner, as before.

Tougard, A., La persecution iconoclaste d'après la correspondance de S. Théodore Studite, in *Rev. des Quest. historiques*, 1891, pp. 80 *sqq.*

IT would have been difficult, if not impossible, under the circumstances, for the Patriarch to have resisted the army's choice of Leo. He therefore tried to make the best of the situation as it was. The new Emperor spontaneously asked the Patriarch for his prayers and support, assuring him of his orthodoxy.[1] The Patriarch

[1] Theoph., 1008b.

attempted to get this assurance reduced to writing and signed by the Emperor under oath. For the moment Leo evaded the issue by deferring the signing until his coronation.[1]

The new Emperor, who is styled Leo the Armenian, was of mixed Syrian and Armenian descent.[2] That is to say, he had much of the same ancestral bias as his namesake the Isaurian. He had been involved in a rebellion promoted by Bardanes against the Emperor Nicephorus, but had extricated himself, subsequently falling into disgrace for losing to Saracen raiders a considerable sum of money belonging to the Imperial treasury.[3] By Michael I he was raised to be strategus of the Anatolic theme,[4] and his own confidential adviser.[5] Even before Michael had abdicated the army of his theme had proclaimed Leo Emperor.[6]

On July 11, 813, Leo was crowned by the Patriarch Nicephorus.[7] The Patriarch attempted again to impose upon the Emperor an attested statement that he would uphold orthodoxy.[8] But it seems as though the Emperor refused to go beyond the unofficial assurance he had already given.[9] For the time he allayed anxiety after his coronation by offering thanks before the celebrated image of Christ on the Chalce Gate, which had been restored by Irene, though this action may have been a mere formality to deceive the orthodox.[10]

Pressing matters claimed his attention. To secure his

---

[1] *Vit. Niceph.*, 77b, followed by Cont. Theoph., 41c, and Gen., 1021c.
[2] ps.-Sim., 664b; add. Georg., 830a; Gen., 1025a.
[3] Cont. Theoph., 24d.
[4] Script. Incert., 1012b.
[5] Cont. Theoph., 2gb.
[6] Script. Incert., 1016b.
[7] Theoph., 1008c.
[8] In a later period Emperors were required to take oath at their coronation that they would defend orthodoxy. But this had not yet become customary.
[9] The authorities are themselves uncertain of what happened. Script. Incert. states that at the coronation a document was produced stating that no action would be taken against the Church nor any alteration permitted in its doctrines as defined by the Holy Fathers. " This the false monarch did not observe, but played the chameleon." Script. Incert., 1016c. But it is not clear that Leo ever signed this document. Cont. Theoph., 41c, says he deferred it μέχρις ἂν ἡ τῆς βασιλείας αὐτῷ τελείως ἀνάρρησις γένηται. Gen., 1021c, agrees ; so does *Vit. Niceph.*, 80a. It is only the less reliable authorities that definitely say that he signed. Leo Gramm., 1037b ; ps.-Sim., 665a ; add. Georg., 824a.
[10] ps.-Sim., 665b.

dynastic succession he saw that Procopia, the widow of the late Emperor, a woman of far greater parts than her husband, was consigned to the cloister.[1] Eustratius and Nicetas, the sons of the Emperor, were devoted to the same vocation. One or both of them were castrated, and Nicetas, who took the name of Ignatius, eventually became Patriarch of Constantinople.[2] The Bulgarian menace fully occupied the first eighteen months of Leo's reign. It was gradually lessened by the activity of Leo, and eventually passed away at the death of the great Bulgarian Czar Crumn. In the latter part of the second year of his reign Leo was discovered to be an Iconoclast.[3] It is possible that he held such views from conviction, as his Syro-Armenian origin might indicate, as well as his equivocal attitude towards the Patriarch's request for a declaration in support of orthodoxy at his coronation. On the other hand, there are strong indications that he adopted Iconoclasm merely as a policy. The revival of popular enthusiasm for the Isaurians before which the orthodox Michael had succumbed, gave Leo more than a hint what was the politic course. He is represented as arguing that only the Iconoclastic Emperors succeeded in founding a dynasty and had died full of honour.[4] He clearly intended to model himself upon the Isaurians, and changed the name of his son Symbat to Constantine with that end in view. The decrees of Nicæa had been mildly administered, and there were still active Iconoclasts in Constantinople.[5] A monk named Symbatios or Sabbatios [6] is alleged to have warned the Emperor that he would not reign long if he adhered to the gods of the She-lion, the Bacchanal, and the Destroyer (ταράξιος), that is, Irene and Tarasius. This looks like a legend. But we get on firm historical ground when we find him seeking advice from others. Leo himself had probably few convictions and little knowledge.[7] The advisers he sought were not " the proper authorities," [8] but three men

---

[1] Script. Incert., 1016d.

[2] Cont. Theoph., 33c, who says that Eustratius was castrated. Gen., 997a, says only Nicetas was so treated. Script. Incert., 1016d, says both.

[3] Script. Incert., 1024c ; Leo Gramm., 1040c.

[4] Script. Incert., 1024c.

[5] *Vit. Ignat., passim.*

[6] Cont. Theoph., 40c ; Gen., 1004c.

[7] τὸ ὄντως δαιμόνων εἴδωλον τὸ τῆς ἀμαθίας ἀνδράποδον τὸ τῆς σκιᾶς ἀφονώτερον. Cont. Theoph., 40c.   [8] *Ib.*

of Iconoclastic antecedents, conspicuous for their birth or learning, all of whom became successive Patriarchs of Constantinople. These were Theodotos Kassiteras, Antony, bishop of Syllæum, and John Hylilas. Theodotos's importance rested on his family connection. He was the son of a patrician, Michael Melissenus, whose sister had been the third wife of Constantine V.[1] He was a layman, popular and of amiable character, but almost entirely illiterate,[2] picturesquely described by George the Monk as " more dumb than a fish." [3] He may be regarded as the chief influence drawing Leo towards the Isaurians, of whom his birth made him a partisan. Through him the Emperor was brought into contact with an ecclesiastic of supple but acute mind, Antony, bishop of Syllæum. This man had had a varied career as teacher of grammar, lawyer, and schoolmaster, had fled to a monastery to " escape his crimes," adopted the name of Antony, became head of the monastery of the Metropolitans, " where he had lived carelessly with young monks and by some strange dispensation of God had been made bishop of Syllæum." [4] The third was the most brilliant of the group. This was John called Hylilas, said to signify the Forerunner (probably of Antichrist), and the Grammarian. He was a member of the family of the Morocharzamii, probably of Armenian origin.[5] His great learning in what would now be called natural science won him the reputation of sorcery, and he was reputed a worker with the devil.[6] He was in minor orders, holding the office of reader at the church of the Palace. Leo is said to have promised him the Patriarchate as the price of his adhesion to an Iconoclastic policy,[7] but it is more probable that he exerted an active and unbought influence upon Leo. For it is said that he read significantly

---

[1] Scr. Incert., 1036a.

[2] μηδὲ παιδευθέντα τῇ γραφῇ ἀλλ᾽ ἢ ἐξ ὀλίγου τινός. *Ib.*

[3] Georg. Mon., II, p. 777.

[4] Scr. Incert., 1025c. It is improbable that he is to be identified with the Antony living κατὰ τὰς Μαυριανοῦ ἔμβολον to whom Theodotos brought the Emperor to receive the promise of a long reign like Leo the Isaurian, if he adopted Iconoclasm. Cont. Theoph., 41a ; Gen., 1005b.

[5] His brother bore the Armenian name of Arsaber. Cont. Theoph., 172.

[6] Scr. Insert., 1025a. He is the one Iconoclast treated with unfailing respect by Theodore Studites. Cf. *Ep.*, II, 168, 194, and 212.

[7] Scr. Incert., 1025a.

in church the words of Isa. xl. 18, 19 : " To whom have ye compared the Lord, and with what likeness have ye compared him ? Has not the artificer made an image or the goldsmith having melted gold gilt it over and made it a similitude ? " " Understand these words, o Emperor," he continued, " and know the truth, which the prophet has revealed unto us. Follow the worship he describes and confound not thyself with overmuch reverences to similitudes." [1] To the advice of these three Leo submitted. [2] That he himself was a complete freethinker with no religious convictions at all is not quite so certain. It is said that he did not even think it proper to mention the name of God at all. [3] But the statement is made in reference to a treaty Leo ratified with the Bulgarians, using the pagan ceremonies and eating their sacrifices. [4] While this points to a cynical disregard for Christian sentiment, it is not in itself decisive.

The bishop Antony was the last of the three to be brought into the counsels of the group. [5] The preliminary steps were taken at Pentecost, 814. In July Antony was introduced and examined, probably as an ecclesiastical expert on the authority for image-worship. He admitted that it was never mentioned in Scripture but was an ancient tradition. " Unless," said the Emperor, " the Gospel and the Apostle definitely say, Ye shall worship my image, I do not accept such worship." [6] The three then set to work to examine the libraries of the monasteries for documentary evidence which would support Iconoclasm. As it was still necessary to proceed cautiously and avoid rousing the suspicion of the monks, they gave out that they were searching for information bearing on alleged warnings the Emperor had received that he had not long to reign. [7]

---

[1] Cont. Theoph., 45c ; Gen., 1009c.
[2] συμμίσταις . . . ἀσέλγεσιν ἑαυτὸν κατεπίστευσεν. Georg. Mon., II, p. 782.
[3] Cont. Theoph., 44d.
[4] Vit. Niceph., 144a.
[5] A curious and unsupported statement is made by *Ep. ad Theoph.* that John fell ill, sought pardon of the Patriarch, and the Emperor had to fall back on the advice of Antony. Antony also compromised with the Patriarch by signing a statement supporting images. This he recanted in the presence of the Emperor, and was anathematised by a council of the Patriarch at which 270 bishops were present. *Op. cit.*, 372d–373b. These incidents may conceivably have occurred in the early part of Leo's reign. But the *Ep. ad Theoph.* is a dubious authority. The incidents may well have been produced to whitewash John, for whom the *Ep.* appears to have an affection.
[6] Scr. Incert., 1028a. 　　　　　　　　　[7] *Ib.*

Eventually the discovery of the records of the Iconoclastic Council of 753 put them on the scent, and they were able to collect a variety of points suitable for popular propaganda.[1] By December, 814, they had made their case complete. The time was now ripe to approach the Patriarch Nicephorus. The Emperor explained to him that image-worship was causing grave offence to the people,[2] it being held the cause of the pagan military successes. He suggested, therefore, either some modification of orthodox practice[3] or some decisive explanation of image-worship which would compensate for the absence of scriptural support. The Emperor proposed a very mild policy. He would remove the pictures in positions low enough to permit gross acts of adoration, accepting those in higher positions as useful illustrations of Christianity.[4] The Patriarch declared that the authority of the Holy Spirit forbade any concession. The Emperor then suggested a conference between the Patriarch and John and Antony, who had discovered in the records authority definitely hostile to image-worship.[5] The exact sequence of events from this point becomes difficult to follow. But it is abundantly clear that Leo proceeded carefully and acted temperately. The Patriarch found himself almost entirely in the hands of Theodore Studites,[6] with whom formerly he had been at variance. It is at first sight a matter of surprise to find that Nicephorus, who had hitherto not hesitated to compromise for the sake of the Emperor, now took a strong stand. He belonged to the moderate party, but his writings show that on the image-question he had definite convictions. By that more than by the influence of Theodore we must probably explain the apparent hardening of the Patriarch's opinion. To be a moderate man does not mean to have no convictions at all.

---

[1] Scr. Incert., 1025b.

[2] *Ib.* 1028b. ὁ λαὸς σκανδαλίζεται. λαός probably means the army.

[3] ποίησον οἰκονομίαν εἰς τὸν λαὸν καὶ τὰ χαμηλὰ περιέλωμεν. *Ib.* The last phrase might mean no more than "remove trifling difficulties," but the *Ep. of Michael II* to Lewis the Pious (p. 479) and Theodore, *Antirrh.*, II, 352d, show that it is intended literally. The compromise Leo proposed was the removal of pictures low enough for the more extravagant acts of devotion.

[4] Imagines de humilioribus locis auferri . . . (of the others) ut ipsa pictura pro scriptura haberetur. *Ep. Mich. ad Lud.*, p. 479 (ed. Werminghoff).

[5] Scr. Incert., 1028c. Up to this point *Vit. Niceph.* is vague and ill-informed. It now becomes more exact.   [6] *Vit. Theod. St.*, 184d.

Matters hastened now to a crisis. The Emperor harped on the troubled conscience of many souls, and the indefiniteness of the authority upon which images stood. The orthodox party with the Patriarch at their head deprecated opening a question which a Council had settled, simply to satisfy frivolous objections.[1] They realised the necessity of organising their forces. They held an all-night vigil of prayer against the Emperor's policy, and some time later convened a meeting at which they pledged themselves to the support of the images.[2] The Emperor still worked for a policy of moderation. Soldiers stoned the celebrated Christ on the Chalce Gate, using very offensive language. The Emperor appealed to the people that the image should be taken down to protect it from such abuse. This was done. But clearly the Emperor gives the impression of trying to preserve the peace, though the chronicler accuses him of being the instigator of the attack on the image.[3] More conferences took place between the Emperor and the Patriarch. What part the advisers of the latter were permitted to take in the conferences is difficult to estimate. Some documents represent Theodore Studites as the principal spokesman, but it may be held as at least improbable that Theodore played openly the exact rôle in which he is depicted.[4] He was without doubt the power behind the Patriarch. The sentiments put in his mouth

---

[1] Scr. Incert., 1028d. Nicephorus was insistent on loyalty to the Council of Nicæa, and that seems to be the basis of his position. *Apol. Min.*, 840c–841b; *Apol. pro. S. Imag.*, 597a.

[2] Scr. Incert., 1029bd; *Vit. Niceph.*, 84c.

[3] Scr. Incert., 1029bd. It was the identical image removed by the Isaurians and bore an inscription : ἣν καθεῖλε πάλαι Λέων ὁ δεσπόζων ἐνταῦθα ἀνεστήλωσεν Εἰρήνη. *Ib.* 1029c.

[4] Neither Scr. Incert. nor *Vit. Niceph.* introduces spokesmen other than the Patriarch. Except the *Vit. Theod. St.* it is only the inferior authorities that bring Theodore into the first place, Georg. Mon., Leo Gramm., add. Georg. and ps.-Sim. The pith of the arguments given to Theodore except in the *Vit.* is extracted from St. John of Damascus. Leo Gramm. and ps.-Sim. add another element of uncertainty in the presence of Euthymius of Sardis. His active connection with the Iconoclastic outburst is placed by the better authority of Cont. Theoph. in the reign of Theophilus. He was a survivor of the Council of Nicæa, but his movements in the reign of Leo can be accounted for. See below, p. 174. In the pictures of the preliminary discussions drawn by the chroniclers we have probably an example of the tendency to bring all the principal actors together and set their opinions one against the other, preferring dramatic to historic truth. Cf. *Vit. Steph.*, *supra*, and *Vit. Niceph.*, 29, where the principal bishops who subsequently suffered are made actors in a preliminary debate with the Emperor.

are characteristic, whether he delivered them exactly in the circumstances alleged or not. The position of the orthodox was that to give up the images was to give up the Faith. The speech assigned to Theodore [1] recapitulates the familiar arguments, much of which touched points not directly raised by the Emperor, such as idolatry and the appeal to the Old Testament. None of them answered the one question which really was asked, What was the authority for the use of images? The nearest Theodore's argument approaches the problem is when he says that for above 800 years the custom of representing Christ has been observed. " Christianity and images have advanced together. It is this ancient custom you are attempting to destroy at a moment's caprice." [2] After all, Theodore is made to say, discussion was futile. Dissent from the Emperor's view inevitably meant punishment. The only course for those in disagreement with him was to follow the old custom of treating heretics and separate from their communion. His last word was that spiritual things belong to priests and doctors, the Emperor's sphere was civil administration. The Apostle had said, God has appointed in the Church first apostles and so forth. He made no mention of Emperors. [3] The narrative proceeds : " Do you then, said the Emperor, cast me out of the Church ? Not I, said Theodore, but the apostle, the friend of the bridegroom. Indeed you have anticipated him and cast yourself out. If you would return, take your stand with us who proclaim the truth." [4] After the dismissal of the conference the Emperor forbade meetings of the monks and ordered them to cease from preaching. Theodore's defiant reply was that he would be silenced only if his tongue were cut out. [5] Even in this account it is easy to

---

[1] *Vit. Theod.*, I, 176 sqq

[2] *Ib.* 177d. In add. Georg., 828a, this argument is attributed to Euthymius of Sardis.

[3] *Vit. Theod.*, I, 181d–184a. The same sentiment is attributed to Theodore by Georg. Mon., p. 779 ; Leo Gramm., 1040d ; add. Georg., 828b. The sentiment is certainly Theodore's (*Ep.*, I, 16), but it is uncertain whether he expressed it in an open conference. It is taken verbally from Jo. Dam., *Or.*, II, 1296c *sqq*.

[4] *Vit. Theod.*, I, 184a.

[5] *Ib.* 184c. With this we should connect Theod. St., *Ep.*, II, 2. The emperor induced some of the abbots to sign a statement promising not to communicate with other monks.

see the moderation of the Emperor.[1] As an account of events this story of Theodore can only be regarded with suspicion. We return to firmer historical ground in following the tentative dealings of Leo with the Patriarch. At Christmas, 814, the Patriarch appealed to the Emperor not to violate the Church, and suggested that his own removal might ease the situation.[2] The Emperor, like a chameleon,[3] that is striving after moderation, deprecated the expulsion of a Patriarch. He made a great effort to secure a compromise. He declared that he only wanted some investigation of the problem to satisfy public opinion. For his own part he believed what the Church believed, giving colour to his words by publicly venerating a crucifix.[4] At the Christmas service it was remarked that Leo venerated the picture of the Nativity on the corporal (ἐνδυτή), but at the Epiphany he avoided doing so.[5] The evident moderation of the emperor won over many of the bishops, in spite of their oath to maintain the faith.[6] Through these bishops he made a final appeal to the Patriarch, threatening now to depose him. The Patriarch only answered that he was bound by the decrees of the Fathers (*i.e.* of the Council of Nicæa). The Patriarch at this point fell seriously ill, and the Emperor charitably waited for the issue of his illness.[7] By the beginning of Lent, 815, the Patriarch was recovering, and his persistence provoked something like a riot in the quarter whence the opposition to images came—the army. A body of soldiers tried to break into the Patriarch's house, and an outrage was only prevented by the patrician and ex-consul Thomas interfering and securing the gates. There can be little question, whatever the explanation of the chroniclers, that on the available evidence, the Emperor did all in his power to protect the Patriarch against popular violence.[8] The Patriarch was now a prisoner in his own

[1] ps.-Sim., 669d, says that after the conference Euthymius of Sardis had his jaw broken and was flogged until he fainted. The unsupported evidence of ps.-Sim. has little value.
[2] Scr. Incert., 1032a. The debates may have taken place not before Christmas, 814, but between Epiphany and Lent, 815.
[3] ps.-Sim., 664b, makes the foolish suggestion that Leo was called chameleon because of his small stature.
[4] Scr. Incert., 1032a.   [5] *Ib.* 1032b.
[6] *Ib.* 1032c. *Vit. Niceph.*, 81a, puts the adhesion of the bishops earlier, and attributes their conviction to bribery and force.
[7] Scr. Incert., 1033a.   [8] *Ib.*

house in charge of the patrician Thomas. The Emperor and his advisers communicated with him in " a halting letter," asking him to appear and answer the case that now was directed not at image-worship but at himself. At first he refused even to admit the bearers of the letter, but at last did so in deference to the patrician who was guarding him. The deputation stated plainly that Nicephorus must choose between some concession to the Iconoclastic party and deposition. He answered that he was quite willing to appear before the bishops of Rome, Alexandria, Antioch, or Jerusalem, but not before a pack of wolves. Nicephorus himself now realised that he must abdicate,[1] while Thomas strongly advised the Emperor to have the Patriarch removed in the interests of all concerned. Being too ill to walk, Nicephorus was carried in a litter to the Forum Melii, " in order," says the chronicler, " that some of the soldiers might kill him." This is a self-evident misstatement, for he goes on to say that it was pitch dark and every one was asleep. The truth was that the Patriarch was removed secretly to protect him from violence. He was taken to the Acropolis, put into a boat, and brought across the water to Chrysopolis (Scutari).[2]

In the morning the Emperor (or in the chronicler's phrase, " the son of perdition ") held a silentium in which he explained that the Patriarch had withdrawn because he could not give any reasonable defence of image-worship. He asked that a new Patriarch might be appointed. It was the Emperor's wish to appoint John Hylilas the Grammarian, whose profound intellect and Armenian connections had commended him to the Emperor But the patricians objected that John was a young and obscure man of lowly birth. That their objections carried weight shows that the Emperor was pursuing a policy of others rather than one of his own. He submitted to their wishes and chose Theodotos, the son of Michael Melissenus, whom we have already had occasion to notice. Theodotus was not only a married layman, but an ex-guardsman of some prowess and a notable trencherman.[3] He was the type of bishop

---

[1] *Vit. Niceph.*, 121–124.
[2] Scr. Incert., 1033.
[3] *Ib.* 1033d. στρατιωτικῷ πέλυκι τῷ βουθοίνᾳ (Hercules) παραβαλλόμενον πρὸς μόνην τὴν γάστερα βλέποντα. *Vit. Niceph.*, 136a. τὸν ἀπὸ σπαθαρίων . . . καὶ τῆς θυμέλης τὴν προσηγορίαν ἐπειλήμμενον. add. Georg., 825d.

N

that was even more offensive to orthodoxy than his opinions. He signalised his accession to the Patriarchate by giving a banquet at which flesh meat predominated, and compelling clerics who had abstained from flesh since their youth, as well as bishops and monks (to whom it was canonically forbidden), to eat of it. Games, laughter, quips, and buffoonery were encouraged in the Patriarch's house.[1] So far as facts allow us to see beneath the surface, it would seem that the leaders of the second Iconoclastic movement were much inferior to those of the first. The Emperor Leo V had none of the sincere attachment of Leo III and Constantine V to the movement. With him it was largely a matter of policy. Apart from John the Grammarian there were no intellects in the party comparable with Constantine of Nacolia and others of the earlier period. Allowing for the exaggeration of a partisan, we shall be forced to admit that Nicephorus has given an apt if rhetorical description of the personnel of the Iconoclastic party of his day.[2] We may pass over the 150 epithets in which he derides them and be content with his description of their more particular qualities. " They never mention resurrection or judgment. They have no consciousness of sin, never ask God's forgiveness, and take no admonition for their soul's salvation. What is wrong with my soul ? say they when one advises them of what is needful." " Many of them are simply gangs of loafers looking for a drink.[3] Large numbers of them are ex-soldiers, either cashiered for misdemeanours or too old for the service, with a fanciful attachment to the memory of Constantine V." [4]

The orthodox leaders did not submit quietly. It was in the last weeks of Lent that the Patriarch was removed. On Palm Sunday Theodore and the Studite monks went in procession round their monastery carrying the sacred pictures and singing, " Thy undefiled image we venerate, good Lord." [5] On Easter Day the new Patriarch was enthroned. Immediately after, probably in Easter week, a Council of the Church was called. Among those invited were Theodore and other heads of monasteries. They

---

[1] Scr. Incert., 1036a.
[2] Niceph., *Antirrh.*, III, 489a *sqq.*
[3] *Ib.* 492a. περισκοποῦσι συχνῶς ἔνθα τε πότοι καὶ συσσίτια γίνονται.
[4] *Ib.* 493a.
[5] *Vit. Theod. St.*, 185c.

replied to the Patriarch in a joint letter [1] drawn up by Theodore, in which they protested against any Council meeting without the true Patriarch Nicephorus or attempting to abrogate the decision of Nicæa ; they further declared that they had behind them the see of Peter.

The synod might be considered a local council of the Patriarch of Constantinople,[2] who presided, supported by the Emperor's son Symbat.[3] On the other hand, the biographer of Nicephorus understood it to be intended to be œcumenical, for he repudiates it on the ground that it was without representatives of the apostolic sees, " as the law of the Church requires." [4] Moreover, its whole aim was to interfere with the decisions of a Council admittedly œcumenical and restore those of another for which the Iconoclasts claimed the same title. Yet there is no indication that this synod expected or attempted to make its decision effective outside the jurisdiction of the Patriarch of Constantinople. It is just to say that at this period there was accepted what neither heretic nor orthodox had visualised before, Constantinople as an independent local church legislating without regard for the rest of Christendom. It was another great step towards the separation of East and West.

The number of bishops present is unknown, and the Acts of the Council have not been preserved. The abbots of Theodore's party refused the invitation to be present. It may be inferred that other monks were invited and accepted. The Council was of brief duration, only two sessions being held.[5] The first session drew up an oath against images and read and confirmed the proceedings of the Council held by Constantine V at Blachernæ.[6] On the following day the bishops who had refused to commit themselves to the Emperor's opinion were brought in and invited to abjure. Their number is unknown. They refused and were trampled on, probably metaphorically, though as they were then consigned to prison they may

---

[1] Theod. St., *Ep.*, II, 1.
[2] The Emperor Michael calls it so, *concilia localia. Ep. ad Lud.*, p. 479.
[3] Scr. Incert., 1036b.
[4] *Vit. Niceph.*, 136b.   [5] *Ib.* 140ab.
[6] *Ib.* ; Scr. Incert., 1036c. It really was a Council to confirm that of 753. Theod. St., *Ep.*, II, 72. Cf. *Ep.*, II, 15. In Theod., 465a, it is called " the Council summoned to confirm that of Blachernæ."

have been subjected to actual ill-treatment.[1] As the dinner-hour was approaching, which the biographer of Nicephorus implies weighed heavily with the Council, a priest of florid eloquence [2] congratulated the Council, and they adjourned. After dinner they reassembled to sign the Definition. All did so, though some disagreed with it.[3] Felicitations to the Emperors and anathemas on the lights of the Church were pronounced by the eloquent cleric already mentioned. The biographer reflects that retributive justice waited upon him, for he was subsequently afflicted with dumbness.[4] The Definition of the Council has been recovered by D. Serruys from an unprinted treatise of Nicephorus preserved in the Bibliothèque Nationale, Paris.[5] In a slightly condensed form it reads as follows :

" The late holy Emperors, Constantine and Leo, considering the proper observance of orthodox belief to be the best public security, sought the honour of Him by Whom they received sovereignty. They summoned a large assembly of spiritual fathers and godly-minded bishops, and condemned the unauthorised and untraditional, not to say useless, practice of making and worshipping images ; preferring worship in spirit and in truth. This synod established and ratified the inspired doctrine of the holy fathers, and following the six Holy Œcumenical Councils, issued canons. Consequently for many years the Church of God remained tranquil, guarding her subjects in peace until the sovereignty passed from the hands of men to a woman, and the Church of God was distressed by a woman's weakness. For at the advice of ignorant bishops she convoked an injudicious assembly and set up the doctrine of painting with material substance the incomprehensible Son and Word of God incarnate. She also laid down in unguarded

---

[1] Theod., 465a.
[2] ἀνθηροφώνου κληρικοῦ προλογίζοντος. *Vit. Niceph.*, 140a.
[3] ὅρου καὶ τοῖς παροῦσιν εἰ καὶ μὴ πᾶσιν ἀρέσαντος. *Ib.*
[4] *Ib.* 140c.
[5] D. Serruys, Les actes de concile iconoclaste de l'an. 815, in *Mélanges d'archéologie et d'histoire.* 1903, vol. xxiii, 345–351, and résumé in Hefele-Leclerq, III (ii), app. iv, 1217–1221. The work of Nicephorus is in Grk. MS., 1250, *Bibl. Nat.*, and was fully described by Banduri in *Fabricius*, vol. VI. It is entitled : ἔλεγχος καὶ ἀνατροπὴ τοῦ ἀθέσμου καὶ ἀορεστοῦ καὶ ὄντως ψευδωνύμου ὅρου τοῦ ἐκκτεθέντος παρὰ τῶν ἀποστησάντων τῆς καθολικῆς καὶ ἀποστολικῆς ἐκκλησίας. It refutes the Councils both of 753 and 815, and the patristic quotations of the Iconoclasts.

fashion that the all holy Theotokos and their fellows, the saints, should be represented in the form of dead figures, and worshipped, defying the vital doctrine of the Church. She defiled our service of worship and decreed that what is due to God should be paid to the lifeless stuff of images ; and these images in her folly she was reckless enough to describe as filled with divine grace, and enjoining the burning of candles and offering of incense, she enforced adoration of them and led astray the simple. But those who offered adoration to lifeless images allowed the folly of their predecessors to lead again to the same heresies ; they either circumscribed in the image that which is uncircumscribable, or they divided the human nature from the divine, correcting one error by another ; in avoiding the irrational they fell into the irrational. For this reason carefully avoiding such doctrine we ostracise from the Catholic Church the unauthorised and illegal manufacture of pseudonymous images ; not led by uncritical opinion but as a just and reasoned judgment we repudiate the adoration of images uncritically defined by Tarasius ; we annul his synod on the ground that it permitted an excessive honour to pictures, in lighting of candles and lamps, offering of incense, and in fact all the reverence that belongs to divine worship. We whole-heartedly accept the holy Council which assembled at Blachernæ in the Church of the Immaculate Virgin under the late pious emperors, Constantine and Leo, as based on the teaching of the fathers ; we keep its decisions intact and decree the making of images to be neither worshipful nor useful. We refrain from speaking of them as idols as there are degrees of evil."

The moderation of this Council reflects the moderation of the emperor. The theology of the period we shall discuss in detail later. The charge of idolatry and the absolute prohibition of images have been entirely abandoned. While forbidding superstitious practices, the Council permitted pictures placed in high positions, so long as lights and incense were not offered before them.[1]

A number of important persons, both clerical and lay, refused to accept the Council's decision. Many of them withdrew to Rome.[2] The Iconoclastic oath was applied,

---

[1] Cf. Michael, *ep. ad Lud.*, p. 479.
[2] *Ib.; Vit. Methodii*, 1248a.

and failure to take it opened the doors of the law courts. In considering the persecution under Leo V it is necessary to remember that the situation was different from the days of Constantine Copronymus. Then Iconoclasm had counted in its ranks most of the intelligence and energy of the empire. Now the advantage lay heavily with the orthodox. In the earlier period a distinct attempt was made to press the Iconoclastic cause throughout the empire, though it apparently made less and less impression the further it advanced from Constantinople. In the second period, though the *Life of Methodius* declares that the whole world subject to the Imperial city was affected,[1] all the records go to show that active measures were confined to Constantinople itself. Constantinople, too, counted for much less than in the days of the Isaurians.

Every effort was made to secure the general conformity of the clergy by appealing to their intelligence rather than by using force,[2] and in this policy John the Grammarian was the principal and most successful agent.[3] Of the secular clergy of Constantinople every one conformed, except a certain Gregory.[4] The bishops proved more obstinate.[5] Their great strength lay in the resistance of the exiled Patriarch Nicephorus. " Few have remained faithful," wrote Theodore to the Patriarch of Jerusalem, " but among them, thank God, is our High Priest." [6] The most conspicuous of those to follow the lead given by the Patriarch was Euthymius, formerly bishop of Sardis. He had been one of the leading members of the Council of Nicæa. In the reign of Nicephorus he had been deposed and exiled for protecting an orphan girl from the attentions of an Imperial strategus.[7] He appears in some of the chronicles taking an important part in the preliminary negotiations between Leo and the Patriarch.[8] Whether this is strictly accurate or not, he clearly was a confessor of

[1] *Vit. Methodii*, 1248a. Cf. Theod. St., *Ep.*, II, 15.
[2] Niceph., *Apol. pro S. Imag.*, 569a.
[3] Theod. St., *Ep.*, 79 (Mai) ; *Epp.*, II, 9, 30.
[4] *Ib. Ep.*, 91 (Mai).
[5] Niceph., *Apol.*, 569c.
[6] Theod. St., *Ep.*, II, 15. Cf. II, 14.
[7] Act. Sanct. Mart. II, 73. See *Echos d'Orient*, V, p. 157. That he was no longer bishop of Sardis is supported by the fact that Theodore Studites refers to a John of Sardis, apparently the bishop. *Ep.*, II, 108.
[8] *Vid. supra*, p. 166.

some note, and is hailed as such by Theodore, together with John, who may well be his successor in the see of Sardis.[1] He was flogged and exiled. The only recorded bishop upon whom capital punishment was inflicted was Theophilus of Ephesus.[2] Many bishops were exiled, Joseph of Thessalonica, the uncle of Theodore,[3] Simeon of Lesbos,[4] Theophylactus of Nicomedia,[5] Ignatius of Miletus.[6] Some were imprisoned, Æmilian of Cyzicus,[7] Michael of Synnada,[8] and probably others. The most curious case was that of an unnamed bishop of Chios. He had joined the Iconoclasts and then repented. He was taken in hand by Theodore, who refused to meet him until he had resigned his see and done penance. Nothing shows the power of Theodore so vividly as this fact, that he actually could put a bishop under discipline and say, " We submitted him to the fit penance." [9] The bulk of the bishops, of course, sided with the Emperor. None of them were figures of importance. A few titles are preserved by Theodore, the bishops of Smyrna, Demetrias, and Chrysopolis, the first of whom is called " very impious," and Gregory, metropolitan of an unnamed see.[10]

The struggle, however, was between the Emperor and the monastic houses. It was the monks under Theodore who led the opposition before and after the Patriarch's deposition. Theodore himself was one of the first to fall after the emperor had exhausted all his powers of conciliation. He had time to order his monks to disperse and seek safety separately before he was himself taken into custody and removed to confinement at Metopa on the borders of Bithynia.[11] Being too accessible to members of his party he was removed to more distant quarters at Bonita in the Anatolic theme, but he was still able even from prison to direct the orthodox campaign. He wrote letters to the faithful, exhorting them and advising them. He wrote to the three Eastern Patriarchs and to the Pope, calling on them to come to the aid of the Faith. He suffered greatly in prison, says his biographer, chiefly because he

[1] Theod. St., *Ep.*, II, 108. Cf. Act. David., 229.
[2] Theod. St., *Ep.*, II, 41, 70.   [3] *Ib. Ep.*, 1 (Mai).
[4] Act. David., 227.   [5] Synax. Eccl. Cple., 519.
[6] Theod. St., *Ep.*, 4, 45 (Mai).   [7] Syn. Eccl. Cple., 875.
[8] *Ib.* 703.   [9] Theod. St., *Ep.*, II, 183, (Mai) 282.
[10] *Ib.* II, 215 ; Mai, 290, 104, 79.   [11] *Vit. Theod. St.*, 188d.

did not cease his propaganda. Three times he was sentenced to flogging, but on at least one occasion his gaoler, either from sympathy or for a bribe, refrained from carrying out the sentence. His confinement, however, was not solitary, for he had with him a faithful brother Nicolaus. He was eventually removed to Smyrna.[1] A persecution that could treat the leader of the opposition so leniently as Theodore was treated was far different even from the attack of Constantine V. The experience of Theodore was typical of the Emperor's policy towards the monks. John the Grammarian devoted himself to winning them to the emperor's cause,[2] and met with great success. The earlier resistance of the monasteries was broken down by the year 817 and large numbers of monks had joined the Iconoclasts.[3] Theodore himself admits not only that many monks joined the enemy but that some of them, like Nectarius, became active agents of the party.[4] A former Studite monk, Leontius, took sides with the Iconoclasts and was made head of the house of Sacccudion.[5] So that it is clear no attack was made on monasticism as such. Some abbots made a formal compliance, secretly maintaining the images. It did not satisfy Theodore. He writes to the hegoumenos Eustratius in severe terms :

" . . . The reports of credible authorities have caused me great pain. I speak of your fictitious subscription. Pardon me if I speak plainly. There must have been some reason if the Imperial officers arrested you and then left you unpunished, or rather let you go free. . . . Do not tell me that your churches have been saved, your pictures kept intact, and the name of our holy Patriarch kept in the Office. That is what others claim who have been caught in the trap. These things could *not* have been kept except at the price of betrayal of the True Faith. What use is it to preserve lifeless buildings and make useless ourselves who are in name and fact the Temple of God ? . . . Perish the whole world of things ; of more account is the certain damnation of soul which is the portion of every pre-varicator." [6]

---

[1] *Vit. Theod. St.*, 189-204.   [2] Thcod. St., *Ep.*, II, 30.
[3] *Ib.* II, 14 ; Mai, 2.   [4] *Ib.* Mai, 10.
[5] *Ib.* II, 31. Among those who temporarily conformed was Nicetas, abbot of Medikios. *Vit. Nicet.*, p. xxvi.   [6] Theod. St., *Ep.*, II, 106.

Monastic life was disorganised but not destroyed.[1] It was upon the monks that the severest measures fell, not because they were monks but because they were the boldest of the orthodox party. Many followed Theodore's bidding and fled, either escaping beyond the reach of the Imperial authority or remaining in hiding.[2] Theodore was particularly careful to warn the orthodox not to throw their lives away, though the Emperor had declared in the early stages of the controversy that the orthodox were deliberately seeking the glory of martyrdom to give credit to their cause.[3] Upon those who persistently refused the overtures of the Emperor's party after the Council of 815 the civil law would be put into operation as heretics according to the terms of the Council. It was here that the resistance produced its largest number of confessors and even some who might claim to be martyrs. In December 816, Thaddeus, a Studite monk, sentenced to 130 blows of the lash, died after the completion of the sentence.[4] Another of the brethren, James, also died in similar circumstances.[5] while a third, Photinus, died in exile, though not from any recorded ill-usage.[6] Others who survived flogging or imprisonment were Makarios of Pelecete,[7] John, abbot of Katharoimon,[8] Hilarion, abbot of Dalmatos,[9] John, abbot of Psicha,[10] and Arcadius, a monk.[11] It is difficult to interpret otherwise than as exaggeration the statement Theodore makes to the Patriarch of Alexandria :[12] " Some have departed, martyrs to the Lord, after being beaten with rods. Some have been sewn in sacks and drowned, as has been related by those who saw them." [13] The simple facts seem to be that the only lives lost in the attack of Leo V were the monks who died under the lash.

The treatment of the historian Theophanes may be taken

[1] Theod. St., *Ep.*, II, 66, 107, 131, 147. [2] *Ib.* II, 44.
[3] *Ib.* and *Vit. Theod. St.*, 181b. [4] Theod. St., *Ep.*, II, 5 ; Mai, 116.
[5] *Ib.* II, 100 ; Mai, 115. [6] *Ib.* ; Mai, 280.
[7] *Vit. Macar.* [8] Act. Sanct. Ap. III.
[9] *Ib.* Jun. I. [10] *Ib.* May VI.
[11] Theod. St., *Ep.*, II, 46. [12] *Ib.* II, 14.
[13] This is stated again by the *Vit. Niceph.*, 141c. It is perhaps explained by a statement in *Vit. Theoph.*, p. 23, ἔστιν ὅτε καὶ νυκτὶ θαλάττῃ παραπεμπόμενοι, the simple meaning of which is that they were deported at night by boat. The same allegation of drowning was made against Constantine V with the same absence of evidence.

as an example of the usual treatment given to monks.
Theophanes, though a man of humble mind, was a person
of note in the Church. The Emperor invited him to join
his party, offering him every advantage for himself, his
monastery, and his friends. For himself, he answered, he
had wanted nothing when young and was not likely to
want anything now he was old and sick unto death, his
monastery and friends would be God's care, who was a
power greater than kings and princes. Theophanes was
handed over to the persuasions of " the chief dialectician
or rather magician " (*i.e.* John), but he remained un-
impressed.[1] The monks of Theophanes' monastery at
Sigriana, near Cyzicus, were dispersed. Theophanes was
imprisoned and suffered greatly owing to the ravages of
kidney disease by which his body was already exhausted.
After two years he was removed to Samothrace, where
twenty-three days later he died, probably early in 818.[2]
The treatment of Theophanes shows how persistent were
the efforts to bring over the monks to the Iconoclastic side.
Those who refused were segregated. But there was nothing
like a systematic suppression of monasticism, as the record
of Leontius already quoted shows. Women in the religious
life were involved as well as men. It is probably such that
the *Life of Nicephorus* declares were publicly stripped
naked, racked and beaten.[3] Theodore refers to two
instances where women inmates of monasteries were
flogged, a number at Nicæa, and thirty in another place.[4]
But the orthodox monastery of which the head was
Euphrosyne, daughter of Constantine VI, and later wife
of Michael II, was not molested.[5] Other sisters were
exiled or deprived of their property.[6] Numbers of the
laity also suffered, both men and women. The patrician
Irene was flogged.[7] For a long time at the beginning of
the movement the only layman implicated was an official
named Gregory, who was confined to the palace.[8] At a
later date Eustratius, a physician, was deprived of part of

[1] *Vit.*, II, Theoph., p. 24.
[2] The first *Life of Theophanes* affirms that Theophanes was given 300
lashes on each of two successive days (p. 12). This detail is omitted in the
second life (attributed to Nicephorus Sceuophylax of Blachernæ), an altogether
more sober account.
[3] *Vit. Niceph.*, 141c.   [4] Theod. St., *Ep.*, II, 91 and 59.
[5] *Ib.* II, 177.   [6] *Ib.*; Mai, 23, 222, 79, 70, 71, 165.
[7] *Ib.* II, 68. Cf. Mai, 148, 270, 16.   [8] *Ib.* II, 55 ; Mai, 185.

his income for refusing to eat with a leading Iconoclast.[1] The ex-consul Thomas (who is probably to be identified with the protector of the Patriarch Nicephorus) was exiled.[2] Officers in the army apparently forced their men to commit themselves by joining in chants with Iconoclasts and eating food they had blessed.[3]

The pictures themselves were removed from the churches and burnt. Sacred vessels embossed with figures were scraped.[4] Theodore even says that altars were overthrown.[5] The records, however, are extremely meagre, and the attitude of the next Emperor, Michael, implies that many pictures were undisturbed.[6] There is great exaggeration in a statement of one chronicler : " Those found in possession of images of Christ or of a saint were punished with dreadful penalties and death, and many noble and illustrious persons were murdered." [7] Iconoclasm pursued its end very cautiously, and there is not a single recorded instance of the infliction of capital punishment. An Iconoclastic Christianity was taught. " Their book is put into the hands of the teachers so that children are brought up in impiety." [8] A systematic watch for secret image-worship was kept, and something like an organised scheme of espionage developed. " Husband and wife fear each other for spies. Informers of all kinds are paid by the Emperor to look out for any one giving an opinion contrary to those established or owning an image or a book in which anything is said about images, or entertaining an exile or helping one of those imprisoned for the Lord. . . . Masters live in terror of their slaves." [9] The ancient hymns that mentioned images were disused and new ones of a heterodox character substituted.[10] The forces of the emperor's party were strengthened by the recall of clergy who had been expelled for canonical offences and by the restoration to communion of those under discipline.[11] The Emperor is said to have informed the bishops that they must regard him as the supreme ecclesiastical authority.[12] This is

---

[1] Theod. St., *Ep.*, Mai, 288. [2] *Ib.* I, 12.
[3] *Ib.* II, 174. [4] Script. Incert., 1036d ; *Vit. Niceph.*, 141a.
[5] Theod. St., *Ep.*, II, 15. [6] Mich., *Ep. ad Lud.*, *supra*.
[7] ps.-Sim., 672a ; Leo Gramm., 1041a.
[8] Theod. St., *Ep.*, II, 14. [9] *Ib.* Cf. Mai, 87 and 117.
[10] *Ib.* II, 15. [11] *Vit. Niceph.*, 141c ; Cont. Theoph., 48a.
[12] *Ib.* 48a ; Gen., 1024a.

probable. It was the attitude of many of the Emperors, though nowhere perhaps so unequivocally stated, and was the answer to the demand for ecclesiastical independence voiced by the Studite monks. A statement made in the *Continuation of Theophanes* that Leo V forbade the use of the title " Saint," [1] standing unsupported by any other authority, looks like a reminiscence of the earlier days.

The progress of the movement could never have shown signs of equalling that of the first period. Moreover, it was effectively countered by Theodore by means of a new feature which he introduced. He organised the opposition. The orthodox party was no longer a scattered body of people whose hearts failed them for loneliness. They were a drilled army lending each other moral courage and compelled to rise to their own highest ideals. Theodore imposed the strictest discipline upon the faithful. He permitted no compromise with heresy. We have noticed already the rigid penance imposed upon a bishop and the grave rebuke administered to an abbot. These were typical of a rule drawn up by Theodore as carefully as the rule of his house, and accepted apparently as readily by the faithful of all classes as if they had been his monks. Theodore imposed his will by moral force. He disclaimed all use of pressure, declaring that he was no more than a priest among his flock with no hierarchical pretensions. [2] But he laid down the sternest law. A priest (or even a deacon) convicted of subscription to Iconoclasm or of communion with Iconoclasts was forbidden to exercise his ministry or even was excommunicated. After penance he might be admitted to communion but not to the exercise of his ministerial functions except by a Council of the Church. He might bless and pray like a monk but not as a priest. [3] Any member of the Studite order who lapsed to the Iconoclasts and then returned was to be debarred from communion until the general restoration of orthodoxy except only *in articulo mortis*. Such were to be regarded not as mere heretics but as blasphemers who had denied the Lord's name on the principle that denial of the image passes to the original. [4] No orthodox person might enter an Icono-

[1] Cont. Theoph., 113a.
[2] Theod. St., *Ep.*, II, 152 ; Mai, 23.   [3] *Ib.* II, 152.
[4] *Ib.* II, 11. ἡ γὰρ τῆς εἰκόνος ἄρνησις ἐπὶ τὸ πρωτότυπον ἀναβαίνει. This is quite an illegitimate development of the celebrated sentence of St. Basil.

clastic church or officiate in one that had passed from them into orthodox hands unless express episcopal permission had been received.[1] The sacraments in no circumstances might be received from the hands of Iconoclasts. If baptism cannot be received from a clerk, it must be performed by a monk or even by an orthodox layman.[2] To increase access to priests, those ordained in Rome, Naples, Lombardy, and Sicily are to be accepted without letters testimonial.[3] The Iconoclastic Eucharist is invalid. It is not the Body of Christ. Nevertheless if inadvertently received it must not be spit out.[4] This advice is probably due to a report circulated that the Iconoclasts seized the orthodox, forcibly opened their mouths, and thrust the Host into them.[5] The simple act of eating with Iconoclasts required penance even though no subscription or communion was involved.[6] Anything like prevarication or reserve was sternly forbidden. An orthodox who says on being accused, I communicate (with the mental reservation " with the orthodox ") is a traitor and is liable to half the penalty of one who goes into communion with Iconoclasts. An orthodox person who swears that he will not venerate images or receive orthodox monks and then repents of his oath and does secretly the right thing shall be excommunicated for three years.[7] The official church of Constantinople was in schism.[8] Theodore appealed from it to the Patriarchs of Alexandria and Jerusalem,[9] above all to the Pope, as " having the first place of all," " the original source of orthodoxy." [10] The Iconoclasts by cutting themselves off from the head (*i.e.* the Pope) and the three other Patriarchs are cut off from Christ.[11] The Pope Paschal I took the matter up so far as to address to the Emperor a

---

[1] Theod. St., *Ep.*, II, 11. Cf. II, 219. [1] *Ib.* II, 24.
[3] ἀκήρυκτοι, *ib.* II, 215. It was a serious canonical offence for priests to leave their diocese without episcopal authority. Cf. Canon 20 of Chalcedon, Canon 17 of Quinisext, etc.
[4] Theod. St., *Ep.*, II, 197 and 24.
[5] *Ib.* II, 32. There is no confirmation of this. Mai, 165, refers to an ancient case of a monk, Matronus, who was forced to a heretical communion, but it was not apparently of the Iconoclasts.
[6] Theod. St., *Ep.*, II, 215. [7] *Ib.* II, 40.
[8] *Ib.* II, 8. He adds, " as it often is in the habit of being."
[9] *Ib.* II, 14 and 15. Probably also to Antioch though no letter survives. *Vit. Theod.*, 191d.
[10] *Ep.*, II, 12, 13 ; Mai, 192.
[11] *Ib.* II, 66.

letter setting out the old arguments in support of images.[1] The other Patriarchs seem to have displayed no particular interest. In a letter of some years later (circa 821)[2] Theodore appears to convey to Thomas, Patriarch of Jerusalem, a hint that he is not as active in his opposition to Iconoclasm as he might be. For five years the struggle went on. Theodore worked for the future, keeping up the morale of the orthodox. By the unflagging energy of his personality, his discipline, and his writings, he effectively prevented the thorough establishment of Iconoclasm that the Isaurians had achieved. A pamphleteer of equal ability, Nicephorus, published the series of writings impressive both in volume and argument to which the Iconoclasts apparently found silence the best answer.[3] The Emperor on his part was no doubt equally persistent. Punishments were inflicted on the recalcitrant. Tongues were cut out.[4] Property was confiscated. Nonconformists were delated by informers. Even foreign rulers (probably the Saracens) were warned of the character of the orthodox fugitives.[5]

The Iconoclastic campaign went on systematically until the death of Leo in 820. At the end of that year there lay

[1] The letter is of no great importance. Part of it has survived. See Mercati, G., *Note di Litteratura biblica e cristiana antica.* (Studi e testi 5.) Rome, 1901, pp. 227–235.

[2] *Ep.*, II, 121. After praising the support given by the Pope he says, οἷς δὲ τοῦτο ποιεῖν ἐξὸν οὔτιποῦ ποιήσασι τοὐναντίον δὲ οὐκ ἔχω λέγειν ὁ τάλας αἰδοῖ τοῦ τῆς μακαριότητος ἡμῶν ἀγγέλον ὅσον ἄν εἴη τὸ καταγόρημα.

[3] Nicephorus' earliest tract against the Iconoclasts is the *Apologeticus Minor,* in which he says it is now more than 120 years since the 6th General Council. That might be dated 813, before the exile of Nicephorus, 845c. In the *Apol. Major* he says that the second Council of Nicæa has been accepted for nearly 30 years (600a), which would date this treatise circa 817. The *Antirrhetici* show signs of broken composition. The earlier portions (1 and most of 2), which consists of a refutation of the work of Mammon, is not really completed. It ends abruptly at 340. It may have been written in Constantinople before the final attack on the orthodox. It was completed on different lines in exile. Only an approximate date, 810–820, can be suggested. The unprinted *Refutation of the Iconoclastic Councils* will be the latest of the polemical writings of Nicephorus. Theodore's anti-Iconoclastic writings have scarcely any indication of date. The letter to his father, Plato, on the veneration of images must be earlier than 812 if Plato is his uncle, the abbot, who died in that year. The *Seven Chapters against the Iconoclasts* is perhaps the skeleton framework for the three *Antirrhetici.* Both deal with the arguments of the period of 815, but no precise date can be fixed.

[4] This may be no more than a rhetorical expansion of Theodore's defiance of the emperor that he would have his tongue cut out before he would be silent. *Vit. Theod. St.,* 184c.

[5] Script. Incert., 1037a.

in prison charged with conspiracy a certain Michael, commander of the cohort of Imperial guards known as the excubitors. His execution had been fixed for Christmas Eve, but the Empress Theodosia dissuaded the Emperor from carrying out the sentence on the eve of his Christmas communion.[1] The postponement proved fatal. Michael was made aware of the situation by Theoktistos, who was allowed access to the prison to arrange for the admission of a priest as confessor.[2] With the connivance of this man Michael got his fellow-conspirators to act. Among them was the keeper of the Imperial Palace (ὁ τοῦ παλατίου παπίας). By him they were admitted into the palace disguised as priests. They ambushed the Emperor as he was going to service on Christmas morning in the Palace chapel.[3] Leo entered in the procession of clerks, for it was his custom to lead the singing, though he had an ugly voice and sang out of tune.[4] The Emperor defended himself with the altar cross, but was cut down and hacked to pieces in a place " where none of his predecessors had died." [5] So, says the chronicler, Michael was brought from prison, heavily chained, and exchanged his bonds for the imperial crown, according to the word of the Psalmist, " Heaviness may endure for a night, but joy cometh in the morning." [6] The corpse of the murdered Leo was buried in the island of Prote and his sons were made monks.[7] Leo had been a capable ruler, as even Nicephorus admitted. Impious as he was, says Genesios, he was absolutely devoted to the affairs of the State.[8] The mildness of his Iconoclastic policy in comparison with that of the Isaurians, coupled with the shortness of his reign and the strength and organisation of the opposition, rendered the new Iconoclasm a thing of slender root. Nor does there seem reason to accept the gloomy summary of Theodore : " What the old heretics never did against Christ is now being done by these men And Christ sleeps and the sea of unbelief rises bringing annihilation." [9]

---

[1] Cont. Theoph., 49a.   [2] *Ib.* 52b.
[3] Leo Gramm., 1041b ; Act. David, 229.
[4] Gen., 1012c ; Geo. Mon., II, 788.
[5] Geo. Mon., *loc. cit.* ; Leo Gramm., *loc. cit.* ; Cont. Theoph., 56b, does deplore the inappropriate scene of the murder.
[6] Leo Gr., 1041c ; ps.-Sim., 680d.   [7] Leo Gr., 1041c.
[8] Cont. Theoph., 44c ; Gen., 1009c.   [9] Theod. St., *Ep.*, II, 31.

CHAPTER X

THE THEOLOGY OF THE SECOND ICONOCLASTIC PERIOD

AUTHORITIES

(a) CONTEMPORARY

1. Theodore Studites. As before, Chap. VIII.
2. *Ep. ad. Theophilum.* As before, Chap. III.
3. Lives especially those of Nicephorus, Theophanes, and Theodore. As before.
4. *Ὄρος* of the Council of 815. See p. 172.
5. Letter of Pope Paschal I to Leo V. See p. 182.
6. Letter of Michael and Theophilus to Lewis the Pious. In M.G.H. Leges Sect. III, Vol. ii, part 2, ed. Werminghoff, pp. 475 *sqq.*
7. Nicephorus as before. Though Nicephorus is actually contemporary with this period he reflects the spirit of the age of the Isaurians and is of more importance for that period.

(b) MODERN

Walch, Schwarzlose, and Bury as before.

IN the second Iconoclastic period the theological problem on both sides had been greatly simplified. In more remote quarters the old crude arguments and precedents still circulated.[1] But among the protagonists on either side these have been tacitly modified. The accusation of idolatry is no longer pressed. "We refrain from speaking of images as idols," says the Council of 815, "because there are degrees of evil." On the Iconoclastic side discussion is focussed on :

(i) The authority for the practice of image-worship.

(ii) The attribution of divine grace to images and the consequent burning of lights and offering of incense before them.

(iii) The interpretation of the Incarnation that images of Christ imply.

---

[1] *Ep. ad. Theoph.* is an example of this.

On the orthodox side these points are met and considerable emphasis is laid on a new one, the independence of the spiritual authority and the primacy of the Roman see. Both sides are much nearer to each other than they had been in the earlier period. The distance separating a moderate image-worshipper like Nicephorus from a moderate Iconoclast like Michael II is very small. There are signs that the picture of our Lord is less in evidence and the pictures of saints and angels more. But the most marked feature is an inclination on each side to lean more heavily than ever upon authority, the Iconoclasts on the Council of 753, the orthodox on that of Nicæa.

The charge of idolatry has not entirely disappeared, but it has lost its sting. The decision of the Council of 815 shows that importance was not attached to it. The Emperor mentioned it at the beginning of his discussions with the Patriarch.[1] Pope Paschal was careful to note that the law against idolatry is a Jewish law with which Christians are not concerned.[2] Though Theodore glances at it [3] it plays little part in his argument. He diagnoses the change of attitude when he draws attention to a certain inconsistency which is now apparent in the Iconoclasts' position. After calling the image of Christ an idol, they are found admitting the picture to be a useful ornament serving the purposes of memorial and record, provided it is not an object of veneration. They are satisfied if the pictures are hung in high positions so that they may not be used for purposes of worship.[4]

The two purely theological questions at issue were the Incarnation and the nature of the relation of a picture to its original. The latter represented the development of the charge of idolatry. It was the real problem of image-worship. Was grace inherent in the picture? There is little doubt that the orthodox saw in symbols a quasi-magical power. We have already had occasion to notice examples cited at Nicæa. The *Epistle to Theophilus* which represents a naive popular view dwells on such things as a picture of the Virgin painted by St. Luke, of which she said

[1] *Vit. Niceph.*, 96.
[2] Ed. Mercati, 231, 232.
[3] *Antirrh.*, I, 333 ; *Seven Chapters*, 485c.
[4] *Antirrh.*, II, 352d. Cf. *ib.* 372a. The Iconoclast says, I am willing to honour the picture of Christ, leaving it in a high place (ἀνωφερῆ ἐῶν).

herself, My grace shall go with it.[1]   We shall see eventually
that the modern Eastern Church clings to the doctrine.   It
was the one doctrinal issue that received a strong impetus
in the second Iconoclastic period.   The more moderate
party, represented by Nicephorus, it is true, seems to have
carefully avoided saying anything that could support this
view.[2]   But the dominant party of Theodore held otherwise.
The Definition of the Council of 815 declares that Irene
had described pictures as " filled with divine grace," a
view supported by the practice of burning lights and incense
before them.   The letter of Michael to Lewis the Pious
corroborates that reading of the orthodox practice.[3]
Theodore goes back to the method of John of Damascus and
upholds philosophically the doctrine that images convey
grace.   To the question, Are the image of Christ and Christ
himself different things ?   Theodore answers that they are
obviously different in fact (κατὰ φύσιν) but that the use of
the same name for both indicates some kind of identity.
Then, says the Iconoclast, is there any divinity in the picture
per se to justify veneration ?   There is not, is the answer,
the actual divinity which is present in the Lord's Body but
a relative one (σχέσις) as in all things animate and
inanimate.[4]   In this explanation Theodore has evaded the
issue, for the veneration of the divinity present in a picture
was certainly not the same as the veneration or respect paid
to God in the works of Nature, a tree or a flower, or even in
a human being.   The picture meant a localisation not only
of the spiritual but of a particular spiritual.   For Theodore
proceeds to say that the channel which conveys the thought
of God is worthy of respect whether it be picture, gospel-
book, cross, or any consecrated object.[5]   This point is
developed further in the second *Antirrheticus*.   The image
cannot be separated from the original.   The Son is the image
of the Father, and the original is venerated in him ; in
the same way the picture is the image of the Son and cannot
be separated from its original.   It is true that no statement
to this effect is found in any creed, but it is an inference
parallel to many inferences drawn from the facts and words

---

[1] *Ep. ad. Theoph.*, 349d.
[2] Cf. *Vit. Niceph.*, 104a–c.   The nearest he gets to it is in accepting the
passage from Basil, *de spir. sanct.* 18 : 45 ; *Antirrh.*, III, 404a.
[3] *Op. cit.*, p. 478.
[4] Theod. St., *Antirrh.*, I, 341–343.   [5] *Ib.* 343.

of Scripture such as that the Holy Spirit is God.[1]   If it be said that the image cannot receive the veneration paid to Christ, the same would apply to the cross which Iconoclasts accept as a true symbol of approach.   The image of Christ is nearer Christ than the cross.[2]   The relationship between the original and the picture is like that between a man and his shadow.[3]   The original and the picture are not separable in person (ὑποστατικῶς), but only in their substance (τῷ τῆς οὐσίας λόγῳ).[4]   This view is simply that a picture or image itself carries the nature of the original.   Externally and accidentally the two are separate but actually and spiritually they are one.   It is a theory that lay behind the views and practice of the early image-worshippers but never was so explicitly stated as by Theodore.   Consequent on this advanced view, Theodore, though not always consistent, advocates a veneration of the image which is at times indistinguishable from the worship paid to the original.   The difference between image and original not being in person but in substance, the image is only inferior in the material of which it is composed.   But it is not the wood or other material that is venerated but the thing signified.   The image apart from its accidents is the same as Christ and will receive an identical veneration.[5]   But he qualifies this elsewhere.   Though the image is in person identical with Christ, he does not regard the image of Christ as actually made into God.[6]   It does not therefore receive the devotion of service paid to the Trinity.[7]   Christ's image is to be

[1] *Antirrh.*, II, 356.
[2] *Ib.* 360.
[3] *Ib.* III, 429b.
[4] *Ep.*, II, 199.   He supports this with a sentence of Dionysius the Areopagite : ἐκατέρον ἐν ἑκατέρῳ παρὰ τὸ τῆς οὐσίας διάφορον. Cf. *Ep.*, II, 23. ἐν καὶ ταὐτὸν τῇ ὁμοιωτικῇ ὑποστάσει ἡ εἰκὼν πρὸς τὸν εἰκονιζόμενον. Cf. also *Antirrh.*, II, 357c, quoting Dionysius that truth is in the likeness, the archetype in the image, differing each in substance.   Theodore uses the words ὑπόστασις, οὐσία as they are used in the Trinitarian theology.   Between Father and Son, he says (*Ep. ad Plat.*, 501b), there is a difference of person (ὑποστατική) but not of nature (φυσική).   Between the Son and his image there is a difference of nature (φυσική) but not of person (ὑποστατική).   He would appear elsewhere to use οὐσία as a synonym for φύσις.   But what he apparently intends to state is that between the image and its original there is a difference in accidents but not in substance.   He adopts the phraseology of Dionysius and identifies it with the phraseology of the Trinitarian formulæ.
[5] οὐκ ἄλλο τί ἐστιν ἡ Χριστοῦ εἰκὼν ἢ Χριστὸς παρὰ τὸ τῆς οὐσίας δηλαδὴ διάφορον. *Antirrh.*, III, 425.
[6] *Ep.*, II, 161. ὡς θεοποιούμενον τὴν Χριστοῦ εἰκόνα.
[7] *Ib.* τῇ Χριστοῦ εἰκόνι οὐ λατρευτέον.

188   A History of the Iconoclastic Controversy

venerated with a relative veneration (σχετικῇ προσκυνήσει),
and in venerating the image we venerate Christ who does
not differ in person (ὑποστάσει) from his image but only
in substance (οὐσία). "For the archetype is reproduced
(ἐμφαίνεται) in the image the one in the other with a
difference of substance (οὐσία), as says the all-wise
Dionysius."[1] To John the Grammarian Theodore explains
further that Christ is venerated not with the image but in
the image.[2] The person of Christ is not divided and another
person (ὑπόστασις) given him is his image. Christ is
venerated and the image is named Christ metaphorically.[3]
But whatever subtlety Theodore may use to state his
position, he more than any writer on the orthodox side
justifies the charge of the Iconoclast that image-worship
meant regarding the image as charged with grace and
mediating the divine in a way that in the minds of the simple
and ignorant was indistinguishable from magic. The
Iconoclast weakened his own position by an illogical cult
of the cross.[4] But Theodore in defending orthodoxy has
admitted the main contention that pictures actually are
held to be endowed with the divine. Theodore logically
followed his own theory when he commended a correspondent for taking the image of Saint Demetrius as sponsor
for his child, on the ground that the original is believed to
be in the image,[5] and when he definitely repudiated the
view that pictures are an indulgence for the imperfect.[6]
While Theodore was not himself a persecutor, for he rejected
violence as a method by which the Church might enforce
its authority,[7] he distinctly refused to admit the possibility
of orthodoxy being consistent with indifference to the claims
of image-worship. It was heretical to be neutral, neither
honouring nor dishonouring the image,[8] and it was heretical
to regard Iconoclasts with indifference or admit them to
communion.[9] His theory of the nature of a picture makes
refusal to venerate the picture actual refusal to venerate
Christ.[10]

[1] Ep., II, 161.   [2] Ib. 194.
[3] οὐ κυρίως ἀλλὰ κατὰ κατάχρησιν. Ep., II, 161.
[4] E.g. Theod. St. Antirrh., II, 357c, 360c; Vit. Theod., 177d.
[5] πῶς οὐχὶ ἐν τῇ εἰκόνι ὁ εἰκονιζόμενος ὁμωνύμως ὁρᾶται τε καὶ εἶναι πιστεύεται.
Ep., I, 17.   [6] Ib. II, 171.
[7] Ep., 23 (Mai).   [8] Antirrh., I, 349.   [9] Ib. 351.
[10] ἧς (εἰκόνος) μὴ προσκυνουμένης ἀνήρηται ὡσαύτως καὶ τοῦ Χριστοῦ προσκύνησις. Ep. ad. Plat., 505a.

The doctrine of the Incarnation continued on both sides to be the central subject of the controversy. Pope Paschal said that God was worshipped through the image exactly as God was worshipped in the Son of God.[1] The picture of Christ is the guerdon of the rule of grace in the Incarnation.[2] Though God remains uncircumscribed, yet the Incarnate Christ is circumscribed. Otherwise the Incarnation is robbed of its meaning. It may be granted that Christ was not a man but man,[3] an idea upon which the Iconoclasts of Theodore's day threw great weight. But Christ was still visible and circumscribed and so capable of being depicted. It is the essence of the Incarnation that matter is not derogatory to the nature of God.[4] The statement that Christ's humanity was generic and not particular—that he was man rather than a man—was the final development of Iconoclastic Christology. It is an orthodox statement but may be given an Apollinarian turn, and is additional evidence that the Iconoclasts still clung to the Monophysite standpoint as the basis of their Christology, Theodore accepted the statement, and replied that even so the particular is present in the universal. Christ was not a phantom but was visible as an individual and therefore can be depicted.[5] But, said the Iconoclast, a picture of Christ implies a self-subsistent manhood, separated from the God-man, and a Nestorian position is reached which introduces a fourth person into the Godhead.[6] Not so, answered Theodore, there is only one person (ὑπόστασις) to the two natures (φύσεις). The Iconoclasts' argument leads to a conflation of the natures,[7] which is Apollinarianism, or else Christ had no true manhood, which is Montanism (*i.e.* Docetism). Theodore has again successfully demonstrated what the earlier stages of the controversy revealed, that the Iconoclasts were definitely Monophysite in Christology. The new argument which the later stage adduced, the generic

---

[1] *Op. cit.*, p. 231.
[2] *Vit. Theod.*, 176.
[3] μηδὲ γὰρ τῶν τινα ἀνθρώπων ἀναλαβεῖν φαίη ἄν τις τῶν εὐσεβούντων τὸν δὲ καθ᾽ ὅλου ἤτοι τὴν ὅλην φύσιν. *Antirrh*, I, 33?d. Cf. *Antirrh.*, II, 356d. To admit Christ's manhood does not make him bare man.
[4] *Ib.* 335.
[5] *Ib.* III, 396d.
[6] φύσιν . . . ἐν ἀτόμῳ θεωρουμένην. *Antirrh.*, III, 397c.
[7] μίαν φύσιν λέγειν τοῦ Λόγου ἐκ δύο φύσεων συγκραθεῖσαν. *Ib.* 401a. Cf. *Ep. ad. Plat.*, 504a.

nature of Christ's manhood, only intensified the Monophysite character of their doctrine and emphasised the
erroneous tendency of their theology. They might go on
calling the orthodox Nestorians or even Arians,[1] but they
were themselves beyond all doubt Apollinarians and
Monophysites.

The supplementary question of the pictures of the
saints would appear to be more prominent in this period
than it has been formerly. The moderate opinion of
Nicephorus was simply that the pictures of the saints recalled
the virtue of those heroes ; men approach them (not their
images) as mediators with God in the same way as they
approach the Emperor through the Imperial officials.[2]
But Theodore would go further. Images of the Virgin
and saints were to him a system of salvation.[3] There was
one veneration paid to God, but there were other kinds of
a. different intention paid to the saints.[4] Ultimately it was
God who was venerated in his servants the saints.[5]

But in these later stages of the controversy the philosophical and theological arguments were subsidiary to the
appeal to authority. It was natural that this should be
so. Nearly a hundred years had gone since the question
had first been raised. On both sides authorities were
abundant. When Leo V reopened the subject, his first
question was, What was the authority for image-worship ?[6]
The Council of 815 described image-worship as " unauthorised and untraditional," and appealed to the Council
of 753 as the definite settlement of the dispute. On the
orthodox side Nicephorus claimed that the Council of
Nicæa was final and incapable of alteration.[7] Since that
Council the image-question was no longer arguable. Those
who went back on that Council denied their own ordination
and had no status in the Church.[8] Theodore went so far as
to declare that for some 800 years Christianity and images
had advanced side by side.[9] Above all, Theodore put forward a new plea, that the authority of the Pope was the

[1] Antirrh., III, 409a.   [2] Vit. Niceph., 104c.
[3] τὸν σωτήριον κόσμον. Antirrh., I, 351.
[4] ἰσοτύπου οὔσης τῆς προσκυνήσεως ἀλλὰ μὴ τῆς διανοήσεως. Antirrh., I, 348d.
[5] Seven Chap., 485.
[6] Script. Incert., 1025d ; ps.-Sim., 668d.
[7] Apol. Min., 840c. Apol. pro S. Imag., 597–600.
[8] Apol. Min., 841b.   [9] Vit. Theod., 177d. Cf. Ep., II, 72.

final one. From Rome the truth can be learnt.[1] So that while the Iconoclasts appeal to Scripture and the Council of 753, the orthodox appeal to tradition, the Council of Nicæa, the Patriarchs, and, above all, the Pope,[2] "having the power from God, as holding the first place of all," and being "the original source of orthodoxy." This acceptance of the Pope as the primary spiritual authority involved a complementary theory, new to Constantinople, a complete repudiation of the right of the Emperor to regulate the affairs of the Church. This theory had been already expressed by St. John of Damascus, and Theodore repeated St. John's words. "The apostle said that God set some in the Church, first apostles, etc. He makes no mention of Emperors.[3] Spiritual things belong to priests and doctors, the Emperor's sphere is civil administration." Even Nicephorus complained of the subordination of the Church to the State.[4] The flight of many of the orthodox to Rome during the attack of Leo V no doubt encouraged this attitude.[5] It was a view that would have surprised orthodox Emperors like Justinian. It developed in the monasteries but only found full scope much later, and then not in the East but in Western Europe. For that reason, though at the time only an abortive agitation, it is one of the important side issues raised by the Iconoclastic controversy.

The more particular authorities to which appeal was made are similar to those cited in the earlier period, but apparently fewer in number and less significant, being overshadowed by the larger appeal to principles and to Councils. They may be classified as appeals to (a) Scripture, (b) Patristic writings, (c) Historical precedents.

(a) Scripture had provided little material to the orthodox side. The Iconoclasts pressed strongly their contention that image-worship found no support in Scripture.[6] Leo declared that he would not accept the legitimacy of the practice unless it was expressly stated in the Gospel and the Apostle, Ye shall worship my image.[7] This position could not be turned. Pope Paschal could only say : If the Scripture says, no one can call Jesus Lord but by the

[1] *Ep.*, II, 129. [2] *Epp.*, II, 12, 13, 66, 129 ; Mai, 192.
[3] *Vit. Theod.*, 181d, 184a ; Georg. Mon., II, 799 ; Leo Gramm., 1040d.
[4] *Antirrh.*, III, 504a. [5] Cf. *Vit. Method.*, 1248a.
[6] *Vit. Niceph.*, 88bc. [7] Script. Incert., 1025d.

Holy Ghost, inasmuch as painting is more durable than speech, no one can paint Jesus as Lord but by the Holy Ghost.[1] Theodore could only taunt the Iconoclasts with their devotion to the Old Testament, reminding them that their own affection for the cross was undermined by the text of Deuteronomy, " Cursed is every one that hangeth thereon " (Deut. xxi. 23).[2] His own view was that the Old Testament was abrogated by the reign of grace, and consequently its rules were inapplicable to Christians.[3] The Iconoclast replied that the New Testament justified reverence to the cross but said nothing of images, citing 1 Cor. i. 18, " The preaching of the cross . . . unto us which are saved it is the power of God," and Gal. vi. 14, " God forbid that I should glory save in the cross of our Lord Jesus Christ."[4] One text reappeared from the Council of 753, and from the attention Theodore gives it must have been the key text of the Iconoclasts. It is 2 Cor. v. 16, " Though we have known Christ after the flesh, yet now henceforth know we him no more." The Iconoclasts, true to their Monophysite attitude, interpreted this to mean that the Risen Christ cannot be represented in visible form. Theodore's answer was that the words really mean that Christ is now known apart from sin and not with fleshly affection.[5] Orthodox weakness in Biblical exegesis is well illustrated by a curious passage in Theodore's *Seven Chapters against the Iconoclasts*. He takes two passages of St. Matthew, xxii. 18, the payment of tribute to Cæsar with the coin bearing Cæsar's image, and xvii. 27, the coin in the fish's mouth, and argues that the tribute money has an image impressed on it : the coin therefore found in the fish's mouth is specially created by the Lord, and when he says, Give unto them for me and for thee, he implies that the coin bears images of Christ himself and of St. Peter.[6]

(*b*) Theodore's party definitely abandoned the appeal to Scripture and took refuge in tradition. The authority for pictures is the long usage of the Church.[7] The whole Christian world since the Ascension had displayed the picture of Christ in the churches.[8] Just as the feasts of the

---

[1] *Ep. Pasch.*, 229.   [2] *Vit. Theod.*, 177d.   [3] *Ib.* 176.
[4] Theod. St., *Antirrh.*, I, 337.   [5] *Ib.* II, 381 *sqq.*
[6] *Op. cit.*, 489c. For another fantastic interpretation of the former passage see Ch. VII, p. 132, *supra*.
[7] *Vit. Theod.*, 176.   [8] Theod., *Ep.*, II, 72.

Gospel story are observed without any direct order, so the incidents they commemorate are recorded in painting.[1] In support are quoted the two inevitable traditional pictures, St. Luke's portrait of the Virgin, and Abgar's portrait of our Lord.[2]

(c) The patristic authorities are less numerous than formerly. They have been sifted out and only the most substantial survived. The Iconoclasts still cited Epiphanius, while Theodore repeated the contention that the extracts attributed to him were spurious, for his disciple Sabinus decorated his church with pictures, and a fellow-Cypriote, Leontius of Neapolis, recorded nothing of an Iconoclastic character of Epiphanius.[3] A passage was cited from Epiphanius to the effect that the reader would do well to reflect whether it is seemly to have God painted in colours. A correct interpretation would refer the statement not to the representation of Christ but of the Godhead.[4]

A passage of Theodotus of Ancyra also reappears. The Nicene council had decided that this was an interpolation. Theodore prefers to refute it by argument. Theodotus had said that pictures were a diabolical invention; it was the virtues of those depicted that called for imitation. Nothing recalls the character of an original, says Theodore, as vividly as a picture. He quaintly illustrates the realistic effect of pictures by an incident of a woman who was delivered of a black child through seeing a negro.[5] A new passage appears from Asterius, *Homily I, On Dives and Lazarus:* "Do not paint Christ. The one humiliation of his Incarnation is enough. . . . But bear with you upon your soul the incorporeal Word." Doctrinally, says Theodore, this passage is unsound. The phrase "incorporeal Word" is not an accurate synonym for the Incarnate Christ. In any case a picture of Christ no more submits him to a fresh kenosis than does the reading of the narrative of the Incarnation.[6]

A passage was also cited from Gregory of Nyssa[7]: "Whosoever venerates a creature though he do it in the

---

[1] Theod. St., *Antirrh.*, I, 339.
[2] Cont. Theoph., 116b ; *Vit. Theod.*, 176 ; *Ep. ad Theoph.*, 349d.
[3] *Antirrh.*, II, 388d. [4] *Ep.*, II, 36. [5] *Ib.*
[6] *Ib.* ἐπὶ δὲ τῆς ψυχῆς σοῦ βαστάζων νοητῶς τὸν ἀσώματον λόγον περίφερε. The passage is conceived in a spirit which undervalues the human life of Jesus.
[7] Theod. St., *Seven Ch.*, 497b. Source untraced.

name of Christ committeth idolatry." In answer to this
Theodore refers to the context, which shows that the passage
referred to the Arians, who alleged Christ was a creature.
It has no bearing on orthodox practice. The same applies
to a phrase quoted from Gregory Nazianzen : That which
is venerated is not circumscribed.[1] This has a particular
reference to the Divine Being. Many objects of veneration
are admittedly circumscribed, the Eucharist, the cross, the
Altar, relics of saints.

The patristic support advanced on the orthodox side
is nearly all old.

1. Basil, p. 137, *supra*.	Theod., 337.
2. Athanasius, p. 138, *supra*.	*Ib.* 360b.
3. Canon of Quinisext, p. 142, *supra*.	*Ib.* 380 ; *Ep.*, II, 72.
4. Gregory of Nyssa, p. 138, *supra*.	*Ib.* ; *Ep.*, II, 199.
5. ps.-Basil, p. 146, *supra*.	*Ib.* [199.
6. ps.-Athan., p. 143, *supra*.	*Ib.* 365bc ; *Ep.*, II,

The following is the new evidence :

7. Dionysius the Areopagite.[2]

" The image reveals the character of the original ; the
truth is in the likeness, the archetype in the image, the one
in the other apart from differences of substance."

This with the passage of St. Basil (No. 1, *supra*) forms
the basal text of Theodore's philosophy of the relation of
the image to its original and therefore of the rational
explanation of image-worship. Not to repeat unnecessarily
what has been said already, it will be sufficient comment here
to notice that Theodore's contention will not stand examination. Symbolically and by convention such a relationship
of image and original as Theodore defines may exist. But
beyond that his argument is mere word-spinning unrelated
to reality.

8. *Vita Pancratii.* Act. Sanct. Ap. III.

" Peter the prince of the apostles said : Bring the picture
of our Lord Jesus Christ and fix it on the tower that the
people may see what form the Son of God adopted." [3]

This piece of hagiography is without historical value.
Pancratius, who is not to be confounded with Pancratius of
Rome, was a Sicilian bishop alleged to have been the disciple

---

[1] Theod. St., *Seven Ch.*, 495c.   τὸ σέπτον οὐ περιγραπτόν.
[2] Theod. St., 501a *et saepe*. The source of the passage is untraced
[3] Theod. St., *Epp.*, II, 42, 72, 199.

of St. Peter. Theodore defends the historical merits of the Life by pointing to a large church in Sicily dedicated to his honour, where the saint still worked miracles.[1]

The number of citations brought as evidence in the second Iconoclastic period is small. It is plain that both sides leaned far more on the more direct and responsible authority of Councils and the Church itself. In the hands of Theodore, too, argument grew over-subtle and passed out of the range of average thought. In spite of the intellectual superiority of Theodore over every other writer on both sides, his theology is less important to the final triumph of orthodoxy than his practical organisation of the orthodox policy. Theologically indeed the second Iconoclastic period is of minor importance. The theoretical issue had been completely argued out by Constantine V and by the Council of Nicæa. Nicephorus was satisfied to restate the case as it had been stated then. That is the reason that Nicephorus, though contemporary with Theodore, is really representative of the earlier age. What original features Theodore was able to add are more dialectical and less related to reality. Something of this has appeared in his view of the relation of the picture to its original. It is very definitely shown in the reasoning which makes up Theodore's *Seven Chapters against the Iconoclasts*. The substance of the work is as follows :[2] Chapter 1 is directed against the charge that in venerating images of Christ, the Virgin, or the saints, Christians are making gods of images. Making a god means to create what does not exist or to believe that images actually are gods. But to make a picture of Christ is not to do this. It is to represent the true God in his Incarnation. What we venerate is not the material but Christ's true nature. Apart from differences of accident (οὐσία), as Dionysius says, the image and the original are the same. In the image of the Virgin we venerate the mother of God and in the saints God whose servants they are. Chapter 2 is addressed to those who ask why nothing is mentioned in the Gospel about the image of Christ. The curious answer to this argument has been discussed.[3] Chapter 3 answers those who say that since in heaven there is no image of man but only the sign of the cross, this is what should be venerated. The

---

[1] *Ep.*, II, 42.   [2] Theod. St., 485–498.   [3] See above, p. 192.

reference is evidently to a constellation. The answer is that there is no man there because the stars were worshipped by pagans, and a figure of a man would have strengthened the practice. The cross is not venerated because it appears in heaven in the form of a constellation but because of him who hung upon it. The image of Christ is not venerated because it was foreshadowed in Adam but because he took human nature of the Virgin. Chapter 4 is entitled Against those who argue that the priest when he signs the infant at the font does not use an image but the sign of the cross, and the title completely describes the argument. The answer is that the priest is himself an image of Christ and applies the sign in imitation of Christ. Chapter 5 is against those who urge that disease and demons are warded off by the sign of the cross and not by images. The answer is similar to the preceding one. The Christian is himself conformed to the image of Christ. Chapter 6 deals with the phrase of Gregory Nazianzen, " That which is venerated is not circumscribed," and Chapter 7 with a sentence of Gregory of Nyssa.[2]

It would seem that Theodore was not satisfied with an academic appeal to the learned only. There exists a collection of epigrams in which he has reduced the doctrine of images to a series of plain statements in iambic verse. It is conceivable that these were only the amusements of his leisure. But as Theodore had an object in all he did, it is more likely that he intended with these to catch the popular ear. We have seen already that the Iconoclasts, probably as early as the reign of Leo III, had been circulating verses enshrining their doctrines. Theodore, a skilled writer of hymns, used his talent to popularise his doctrines. The following are typical examples :

1. On the Holy Pictures.[3]

Christ's picture which you stand before
Is also Christ (by metaphor).
Though two in kind, they're one in name ;
The reverence paid them is the same.
Who honours the picture, worships Christ ;
Who honours not hath Christ despised,
A fool who forbids us to adore
The face of Him that manhood bore.

---

[1] See above, p. 194.   [2] *Ib.*   [3] Carm. 30, 1792b.

2. On the Holy Pictures.[1]

In a picture here Christ's features you may scan,
For, though essential God, he was made man.
Who on his image cannot thole to look
Believes the Incarnate Christ was but a spook.

3. On the Holy Theotokos.[2]

O Mother of the Lord, in love and fear
I venerate thy picture painted here.
For thou with such abounding grace art fraught
That by thine image miracles are wrought.

With Theodore the theoretical statement of the controversy ended in the East. The toleration of Iconoclasm
in the reign of Michael the Amorian and its temporary
revival under Theophilus were not theological. The
restoration of orthodoxy and its final triumph also came
about in an atmosphere nearly entirely political. It was
only in the West that the theological controversy went on,
where the Frankish scholars were bringing the zest of their
newly found learning into theology.

APPENDIX TO CHAPTER X

List of Patristic Citations

The following are the principal passages of the Fathers cited
by Theodore on the orthodox side. (*a*) signifies that the passage
was also cited earlier. See above, Chapter VII.

Fourth Century.

Gregory Nazianzen (328–390)
  (*a*) Carmen, xviii.   .   .   . 468d ; *Ep.*, II, 36
Athanasius (328–373).
  (*a*) Quæst. ad Antioch, 39   . 468c
  (*a*) *Or.*, III, contr. Arian, i and 5   360b
ps.-Athanasius.
  (*a*) de pass. imag. Christi .   . *Ep.*, II, 199
Basil (330–379).
  (*a*) de spir. Sanct., 18   .   . 337
  (*a*) hom. xx in xl martyr.   . 445d
  (*a*) hom. xviii in Gord. Martyr. . 445d

---

[1] Carm. 34, 1793a.   [2] *Ib.* 35, 1793b.

ps.-Basil.
   (*a*) Serm. in Balaam.   . . *Ep.*, II, 36, 199
Gregory of Nyssa (335–394).
   (*a*) Serm. on Godhead of Son . *Ep.*, II, 199
John Chrysostom (344–407).
   (*a*) Serm. I de div. utr. Test. . 469a ; *Ep.*, II, 36
   (*a*) Serm. in Melet. .   .   . 373b ; *Ep.*, II, 41
   Hom. xi de Romano   . . *Ep.*, II, 41
Cyril of Alexandria (370–444).
   (*a*) Thes., 12 .   .   . 364a
   Untraced passage   .   . 469b

Sixth Century.

Dionysius the Areopagite (circa 530)
   Untraced passage   .   .   . 357, 501
   de coel. hier., 1 : 3 .   . 468c ; *Ep.*, II, 36
   (*a*) de div. nom.   .   . *Ep.*, II, 65

(*a*) *Acta Maximi* (580–662)   . . *Ep.*, II, 65

Seventh Century.

Sophronius (d. 638).
   (*a*) de martyr. Cyr. et Joann. . 364c

(*a*) *Canon 82 of Quinisext.* (692) . 380a ; *Ep.*, II, 72

Unknown Date.

Vit. Pancratii . . . . . *Ep.*, II, 42, 72, 199

CHAPTER XI

ICONOCLASM UNDER THE AMORIAN DYNASTY

AUTHORITIES

As for Chapter IX.

THE accession of Michael raised the hopes of the leading image worshippers. Theodore took an early opportunity of addressing him as "a new David, a second Josiah, the Emperor of the reign of peace." [1] These hopes were largely illusory. The new Emperor, Michael II, called the Stammerer (Balbus), was a man of lowly origin, whose previous history had predisposed him to an attitude to religion almost unique in the records of the Empire. He had been brought up in Amorium, where large numbers of Jews and Athingani were found. In addition there was a quasi-Judaic sect who were baptised but accepted all the Mosaic law except circumcision. Michael had been brought up in this sect, but either abandoned it or modified it to a more definite mixture of Judaism and Christianity. [2] It is recorded that he treated the Jews with great favour, reducing their taxation. [3] At one time he fixed the Sabbath as a fast, at another he attacked the scripture by denying a resurrection. He declared there was no devil, for Moses had taught nothing of one. [4] He ordered oaths to be taken only in the name of God. He complained that the Passover was celebrated wrongly at the wrong time, [5] and included Judas (probably because his name seemed to mean "the Jew") among the saved. [6] Such is the picture of Michael's religion

[1] Ep., II, 74.
[2] Cont. Theoph., 56d. There is nothing inherently improbable in the existence of such a sect in Phrygia, the home of religious eccentricity.
[3] Ib. 61d.   [4] Ib.
[5] This fact probably makes Vit. Ignat. attach him to the obscure Novatianist sect called Sabbatiani.
[6] Cont. Theoph., 64a.

depicted by the Continuators of Theophanes. It must, however, be received with considerable reservation, for the Continuators made it their business to depreciate the Amorian dynasty in the interest of Basil the Macedonian. Michael is here represented as a Jew or a Mohammedan, but in no very obvious sense as a Christian at all. While none of the details supplied by the history of his dealings with orthodox Christians confirm the peculiar tenets attributed to him by the Continuators and the Emperor's own letter to Lewis the Pious plainly contradicts them, he remains a somewhat liberal freethinker with a definite anti-clerical bias. The writer of the *Epistle to Theophilus* calls him a kindly and peaceable Emperor, which is not an unfair description of his policy.[1] He certainly inaugurated his reign by proclaiming a general amnesty. Prisoners were released and exiles restored,[2] among whom were the members of the orthodox party. Theodore himself returned, eventually establishing himself with Nicephorus at Chalcedon.[3] Methodius (later to be Patriarch) came back from Rome to Constantinople.[4] But they soon found that from their standpoint it was a phantom freedom, and the new Emperor was to all intents an Iconoclast.[5] It is possible that the death of the Patriarch Theodotus coincided with Michael's accession. Theodore and Nicephorus opened a correspondence with the Emperor to advance their cause. Several letters of Theodore's belong to the early months of the new reign. In the letter congratulating the Emperor on his restoration of the exiles he took the opportunity of urging a reconciliation to Christ (*i.e.* a restoration of images). In particular this could be effected by uniting with Rome " the head of the churches," and through her with the three Patriarchs.[6] He repeated the request in a letter addressed to the Emperor in the name of the hegoumenoi,[7] in which he asked for an interview in order to state the orthodox case, but he definitely refused to meet the Iconoclasts, and repeated his opinion that in case of doubt the decision of Rome should be sought, inasmuch as she is the supreme head (κορυφαιοτάτη) of the Churches, in virtue of the promise to Peter the first occupant of the see. Meanwhile Theodore

[1] *Ep. ad. Theoph.*, 377C. τὸν πραότατον καὶ γαληνότατον βασιλέα.
[2] Theod. St., *Ep.*, II, 74.   [3] *Vit. Theod.*, 208a, 220a.
[4] *Vit. Method.*, 1248c.   [5] *Vit. Niceph.*, 145C.
[6] *Ep.*, II, 74.   [7] *Ib.* 86.

wrote also to high imperial officials, to the logothete Pantoleon,[1] and to the general logothete Democharis,[2] asking them to use their influence to win the Emperor to the orthodox side. The ex-Patriarch Nicephorus, probably with special reference to the vacancy in the patriarchate, wrote to the Emperor to explain the antiquity of image-worship and warn him of the fate that had befallen his predecessor.[3] The Emperor gave his formal answer [4] : " As far as they are concerned who before us have investigated the Church's doctrine, they will have to answer to God whether their conclusions are good or bad. For our part we have ordained to maintain the Church as we found it. To make this clearer we have ordered that in future no one shall attempt to speak in public either against images or in their defence. The synod of Tarasius, the ancient synod of Constantine, and the synod recently summoned under Leo, shall alike be obliterated. Everything that recalls the images is to be buried in profound silence. If he who has thought fit to write and speak on these matters wishes to preside [5] over the Church, still holding his opinions, he is at liberty to return, provided that for the future he maintains absolute silence on the rightness of images and their worship." The way was open to Nicephorus to return, but any attempt to compromise was checked by Theodore, who was now at Chalcedon with the ex-Patriarch.[6] To Theodore's request that the Emperor should restore the exiled bishops to their sees and expel the interlopers, and to his general plea for the images, the Emperor replied that Theodore's views might be right but they were unacceptable to him. He had never venerated any image. " I must remain what I am, and you can abide as you are and follow your own opinions. I will hinder no one. I will not permit you to erect images inside the city ; but outside you may put them where you please." [7] The policy of the Emperor was sealed

[1] *Ep.*, II, 81.   [2] *Ib.* 82.
[3] *Vit. Niceph.*, 148a. Cf. Cont. Theoph., 61b, which seems an independent source. The other chronicles are all based on *Vit. Niceph.*
[4] According to Leo Gramm., 1044a, it was in a *silentium*. If it was in a letter the contents must have been made public.
[5] *I.e.* Nicephorus. The words following seem to imply that the see of Constantinople was vacant, and that it was open to Nicephorus to return to it on the terms described.
[6] *Vit. Theod. St.*, 220a.
[7] *Ib.* 221b.

P

before Whitsuntide, 821,[1] by the appointment of Antony of Syllæum to the Patriarchate vacant by the death of Theodotus. The orthodox persisted in their efforts. Methodius (later to be Patriarch) arrived from his exile in Rome with a dogmatic epistle from the Pope urging the restoration of the Patriarch Nicephorus. Michael, after reading the document, is said by the biographer of Methodius to have sentenced the bearer to seventy lashes and exiled him to the island of St. Andrew near Acrita.[2] It is possible that, after failing to secure an agreement, Michael worked off his exasperation on the orthodox party. For the Continuators of Theophanes say that as he consolidated his power he took measures against the Christians, inflicting penalties on the monks and exiling others of the faithful.[3] If this was so it can hardly fail to be connected with the very serious political outbreak at the beginning of Michael's reign led by a mysterious person named Thomas. This rebellion had many of the features of a social revolution, while orthodoxy was one of Thomas's rallying cries, for he had himself crowned by the Patriarch of Antioch to ensure the act being performed by an orthodox prelate. Fearing that the orthodox appeal of Thomas would win the participation of Theodore and his monks who had retired to the monastery of Crescentius near Nicomedia,[4] Michael ordered them to return to Constantinople.[5] There they were forced to remain until the year 823, when the rebellion was finally crushed. The Emperor then made another attempt to secure acceptance of the policy of toleration. Theodore answered that he could not entertain any proposal which would involve him in meeting heretics to discuss the faith, and that secondly this was a spiritual matter which could only be settled by spiritual authority, that is to say, it did not come within the Emperor's jurisdiction at all.[6] In a letter to Leo the sacellarius,[7] he restated his whole position in detail. The

---

[1] The dates of the death of Theodotos and of Antony's succession are unknown. ps.-Sim., 681c, says vaguely κατὰ τὸν καιρὸν τοῦτον (*i.e.* the beginning of Michael's reign) Antony held the see. Add. Georg., 852a, mentions Antony as Patriarch performing the marriage ceremony of Theophilus on Whitsunday, 821.

[2] *Vit. Meth.*, 1248c ; Cont. Theoph., 61c.

[3] *Ib.*

[4] *Vit. Theod. St.*, I, 221b ; *Vit.*, II, 317d.

[5] *Ib.*, II, 320a.

[6] Theod., *Ep.*, II, 199.   [7] *Ib.* II, 129.

matter in dispute was not one for the arbitration of the Emperor but for the apostles and their successors, of whom the first is the bishop of Rome, the second the bishop of Constantinople, and then those of Alexandria, Antioch, and Jerusalem. Emperors and princes can only support and approve the bishops' doctrinal definitions. It was for that reason that the Iconoclastic doctrines are rejected. They were wrongly passed in council under violent pressure from Constantine (V) and Leo (V). The way to peace was that the heterodox should leave the Church, the Patriarch Nicephorus return to his see, and a Council be held in which at least representatives of the other Patriarchs should take part. The Patriarch of the West could be present if only the Emperor would permit it. The Pope was supreme in a General Council. And if there was any doubt about the faith as presented by Nicephorus because of his association with the Studite party, as the Emperor alleged, then Rome could be approached *by other channels* and the faith in its true form received thence. It says much for Theodore's authority and for Michael's desire for peace that he actually followed part of this advice. From the reference to Nicephorus in this letter and from the care with which Theodore's biographer dwells on the Patriarch's affection and respect for Theodore,[1] it appears that there was a prevalent opinion that Nicephorus was a tool in the hands of the more masterful monk. The Emperor did address a request to the Pope. He did not do it in terms that Theodore would have approved, and he made his approach through a channel which shows his view of the position of the Church. He wrote to the Frankish Emperor Lewis the Pious, probably believing that the bishop of Rome would stand in the same relation to Lewis as the Patriarch of Constantinople did to himself. He assumed that the Pope would obey the Emperor of the West. The letter[2] is dated 10th April, 824, and is addressed " to our beloved and honourable brother Lewis." Michael relates the circumstances in which he came to the throne, making the best of his case and representing the fall of Leo as due to Thomas's rebellion.[3] " We, seeing the persistence and guile of that devil and murderer (Thomas) and how the

---

[1] *Vit. Theod.*, 224. [2] ed. Werminghoff (M.G.H.), pp. 475 *sqq.*
[3] The origin of the rebellion is so obscure that the case made out by Michael may not be without foundation.

Christians were being seduced by him, put our hope and virtue in Christ the true God,[1] our helper and support, and with perfect faith moved our state against the tyrant." After recording his successful settlement of the rebellion, he explains that this is the first opportunity he has had of expressing to Lewis his brotherly mind and peaceful intention, which he does by an embassy including several ecclesiastics, Nicetas metropolitan of Myra, Fortunatus archbishop of Venice, and a deacon Theodore. He then relates that many clergy and lay people have become alienated from the apostolic tradition, giving details of image-worship which we have already noticed. He points out that a local synod (*i.e.* that of 815) has forbidden such practices and permitted only pictures in a high position as having the same use as scripture.[2] Those who refused to accept the local councils have fled to old Rome and injured the Church by calumny. " In contradiction of them we wish to state our orthodoxy ; we hold inviolate and not merely with lip assent the holy creeds and the six General Councils." The doctrine of the Trinity is stated carefully to avoid any hint of Monophysite unorthodoxy.[3] " We have sent a letter to the most holy Pope of old Rome with a gold gospel-book decorated with precious stones, a gold paten and chalice similarly decorated, an offering to the church of St. Peter, the prince of the apostles, to request his prayers for ourselves and you." A gift of valuable stuffs is sent for Lewis, and he is requested to forward the messengers on their way to Rome and request the Pope to expel from the city the false Christians who calumniate the Church (*i.e.* the image-worshipping refugees).

It appears that the actual negotiations with the Pope were to be carried on through Lewis. The details of the action taken by Lewis will be examined in another chapter. He stated his own view to Pope Eugenius II, and suggested that a Papal embassy might be sent to Greece with a Frankish embassy " to assist them."[4] No record survives of the sequel. But it is not difficult to surmise that the moderate Iconoclastic position in which Lewis and Michael

---

[1] This hardly supports the chroniclers' view of Michael's religion.
[2] This view Theodore definitely repudiates. *Ep.*, II, 171.
[3] Divinitatis et humanitatis duas voluntates et operationes gloriamur, p. 479.
[4] Ep. Lud. ad Eug. Werminghoff, p. 534.

were at one received no more support at Rome than the policy of Constantine Copronymus himself. Michael's attempt at conciliation failed. After 823 Theodore withdrew, probably voluntarily, and died in 826 on one of the islands in the Black Sea.[1] Two years later the ex-Patriarch Nicephorus and, in October, 829, the Emperor also died. Probably after 824 the Iconoclastic party was supreme at least in Constantinople. No monastery was free from Iconoclasm at this period, says the biographer of Methodius.[2] Ignatius, the deacon, pupil and biographer of the Patriarch Nicephorus, conformed to Iconoclasm about this time.[3] Theophilus, the Emperor's only son, was brought up an Iconoclast under the tutelage of John the Grammarian. The Emperor himself gave support to the Iconoclastic cause by taking as his second wife Euphrosyne,[4] daughter of Constantine VI, the last of the Isaurians. This in itself angered the orthodox, for not only were second marriages canonically discouraged, but Euphrosyne had already taken vows from which she had to be absolved by the Patriarch. In the phrase of the chronicler, "the Emperor embraced fornication."[5]

Michael played in the second Iconoclastic period much the same part as Nicephorus had played in the first. Both affected a moderate policy in religion. Like Nicephorus, Michael was unfortunate in war. In his reign Crete, Sicily, and Southern Italy fell to Saracen raiders.[6] But in spite of this and in spite of being so illiterate that one could read a book in the time it took him to spell out his own name,[7] he could hardly have been so boorish and incompetent as the biassed chroniclers of the Macedonian house allege. He succeeded in founding a dynasty, and left behind him a son who cuts one of the most striking figures in the history of the Empire.

This son, Theophilus, succeeded on 10th October, 829. He is a character of a Stevensonian cast, with a taste for dramatic situations and artistic display. With these he

---

[1] The data in the *Vit. Theod.* make 826 probable. He died on 11th November, a Sunday, with which 826 agrees. *Vit.*, 229b.

[2] *Vit. Meth.*, 1249c.

[3] *Vit. Niceph.*, 156.

[4] She may have been orthodox like her mother. There is no evidence that she exercised any influence on the religious life of her time.

[5] Cont. Theoph., 64a.

[6] *Ib.* 97a.

[7] *Ib.* 64a.

combined a definite Iconoclastic conviction, fostered by his tutor, the ablest of all the Iconoclastic leaders, John the Grammarian. The details of his reign are the least clear in the whole of the Iconoclastic period, for we lose the guidance of nearly all the contemporary writers. The best of the orthodox biographies came to an end with the deaths of Theodore and Nicephorus. George the Monk, who was contemporary with Theophilus, being left to his own devices to collect his material, devotes three and a half pages to the reign of Theophilus, two of which are a catena of citations from Gregory Nazianzen's *Invective against Julian.* We can only check the chroniclers by a number of minor Lives of Saints, the only one of which possessing first-class value is the contemporary *Life of Methodius,* afterwards Patriarch. George hails Theophilus as "the new Belshazzar, god-hater, insulter of saints, destroyer, profane," [1] while with an ingenious play on his name the biographer of Methodius describes him as a better lover of paganism than of God. [2] At the same time the writer of the *Epistle to Theophilus,* probably in Syria, was optimistic enough to appeal to him at the beginning of his reign to walk in the ways of pious emperors like Constantine and Theodosius, who were patrons of the monasteries. [3] He tolerated the image-worship of his wife Theodora, [4] and released Methodius from prison in order to enjoy his learning. [5] The evidence shows Theophilus a very active enemy of the monks. But it is questionable whether he pressed the Iconoclastic policy outside Constantinople itself. There is no reason to doubt, and indeed every fact leads us to accept, the religious outlook attributed to Theophilus by his wife after his death. She said that he was a mild Iconoclast, having inherited from his forefathers a slender root of the heresy, but was led further by the Patriarch, who was responsible for the persecution. [6]

Theophilus reigned for twelve years, but it is difficult to fix the ecclesiastical events of his reign in any exact chronology. He began his reign by punishing the associates of his father who had been concerned in the murder of Leo V. He made a dramatic appeal in a public assembly in

---

[1] Georg. Mon., II, 797.
[2] ἐθνοφίλου μᾶλλον ἢ Θεοφίλου.   *Vit. Method.,* 1249c.
[3] *Ep. ad. Theoph.,* 380d.   [4] Cont. Theoph., 105.
[5] Gen., 1088b.   [6] Cont. Theoph., 164.

the Hippodrome, holding in his hand the candlestick or altar-cross with which Leo had defended himself, and asking what should be the punishment of those who smote the Lord's anointed in the house of God. The assembly cried, Death.[1] Some of the chroniclers explain the motive of his act as sympathy with the religious views of Leo,[2] not a very convincing suggestion. The causes which had led to the accession of Michael are far from clear. Michael's own statement that the rebel Thomas had something to do with it may be true. Michael may have been a tool who revealed a capacity not suspected by his principals. The executions carried out by Theophilus may then have been the last act in the settlement of Thomas's partisans. There is no indication that Theophilus showed any strong Icono-clastic policy before John Hylilas became Patriarch. This took place in 832,[3] on the death of Antony. All that the chroniclers say points to John as the real Iconoclast behind the outbreak which followed. He is the " new Jannes and Jambres, by common report addicted to divination and all kinds of impiety." [4] He is the " magicarch and demoniarch rather than Patriarch, the new Apollonius or Balaam . . . a fit instrument of the devil." [5] He built a house in the suburbs and by sacrifice consulted demons and advised the Emperor of the future.[6] Behind these fantastic statements we can read that John possessed wide and rare learning and was the Emperor's adviser. Nor is it a very difficult inference that his advice led the Emperor into a stronger policy against images. Before the consecration of John the policy of Theophilus is described in vague terms. " Under a profession of public order he injured faith and piety beyond his predecessors." [7] But after John had become Patriarch a definite decree was issued, prohibiting the painting of sacred pictures with colours.[8] Sacred pictures

---

[1] ps.-Sim., 688a.
[2] Add. Georg., 852b ; Leo Gramm., 1045d.
[3] The date is given by Cont. Theoph. as Sunday, 21st April. This is almost certainly 832, a year in which 21st April fell on Sunday. No attention is to be paid to the worthless chronology of ps.-Sim. (696d), which gives the year as the eighth of Theophilus' reign, *i.e.* 836.
[4] Leo Gramm., 1053a.
[5] Georg. Mon., II, 798–799.
[6] Leo Gramm., 1053b.   [7] *Ib.* 1048a.
[8] *Ib.* 1053a. Cont. Theoph., 113b, appears to misdate this, attributing it to Michael.

in churches were replaced by birds and beasts.   Resistance followed.   For an attack was made on the monks.   No monk was allowed free access to the city and monasteries were suppressed (probably within Constantinople).   Some of the religious died of hardship, others concealed their calling, and others forsook it.[1]   This was clearly a reversal of the tolerant policy which had been followed not only by Michael but by Theophilus as Michael's colleague.   The persecution which followed is probably confined to the years 832–836.[2]   It was directed against those who resisted, and painters, who, it must be remembered, were mostly monks, were conspicuous victims.   The monks of the Abraamite monastery argued with the Emperor on the antiquity of image-worship, irritated him by their freedom of speech, and were flogged and exiled to the oratory called Phoberon on the Euxine.[3]   A monk named Lazarus, who was a notable painter, persisted in still painting sacred pictures.   Red-hot plates of iron were applied to his hands.   Eventually released at the entreaty of the Empress he escaped to Phoberon, where he painted the picture of the Forerunner, which the chroniclers declare still works miracles.[4] Euthymius, bishop of Sardis, the last survivor of the council of Nicæa, who had probably been banished from Constantinople by Michael as an unremitting champion of orthodoxy, died under the lash in the reign of Theophilus, probably in 834.[5]   He is the only bishop who is recorded among the victims, and probably had not held his see for many years.[6]   Otherwise it was only monks that suffered.   " The Emperor confined in prison Michael, syncellus of the Church of Jerusalem, and many other monks, hoping to tame them by long ill-usage." [7] Methodius, who had been permitted to return from exile at the end of Michael's reign, was accused of causing strife, and the fact that he had brought Papal documents to Constantinople was raked up against him.   He answered

---

[1] Cont. Theoph., 113c.
[2] The episode of the brothers Theodore and Theophanes is dated in the *Vit. Theoph. Grapt.*, 14th July, 836.
[3] Cont. Theoph., 116b.
[4] *Ib.* 117.
[5] *Ib.* 61c ; Act. David., 237.
[6] See above, p. 174.
[7] Cont. Theoph., 117 ; Gen., 1085b.

truculently that if the image of Christ was so derogatory to Christ's dignity, the image of the Emperor might with advantage be abolished in the interest of the Emperor's dignity. He received for this six hundred lashes and was thrown into the palace dungeons. He was brought out by the orthodox, hardly without the connivance of the Emperor, and was kept in the palace, where he secured converts in the imperial entourage and caused the Emperor himself to modify his fury.[1] But the Emperor's fury must have been much less vigorous than the biographer of Methodius allows, for Genesios records that it was the Emperor himself who released Methodius from prison and kept him in the palace to enjoy the great pleasure of his learning and scientific knowledge, little as he cared for his theology.[2] The most famous of all the confessors under Theophilus were the two brothers Theophanes and Theodore.[3] They had come from Palestine to Constantinople probably to escape the Arab invasions (circa 812/813).[4] Theophanes had some reputation as a poet. They had probably been already exiled in the reign of Leo V. But now, according to one narrative, they were again in Constantinople, and were permitted to dispute with the Emperor, who misquoted a text from Isaiah. In rage at being convicted of error he ordered Theophanes to be flogged and twelve iambic verses of the Emperor's composition to be tattooed on his face. Another version of the story makes the brothers the aggressors in ridiculing the Emperor's religion. The Emperor pointed out that they had come uninvited from Palestine and might be expected to respect the ruler of the country they had adopted. In this version both were tattooed, and the brothers made the dignified retort that the Emperor might write what he would, he would have to read it again before the great Judge. But their own story as preserved in their Life shows them not so much attacking the Emperor as leaders of the opposition to his policy. They were first imprisoned, scourged, and exiled to Proconnesus, and then recalled. They refused to answer the Emperor's questions, and the infamous

---

[1] *Vit. Meth.*, 1252.
[2] Gen., 1088b.
[3] *Vit. Theod. Grapt.*, M.P.G., 116 ; Cont. Theoph., 117 *sqq.* ; ps.-Sim., 701 ; add. Georg., 868 ; Leo Gramm., 1060a.
[4] Vailhé, S., St. Michel et deux frères Grapti, in *Revue de l'orient chrét.*, vol. VI, p. 331.

punishment was ordered.[1]   The iambic verses of this bizarre incident ran as follows :

> That city all desire to see, where trod
> The holy feet of Christ, the Word of God,
> In compassing the world's salvation.
> But these vile tools of superstition,
> Born in the precincts of that holy place,
> Wrought therein deeds, discreditable and base,
> Out of their misbelief and impiously.
> Till like apostates they were forced to fly,
> And secretly to the Imperial city came,
> Bringing their lawless folly still with them.
> And this is the reason we expel them now
> Condemned as rogues and branded on the brow.

Theodore died in exile, but Theophanes survived and became metropolitan of Nicæa.[2]

The hand of the Patriarch behind the Emperor was the real Iconoclastic force. All the indications point to a decline in the appeal of Iconoclasm. The Empress Theodora was known to be an image-worshipper. A story is told that a privileged palace buffoon named Denderis found the Empress kissing images and was told by her that they were dolls. She explained to the Emperor that Denderis had only seen herself and her children reflected in a mirror, but she gave Denderis a whipping, and when the Emperor asked him again about the dolls, he put one hand on his lips and the other behind him and whispered, " Hush, hush, not a word about dolls." [3]   The significance of the story is clearly that Theophilus knew all about the private views of the Empress and tolerated them, even granting her favours on behalf of notorious image-worshippers like the painter Lazarus and perhaps Methodius. Between the affair of Theophanes and Theodore in 836 and the Emperor's death in 842 we hear nothing of religious disorder. The ease with which orthodoxy was restored and the indifference with which the populace and the army saw the tomb of Constantine the greatest of the Iconoclasts desecrated show that Theophilus had made no very strong attempt to press these views on his subjects, however sincerely he might hold

---

[1] *Vit. Theod. Grapt.*, 673. A picture of the incident is in the Madrid MS. of Scylitzes. See Beylié, *L'Habitation byzantine*, p. 122. The composer of the verses is said in the *Vita* to be one Christodoulos.
[2] Cont. Theoph., 176a ; ps.-Sim., 704d.   [3] Cont. Theoph., 105.

them himself, whether it was the will he lacked or the means of enforcing his will. In this connection a sentence of Finlay's is suggestive : " The government of the earlier Iconoclasts reposed on an army organised by themselves and ready to enforce all their orders ; but in the time of Theophilus the army neither possessed the same power over society nor was it equally devoted to the Emperor." [1] One fact has given an exaggerated place to Theophilus as an Iconoclast. That is the sadistic cruelty of the methods of punishment inflicted on Lazarus and the Grapti. This may have significance in emphasising the vein of extravagance which in other ways also he displays, but it does not imply what it is made to imply,[2] a stronger zeal for Iconoclasm than his predecessors. The conclusion, indeed, would seem to be that Theophilus the last was also the least of the adherents of a definitely Iconoclastic policy, and in that policy he acted more under the influence of the Patriarch John than *proprio motu*.

[1] *Op. cit.*, p. 138.   [2] *E.g.* by Pargoire.

CHAPTER XII

THE END OF THE CONTROVERSY IN THE EAST

AUTHORITIES

As for Chapter IX.

W HEN Theophilus died of dysentery in 842, his son
Michael was but three years old, and the regency
fell to Theodora the Empress-mother. The doom of
Iconoclasm had long been sounding. Theophilus had been
singularly unfortunate in war ; his persistent failures were
openly attributed to his religious opinions.[1] Iconoclasm
itself was a declining force. The Studite monks, though
possessing no leader of the talents of Theodore, had gained a
tactical advantage which was even more valuable. They
had obtained an influence in the palace through Theoctista,
mother of the Empress.[2] The Empress herself was a loyal
image-worshipper and had brought up her five daughters
in the same faith.[3] Most important of all, there were signs
that a popular outbreak in favour of orthodoxy was
imminent. Before his death Theophilus anticipated trouble
from an orthodox believer of Persian descent named
Theophobus, a general in the army, and had ordered his
secret execution.[4] Between the Studite monks [5] and the
fear of a rising the advisers of the Empress were not long
in deciding that the restoration of orthodoxy would be a
politic move. These advisers, who had been nominated in
the will of the late Emperor, were Theoktistos, patrician,
keeper of the imperial purple ink, and logothete of the cursus,
Manuel, magistros and domesticus of the scholarii, uncle of

[1] Cont. Theoph., 101a.
[2] Gardner, *Theodore of Studium*, p. 196.
[3] Cont. Theoph., 105a.
[4] Gen., 1065c.
[5] The monks and other exiles returned, probably without decree, immediately after the death of Theophilus.

the Empress, and Bardas her brother.[1] There was a
conflict of opinion among the three. Manuel was inclined
to take no action. Possibly, as Finlay surmises, he was
himself an Iconoclast.[2] At all events, he feared the leading
laymen who surrounded the Patriarch.[3] Theoktistos was
urgently pressing the Empress to act. The Empress was still
strongly under the influence of her late husband. Not only
did she fear the strength of the Patriarch's party, but she
put the case plainly : " My husband was a man of understanding who knew what was politic. Are we to abandon
his policy ? "[4] Meanwhile Manuel had been induced to
change his opinions. The story is that he fell ill and the
Studite monks promised him restoration of health if he would
restore the images. That the Studites won Manuel by this
appeal is unlikely. He discovered something which caused
him graver misgivings, danger of a revolution.[5] To this
plea the Empress yielded. She agreed that a meeting of the
orthodox should take place at the house of Theoktistos to
investigate the doctrines of orthodoxy.[6] This meeting probably decided on the restoration of orthodoxy. The restoration was carried out rapidly but cautiously [7] a year after the
death of Theophilus.[8] Many bishops and priests conformed,
others were expelled.[9] It was the Patriarch who caused
most anxiety, for the Patriarch was not only the head of the
party, he was the greatest personality of Constantinople.
The drungarius of the Watch, Constantine, was entrusted
with the message asking him to accept image-worship or
abdicate.[10] The Patriarch, so the story runs, having read

---

[1] On the incidents leading to the restoration of images George the Monk,
though a contemporary authority, is without value. Instead of exact information he gives vague declamation. The account of Genesios seems best. The
Continuators of Theophanes are inclined to exaggerate the importance of
Manuel and the enthusiasm of the Empress for the change. Cedrenus has a
value here, for by following Genesios he shows that he considered his account
the best.

[2] Bury, however, suggests that the interest taken by the Studite monks in
Manuel mark him as a secret image-worshipper. *East. Rom. Emp.*, p. 146.

[3] Gen., 1092a ; Ced., I, 1024b.   [4] Gen., 1092c.

[5] *Ib.* 1093a. In Gen., Manuel hints at this. Ced., I, 1025b, interprets
his hint in plain language as " imminent danger to the dynasty and the life
of the Empress."   [6] Gen., 1093a.   [7] *Ib.*

[8] *Vit. Ioannicii*, 320. The date marks the end of the restoration. The new
Patriarch was consecrated in March, 843, and on the 11th March the first
Feast of Orthodoxy was celebrated in honour of the restored images.

[9] Gen., 1093a ; Theoph., *Or. de exilio Niceph.* (M.P.G., 100), 164a.

[10] Cont. Theoph., 164d.

the message and dismissed the messenger, proceeded to wound himself with a knife and spread the rumour that he had been assassinated by order of the Empress. The truth was discovered through a servant, and the Patriarch retired to his celebrated house in the suburbs, the scene of many scandals invented for him.[1] The Patriarch gave less trouble than might have been expected. To his see there was appointed Methodius,[2] who had long been an inmate of the palace, and may be supposed to have been admitted to the imperial counsels.

After the work of restoration had started, a formal Council of the Church was held at Constantinople,[3] probably early in 843. Information concerning this council is vague and uncertain. Its proceedings are summarised in the not very reliable Vetus Synodicon : " Theodora and Michael summoned a divine and holy local synod in the house of the Keeper of the Ink and degraded the disreputable John from the see and appointed Saint Methodius Patriarch ; they confirmed the seven Holy Councils and restored the sacred images to the veneration which was formerly their due." [4] Probably the Council was a meeting of bishops summoned when all the work was done, to ratify the acts of the Empress, particularly the expulsion of John and the appointment of Methodius. It would be at that meeting that Theodora adroitly saved the memory of her husband from official condemnation. She asked that his name should be kept free from blame, that is, not included in the anathemas. Otherwise she could not consent to the restoration of orthodoxy.[5] Methodius replied that the fate of Theophilus was not in his hands. Much as he would wish to repay a benefactor, especially when the benefactor is a prince, those who had departed this life in the hope of damnation, bearing their own open condemnation, were beyond the reach of any absolution of his. The Empress replied with a solemn affirmation that the Emperor before his death had repented

---

[1] Cont. Theoph., 166b, 172.
[2] *Vit. Meth.*, 1253a.   [3] Georg. Mon., II, 802.
[4] Fabricius, *Biblioth. Grœc.*, vol. XI, p. 253. The only significant words are ἐν τοῖς Κανικλείου, which would identify the Council with one of the meetings at the house of Theoktistos. The attitude of the Patriarch John must have been ascertained before the Council.
[5] Cont. Theoph., 168a.

and asked for the images, which she had held up for him to kiss. On hearing this the bishops, balancing their doubts of the accuracy of this story against the thought of the exemplary piety of the Empress,[1] agreed to pray for the Emperor and gave a written security that his name would not be included in the anathemas. Accordingly, the restoration of orthodoxy was formally celebrated on the first Sunday in Lent (11th March), 843, a celebration the Eastern Church still observes under the name of the Sunday of Orthodoxy. Heretics were proscribed throughout the world, and John, in particular, was marked out for condemnation. He had been removed to a monastery.[2] There he displayed his attachment to his principles by having the eyes of a picture cut out.[3] For this exploit he was flogged and narrowly escaped blinding.[4] He next proceeded to attack the new Patriarch, bribing a woman to say that Methodius had debauched her. The charge was heard before the Empress. The Patriarch gave a demonstration which showed him to be physically incapable of debauching any woman.[5] Even so Manuel, who perhaps still in some measure regretted the past, was not satisfied until he compelled the woman to confess that she had been bribed to bring a false accusation.[6] The proper reverence to the images, says George the Monk, was then finally restored.[7] It was never again overthrown in the East. John the ex-Patriarch is heard of no more. He was dead before 866, for in that year his tomb was desecrated.[8] There is hardly adequate material for arriving at a just estimate of the singular character of the Patriarch John. His wealth and magnificence, his patronage of architecture and mechanical science, won him the esteem of the Emperor Theophilus, who learnt to share his tastes. They roused wonder even in the caliph to whom John went as imperial ambassador. To the populace he was a necromancer, practising many varieties of sorcery but most skilful

---

[1] Cont. Theoph., 168c.
[2] Of Clidion at Stenos, says Leo Gramm., 1061a.
[3] Cont. Theoph., 172.
[4] *Ib.*; Gen., 1096c. ps.-Sim. erroneously says that he was blinded (713b). The Empress expressed the opinion that blinding was what he deserved. Gen., *loc. cit.*
[5] Cont. Theoph., 173b ; Gen., 1097b, who says that the woman was mother of Metrophanes, bishop of Smyrna, a touch adding verisimilitude to the story.
[6] Cont. Theoph., 176a.
[7] Georg. Mon., II, 803.   [8] Leo Gramm., 1081a.

with the divining bowl (λεκανομαντεία). His private residence was the mysterious laboratory of crime. There he was reputed to keep for his evil purposes nuns and women, the assistants of his craft or the victims of his lusts.[1] But of the real man behind this legendary figure nothing remains. His theology and his religious convictions are unknown. The last of the great Iconoclasts, John is the one about whom we know least.

The triumphant image-worshippers carried themselves confidently, almost insolently. The painter Lazarus restored the image of Christ on the Chalce Gate, which had been removed by Leo the Armenian. When he was asked by Theodora to forgive Theophilus, he replied : " God is not unjust to forget our love and our labour towards him and prefer his hatred and surpassing madness." [2] Theophanes with the branded face had risen to be metropolitan of Smyrna. He was present at the imperial banquet at which the restoration of orthodoxy was celebrated. The Empress tried to make some awkward apology to him, but he only answered tactlessly : " For this writing I shall indict your husband and Emperor at the incorruptible tribunal of God." The Empress burst into tears, crying, " Is this your promise and the agreement you have endorsed ? " " No, no," interrupted the pacific Patriarch, " our promises still stand. These men's contempt is of no account." [3]

The Patriarch might be pacific towards the Empress, but he admitted no compromise with the decisions of her Council. The weakness of the restoration of orthodoxy under Irene had been the lenient handling of the Iconoclastic clergy by Tarasius. Methodius took precautions that there should be no repetition of this mistake. He ordained an unprecedented number of men to fill the place of the nonconforming Iconoclasts, making orthodoxy compensate in the candidates for the lack of other qualifications.[4] The miserable reign of Michael the Drunkard showed no sign of reaction. In 865, a Russian fleet appeared in the neighbourhood of Constantinople. It was shattered by a storm, and the universal opinion was that the storm was produced by the application

[1] Cont. Theoph., 172. See Bréhier, L., Un patriarche sorcier a Constantinople, *Revue de l'orient chrét.*, 1904.
[2] Cont. Theoph., 117c.
[3] *Ib.* 176a.   [4] *Vit. Meth.*, 1257b.

to the waters of the image of the Virgin of Blachernæ.[1] It would appear that the Iconoclasts had lived in vain. In the following year occurred an incident, small in itself, but symbolical of the end of Iconoclasm. The tomb of Copronymus, greatest of the Iconoclasts, was broken open. The corpse was removed and wrapped in a sack. The body of the Patriarch John was also removed from its grave. At the public horse-races both bodies were exposed and beaten, and finally burnt at the place of Maurianos.[2] There is no record of either protest or opposition.

Faint echoes of the controversy did sound for a time. In 861 Pope Nicholas I,[3] to whom appeal had been made in the disputes over Photius, notices the allegation of the Greek envoys that anxiety was acute in Constantinople because of a revival of Iconoclastic views, but the absence of supporting facts, and the indifference which accompanied the violation of the tomb of Constantine, suggests that the plea was a disingenuous attempt to enlist the sympathy of the Pope in an entirely different matter. The eighth General Council, held at Constantinople in 869 to condemn Photius, dealt incidentally with the matter. There was no suggestion that Photius had any affection for Iconoclasm. On the contrary, it was one of the few points upon which he was in harmony with his opponents.[4] The Council probably took the opportunity of giving Iconoclasm a parting kick. Four persons of Iconoclastic leanings were summoned before the council and required to recant. Three of them obeyed. The fourth, Theodore Krithinos, clung to his opinions, and the anathema was pronounced against him. The third Canon of the council was directed against Iconoclasm. It decreed that the honour paid to the image of Christ should be the same as that paid to the book of the gospels. Pictures gave the illiterate what books gave the learned. The honour paid to them according to ancient tradition passes to their originals. " Whoever, therefore, does not venerate the image of the Saviour Christ, may he not see his face when he shall come in the glory of his Father. We venerate also images of the Virgin, the angels, and the saints. Those

[1] Leo Gramm., 1073b.
[2] *Ib.* 1081a.
[3] Mansi, XV, 161.
[4] Neander, E. Tr., vol. VI, p. 288.

Q

who do not so be they anathema by the Father, the Son, and the Holy Ghost."[1]

The orthodox view never changed in the East. It remains to-day what it was in the eighth century, at its highest a sacramental theory of the relation of original and copy, at its lowest an instrument of the most puerile superstition.

Two illustrations may serve to emphasise this. The first is the answer of the Council of Bethlehem in 1672 to the Calvinistic leanings of Cyril Lucar, the second are some contemporary extracts. Cyril had accepted the bearing of the second commandment on images, and suggested that images of Christ and the saints were permissible, but that worship and service to them were forbidden in Scripture.[2] The Council stated that the correct doctrine required men to adore, honour, and kiss the images of our Lord, the Virgin, the saints, and the angels, and the Holy Spirit represented as a dove. It roundly declared that the use of the word "idolatry" in connection with such adoration was foolish and frivolous. "For we worship with latreia the only God in Trinity and none other. . . . But the holy images we adore relatively since the honour paid to them is referred to their prototypes." The Council comments severely on the loose application of words of Scripture apart from their context, instancing the cherubim and brazen bulls as necessary factors to be taken into account in any consideration of the relation of the second commandment to pictorial representation ; secondly, it alleged that opinions expressed by holy men against image-worship referred to latreia not to the correct veneration. It adhered to the seventh General Council and anathematised the opinion that the adoration of images meant the payment of latreia to images. The Council, while insisting on image-worship, accepted the principle which Theodore Studites would have denied, that pictures served as the books of the illiterate.[3]

For contemporary evidence the following is interesting. The reformation of the Greek Calendar produced in 1924 this expression of opinion. "I tell you the truth," said one

[1] Mansi, XVI, 161. The canon was reaffirmed by the council held at Constantinople in 879. Mansi, XVII, 494. Cf. Walch, vol. X, p. 808.
[2] The Acts and Decrees of the Synod of Jerusalem. Trans. Robertson (London, 1899), pp. 213, 214.
[3] *Op. cit.*, pp. 156 *sqq.*

charming old specimen [of the conservative type] . . . " the Panagia does not like this new calendar. More, St. George does not like it either. There was a concessionist priest who sang the office of St. George before the saint on the new-fangled day—and the saint fell down flat on the ground." In the same year it is reported that on the occasion of a serious forest fire in the neighbourhood of the monastery of Khiliandari in Mount Athos, " the monks in despair of all human aid brought out their most sacred eikon, 'Our Lady of the three Hands,' and put it in the path of the fire. On the instant the wind changed, the fire was driven . . . back on the already devastated area, where it soon went out for lack of fuel." [1]

We may in conclusion attempt to summarise the effects of the controversy on the Eastern Church. In religion, the results were entirely negative. The conflict with Iconoclasm was the last time that an influx of new thought seriously invaded the Church in the East. In the act of resisting the invasion, Eastern Christianity finally demonstrated the policy which it had indicated even as early as the fifth century—the complete stereotyping of doctrine. Henceforth for the Eastern Church the seventh Council marks the close of the canon of doctrine exactly parallel to the closed canon of Scripture. There can be no further addition even in the way of development. After St. John of Damascus theology in the East means exegesis in a sense unknown in Western Europe. " The radical affliction from which the Orthodox Church suffers is arrested development." [2] The Iconoclastic controversy was the occasion which finally gave the East this character.

Socially and politically the controversy produced the isolation of the East from the rest of Christendom. Other facts contributed to this end, and the ultimate causes were no doubt more deeply seated. But the incidents of the Iconoclastic controversy widened the breach beyond repair. The relations between Constantinople and Rome never recovered from the events of the reign of Constantine V. When Irene restored orthodoxy she neither revoked the

[1] Both incidents are recorded, apparently seriously, in *The Christian East*, September, 1924, p. 144. For similar beliefs in contemporary Russia, see " The Phenomenal Renewal of Eikons," *The Christian East*, June, 1925, pp. 94 *sqq.*
[2] Fortescue, Adrian, *The Orthodox Eastern Church* (London, 1920), p. 393.

decree which deprived the bishop of Rome of his jurisdiction over South Italy and Illyricum, nor did she make any pretence of restoring the Papal patrimonies. Pope Hadrian wrote to Charles with some bitterness about this failure. He says that he gives the Emperor at Constantinople warning that if the dioceses and patrimonies are not restored he will be declared a heretic.[1] But Constantinople did nothing, and it is easy to see that the Papal toleration of the eccentric views of the Franks owed something to Constantinople's indifference to the Pope's territorial claims. Theodore and his party, alive to the fact that Rome was the ideal centre of unity, advocated incessantly a policy new to the local self-sufficiency of Constantinople. They called on the Emperor and the Church to take for their teacher Rome, the head of Christendom. They called in vain. Constantinople might appeal to Rome when it suited her, when she had something to gain and nothing to offer—for example, in the Photian disputes. But local jealousy never permitted any sincere intercourse. When Theodora restored orthodoxy she asked for no opinion or co-operation on the part of Rome. The Patriarch Methodius, who had once brought letters from Rome appealing for the restoration of the true faith, apparently had no thought for Rome in the day of success. The final breach between the Churches was postponed, but it was virtually complete in the ninth century.

Though the Iconoclasts failed entirely to achieve the objects for which they contended, the effects they did achieve were both greater and more permanent than might be supposed. Iconoclasm, says Diehl, produced in Art a return to primitive models and a greater realism. Animal and conventional decoration is its most conspicuous subject matter. " On répète volontiers que les iconoclastes ont anéanti l'art. Ce qui vient d'être indiqué montre amplement combien ce reproche est peu justifié. Mais il y a plus. On ne saurait même dire avec vérité qu'ils aient anéanti l'art religieux." [2] In the earlier stages the new art apparently copied from the Hellenic tradition preserved in Egypt. Under Theophilus it turned to Persia.[3] The effect was that there came a temporary renaissance of Byzantine

---

[1] Mansi, XIII, 808.   [2] Diehl, C., *Manuel d'Art byz.*, p. 352.
[3] Bréhier, L., *L'Art chrét.*, pp. 122, 123.

art which makes it fair to say that to Iconoclasm Byzantine art owes its second golden age.[1] Examples of the new, freer, and more realistic art are to be seen in the satirical illustrations of several psalters of the ninth–eleventh centuries.[2] Nothing could be more lively than the picture of " I will not sit among the ungodly " (Ps. xxvi. 5), showing John the Iconoclast rolling at the feet of Methodius.[3] Nothing could be more unlike the eventual type of religious picture which the East produced. This, the official Image, was the old hieratic picture stereotyped. The doctrine of the relation of the picture to the original forbade all individuality. And so there became established the featureless conventional face of the eikons.[4] At the same time the contentions of the Iconoclasts eventually carried into religious art a curious compromise, a great affection for low relief and the total disappearance of the statue proper. It took some generations for this to be firmly established. The universal practice of the Eastern Church to-day is to employ only sacred pictures flat or in low relief. Sculptured figures in the round are practically unknown. A few church decorations of the Iconoclastic period survive. In these the cross is a conspicuous object among the mosaic ornamentation. The best example is the apse of the church of St. Irene in Constantinople.[5]

[1] Diehl, *op. cit.*, pp. 359 *sqq.*
[2] Examples are the Chloudof Psalter in the monastery of St. Nicholas, Moscow, a Studite Ps. in Br. Mus. (Add. MSS. 19352), Ps. of the monastery of Pantocrator, Mt. Athos. Reproductions are given in Gardner, Bréhier, and Dalton, *op. cit.* For a list of Iconoclastic illustrations, see Tikkanen, J. J., *Die Psalter illustration in Mittelalter*, vol. I.
[3] From Pantocrator Ps., Bréhier, *op. cit.*, p. 125.
[4] Bréhier, *ib.*
[5] Illustrated in Dalton, *op. cit.*, p. 385 Another example occurs in St. Sophia, Salonika. Bréhier, *op. cit.*, p. 123.

CHAPTER XIII

ICONOCLASM AND THE FRANKS—(i) CHARLES THE GREAT

(a) AUTHORITIES

1. *Libri Carolini.* For this see below, Text. ed. Heumann, Hanover, 1731. Also M.G.H. ed. Bastgen, 1924. On the Caroline Books the most accessible writers are Hefele and the articles in Hauck, R.E. Perceval, *The Seven Œcumenical Councils*, on this subject is very misleading. Pope Hadrian's reply to Charles is found in Mansi, XIII, 759 *sqq.*

2. Council of Frankfort in Mansi, XIII, 863.

3. Council of Paris, M.G.H. Leges. Sect. III, vol. ii, part 2, ed. Werminghoff.

(b) MODERN

All writers on the Carolingian Age touch the subject, but little has been added to the very lucid and judicious account given by Neander, vols. v and vi. See also articles on the principal persons in Hauck, R.E.

(i)

WHEN Constantine V died in 775, a new situation had developed in the West. From that time onwards there were three parties involved—Constantinople, the Pope, and the Frankish Empire. No two of them were completely in harmony. The religious problem was inextricably involved with politics. The position of the Pope was particularly obscure. He had committed himself politically to the Franks. He might find himself in religious union with Constantinople and in religious discord with Charlemagne, but political loyalty came first. So that he was found tolerating in Charles what he had condemned in Constantine. Dogmatic orthodoxy in Constantinople was insufficient to counterbalance political orthodoxy in Frankland. In the later stages of the Iconoclastic dispute the Pope gave an official friendship to the orthodox of the Empire, but his real fellowship was with the heterodox Franks.

The relations of the Empire and the Franks, on the other hand, were on the whole friendly. But the two Empires had so little in common and came so little into contact with each other that there was usually no occasion for any definite attitude.

At the time of the death of Constantine V Charles had overthrown the Lombard kingdom and Northern Italy was part of the Frankish empire. The Exarchate and Pentapolis, nominally still the dominions of Constantinople, had been bestowed on Rome by Pippin. The donation was renewed by Charles, and he, through the Pope, was the actual ruler of Rome and the Exarchate. Southern Italy and Istria remained loyal to Constantinople. When, in 780, orthodoxy was revived in Constantinople, the actions whch had been taken by the Franks made complete political friendship between Rome and Constantinople difficult. It was recognised at Constantinople that Charles rather than the Pope was the important person, and in 781 negotiations were opened for a marriage between the young Emperor Constantine and Hrotrud, daughter of Charles. After a successful beginning the negotiations broke down, and in 787 relations between the emperor and the king became strained. Indeed, a mild state of war broke out.[1] The Franks raided the borders of Beneventum and a Greek fleet was active on the coast. For the strained relations between the empires Charles threw some blame upon the Pope. It was in these unfavourable circumstances that the Council of Nicæa met in 787. At that Council there were no Western representatives except the two Papal delegates. The plain fact was that Western Europe had no concern in the matter at issue. The Pope's interest in the Council centred not on doctrine but on prerogative and temporalities. For the rest of Western Europe there was no image question. The pronouncements on the subject by the Vatican Councils had been a demonstration against Constantinople, not a decision required by any actual facts of the Church in the Western countries. The Pope regarded three points as essential to the restoration of orthodoxy in the East:

(i) That the decisions of the Council of 753 should be rescinded ;

(ii) That the Papal patrimonies should be restored ;

(iii) That the dioceses of Southern Italy and Illyricum should return to the Roman jurisdiction.

[1] Hodgkin, VIII, p. 15.

After the Council Pope Hadrian I informed Charles that he was dissatisfied on the second and third points, and unless his demands were met he would decree the Emperor in Constantinople a heretic.[1] But the Pope asked in vain. It may be best to follow this issue to the end before discussing the image question in the West.

After the Nicene Council the position was that—

(i) Relations between Rome and Constantinople were strained because of Irene's failure to meet the Papal territorial requirements.

(ii) Relations between Constantinople and the Franks were openly hostile because the Franks were plainly becoming a rival power threatening the imperial dominions.

Charles, on his part, was alive to his equivocal position. He had been piqued by the attitude of Irene. Between 790 and 800 he delivered a series of calculated insults. In 790 the *Caroline Books*, and in 794 the Council of Frankfort, attacked Irene's theology. In 799 Charles meditated a more material attack by planning an expedition against Sicily. The coronation of Charles by the Pope in 800 altered his tactics. He became anxious to conciliate Constantinople. The Pope had committed him to a position he had not sought. He was now unequivocally a rival Emperor. The image question did not greatly exercise the Papal policy. Hadrian could overlook Charles's theological polemics because in his mind " all roads led eventually to the question of the patrimonies of St. Peter." [2] By crowning Charles Hadrian's successor Leo III settled the question at the cost of definite estrangement between Rome and Constantinople. Later Popes might have theological dealings with Constantinople, the party represented by Theodore might proclaim the primacy of Peter, but the official attitude of Constantinople was indifference to the Papacy except when occasion made Papal support a useful expedient. The orthodox Empress Theodora ignored Rome as openly as the Iconoclast Theophilus.

Charles, however, adopted after his coronation a more conciliatory attitude to Constantinople. Abandoning his designs on Sicily he entered into fresh negotiations for a marriage—now between himself and Irene. This would have restored the unity of the Empire, an ideal which still

[1] Ep. Had., Mansi, XIII, 808d.   [2] Hodgkin, VIII, p. 19.

held good. For it was almost an axiom both in the East and the West that there could be but one Roman Emperor. The scheme was opposed by Aetius and collapsed with the fall of Irene in 802. Charles still sought friendly relations with Constantinople, and in 803 sent a draft treaty to Nicephorus, which was never signed. Intermittent hostilities over Venetia followed. Eventually, in 812, the Emperor Michael recognised Charles as Basileus.[1] The relations between Constantinople and the Frankish Empire were henceforth similar to the relations between Constantinople and the Papacy. The Eastern Emperors did not consider their concession to be permanent. " It became hereafter a principle of their policy to decline to accord the title of Basileus to the Western Emperor unless they required his assistance or had some particular object to gain." [2]

Against this political background we can now examine in detail the Western disputes about the images. The general position was—

(i) The question was academic and owed its vagaries to matters of policy or personal taste, because, strictly speaking, there was no image question in Western Europe. Between the episode of Serenus of Marseilles at the end of the sixth century and the publication of the *Caroline Books* at the end of the eighth there does not appear to be any evidence whatever of any local controversy or even expression of opinion in Western Europe on the use or abuse of pictures.[3] The question was introduced *in vacuo* and was carried on in the spirit of a debating society where no real issues were involved. It was only afterwards that an operative Iconoclasm appeared with Claudius of Turin, and it is very doubtful if the spiritual affinities of Claudius were with Eastern Iconoclasm at all.

(ii) Pictures and images of saints rather than of Christ were the more regular Western use, and, as Harnack says, whereas in the East image-worship grew out of Christology, in the West it was part of a system of intercessors and helpers in need.[4]

---

[1] Bury, *East. Rom. Emp.*, p. 325. Previously Charles had been to Constantinople ῥήξ only.

[2] *Ib.*, p. 326.

[3] Apart, of course, from the two Vatican councils and the synod of Gentilly, which were pronouncements on the Greek situation.

[4] *Hist. of Dogm.*, E. Tr., V, p. 308.

(iii) When once controversy had been artificially aroused it found the question of relics as vital as that of pictures.

No doubt the temperament of Western Europe approached Christianity differently from the East. The farther from the Mediterranean Christianity advanced the more marked this difference. It is doubtful if images ever received West of Rome the mystical regard they obtained in the East. Of course, pictures and images were equally common in West and in East. One of the earliest apologists for their use was the Western bishop Paulinus of Nola (409–431), who justified them as valuable instruments of instruction.[1] Already the practices of the East were raising alarm in the West. The Spaniard Vigilantius (died 420) at the beginning of the fifth century paid a visit to the Holy Land, and by what he saw was moved to vigorous protest against the worship of images as a breach of the Mosaic law which Jesus came to fulfil. His protest covered a large field of nascent abuses besides images, relics, ascetic observances, and even clerical celibacy. Vigilantius found a bitter opponent in St. Jerome, who succeeded in branding him with the stigma of heresy. In many ways Vigilantius anticipated by four centuries Claudius of Turin, brought up like himself in the shadow of the Pyrenees. In spite of a strain of extravagance Vigilantius excellently illustrates the temperamental difference between East and West on the image question, for Vigilantius is a genuine Western, while St. Jerome was by all his associations much more akin to the Easterns.[2] Long after the practice of image-worship was established in the East no such questions had arisen in the West. Pictures of Martin of Tours and Paulinus of Nola were introduced into Gallic churches during their lifetime, a fact which is decisive against image-worship.[3] Superstition, however, was not far away. It was in Rome that images of St. Simeon Stylites were used as mascots,[4] and in the sixth century Gregory of Tours (d. 594) had begun to tell stories of

[1]   propterea visum nobis opus utile, totis
            felicibus domibus pictura illudere sancta
            . . . sanctasque legenti
            historias castorum operum subrepit honestas
            exemplis inducta piis.—Paul., *nat.* ix.
[2] On Vigilantius, see Fremantle, W. H., in D.C.B. s.v.
[3] Paulin, *Ep.*, 32.   [4] *Vid. supra*, p. 21.

miraculous pictures.[1] Nevertheless, there was something like an official decision, supported by popular opinion, that pictures were means of instruction and not objects of devotion. St. Augustine (354–430) many times in the course of his writings expressed this view, admitting that many pretended Christians worshipped pictures, but denying them a true knowledge of the religion they professed.[2] The matter was definitely settled for the West by Gregory the Great in the affair of Serenus, bishop of Marseilles (595–600). Serenus had found that pictures in his diocese were being used for adoration, and had incontinently thrown the pictures out of the church. Pope Gregory wrote, praising his zeal against the worship of created things, but regretting its intemperate display.

" We are of opinion, however, that you should not have destroyed the effigies. A picture is introduced into a church that the illiterate may at least read what they see on the walls, though they may be unable to read the same in writing. You should, therefore, my brother, have preserved the pictures while safeguarding them from popular worship, that the illiterate might have the means of acquiring a knowledge of history whilst the people might be prevented from committing the sin of worshipping a picture." [3]

The same Pope wrote to Secundinus, a hermit otherwise unknown :

" We have sent you the effigies which you asked to be forwarded by the deacon Dulcidus. Your request gave us great pleasure ; for it shows you seek with all your heart and intention him whose image you desire to have before your eyes, that the daily visible sight of it may keep your devotion active. . . . I know that you do not seek the image of our Saviour that you may worship it as God, but that by bringing to mind the Son of God you may keep warm in the love of him whose image you desire to have before you. We bow before it not as before divinity but we worship him of whom we are reminded by the picture that shows his birth or his person or his throne." [4]

[1] *de mirac.*, 22, 23.
[2] *de moribus*, I, 34, 74. Cf. *de cons. evang.*, I, 10, 16, *enarr. in ps. cxiii*, *serm.* 2, 4, etc. In the Libellus of the Synod of Paris there are 34 citations from St. Augustine deprecating any worship of images.
[3] Greg. Mag., *Ep.*, IX, 105. Cf. XI, 13.
[4] *Ib.*, IX, 52.

When Augustine of Canterbury had carried before him a picture of Christ,[1] he provided a good illustration of the accepted use of pictures and images in the West. They were ornaments of the Church and useful aids to devotion. Western Europe had never been torn by the Monophysite struggle, and to that more than to any single fact it owed a complete freedom from any difficulties about images and apparently a no less complete freedom from the more violent extravagances that surrounded the Iconoclastic struggle in the East. That explains the position in the West during the first Iconoclastic period. The Popes refused the innovations of Leo III and Constantine V in the spirit in which Gregory the Great rebuked Serenus. When the Council of Nicæa restored orthodoxy, it could make no difference in Western Europe, for orthodoxy had suffered no reverse. Then came *à propos* of nothing in their own religious situation a definite pronouncement on images from the Franks. The history of the *Caroline Books* and the synods of Frankfort and Paris is a singular one. When all factors are taken into account it appears that the earlier Frankish pronouncements on images were not related to any actual situation of the time, but were a theoretical view based on three things—

(i) A failure to grasp the atmosphere of the controversy and the ideas Christological and philosophic in which it developed in Constantinople.

(ii) A corresponding inability to appreciate the meaning of the decisions of Nicæa.

(iii) A personal hostility felt by Charles for Irene with a consequent readiness to find Constantinople always in the wrong.

To these may be added a fourth factor, the self-reliance and sense of power which characterised the young and exuberant Frankish Church.[2] The effect is that the Western dispute is a logomachy rather than a reality.

(ii) THE CAROLINE BOOKS

After Pope Hadrian I had received the Report of the Council of Nicæa, he forwarded the same in a Latin trans-

---

[1] Bede, *Hist. Eccl.*, I, 15.
[2] On the last feature cf. Harnack, *Hist. Dogm.*, E. Tr., V, 305 *sqq.*

lation to Charles. The translation, according to Anastasius, was so barbarous that much of it was unintelligible.[1] Charles found cause for complaint in the record and made a series of notes of his objections, which were eventually sent to the Pope as a " Capitulare adversus Synodum." This has not survived. The Pope's reply is the celebrated Epistle of Hadrian.[2] The *Caroline Books* are extant, and a reference to them occurs in Hincmar of Rheims (ninth century), who cites a passage from Book IV, 28, and says that he read it in a large volume against the Seventh Council which was sent by Charles to Rome.[3] The exact relation of the extant *Caroline Books* to the original *Capitulare* is a difficult problem. Probably the *Caroline Books* are a revision of the original document. It has been thought that the hand responsible for the *Caroline Books* was Alcuin's. It is true that Charles seems to have appealed to him, and Alcuin wrote from Britain, with the authority of the British bishops behind him, a summary of the Scriptural authorities definitely unfavourable to images,[4] and subsequently Charles commended Alcuin to the Synod of Frankfort as an adviser ; but this evidence is too slender to justify any conclusion.[5] We may perhaps be satisfied to say that Charles's arguments against Nicæa were originally sent to Rome by the hand of Angilbert in 792 or

[1] Mansi, XII, 981c. Fragments survive, cited in the *Caroline Books* and in the letter of Hadrian to Charles. Mansi, XIII, 759 *sqq.* That a Latin translation was all Charles had is plain from *Caroline Books, e.g.* a latinæ locutionis integritate penitus extraneum et a sensuum regulis et alienum. *Lib. Car.*, IV, 14 (p. 489). Cf. IV, 15 (p. 494).

[2] *Ib.* That the *Caroline Books* are not the Capitulare is proved by (i) the fact that they are not called so. (ii) In the Capitulare it is evident from Hadrian's letter the arguments had cross references to the sessions of the Council to which they referred. No such references exist in the *Caroline Books*. (iii) The contents. *Lib. Car.*, III, 3, is called chapter I by Hadrian. Mansi, XIII, 760b. (iv) Three whole sections discussed by Hadrian are not found in *Lib. Car.*, Mansi, XIII, 800e, 804e, 808b. (v) The Pope's reply refers to nothing in the last half of Bk. IV of *Lib. Car.*, a fact which is strong evidence that this material was added after the Capitulare was sent to Rome.

[3] Hincmar, M.P.L., vol. 136, col. 360. de eius destructione non modicum volumen quod in palatio adolescentulus legi ab eodem inperatore Romam est per quosdam episcopos missum.

[4] So Roger of Hoveden (twelfth century). See Collier, *Eccles. Hist.*, I, 327.

[5] The editors of Alcuin, Jaffe and Dummler believed they could trace Alcuin's style in the *Lib. Car.* Monum. Alcuin., p. 220n. Stubbs also accepted Alcuin's authorship. D.C.B., s.v. Alcuin. Cf. Hauck, R.E., X, 90.

794,[1] and that in a revised form they are what we know as the *Caroline Books*

Beyond the testimony of Hincmar already cited and a reference to Charles's refutation of Nicæa contained in the Libellus of the Synod of Paris in 825, the *Caroline Books* remained unnoticed for several centuries. Steuchi, the Papal Librarian (d. 1550), mentioned in his work on the Donation of Constantine that the Palatine Library possessed an ancient MS. in the Lombard hand of a work of Charles on images.[2] In 1549 the Caroline Books were printed at Paris in one volume 16mo from a MS. alleged to exist "in one of the oldest and most famous churches of Gaul." There was no editor's name or place of publication given, but it was the work of Jean du Tillet, subsequently bishop, first of St. Brieux and then of Meaux. The text of this edition was reprinted by Goldast in his collection of Imperial decrees on Images (Frankfort, 1608), and by Heumann (Hanover, 1731). Froben Forster, in 1759, sought the original MS. in Rome, but Cardinal Passionei informed him that it could not be found. The MSS. of Tillet and Steuchi have not been definitely identified, but Vat. 7202, discovered by Reifferschied in 1866, corresponds with the text of Tillet. A second MS. is in the Arsenal Library, Paris, Number 663.[3] The title of the work is "Caroli Magni contra synodum quæ in partibus Græciæ pro adorandis imaginibus stolide sive arroganter gesta sunt libri quattuor." This is not a very complete description of the contents. For the books attack the Iconoclasts as well as the orthodox of Nicæa.[4] They are indeed a lively and on the whole a sound statement of the common-sense view that pictures are not

---

[1] Angilbert was present in Rome in both years. Hadrian died in 795, which marks the extreme date at one end. 792 seems a likely date, in which case the reply of the Pope did not satisfy Charles, and the Council of Frankfort in 794 was the answer to the Pope's letter. The *Lib. Car.* date themselves "about three years" after the Council (ed. Heumann, Præf., p. 8), but this may well be the date of Charles's first draft, which was subsequently revised. The following is a rough scheme of dates. 789/790 Charles received the report of Nicæa and made his first notes. They were put together with references to the Acta of Nicæa and sent to Rome in 792. The material was more carefully worked up for circulation among the Frankish bishops before the Synod of Frankfort, and in this form they are the *Lib. Car.* known to us.

[2] He cites a passage from I, 6, antequam discutiendum, etc.

[3] Krüger's *Handbuch*, II, p. 30.

[4] Both, they say, go off at the deep end. utrique præcipites per abrupta discurrant. I, Præf., p. 9.

objects of any kind of worship, but pleasant and useful ornaments. Apart from the light thrown by the arguments on the Frankish standpoint, it is not unlikely that Charles has incorporated material collected from the propaganda of the Iconoclasts of Constantinople. He is certainly well informed about details of church life there.[1]

The *Caroline Books* are the most complete and rational of all the statements made on the subject of images. It is true that in one passage what was said at Nicæa is completely reversed. Constantine, bishop of Constantia, is made to say : " I take up and embrace with honour the holy and venerable images with the service of veneration that I give to the consubstantial and life-giving Trinity," [2] anathematising those who denied this. Really Constantine had said that he did *not* honour the images with the veneration paid to the Trinity. Charles's text misled him here. But it would be a misreading of the polemic to suppose that this one misinterpretation coloured the whole of Charles's impression of the Nicene Council. Only a single chapter is devoted to it, and if it were removed the indictment would be no weaker. Charles certainly does not write as though his attack was built on this one argument.

Nor does this error stand alone. The phrase Qui conregnat Deus nobis, God our co-regent, is attributed to Irene, who is consequently charged with blasphemous arrogance. It was really used by the Council.[3] The analogy between images and the stones set up in Jordan by Joshua is attributed to the Oriental priest John. It was really advanced by the Papal delegate in a citation from Leontius of Neapolis.[4] The Council of Nicæa is charged with asserting that the apostles instituted image-worship. The Council did not make any explicit statement to that effect. The most it said was that image-worship went back to Apostolic times.[5] In commenting on a quotation from

---

[1] *E.g.* a popular description of Tarasius, qui *ut fertur a populari conversatione* ad sacerdotale culmen a militari habitu ad religiosum, etc., I, 20, p. 110, a report of Frankish ambassadors that many churches in Constantinople are roofless, IV, 3, p. 432. The argument that no act of consecration is made upon an image, I, 2, p. 34, was a point made by the Iconoclastic Council.

[2] secundum servitium adorationis quod . . . Trinitati emitto. III, 17. Cf. Mansi, XII, 1148.

[3] *Lib. Car.*, I, 1 ; Had., *Ep.*, 804d ; Mansi, XIII, 480.

[4] *Lib. Car.*, I, 21 ; Had., *Ep.*, 797e ; Mansi, XIII, 51.

[5] *Lib. Car.*, I, 25 ; Had., *Ep.*, 777c.

Asterius of Amasea, one of the bishops remarked that the father himself (*i.e.* Asterius) had commended the painter of pious pictures. Charles carelessly interpreted the father as God the Father and declared that Scripture contained no such statement.[1] A passage on the Eucharist taken from the proceedings of the Iconoclastic Council of 753 Charles attributes to Nicæa,[2] and he does the same with a passage which spoke of the Emperors as ministers like the apostles, made wise with the Holy Spirit.[3]

The occurrence of such errors shows that the spirit of the *Caroline Books* is a determination to find Nicæa wrong rather than to submit its proceedings to a careful examination. That view is only deepened by a detailed analysis of the argument of the Books. Petty verbal criticisms and sound reasoning are jumbled together. The case is presented unsystematically. So that it is difficult to set out the indictment in a connected sequence.

"Both rulers and clergy in the East," says Charles,[4] "have been inflamed by the swollen ambition of windy arrogance and an unchecked passion for empty praise to forget healthy and sober doctrine and . . . by nefarious and ill-advised synods to attempt to impose on the Church what the Saviour and the apostles, as far as our knowledge goes, never imposed upon it." . . . "A few years ago there was held in Bithynia [5] a synod of such short-sighted perversity that it ruthlessly swept away all pictures that had been set up by them of old time to decorate churches or to recall the past ; what the Lord ordained concerning idols they interpreted of all images, not knowing that 'image' is a class and 'idol' a species, and while species can be included in class, class cannot be included in species. . . . Image is used of that which stands for something else, idol of that which stands for itself. . . . About three years ago another synod was held in those regions by the successors of those who assembled in the first, indeed by many of those, it is said, who were actually present at the first ; which, far as it was from the former in purpose, was not far

[1] *Lib. Car.*, III, 22 ; Had., *Ep.*, 798e ; Mansi, XIII, 18.
[2] *Lib. Car.*, IV, 14; Mansi, XIII, 262. Cf. *Lib. Car.*, II, 27 ; Had., *Ep.*, 778a.
[3] *Lib. Car.*, IV, 20 ; Mansi, XIII, 226.
[4] I use Charles = the *Caroline Books* for the sake of simplicity.
[5] *I.e.* at Hieria.

from it in error. . . . This Council anathematised and abhorred the former Council and its conveners and enforced the worship of the images of which the first Council had not permitted even the sight, and wherever in Scripture or in the commentaries of the fathers they found image mentioned they perverted it to support their own arbitrary intention of worship. . . . They identified ' possess ' and ' worship ' in the same ridiculous way as the first Council had identified ' image ' and ' idol.' In fact, they are even less accurate, for *image* and *idol* are words of the same classification, while *possess* and *worship* have no common element. . . . A new principle is thus brought into the Church, which is equivalent to an act of schism. We therefore appeal to Scripture, the fathers, and the six General Councils, and reject the innovation. . . . For that reason we feel called to write against the written conclusion of that Council, and we do so with the consent of the bishops of our kingdom. . . . We refuse with the first Council to destroy the images or with the second to worship them." [1]

The general attitude of Charles was that the fear of God is shown not, as was alleged at Nicæa, in the veneration and worship of images but in the will and pursuit of the commands of God.[2] If colour is needed to show the fortitude of the Lord, as John the priest said at Nicæa, the men of old like Abel and Enoch never saw it, nor is it to be seen where the art of painting is unknown. It is Christ and not colour that reveals his fortitude. Those who need pictures to recall Christ will soon forget him.[3] The Council accepted the statement that the picture of the Virgin and the Child arouses veneration in any but a disordered mind. On the contrary, says Charles, it is more reasonable to say that the disordered mind is reflected in paying to a picture the veneration due to the Creator. Such a picture might really represent Sarah holding Isaac or Venus holding Æneas.[4] Such mistakes can easily occur. The more beautiful picture is likely to be thought the more wonderful, and poor folk with no competent artists will be deprived of these privileges of the faith, if such they are reckoned.[5]

[1] *Lib. Car.*, Præf.
[2] *Ib.*, III, 28 ; Had., *Ep.*, 795a ; Mansi, XIII, 54.
[3] *Lib. Car.*, IV, 2 ; Had., *Ep.*, 795b ; Mansi, XIII, 71.
[4] *Lib. Car.*, IV, 21 ; Mansi, XIII, 362.
[5] *Lib. Car.*, IV, 27.

The strength of the *Caroline Books* lies in the vivid sense of reality with which they are infused. This is seen not least in the liveliness of the personal attack. Tarasius the Patriarch is treated with small respect, "a man reported to have been advanced in some extraordinary fashion from ordinary life to the highest possible rank, from the tunic to the cassock, from the circus to the altar, from the wrangle of debate to the pulpit, from the rattle of arms to the celebration of the holy mysteries." He is told that if he appeals to the Cherubim on the Mercy Seat as a model for images, the best thing he can do is to introduce a replica of the Jewish sanctuary into his church.[1] Leo of Phocia, the reclaimed Iconoclast, is described as displaying a folly in his scriptural quotation equal to his own silly behaviour in shedding tears for his past.[2] John the Oriental priest is written down as incorrigible in his loquacity, though but a priest (*i.e.* not a bishop).[3] Irene is told bluntly that a woman has no right to teach in a Council. She is forbidden in Scripture and by the law of Nature itself. "For the weakness of her sex and her instability of mind forbid that she should hold the leadership over men in teaching or preaching." [4] Epiphanius the deacon, who read the refutation of the Iconoclastic Council, is described as an empty babbler,[5] somewhat unfairly, for he was merely the official reader. The arrogance of the Council and its vainglorious language is worked up as a definite indictment rather than a casual insult. The Council blasphemously claimed God as its co-regent.[6] The emperors spoke of God choosing "us who seek his glory in truth." [7] They described God as though he asked favours of men. "We ask your fatherhood and above all God asks." [8] The Council throughout showed a lack of kindliness and patience, speaking

---

[1] *Lib. Car.*, I, 20 ; Mansi, XIII, 6. Cf. *Lib. Car.*, III, 2.
[2] *Lib. Car.*, I, 25 ; Had., *Ep.*, 773e ; Mansi, XIII, 55.
[3] multiloqua procacitate. *Lib. Car.*, II, 4.
[4] *Ib.* III, 13 ; Had., *Ep.*, 783e ; Mansi, XII, 1001 ; XIII, 414. The Pope quotes in justification Helena, wife of Constantine I, holding a Council of Jews and Christians at Rome, Pulcheria sitting with Marcian at the fourth council, and women ministering to Christ.
[5] *Lib. Car.*, IV, 16, 17.
[6] *Ib.*, I, 1. Cf. III, 14 ; Had., *Ep.*, 790b.
[7] *Lib. Car.*, I, 2 ; Mansi, XII, 985.
[8] *Lib. Car.*, I, 4 ; Had., *Ep.*, 796d ; Mansi, XII, 985. The Pope quotes the not very convincing parallels, Luke xxii. 32 ; 2 Cor. v. 20, to show that God (Christ) "rogat."

unadvisedly with their lips,[1] and recklessly anathematising the Catholic Church. Agapius of Cæsarea could insolently speak of the Scriptures as *our* Holy Scriptures,[2] and the Council, with similar insolent ignorance, could speak of making Christ their head, whereas it is Christ that chooses men, not men that choose Christ.[3]

The reasoned arguments of the *Books* will be appreciated most effectively if they are grouped together. They may be represented under the following heads [4] :

I. Terms defined. (*a*) Image. (*b*) Worship.

II. Appeals to Authorities. (*a*) General. (*b*) Scriptural. (*c*) Patristic.

III. Points of doctrine raised by the image question.

I. Terms defined. (*a*) The nature of a picture.

CHARLES : A distinction should be drawn between image (imago), similitude (similitudo), and analogy (æqualitas). The image-worshippers tend to identify the three. An image is something that exists apart from that which it represents and admits of no degrees.[5]

The POPE : Every simple soul knows that, as St. Ambrose points out, Christianity is not a matter of philosophy or dialectic.[6]

The relation of image and original.

CHARLES : It is wrong to say that honour paid to the image passes to the original. Images are legitimate for their historical value as reminders of the past and as decorations for churches. But they are apt to be a snare for the ignorant.

The POPE : The statement criticised is St. Basil's, whose orthodoxy none would question.[7]

CHARLES : A ridiculous and false statement was made by the priest John : Whoever venerates an image and says that it is Christ (Hic est Christus) commits no sin. He does commit sin, for he is telling an obvious lie unless Hic is an adverb of place.

The POPE : Christ as divine is not limited in space or

[1] *Lib. Car.*, III, 12.
[2] *Ib.* III, 19 ; Had., *Ep.*, 794e ; Mansi, XII, 1088.
[3] *Lib. Car.*, IV, 24 ; Mansi, XIII, 460.
[4] The reply of Pope Hadrian is adjoined to complete the account.
[5] *Lib. Car.*, I, 8.
[6] Had., *Ep.*, 781d.
[7] *Lib. Car.*, III, 16 ; Had., *Ep.*, 790d ; Mansi, XII, 1145 ; XIII, 71.

time like material bodies. He can therefore be in likenesses
as St. Augustine shows.[1]

(*b*) The word WORSHIP.

CHARLES: Let us examine the examples of adorare quoted
from the Old Testament. Gen. xxiii. 7 : Abraham bowed
himself (adoravit) before the people of the land. Ex. xviii. 7 :
Moses did obeisance (adoravit) at meeting his father-in-law.
This is not the worship paid to God, as the story of Paul
and Barnabas (Acts xiv. 14) shows. Nor is even the respect
shown to human beings a justification for showing the same
respect to pictures. St. Peter does not say Love the pictures
of the brotherhood (1 Peter ii. 17), or Be subject to the
pictures (1 Peter ii. 13).

The POPE : St. Augustine lays down the principle that
words are used in Scripture with a different significance.[2]

CHARLES : There is no reason in the argument that
because Jacob blessed (adoravit) Pharaoh (Gen. xlvii. 7)
but not as God, therefore we worship an image but not as
God.

The POPE : Scripture teaches us to bless, and we know
that we are only truly blessed because of the crucifixion of
the Incarnate Christ.[3]

CHARLES : The adoration paid by Nathan the prophet
to King David (1 Kings i. 23) is the respect paid to authority.
It is no argument for paying worship to images.

The POPE : The Fathers tell us there is a mystical meaning to Scripture, and David is a symbol of Christ.[4]

CHARLES : There is a difference between showing
respect to a man in greeting him and venerating pictures.
God sent his son into the world for the sake of men, not for
the sake of pictures. " Men who proclaim in Holy Writ
inside the church that God alone is to be worshipped and
then summon synods to promote the worship of images
must beware lest they disturb the peace by internal war,
and wreck our welfare by their error as surely as by civil
strife." [5] In a later passage [6] Charles criticises the decision

[1] *Lib. Car.*, IV, 1 ; Had., *Ep.*, 799e. Mansi, XIII, 71.
[2] *Lib. Car.*, I, 9 ; Had., *Ep.*, 770d ; Mansi, XIII, 46, 54, 406.
[3] *Lib. Car.*, I, 14 ; Had., *Ep.*, 772a ; Mansi, XIII, 46, 406.
[4] *Lib. Car.*, I, 22 ; Had., *Ep.*, 798b ; Mansi, XIII, 100.
[5] *Lib. Car.*, II, 24. Not in Hadrian's *Ep.*
[6] *Ib.* IV, 23 ; Mansi, XIII, 403.

of the Council that veneration implied kissing the sacred pictures because the word προσκύνησις, προσκυνεῖν, was used, meaning either " to kiss " or " to venerate." Charles denies that adorare, osculari, and amplecti are synonymous. The Greek view was based on the word προσκυνεῖν, a fact that Charles, either through ignorance or deliberately, failed to grasp.[1]

II. Authorities. (a) The general nature of Authority and the field of appeal.

Charles very strongly insisted that authority for ecclesiastical custom must be sought in Scripture and in the Fathers interpreting apostolic tradition not whimsically but in a fashion that represented the mind of the whole Church.

CHARLES : The Greeks have attempted futilely and recklessly to anathematise the Catholic Church for not worshipping images. They should first have investigated the doctrine of every part of the Church before they, a part only of the Church, ventured to enforce on the whole body a practice which is supported neither by the apostles nor their immediate successors.

The POPE : They have not anathematised the whole Church but the heretics who dissent from the doctrine of the whole.[2]

CHARLES : They call their Council œcumenical, but it plainly was not a gathering of the whole Church, and its resolutions are at variance with those of the Fathers.[3]

CHARLES : The Church of Rome is above the rest, and must always be consulted on matters of faith. Scripture and doctrine are authenticated by Rome.[4]

CHARLES : Images have no ancient authority, and indeed are contrary to all the evidence of Scripture, which is insistent on the necessity of worshipping God only. That view is incompatible with any sort of image-worship.[5]

[1] *Lib. Car.*, IV, 23 ; Mansi, XIII, 403. Not in Hadrian's *Ep.* The Latin translation of the Council is here more than usually barbarous, and in some measure may explain Charles's inability to grasp the point, *e.g.* the words κυνεῖν and προσκυνεῖν are represented by participo and adoro, destroying their point completely.
[2] *Lib. Car.*, III, 11 ; Had., *Ep.*, 783d ; Mansi, XIII, 379, 398.
[3] *Lib. Car.*, IV, 28. Not in Had., *Ep.*
[4] *Lib. Car.*, I, 6. Not in Had., *Ep.*
[5] Imagines vero omni sui cultura et adoratione seclusa utrum in basilicis, propter memoriam rerum gestarum et ornamentum sint an etiam non sint nullum fidei catholicæ adferre poterant præiudicium quippe cum ad peragenda

The POPE : St. Augustine says that the external form and the interior spirit alike are necessary.[1]

CHARLES : The veneration of images never was, as they vainly claim, ordained by the example or ordinance of the Apostles, nor does the New Testament mention any act of veneration beyond mutual greetings of respect, illustrated by the incidents of Peter and Cornelius, John and the angel, Saul at Lycaonia.

The POPE : Dionysius the Areopagite was of the age of the Apostles, and is mentioned in Acts. His testimony has been accepted by the Popes.[2]

CHARLES : For a grave matter we need the support of authentic evidence from Scripture or the Catholic Fathers. Theodore of Myra was satisfied with the dreams of his archdeacon. Dreams are not evidence.

The POPE : The future has been revealed in dreams both under the old and new dispensations.[3]

CHARLES : When it is argued that honour paid to the Emperor's image is a precedent for honouring the image of Christ, the answer is that precedents must be good and worthy. Pagan licence is not a foundation for Christian practice. The Apostle does not say, Be ye imitators of the Emperor, but Be ye imitators of me as I am of Christ.[4]

CHARLES : The Council draws an analogy between images and animal sacrifice. Animal sacrifice was practised in the Old Testament, though a heathen custom. Similarly, images may be pagan and yet legitimate to Christians. This argument is a complete *non sequitur*. The pagan custom of animal sacrifice in the Old Testament is no justification for following the heathen in worshipping images. Further, even the heathen did not originally worship images. They set them up as memorials of dead heroes and gradually raised them to divine honour.[5]

(*b*) The appeal to Scripture.

The argument and the strength of the *Caroline Books*

nostræ salutis mysteria nullum penitus officium habere noscantur.   *Lib. Car.*, II, 21.

[1] *Ib.*; Had., *Ep.*, 785b; Mansi, XIII, 398, 415.

[2] *Lib. Car.*, II, 25; Had., *Ep.*, 777c.   The pseudo-Dionysius to whom the Pope refers was, of course, a sixth-century writer.   The support of the Popes was the ruling of the Vatican Councils of 731 and 769.

[3] *Lib. Car.*, III, 26; Had., *Ep.*, 793e; Mansi, XIII, 34.

[4] *Lib. Car.*, III, 15; Mansi, XII, 1068.   Not in Had., *Ep.*

[5] *Lib. Car.*, IV, 18; Mansi, XIII, 275.   Not in Had., *Ep.*

rests on the appeal to Scripture. The strength of the argument lies in the method of interpretation. Charles is much further from the traditional quasi-allegorical school than the theologians of the Council. He has some sense of the need of setting a passage in its context and expounding it literally. Frequently, simple as this method seems, it is a break with tradition. The Pope almost invariably takes refuge in patristic (*i.e.* traditional) interpretation. But at the time it is probable that the Pope's method would represent the mind of the Church,[1] Charles's only a rash innovation. " This letter of Adrian's," says Collier, " did no execution, as one might expect from the contents of it." [2] So it would appear even to the eyes of the seventeenth century, less obviously so in the eighth. Further, Charles weakened his effectiveness by a mass of pettifogging objections to the indiscriminate quotation of texts with which the Fathers of the Council decorated their speeches. These were not intended to be interpretations of Scripture, and Charles's lack of discrimination reduces the force of his attack on the genuine misinterpretations. Throughout the *Books* Charles consistently lost ground by attempting to disprove too much.

CHARLES : Gen. xxix. 18. The pillar Jacob set up was not an image nor did Jacob worship it, as was implied at the Council.

The POPE : Figurative interpretations of Scripture are endorsed by the Fathers. St. Augustine so interprets this same passage.[3]

CHARLES : Gen. xxxii. 24. The angel wrestling with Jacob was not described as the Council alleged "in the form of a man," nor has the incident any bearing on images.

The POPE : St. Gregory and St. Augustine both accept the interpretation " in the form of a man." [4]

CHARLES : Gen. xxxvii. 33. Jacob is said to have kissed Joseph's coat and laid it on his own eyes (osculatus est cum lacrymis et propriis oculis imposuit). This has no bearing on image-worship nor does it occur in the Hebrew text.

[1] See *e.g.* Had., *Ep.*, 781c, where he states explicitly that the general method of interpretation is not the Council's but St. Augustine's.
[2] *Eccl. Hist. of G. Brit.*, I, 331.
[3] *Lib. Car.*, I, 10 ; Had., *Ep.*, 780d ; Mansi, XIII, 7 ; XII, 1064.
[4] *Lib. Car.*, I, 11 ; Had., *Ep.*, 797b ; Mansi, ib.

The POPE : Some fathers read the text so. There are many examples in patristic writings of readings not found in our translation from the Hebrew.[1]

CHARLES : Gen. xlvii. 31. The analogy from Jacob worshipping the top of Joseph's staff is unsound. Jacob paid reverence not to the wood but to Joseph by means of the wood.

The POPE : St. Augustine interprets the staff as a true type of the Cross.[2]

CHARLES : Images cannot be justified by the Mercy Seat, the Cherubim, and the Ark. These were not ordered to be objects of worship or even records of the past, but signs of future revelation in Christ.

The POPE : They are accepted as support for images by the authority of our predecessors.[3]

CHARLES : Ex. xxxi. 2-6. Bezaleel and Aholiab cannot be cited as witnesses in support of image-worship. There is no ground for holding the work of silver and gold, in which these men were skilful, to be objects of worship. Bezaleel, which is interpreted " in the shadow of God," represents Christ, his assistant Aholiab represents the apostles and apostolic men.

The POPE : The Councils of our predecessors accepted the reference.[4]

CHARLES : Num. xv. 38. It is argued that since it was ordered that blue fringes should be worn as a reminder of the commandments, much more is it legitimate to use a picture of the saints to show us the end of their conversation and to make us imitate their faith according to the apostolic tradition. But the fringes were not appointed for worship, but for a reminder that we should be dressed in justice and holy conversation. Matt. xxiii. 5 condemns the misuse of fringes, parallel to which is the image-worshippers' misuse of images. The phrase " according to apostolic tradition " is not correct. The apostolic tradition (Heb. xi., Eph. v., 1 Cor. xi.) is that the end of the conversation of the saints is to be seen not in their pictures but in their virtues.

[1] *Lib. Car.*, I, 12 ; Had., *Ep.*, 771a ; Mansi, XIII, 46.
[2] *Lib. Car.*, I, 13 ; Had., *Ep.*, 771c ; Mansi, XII, 46, 1064 ; XIII, 115. The text is that of the LXX.
[3] *Lib. Car.*, I, 15 ; Had., *Ep.*, 781a ; Mansi, XIII, 1064. Cf. *Lib. Car.*, II, 26 ; Had., *Ep.*, 785d.
[4] *Lib. Car.*, I, 16 ; Had., *Ep.*, 792d ; Mansi, XIII, 250.

The POPE : The opinion of our predecessors in the Councils already mentioned answers this argument.[1]

CHARLES : The analogy of the brazen serpent is unsound. The brazen serpent was set up by the Lord's explicit orders ; not so the images of saints. The Son of Man himself alone is said to be lifted up like the serpent (John iii.). Moreover, when the serpent became an object of worship it was destroyed by Hezekiah. To that superstitious worship image-worship is an exact parallel.

The POPE (getting out of temper) : This has been settled by the opinion of our predecessors. But for the satisfaction of unbelievers and for the guidance of the Franks we may add the following : Are we to believe that the people of Israel were freed from their calamity by looking at a brazen serpent and to doubt our own salvation as we behold and venerate the figures of Christ our God and the saints ? God forbid that we should give way to the impious madness of such recklessness.[2]

CHARLES : Image-worship cannot be supported by the stones that Joshua set up by Jordan. For the text of Scripture tells us that the purpose was not that the stones should be worshipped but that they should be a memorial of the drying of Jordan, with a mystical reference to Jesus, to baptism, and to the twelve apostles.

The POPE : Many patristic passages show that the external symbol brings the mind to the inner truth.[3]

CHARLES : Solomon's oxen and lions in the Temple are no support for image-worship, for the Old Testament should be interpreted mystically. The oxen and the lions represent the apostles and their successors, who unite the gentleness of the ox with the fierceness of the lion.

The POPE : But our predecessors have accepted the analogy.[4]

In order to show Charles's method the following selection of criticisms of casual Scriptural quotations occurring in the proceedings of the Council is given :

CHARLES : Ps. xi. 3 (xii. 2). "They talk of vanity every one with his neighbour." These words are not intended

---

[1] *Lib. Car.*, I, 17 ; Had., *Ep.*, 797c ; Mansi, XIII, 114 *sqq.*
[2] *Lib. Car.*, I, 18 ; Had., *Ep.*, 772c ; Mansi, XII, 1065 ; XIII, 167.
[3] *Lib. Car.*, I, 21 ; Had., *Ep.*, 797e ; Mansi, XIII, 51.
[4] *Lib. Car.*, II, 9 ; Had., *Ep.*, 805e ; Mansi, XIII, 43.

to describe the Iconoclasts.   They refer to the Pharisees and
the Jews who rejected Christ.   They might appropriately
be used to describe those who summon assemblies to buttress
up image-worship.

The POPE :   The words can be applied to the Iconoclasts.[1]

CHARLES :   Ps. xxv. 8 (xxvi. 8).   " I have loved the
habitation of thy house " (*decorem domus tuæ*).   The Council
by *decorem* understood " images."   But the next clause, *locus
habitationis gloriæ domini* ("the place where thine honour
dwelleth "), is decisive against any materialistic interpretation.   Surely the anchorites like Antony and Hilarion, who
lived in huts and had no decorated churches, loved *decorem
domus domini*.[2]

CHARLES :   Ps. lxxiii. 3 (lxxiv. 4).   " That thou mayest
destroy every enemy which hath done evil in thy sanctuary."
The reference is not to the Iconoclasts.   It is foolish to appropriate to the opponents of image-worship what was said
long ago of the spoilers of the Temple in Jerusalem.

The POPE :   But the words may be applied to them if we
understand sancta to describe all consecrated things.[3]

CHARLES :   Ps. lxxxiv. 11 (lxxxv. 12).   " Mercy and
truth are met together."   The Eastern priest John applied
this figure to the co-operation of Pope Hadrian and Tarasius.
It might legitimately describe the union of the Old Testament and the New Testament.   But, as used by John, it
is a twisting of sacred words to support superstition and is
grossly flattering.

The POPE :   The reference is appropriate.   God has had
mercy on Constantinople and Constantinople has met the
Holy Apostolic See which always holds to righteousness, as
it is written, Iustitiæ sedes fidei domus, aula pudoris.[4]

CHARLES :   Cant. ii. 14.   " Let me see thy countenance "
(*faciem*).   This they have applied to looking at images.   If
the word *faciem* is to be understood literally all the phraseology of Canticles must be interpreted in the same way.

The POPE :   Rightly so.   Cant. is admittedly interpreted in reference to Christ, and the sight of the sacred
pictures is a relevant example.[5]

---

[1] *Lib. Car.*, I, 26 ; Had., *Ep.*, 774b ; Mansi, XIII, 222, 326.
[2] *Lib. Car.*, I, 29.   Not in Had., *Ep.* ; Mansi, XII, 1065.
[3] *Lib. Car.*, II, 1 ; Had., *Ep.*, 766c ; Mansi, XIII, 130.
[4] *Lib. Car*, II, 4 ; Had., *Ep.*, 774c ; Mansi, XIII, 1085.
[5] *Lib. Car.*, II, 10 ; Had., *Ep.*, 769b ; Mansi, XIII, 221.

CHARLES : Matt. v. 15. "No man lighteth a lamp." It is the height of folly to quote this against Iconoclasm. It plainly means that the disciples were to proclaim their message boldly.

The POPE : The lamp is the Catholic faith, as the Fathers show (and the Iconoclasts were suppressing it).[1]

CHARLES : John the Eastern priest identified the angel pursuing a host of barbarians in a picture described by St. John Chrysostom with the angel who smote the Assyrians encamped around Jerusalem. Apart from the fact that the passage has no bearing on image-worship, there is no ground whatever for the identification. Besides, the Assyrians were not encamped around Jerusalem.

The POPE : It was a private interpretation of John's, and he only put it interrogatively.[2]

(c) Criticism of interpretations of the Fathers.

This is one of the strongest features of the *Caroline Books*. The weakest of the passages are unerringly dropped on, and the special pleading introduced into the interpretation is well riddled.

CHARLES : St. Sylvester, bishop of Rome, is quoted as sending pictures of the apostles to the Emperor Constantine. There is no indication that he ordered the emperor to worship them. We do not condemn the practice of having pictures.[3]

CHARLES : The life and preaching of Gregory of Nyssa are unknown to us. Yet they adduce evidence from him to support their errors. Works attributed to him must be treated as secondary authorities.[4]

CHARLES : The evidence adduced from the Canon of the Sixth Council on depicting Christ as a Lamb has no bearing on image-worship.

The POPE : This evidence was brought to show that at the period of the Sixth Council images and pictures were held in honour.[5]

[1] *Lib. Car.*, II, 12 ; Had., *Ep.*, 776a ; Mansi, XIII, 210.
[2] *Lib. Car.*, III, 20 ; Had., *Ep.*, 780b ; Mansi, XIII, 10.
[3] *Lib. Car.*, I, 13. Not in Had., *Ep.* ; Mansi, XII, 1060.
[4] *Lib. Car.*, II, 17. Not in Had., *Ep.* ; Mansi, XIII, 10. This is an unjustifiable scepticism on the part of Charles.
[5] *Lib. Car.*, II, 18 ; Had., *Ep.*, 777a ; Mansi, XIII, 40. Charles also impugns the text of the Canon as cited, but this apparently was due to the vicious text he had before him.

CHARLES : The statement of St. John Chrysostom on the honour paid to the Emperor's image is not a true analogy for image-worship. The reference is to a pagan superstition. The analogy as applied to Christianity sees in Christ the image of God, and so St. John himself applies it.

The POPE : Our predecessors have accepted the analogy in reference to images of Christ.[1]

CHARLES : No authentic writings attest the story of the man restrained from adultery by the image of a certain Polemon. Even if the story were true it would no more justify a general veneration of images than the incident of Balaam's ass would justify a general veneration of animals. It is not parallel to the Lord's healing of the woman with the issue as they argue. Our Lord's miracle has a parabolic meaning.

The POPE : The story has the evidence of Gregory Nazianzen behind it.[2]

CHARLES : The Council has interpolated the text of the Fathers with apocryphal incidents and absurd follies.

The POPE : As a matter of fact, they exposed the apocryphal evidence used by the Iconoclastic synod.[3]

CHARLES : They related a foolish tale of a penitent who made an oath to a demon and then broke it. His Abbot is convicted of madness in saying that it was better to frequent every brothel in the town than to refuse to venerate an image of the Lord and his mother. The folly of the penitent in his dealings with the demon is even surpassed by the moral obliquity of the Abbot's advice.

The POPE : This story has the authority of St. Sophronius, whom no true Christian would disregard.[4]

CHARLES : The letter attributed to St. Symeon addressed to the Emperor Justinian is inconsistent with Christian standards, first in saying to the Emperor, " Your divine ears," and secondly, in preventing the Emperor from exercising mercy.

The POPE : St. Ambrose addressed Gratian as *Sancte imperator*. The phrase " divine " ears means ears open to the divine word. The saint did not prevent the Emperor showing mercy, but claimed a reasonable punishment should be inflicted. It was just anger.[5]

[1] *Lib. Car.*, II, 19 ; Had., *Ep.*, 798d ; Mansi, XIII, 67.
[2] *Lib. Car.*, III, 21 ; Had., *Ep.*, 791e ; Mansi, XIII, 14.
[3] *Lib. Car.*, III, 30 ; Had., *Ep.*, 784d.
[4] *Lib. Car.*, III, 31 ; Had., *Ep.*, 794c ; Mansi, XIII, 194.
[5] *Lib. Car.*, IV, 5 ; Had., *Ep.*, 766e ; Mansi, XIII, 159.

CHARLES : No text of Scripture preserves their allegation that Jesus sent his portrait to Abgar. It is an apocryphal story and even so does not support image-worship.

The POPE : The current report of the faithful is worthy of credence, as our predecessor Stephen has ruled. The tradition is accepted in the letter of the three Patriarchs.[1]

CHARLES : Anonymous lives of the Fathers are not proper evidence for matters of dispute.

The POPE : St. Augustine shows that anonymous writings, though not read in church, are perused by the orthodox and ascribed to probable writers. Passions of martyrs are even canonically accepted for reading in church on the martyr's festival.[2]

CHARLES : A story was cited of a monk who lighted a candle before an image of the Virgin and found it still burning even after six months. A story like this, with no date, time, or place, has no authority. A miracle is not necessarily the work of God ; it may be due to demons. Nor is the instrument of a miracle *ipso facto* an object of veneration.[3]

CHARLES : The legend that grass of healing power grew at the foot of the statue erected by the woman with the issue is the fruit of superstition. A miraculous power needs more evidence than this.[4]

CHARLES : The criticism aimed at Epiphanius is ill-directed. It was argued that he could not have been a destroyer of images because his disciples in Cyprus decorated with pictures the church called after him. But the question is not about images but image-worship, and Epiphanius cannot be held responsible for his disciples.[5] So, when it is argued that if Epiphanius had thought image-worship a heresy he would have included it among the eighty heresies he described, it might as aptly be claimed that if he thought neglect of image-worship a heresy he would have included it in his list. As a matter of fact, his epistle to the Bishop John is a definite attack on images. In his account of Simon Magus he notices that Simon gave effigies of himself and his companion Selene for veneration, and in his account

---

[1] *Lib. Car.*, IV, 10 ; Had., *Ep.*, 768b ; Mansi, XII, 964 ; XIII, 191.
[2] *Lib. Car.*, IV, 11 ; Had., *Ep.*, 800a.
[3] *Lib. Car.*, IV, 12. Not in Had., *Ep.* ; Mansi, XIII, 194.
[4] *Lib. Car.*, IV, 15. Not in Had., *Ep.* ; Mansi, XIII, 267.
[5] *Lib. Car.*, IV, 19. Not in Had., *Ep.* ; Mansi, XIII, 295.

of Carpocrates he notices the pictures of Jesus, Paul, Homer, and Pythagoras venerated by Marcellina. Had he been familiar with image-worship as a legitimate act he would not have called attention to it as a practice of heretics.[1]

III. As Charles makes his indictment as sweeping as possible he introduces a good deal of indiscriminate doctrine into his attack. The following points deal with matters not directly at issue, but apparently felt by Charles to be too good to be left unmade :

(i) The relation of Nicæa to historical Christianity.

CHARLES : The Council has anathematised its own parents. If their predecessors were heretics, they themselves are the children of heretics, taught and consecrated by heretics, and thereby their own ecclesiastical acts are invalidated.

The POPE : Authority (Scriptural and patristic) shows the principle of individual responsibility for oneself and not for others, whether parents or children.[2]

(ii) Heretical tendencies shown by members of the Council.

CHARLES : Theodore of Jerusalem used expressions in his letter which savoured of Arianism. He spoke of the Father having no beginning but the Son having no other beginning but the Father, which might imply a subordination of the Son.

The POPE : The statements are not out of harmony with the orthodox doctrine of the subordination of the Son.[3]

CHARLES : Tarasius[4] used the word contribulus to describe the Holy Spirit in relation to the Father and the Son.

The POPE : Sophronius used the same expression.[5]

(iii) The rites of the Church.

1. The Procession of the Holy Spirit.

CHARLES : Tarasius said not that the Holy Spirit proceeds from the Father and the Son but from the Father

---

[1] *Lib. Car.*, IV, 25. Not in Had., *Ep.*; Mansi, XIII, 294.
[2] *Lib. Car.*, II, 31 ; Had., *Ep.*, 782e ; Mansi, XIII, 398, 415. Cf. *Lib. Car.*, IV, 7 ; Had., *Ep.*, 784e ; *Lib. Car.*, IV, 22.
[3] *Lib. Car.*, III, 4 ; Had., *Ep.*, 764 ; Mansi, XII, 1136.
[4] Really Theodore of Jerusalem.
[5] *Lib. Car.*, III, 5 ; Had., *Ep.*, 787 ; Mansi, XII, 1135.

through the Son. This phrase does not safeguard the faith. It would not be correct to say the Son was born per hominem instead of ex homine. The phrase might suggest an Arian view, that the Holy Spirit was a creature made like other created things per filium. The temporal mission of the Holy Spirit is through the Son, but that his procession should be so has a queer sound. The Holy Spirit procedit nascendo, procedendo non nascitur.

The Pope answers courteously, with full patristic citations, that Tarasius' expression is correct.[1]

2. The Nature of God.

CHARLES: They circumscribe God when they say, " We worship and venerate them (*i.e.* images) as the abode of God (sicut locum Dei)."

The POPE : The Fathers teach that God is everywhere.[2]

3. Miracles.

CHARLES : The belief that images have worked miracles does not justify image-worship. Miracles have been wrought by the fallen angels and their allies and by magic. Even the instruments of God's actions are not venerated. Moses did not venerate the burning bush or Aaron's rod. Much less are all objects of a class venerated because one has been the instrument of a miracle. Would you venerate every jawbone of an ass because one in Samson's hand wrought a miracle ?

The POPE : The worship they are to receive is only the kiss and veneration. It is not the worship paid to God.[3]

4. Relics.[4]

CHARLES : Images are not parallel to relics of the holy martyrs, as they attempt to maintain, for relics are either of the body or of what were in the body or about the body of a particular saint. Images are not believed to have been or likely to be part of the body or near the body of those to whom they are ascribed.

The Pope entirely misses the point, quoting authorities for reverence to relics which Charles had accepted.[5]

[1] *Lib. Car.*, III, 3 ; Had., *Ep.*, 760b ; Mansi, XII, 1121. Cf. *Lib. Car.*, III, 8.
[2] *Lib. Car.*, III, 27 ; Had., *Ep.*, 805b ; Mansi, XIII, 46.
[3] *Lib. Car.*, III, 25 ; Had., *Ep.*, 784b ; Mansi, XIII, 23, 47.
[4] Relics held in the West much the position of images in the East.
[5] *Lib. Car.*, III, 24 ; Had., *Ep.*, 785e ; Mansi, XIII, 379.

5. The Cross.

CHARLES : The cross is not parallel to images. It was the instrument of redemption, and is authorised by many New Testament references such as " Let him take up his cross and follow me " (Matt. xvi. 24). Images are neither.

The Pope quotes from the fathers to show that both the cross and images are symbols of Christ.[1]

6. The Scriptures.

CHARLES : Images cannot be objects of veneration as the scriptures are. The scriptures are the recognised revelation of God, images are derived from the heathen. It is " whatsoever things were written aforetime . . ." not whatsoever things were painted. The scriptures and not pictures are the rule of life (norma per quem instruitur).

The POPE : But Pope Gregory, writing to Serenus of Massilia, puts pictures on the level of scripture, and so do other fathers.[2]

7. Lights and Incense.

CHARLES : The Council says that none need be offended because lights and incense are offered before pictures of the saints. But it is an offence to offer to senseless things what is due to God. Besides, the true devotion of the Greeks is not great, for our ambassadors report that many of their churches are roofless. It is the custom of our country not to burn incense to images but to make our churches magnificent.[3]

The Frankish *via media* between Iconoclasm and the decisions of Nicæa is seen in the following, which may be considered a summary of the case :

CHARLES : Either to worship or to break an image is contrary to the doctrine of Gregory, bishop of Rome, in his letter to Serenus.

The POPE : But Gregory in his letter to Januarius, bishop of Calare, does not condemn reverence for images.[4]

CHARLES : We are as much opposed to destroying images as to venerating them. We consider, however, that it is

---

[1] *Lib. Car.*, II, 28 ; Had., *Ep.*, 804a ; Mansi, XIII, 379.
[2] *Lib. Car.*, II, 30 ; Had., *Ep.*, 786e ; Mansi, XIII, 379.
[3] *Lib. Car.*, IV, 3. Not in Had., *Ep.* ; Mansi, XIII, 123, 378.
[4] *Lib. Car.*, II, 23 ; Had., *Ep.*, 781e.

a great exaggeration to compare those who contemn images to Nebuchadnezzar when he cast the bones of the kings of Judah from their sepulchres, put out the eyes of the king, killed his sons and removed the Cherubim from the Temple.

The POPE : But Pope Gregory has shown that images are not to be contemned but venerated.[1]

CHARLES : We agree that acts of Iconoclasm like that related by the deacon Demetrius are rightly described as careless and irregular (incaute et inordinate).

The POPE : The Fathers of the Sixth Council stigmatised the mutilation of documents as heretical.[2]

CHARLES : People who find it necessary to erect images to keep alive the remembrance of the saints or even of the Lord himself must have poor memories.

The POPE (evidently out of temper) : And St. Jerome says that such men in seeking to blame the incapacity of others reveal their own. They need purging.[3]

So much for this free-spoken attack. Apart from its bearing on the Iconoclastic struggle, it is an interesting picture of the little reverence that the younger nations had as yet either for the Papacy or the authority of a General Council.[4]

The document of which the *Caroline Books* are the expansion was received by the Pope and answered by him on the lines indicated by the quotations from his letter given already. It will be very plain that Hadrian did not shine in controversy. Frequently he misses the point of

[1] *Lib. Car.*, IV, 4 ; Had., *Ep.*, 795c ; Mansi, XIII, 174.
[2] *Lib. Car.*, IV, 8 ; Had., *Ep.*, 795e ; Mansi, XIII, 183.
[3] *Lib. Car.*, II, 22 ; Had., *Ep.*, 800b.
[4] The scandal that such a spirit provoked is shown in a chapter added to the *Lib. Car.* by another hand. This chapter (*Lib. Car.*, IV, 29, in Goldast's edition) states that the Pope is to understand that the writer follows the opinion of Pope Gregory to Serenus : Adorare vero eas (sc. imagines) nequaquam cogimus qui noluerint, frangere vel destruere eas etiamsi quis voluerit non permittimus. But the text of Gregory actually reads, et quidem zelum vos ne quid manufactum adorari possit habuisse laudavimus sed frangere easdem imagines non debuisse iudicamus . . . and again, et si quis imagines facere voluerit minime prohibe, adorare vero omni modo devita. The citation of Gregory misrepresents his actual ruling and contradicts the opinion already expressed in the *Lib. Car.* This chapter was first brought to light by Binius. It is absent from the original text of *Lib. Car.* and from most MSS. of Hadrian, *Ep.* Goldast summarises correctly : aut spurium esse hoc capitulum atque a Romanis adulatoribus confictum aut probam sententiam ab improbis editoribus depravatum (*op. cit.*, p. 588).

his opponent's argument altogether. Practically never does he meet him. Instead he falls back on authority. But the Pope takes the attack much more kindly than might have been expected. Partly, no doubt, he was aware that the image-question had no practical interest in his sphere of influence, while he himself was a man of no intellectual power or curiosity. Partly the dioceses transferred to Constantinople and the patrimonies of Peter were more important to him than academic debates on abstract doctrine. The conclusion of his reply to Charles emphasises this.

" We have made as yet no reply to the Emperors, fearing they may return to their error. We exhorted them long ago about the images and the dioceses of the archbishops which . . . we sought to restore to the Holy Catholic and Apostolic Roman Church, which they sequestered together with our patrimonies at the time they overthrew the holy images. To those exhortations they never replied. They have returned in one point from their errors, but in the other two they remain where they were [*i.e.* the dioceses of South Italy and the patrimonies]. . . . If your God-protected Royal Excellency agrees we repeat our exhortation [to Constantinople], expressing gratitude that the holy images are in their former state. But as to the dioceses of our holy Roman churches . . . and the patrimonies we warn the Emperor solemnly that if he does not restore them to our Holy Roman Church, we shall decree him a heretic for persistence in this error." [1]

Charles replied by getting the Council of Frankfort to support him. This Council met in June, 794, to discuss Adoptianism. It was largely attended by bishops from all the Frankish dominions, Italy, Gaul, and Germany, including two Papal delegates, the bishops Theophylact and Stephen. [2] Even some British monks were present as advisers. [3] Fragmentary information alone survives. The question of the images was introduced incidentally. The *Annals of Einhard* say that " the Council recently held in Constantinople under Herena and Constantine her son, and styled the Seventh General Council, was declared null

---

[1] Had., *Ep.* ; Mansi, XIII, 808c.   [2] Mansi, XIII, 863.
[3] . . . necnon et de Brittanniæ partibus aliquos ecclesiasticæ disciplinæ viros convocavimus. *Ep. ad. Elipand*, cited Werminghoff, p. 159.

by universal consent and refused the titles Seventh and General." [1] The second Canon of Frankfort which survives reads : The question was introduced of the recent synod of the Greeks on the worship of images held at Constantinople. There it was laid down that those who refuse to pay service and veneration to the images as to the divine Trinity (ita ut deificam Trinitatem) should be judged anathema. Our most holy fathers, absolutely refusing that service, held them (*i.e.* the Greeks) in contempt and unanimously condemned them.[2]

The reference to the Holy Trinity shows that Charles still, either maliciously or ignorantly, believed that the same kind of worship was to be paid to images as to the Trinity. It is usually suggested that Charles was still misled by the erroneous translation of the proceedings of Nicæa, and condemned something that was never sought or practised. It is more likely that he obstinately refused to see the possibility of degrees of veneration. To him there was only one kind of religious veneration possible ; whether paid to the Trinity or to images it was the same.[3] Some of the older historians made desperate efforts to prove that the Council of Frankfort had not rejected Nicæa,[4] because the Council condemned was described as meeting in Constantinople. To Charles Constantinople meant the Empire in the same way as its subjects are always called Greeks. There can be no room for reasonable doubt that the Council of Frankfort went out of its way to condemn Nicæa, not in the ordinary course of its business, but deliberately, no doubt to satisfy the desires of its president Charles to speak his mind to the Papal delegates. Charles apparently had the last word, and the subject of Images disappeared from Western debate for a quarter of a century.

(iii) Lewis the Pious and the Empire

That the image-question was not indigenous to the West is shown by the fact that in the years when there

---

[1] *Ann. Einh.* (ed. Kurze), p. 95.

[2] Mansi, XIII, 909d ; Werminghoff, p. 165.

[3] Leclerq is almost certainly correct in concluding that the *Lib. Car.* refuse any kind of cult to images. Hefele-Leclerq, III (ii), 1070n.

[4] The ingenious special pleading of Binius may be read in Mansi, XIII, 914 *sqq.*, and in Perceval, who (p. 584) is in sympathy with it.

were few relations between the West and Constantinople, the image-question in the West was dead. The second Iconoclastic outbreak took place in Constantinople, but it made no impression beyond the Adriatic, until the Emperor Michael II reopened relations with the West by writing to Lewis the Pious on April 10th, 824. The substance of that letter we have already examined. The occasion was pacific. Refugees from the Iconoclastic outbreak had fled to Italy, whence they were carrying on propaganda against Constantinople. Michael desiring a peaceful settlement wrote to ask Lewis to intervene with the Pope to get these active agents expelled from Rome.[1] Michael gave a full account of the religious situation in Constantinople, and sought a basis of unity in the doctrine of the Six General Councils, which he probably thought would represent the Frankish position. The Imperial embassy was entertained by Lewis on November 17th, 824, at Rouen.[2] No record tells us what exactly Lewis set out to achieve after reading Michael's letter. But what appears to have been his scheme was this. Judging from the letter and the conversation of the Imperial envoys that Michael and the Franks held the same views, he decided to approach the Pope and persuade him to substitute the *via media* for the decision of Nicæa.[3] Lewis sent to the Pope, Eugenius II, Freculphus bishop of Lisieux, and a certain Adegarius, probably to begin the negotiations. They met the Pope, talked and obtained his permission to investigate the matter.[4] A synod accordingly met at Paris, November 1st, 825, to collect the evidence against images and draw up the Frankish case.[5] What exactly was the nature of the assembly is not clear. It seems to have been a select Committee of the Emperor's advisers rather than a Council. Many of the members were ignorant of the subject of inquiry until they reached Paris.[6] But its findings were referred to as authoritative pronouncements by later writers. Walafrid Strabo says that the Greek error was confuted under Lewis in synodal writings,[7]

---

[1] Werm., p. 480.
[2] *Ann. Einh. ad ann.* 824.
[3] Werm., p. 482.
[4] *Ib.*, pp. 532, 534.
[5] *Ib.*, p. 483.
[6] *Ib.*, p. 483.   They do not speak of themselves as a Council but as servi et fidelissimi oratores vestri. *Ib.*, p. 481.   Orator = King's deputy.
[7] Scriptis synodalibus.   Wal. Str., *de exord.*, 8.

while Dungal, who is no enemy of images, refers to this
assembly as one that has settled the question definitely,
even for the least intelligent.[1]

The assembly first made a short memorandum on the
history of the controversy over the Council of Nicæa.
The preliminary letter sent by Pope Hadrian to Irene they
considered rightly reprimanded the action of those who
presumed to destroy the images. On the other hand, he
was ill-advised in ordering a superstitious veneration for
them.[2] Their own view was that it is legitimate to set
up pictures but wrong to worship them. The patristic
evidence cited by Hadriar they thought irrelevant to the
issue involved. In consequence of the Pope's letter a
Council was held which in enjoining the worship and
veneration of images, giving them the name of holy, and
claiming to get sanctity from them,[3] fell into error as serious
as did the other Council which decreed the abolition of
images. This Nicene Council, in order to support their
contention, misconstrued passages of the Fathers, violating
both their meaning and the intention of the writers.[4]
The Emperor Charles had this Council examined and found
many faults, upon which he sent heads of notes to Pope
Hadrian for correction. The Pope out of favour to the
Council wrote a defence of a character that served his
purpose rather than the demands of truth.[5] His defence
was quite unsatisfactory, but he concluded by stating that
he held to the position defined by Pope St. Gregory, which
shows that he went wrong in ignorance rather than malice.[6]
The meeting then read the Emperor Michael's letter and
received from Freculphus a report of his discussion with
the Pope. They considered that what was wanted was a
statement of a *via media* of truth, between a complete
destruction of images and a superstitious worship.[7] The
Pope they thought would respect the influence of Lewis,

---

[1] Dung., 468c.

[2] Sic indiscrete noscitur fecisse ineo quod superstitiose eas adorare iussit.
Werm., p. 481.

[3] Qui eas non solum coli et adorari et sanctas nuncupari sancxerunt
verumetiam sanctimoniam ab eis se adipisci professi sunt. *Ib.*

[4] Violenter sumpserunt et eidem suo operi incompetenter aptaverunt
quoniam non eo sensu quo dicta nec eo intellectu quo a sanctis patribus
exposita ab illis esse produntur prolata vel intellectu. *Ib.*

[5] Respondere quæ voluit non tamen quæ decuit conatus est. *Ib.*

[6] *Ib.*, p. 482.   [7] *Ib.*

the authority of the Papal see, and the evidence of the truth.[1]

The assembly then made an extensive collection of patristic evidence.[2] This they submitted to the Emperor, apologising for deficiencies due to lack of time. Two bishops, Halitgar of Cambrai and Amalarius of Metz, brought this to the Emperor with the official libellus of the assembly. The tenor of their conclusions was that pictures of saints are not to be foolishly injured or contemned, nor, on the other hand, are they to be worshipped or venerated. They are to be treated as memorials of what they represent, according to the Catholic and unequivocal statement of St. Gregory.[3] " We consider that the holders of the see of St. Peter should be treated with every respect. At the same time we know, some of us by what we have seen and others by report, of the superstitious regard the Popes pay to pictures. We desire to express ourselves against the destruction of pictures and so influence those of the other party to accept our guidance on their practice." [4]

Two model letters were enclosed for Lewis to send to the Pope, one to the Pope in Lewis' own name and one in the Pope's name to Michael.[5] To the Pope it was proposed to say that the mission of the Church is peace. " The demands of human reason should not be refused except in matters beyond the pale of human discussion. The disagreement in the East on images we believe can be settled reasonably, and to that end we have made a collection of patristic evidence. The proper guardian of the Church's peace beyond all question is the Pope. It is with full recognition of that fact that we lay before you the information we have collected, partly in writing and partly to be expounded to you verbally by your sons our brethren (*i.e.* the bishops bringing the letter to the Pope)." [6]

To the Emperors Michael and Theophilus the substance of the proposed letter ran as follows (written in the person of the Pope) :

" As the agent of St. Peter and St. Paul I call you to the

[1] Werm., p. 483.   [2] For a detailed examination of this, see Appendix.
[3] Werm., p. 484.   [4] *Ib.*
[5] *Ib.* pp. 521-528. A lacuna occurs before the first, and the beginning of the letter to the Pope seems to have been part of what is lost.
[6] *Ib.* pp. 521-523.

cause of peace. I beg you to listen as the God-ordained Roman Emperors."[1] They appeal to the three principles of (i) reason, (ii) authority, (iii) counsel.

(i) Reason. The Frankish Council and clergy desire peace to reign in the two kingdoms which God has set up (*i.e.* the Eastern and Western Empires). They state that in their own kingdom there is no ancient ruling on images. Any one who has wished to make a religious picture as a pious memorial has been at liberty to do so. On the other hand, they realise that contrary customs may prevail elsewhere, and they urge that there should be no compulsion either to have or not to have pictures. Those who have them should be warned against an illegitimate worship of pictures and those who dislike them should be warned against damaging them.[2]

(ii) Authority. The opinions of Gregory are tabulated. His view may be stated as : We do not prostrate ourselves before the picture as a divinity, but we venerate it (*adoramus*). The first statement is the significant one.[3]

(iii) Counsel. The counsel of God is peace and charity (John xiv. 27 ; 1 Cor. xiii. 3). There is a certain lack of wisdom in the disunion displayed among the Greeks. Mercy should be shown to the image-worshippers to reconcile them. Bitterness has been caused by the mistaken policy of the Emperor, who thought that error could not be corrected without a total destruction of images. The true policy is to regard images as a means of pious recollection for the educated and of instruction for the ignorant.[4] The policy of violence on both sides has led to a series of exiles, sufferings, mutilations, and even murders. It is the deception of the devil that leads to this, as it was the devil who deceived Irene.[5]

Lewis received the report of the Council on December 6th, 825.[6] After reading it he sent the patristic excerpts to Jeremy, archbishop of Sens, and Jonas, bishop of Orleans, who were to bring the matter personally before the Pope. The emperor wrote a covering letter in which

---

[1] Sublimiter a Deo exaltati inperatoris Romani. Werm., p. 523.
[2] *Ib*. pp. 525–526.   [3] *Ib*. pp. 527–429.
[4] Scientibus pro pia memoria nescientibus vero pro doctrina utiles erant. *Ib*. p. 531.
[5] Herenam videlicet cum filio tam pestifera inlusione decipiens. *Ib*. p. 532.
[6] *Ib*. p. 532.

he asked the two bishops to select the most suitable passages, for choice those which gave clearest indication of general agreement and those the Pope will be unable to reject. He advises them that they must not force the Pope into any irrevocable decision by undue opposition ; rather they must make any concessions that will bring him to the side of moderation. They must make things better, not worse. If they fail and the Pope expresses a wish to send envoys to Greece, they are to ask permission for Frankish envoys to accompany those of the Pope, and inform Lewis at once, in order that Halitgar and Amalarius may be despatched on the mission.[1]

The two bishops revised the collection of authorities.[2] They proceeded to Rome with a letter to the Pope from Lewis and Lothair.[3] In this the Frankish Emperors said that they realised the duty of assisting the Church's pastors, and they now submitted the result of the inquiry, permission to hold which they had previously sought from the Pope. They hoped he would confer with the bishops who brought the letters, and in no sense suppose that the Emperors were attempting to teach him. Their one desire was that the Pope should endeavour to bring peace into Greece, and if he sent an embassy thither he would graciously permit them to send one with it, in no disparagement but to assist the others.

There complete darkness falls. Nothing is known of the attitude of the Pope or of the events that followed. Halitgar and another Frank, the destined envoys, apparently were sent to Constantinople,[4] but again their purpose is unknown. It can only be conjectured that the Pope Eugenius saw no reason to depart from the decisions of Hadrian, and was not greatly concerned with Constantinople. So ends the Frankish share in the Iconoclastic struggle. The last incident was no more than an attempt to settle the problem in Constantinople. It had no reference to the Frankish Church. Lewis continued the rôle affected by Charles, that of the disinterested spectator trying to compose a quarrel between two other people.

[1] Werm., pp. 532, 533.
[2] The revision is probably the Epitome of the Libellus of the Council of Paris designated E by Werminghoff, pp. 535 *sqq*.
[3] *Ib.* pp. 533, 534.
[4] *Vit. Hlud. pii.*, M.G.H., II, p. 631.

The Papacy was already giving signs of an equally traditional attitude, that of maintaining a settlement long ago accepted by the see of Peter, which others futilely regarded as still open.

APPENDIX TO CHAPTER XIII

ON THE AUTHORITIES COLLECTED BY THE COUNCIL OF PARIS

The patristic authorities collected by the Council of Paris are in two versions. The earlier [1] represents the collection as made by the Council. It consists of 76 passages arranged under heads, followed by 44 not arranged, and in some cases repeating citations already made in the first group. Apparently there is a lacuna at the end of the 44 from which further extracts have disappeared.[2] The second version [3] represents the material revised by the bishops Jeremy and Jonas and sent to the Pope. It consists of 53 passages ; two of them do not appear in the former collection, but they may have been in the section believed to be lost.[4] Western authorities like Augustine preponderate, and the subject is treated both more exhaustively and more intelligently than in the East. The definite theses illustrated are :

(i) That pictures should not be attacked, whether displayed in buildings or on the sacred vessels.[5]

(ii) That it is improper to offer worship to images.[6]

All the important passages of the Western theologians are in the collection, like Paulinus of Nola in praise of painting,[7] Gregory the Great on the affair of Serenus of Marseilles,[8] as well as many from Eastern sources. There is a marked avoidance of the less authentic writings and legends to which Nicæa appealed. Principles are emphasised in a way quite strange to the controversial method of Constantinople. St. Augustine [9] is quoted, for example, as saying that what is made

---

[1] Werm., pp. 484–520.

[2] *Ib.* p. 520.

[3] *Ib.* 535–550.

[4] They are (i), p. 541, a passage from John Chrysostom otherwise unknown, said to be from *Hom. XII on Ep. to Heb.* ; (ii) p. 543, Aug., *de Civ. Dei*, VII, 27, 2.

[5] Werm., pp. 485 *sqq.*, 535 *sqq.*

[6] *Ib.* pp. 489 *sqq.*, 547 *sqq.*

[7] *Ib.* p. 486.

[8] *Ib.* p. 488.

[9] *Ib.* p. 493. Aug., *de quant. anim.* 2.

by man is mortal and not like God's creation immortal, and this is applied as a principle against the desire of the Nicene Council to make images a necessary mediation. Broadly the position supported is that of the *Caroline Books*. The following is a list of the citations :

(*a*) signifies that the passage was also cited as an authority in the East.

Third Century

Origen (189–254).
Hom. 8 in Ex. 20 . . . . . . Werm., p. 490
Hom. 6 in Ex. 15 . . . . . . 541, 491
Expl. Ep. Paul ad Rom. 1 : 1 . . . . 545, 495
Lactantius (250–330).
Inst. Div. I. 20 : 20–24 . . . . . 542, 491
ib. II, 6 : 1, 17 : 9, 18 : 1, 18 : 2–3, 3–7 . . 542, 492

Fourth Century

Eusebius (265–340).
(*a*) Hist. Eccl. VII, 15 . . . . . 484, 536
ib. IX, 9 . . . . 502, 550
Athanasius (295–373).
Quæst. ad Antioch. 39 510
de Incarn. Verb. Dei 1 and 14 513
(*a*) Or. 3 adv. Arian. 1 and 5 516
Epiphanius (320–403).
Unknown source 510
(*a*) ad Johann. (*Hier.* Ep. 51) . . . 498, 547
Basil (330–379).
(*a*) de Spir. Sanct. 18 : 45 510
(*a*) Hom. XIX in XL martyr. 2 . . . . *ib.*
(*a*) *ps.-Basil*. Ep. 360 . . . . . . *ib.*
Ambrose (333–397).
(*a*) de Incarn. dom. sacr. 7 : 75 513
ps.-Ambrose, Comm. in ep. Rom. Amb. app. 33 . 493, 543
ib. Comm. in ep. 1 Cor. *ib.* 138 . . 498, 548
Gregory of Nyssa (335–394).
(*a*) Serm. in Abrah (not extant).. . . 538, 486, 513
(*a*) another passage (not extant) . . 486, 513
Jerome (342–420).
Comm. in Daniel 3 : 18 . . . . . 541, 491
Comm. in Ez. 8 : 11 . . . . . 542, 491
Comm. in Jer. 9 : 14 . . . . . 547, 497
Quæst. Heb. in Gen. 47 : 31 499
John Chrysostom (344–407). . . .
Hom. 1 de cruc. 1 : 48 . . . . . 504, 549
(*a*) unknown 510
Hom. xii Ep. Heb. (otherwise unknown) . . 541
ps.-Chrys. Hom. in 50 Ps. (Op. V. 572) . . 485, 537
ib. Serm. in ven. cruc. (Op. II, 812) . . *ib.*

CHAPTER XIV

ICONOCLASM AND THE FRANKS—(ii) THE AFFAIR OF CLAUDIUS OF TURIN

(a) AUTHORITIES

1. Claudius of Turin. His own writings against images have not survived, but fragments are preserved by Dungal and by Jonas of Orleans. His affair is the basis of the treatment of the image-controversy in all the following :
2. Dungal Reclusus. *Responsa contra perversas Cl. Taurin. ep. sententias.* M.P.L., 105.
3. Agobard, *Liber contra eorum superstitionem qui picturis et imaginibus sanctorum adorationis obsequium deferendum putant.* M.P.L., 104.
4. Jonas Aurelianensis Ep. *De cultu imaginum libri iii.* M.P.L., 106.
5. Walafrid Strabo. *De exordiis et incrementis quarumdam in observationibus ecclesiasticis rerum.* M.G.H. Leges II, Capit. regum Franc., II, ed. Krause, pp. 473 *sqq.*
6. Hincmar of Rheims. His writings on Iconoclasm have disappeared ; all the available information is contained in Hincmar, *Opus lv adv. Hincmar Laud*, Ch. 20, in M.P.L. 126, and in Flodoard, *Hist. Eccles. Remens.*, III, 29, in M.P.L. 135.

(b) MODERN WRITERS

The best accounts are, as for Ch. XIII, those of Neander and articles in Hauck, R.E.

A LL Western discussion of the image controversy had been academic, the expression of outside opinion on the affairs of Constantinople. But there arose about the time of the synod of Paris a purely Western outbreak of Iconoclasm, which produced a large quantity of controversial writing and some considerable stir. At first sight it would seem attractive to connect this affair with the investigations conducted by the synod of Paris. But on examination this proves not to be the case. The whole episode was connected with Claudius of Turin, and he in his turn represents the influence not of Eastern theology but of the Adoptianism of Spain. At the same time the ideas of Claudius may be traced ultimately to the same Asiatic monotheism as the Iconoclasm of the East. It reached Claudius through the Mohammedans of Spain, who may be considered indirectly responsible for the theology underlying Adoptianism. The Spanish authors of that heresy seem to have been seeking to present a pure and rational Christianity in the face of Moslem criticism. From those teachers Claudius learnt the views which he himself developed. So that we have the interesting phenomenon of another stream of Iconoclastic development virtually independent of the main channel.

Claudius was of Spanish origin and had been a pupil of the greatest of the Adoptianists, Felix of Urgel. The character of Adoptianism it is beyond our province to examine. It originated in Spain and was a rationalistic Christology, Nestorian or even Arian in spirit. Felix of Urgel was its most persistent advocate and was the main instrument in bringing it into contact with the Franks ; his see town of Urgel was in the Spanish mark which was added to the Frankish dominions in 780. Though Claudius was a favourite pupil of Felix, he apparently was regarded as orthodox.[1] He appeared at the court of the Aquitanian kings in 811, and about 816 was made bishop of Turin by Lewis because of his skill in expounding the gospel, in which the Italians were greatly deficient.[2] From the few writings of Claudius that have survived it is apparent that his theology was a highly developed Augustinianism, the closest affinities with which are to be sought in the theologians of the Reformation.[3] The condition of his new diocese roused in Claudius something like horror. The devotion of the Italians to images was particularly revolting to him, a fact which confirms what we have seen already,

---

[1] Jonas says that he was an Arian (*de cult.*, 308a), but the charge lacks evidence, and Cave is probably right when he says " id ex invidia aut disputationis æstu profectum crediderim." *Script. Eccl. Hist. Litt.*, II, p. 16.

[2] Jonas, *de cult.*, 306b.

[3] Epistolæ primæ Pauli apostoli quam misi quia tota inde agitur ut merita hominum tollat unde maxime nunc monachi gloriantur et gratiam Dei commendat. *Præf. in comm. ad ep. S. Paul.* M.P.L. civ., 840b. Gratia autem est quia nullo merito nec opere salvamur. *Expos. Ep. ad Phil.*, *ib.* 912d. Augustinum assumit . . . Hieronymum maxime præ ceteris exprobat. Dungal, 480a.

that the Franks paid little attention to the use of pictorial representations.[1] Claudius accordingly began a single-handed attack on the images throughout his diocese,[2] removing them with his own hands. Nor did his zeal stop there. The cross also fell under his censure as well as such established Catholic practices as the invocation of saints, penitential pilgrimages to Rome, the honour of the Apostolic see, and the monastic life.[3] Eventually even the friends of Claudius outside the diocese took alarm. One of them, Theodemir, abbot of Psalmody in the diocese of Nismes, to whom Claudius had dedicated many of his writings, considered the theology of Claudius' *Commentaries on St. Paul's Epistles to the Corinthians* so reprehensible [4] that he brought it to the notice of the authorities. Claudius protested, and Theodemir replied with definite charges. In answer Claudius wrote an *Apologeticum atque Rescriptum adversus Theutmirum Abbatem*. This was the work in which Claudius' Iconoclastic doctrine was set out. It was extant in 1461 in a MS. in the monastery of Bobbio, which has now disappeared, and apparently as late as 1608 it was known to Papirius Masson, the editor of Dungal. A few fragments alone survive, preserved in the writings of Dungal and Jones.[5] It was a book of considerable length, far longer than the Psalter.[6] It was very intemperately written.[7] Indeed, the tone and temper of Claudius are indicative of a mind neither conciliatory nor constructive. He failed to be reasonable, says Jonas, in correcting his flock, with the result that he caused offence and made himself unpopular.[8] He called his opponents

---

[1] Superstitiosæ imo perniciosæ imaginum adorationi . . . ex inolita consuetudine deditum esse. Jonas, 310d. Cf. Dungal, 460d. The official Papal view of the Frankish attitude may be seen in the preface of Anastasius to the Acta of Nicæa. He says that some Gauls did not accept images quibus utique nondum est harum utilitas revelata. Mansi, XII, 983.

[2] Dungal, 460d.

[3] *Ib.* 459 *sqq.*

[4] Pervenit ad manus meas epistola ex Aquis . . . qualiter tu librum tractatus mei quem tibi ante biennium præstiti in epistolas ad Cor. episcoporum iudicio atque optimatum damnandum ad eundem iam dictum palatium præsentari feceris, quem tractatum ibidem non damnandum sed scribendum amici mei non solum humaniter sed etiam amabiliter susceperunt. Claud., *Quæst. xxx super libr. Reg.*, 811a.

[5] Collected in M.P.L., 105, 459 *sqq.* The date was after the death of Pope Paschal (824) and during the Papacy of Eugenius, before 827, when Dungal wrote his reply, 468b.

[6] Jonas, 312c.   [7] *Ib.* 313.   [8] *Ib.* 311a.

limbs of the devil,[1] described the churches of Italy as filled
with the filth of offerings and with images,[2] and designated
the worship of saints as a worship of demons.[3] A council
of bishops (called perhaps in response to Theodemir's
appeal for an investigation of the doctrine of Claudius) he
called a congregation of asses and refused to attend.[4]
Pope Paschal was the Scribe and Pharisee sitting in Moses'
seat.[5] Claudius accepted those of the Fathers that suited
his purpose and treated with contempt those whose faith
and doctrine he rejected. Augustine was his chief favourite,
Jerome his chief dislike.[6] The clumsy and ungrammatical
style of his writing which is self-evident in his surviving
work, is noticed by Jonas, himself one of the most reasonable
and pleasant of scholars. The conclusion that may be
drawn from the style of Claudius is that he wrote in a
violent temper. The *Apologeticum* appeared about 825–827,
the period of the synod of Paris, but it had no apparent
relation to that assembly, nor any connection with the
controversy in the East. Dungal wrote his reply in 827.[7]
But no penal measures were taken against Claudius, and he
apparently continued his Protestant activities up to the
date of his death (circa 840), when he left a party of disciples
behind, marked by Arian as well as Iconoclastic tendencies.
It was sufficiently strong to make Jonas, archbishop of
Orleans, think it worthy of refutation in a reply to the
Apologeticum of Claudius.[8]

The contents of Claudius' polemic were as follows :[9]

(i) Pictures and images. He says that when he came
to Turin, he found all the churches, contrary to order,
filled with images which every one worshipped (colebant).
Accordingly he began to destroy them single-handed, and
had not the Lord helped him all men would have swallowed
him up quick. The second commandment forbade not
only the gods of the heathen but any pictorial representation
that may be devised by human intelligence. If images are

---

[1] Membra diaboli. Jonas, 313b.
[2] Sordibus anathematum et imaginibus. *Ib.* 315b. Jonas understood
anathemata as " accursed things," but perhaps Claudius' word only means
" votive offerings."
[3] Dæmonum cultum. *Ib.* 325d.   [4] Dungal, 529a.
[5] *Ib.* 464c.   [6] *Ib.* 480a.
[7] He gives the date as two years after the synod of Paris, 468b.
[8] Jonas, 307a.   [9] Dungal, 459 *sqq.*

T

admittedly not gods but representations of saints, there can be no veneration of them without assigning to them the honour due to God. Such would be a worshipping of the creature rather than the Creator. Man was made by God upright to look up to heaven, not to crawl with body bent earthward towards the image.

(ii) The Cross. Devotion to the cross is devotion to that object in our Lord's life which unbelievers credit who believe nothing of the resurrection. It suggests belief only in a suffering Christ. Remember the Apostle : " Though we have known Christ after the flesh, yet now know we him no more." [1] If the cross is venerated, why not venerate all that touched the Lord, virgin wombs, stables, swaddling clothes, ships, the ass, lambs, lions,[2] stones,[3] thorns, and spears. God bade us bear the Cross, not venerate it.

(iii) Intercession of saints. God said Noah, Daniel, and Job should save neither son nor daughter. That settles the intercession of the saints.

(iv) Penitential journeys to Rome and the Apostolic see. It is apostolic teaching and not succession to an apostolic see that constitutes an apostolic church.

The earliest reply to Claudius is that of Dungal. Dungal was an Irish monk,[4] one of those learned men that the mediæval Irish church sent to the continent of Europe. He was sent to Pavia by Lothair to organise the schools, and became the chief of the teachers of Italy (circa 823). He was thus at close quarters with Claudius, and his reply to the Iconoclasm of Claudius followed closely upon the original polemic.[5] Dungal's treatise bears the title *Dungali responsa contra perversas Cl. Taurin. Ep. sententias.* It is marked by great learning, but is rather crabbed and heavy. The basis of his argument is that the opinions of the council of Paris in 825 showed conclusively that divine honour was not paid to saints or images or indeed to anything but God. The authorities are Gregory to Serenus of Marseilles, Paulinus of Nola, and Gregory of Nyssa.[6]

---

[1] Notice this new application of the favourite Iconoclastic text.
[2] From the designation of Christ as the Lion of the tribe of Judah.
[3] From the rocky tomb.
[4] He is usually designated " reclusus," which may imply that before his active life he had been a hermit.
[5] It was written in 827. Dungal, 468b.   [6] *Ib.* 468–470.

Dungal thus maintains the orthodox tradition of refuting Iconoclasm by appealing to authorities. The prohibition of images he says was removed as soon as God felt that the people would use them to his honour, as is shown in the cherubim and the brazen serpent.[1] He quotes the authorities cited by the Council of Paris to show that neither the pictures nor the relics of the saints are venerated as God, nor is sacrifice offered to them. They are venerated in God and the divine help is sought through their intercession.[2] As to the cross, the text cited by Claudius, If we have known Christ after the flesh, etc., is entirely inappropriate. " The flesh " means corruption and mortality. It would be far more appropriate to quote, God forbid that I should glory save in the cross of our Lord Jesus Christ.[3] "Holy angel, holy man, or holy cross we venerate and worship for a variety of merits, that is to say, we humbly honour, love, and embrace them because of God, and in God in a far different fashion from that in which we worship and venerate God himself." [4] The main topic of Dungal's book is the cross. In defending the adoration of it he elaborates all the traditional patristic arguments. The cross is prefigured in the Old Testament in the wood laid upon Isaac [5] and in the sign Tau in Ezekiel.[6] The thread let down by Rahab signifies the blood of the cross.[7] St. Paul's " length and breadth and height " is the cross, as is the sign of the son of man in heaven (Matt. xxiv. 29).[8] The argument of Dungal finally loses itself in this kind of exegesis. Paul saved 276 souls in the shipwreck, and after he has begun to be with Christ, is he going to shut his lips and be silent for those who throughout the world have believed through his gospel? [9] Dungal reveals himself as a man of great learning according to the standard of the day, but he hardly comes to grips with the rationalistic arguments of Claudius.

Dungal's reply was unofficial. The official answer, composed probably at the request of the Emperor, is that of Jonas, bishop of Orleans (821–843). We have already

---

[1] Dungal, 471a. [2] *Ib.* 472b–476b.
[3] *Ib.* 478a. [4] *Ib.* 481c. [5] *Ib.* 486d.
[6] *Ib.* 488d. Ezek. ix. 4. The Tau is a reading of the OL preserved by Tertullian (*de jej.* 11). It is not in the Greek text of LXX, but in Aquila's and Theodotion's versions.
[7] Dungal, 488a. [8] *Ib.* 487b, 490c. [9] *Ib.* 498b.

met him at the Council of Paris and as the fellow-delegate
of Jeremy of Sens to Pope Eugenius. His book against
Claudius, *de Cultu Imaginum libri tres*, is dated 840.
Jonas was engaged in writing it when news of the death
of Claudius reached him and he abandoned his plan.
But on hearing that Claudius had left disciples he resumed
his work.[1] The tone of Jonas is extremely courteous and
kindly, his position so moderate, that Baronius is constrained
to enter a warning against his inadequate orthodoxy.[2]
He represents well the Frankish tradition on the image
question. He dissents from Claudius not on principle but
on method. Claudius ought to have followed the advice
of Serenus of Marseilles or the example of St. Paul, who at
Athens did not overthrow the idols with which he found
the city filled.[3] Instead of attacking the abuses of Italy in
intemperate language, he ought to have reasoned with the
ignorance of the people.[4] The argument of Claudius based
on the second commandment is improperly applied to the
pictures of saints.[5] The pictures like the golden Cherubim
and Solomon's oxen and lions were never intended to be
objects of worship. The word " adoro " is equivocal, for it is
used indiscriminately for all kinds of veneration.[6] Jonas
agrees that the view current in the East is untenable, for it
implies a divinity inherent in the picture.[7] But he finds
the language of Claudius exaggerated. The veneration
of saints is not a worship of demons or idolatry. Those
who pay this veneration believe in the Trinity.[8] Relics
of saints should not be compared to bodies of beasts, stones,
and wood. It is well to recollect the piety with which
Christians have always sought out the corpses of martyrs
and the miracles they have worked.[9] The same spirit of
exaggeration is shown by Claudius in complaining that

[1] Jonas, 307ab.
[2] Non tamen e castris ecclesiæ orthodoxæ a qua errore pristino ex parte
dissentit militavit. Bar. ad ann. 825.
[3] Jonas, 311a.   [4] *Ib.* 315d.
[5] It is worthy of notice that the Frankish discussion almost always turns
on pictures of saints. Representations of Christ were probably very un-
common among the Franks.
[6] Jonas, 318, 319. Aug., *de civ. Dei*, X, 1, and other passages cited in
support.
[7] Non putamus imagini quam adoramus aliquid inesse divinum sed
tantummodo pro honore cuius effigies est tali eam veneratione adoramus.
Ib. 325c.
[8] *Ib.* 326.   [9] *Ib.* 328.

veneration to the cross is the mark of an obsession with the Passion of Christ. The cross is traditional everywhere, in the church and in its service books. Among other examples Bede's narrative is quoted in which Augustine is described landing in England with a silver cross and the picture of Christ. The special honour paid to the cross and not to the ass and other objects named by Claudius is based on the special significance given to the cross both in the Old Testament and the New Testament, a significance not given to the other objects. It is not to the cross itself that the honour is paid but to him who won his victory on the cross.[1] As to the pilgrimages to Rome their value lies in the motive with which they are undertaken.[2]

That the moderate attitude of Jonas was the official one in the Frankish church is shown by three other conspicuous writers of the period, who deal with the image question in a more general fashion, without exclusive reference to the views of Claudius. These are Agobard, bishop of Lyons, Hincmar, bishop of Rheims, and the monk Walafrid Strabo.

Agobard, who was born in 779, after some time spent as a child in Spain, returned to Gaul in 783 and became bishop of Lyons (814/816), dying about 840. He was a liberal of enlightened views who took a definite stand against the judicial practices of the ordeal and trial by combat. His views on the image question are indicated by the title of his book, *Liber contra eorum superstitionem qui picturis et imaginibus sanctorum adorationis obsequium deferendum putant.* There is no internal evidence of the occasion which called forth this document. The absence of any reference to particular events would suggest that it ante-dated the activity of Claudius. It most probably originated from the discussions of the Council of Paris in 825. Agobard takes the second commandment for his text, and argues definitely against the legitimacy of any kind of cult of images. The invisible and incorporeal are superior to the visible ; the man of faith must pass from the flesh to the soul, from the body to the spirit, from the visible to the invisible, from the world to God. The body and flesh are inferior to the soul and spirit, still more inferior are the creations of human and carnal pride, among which are to be included the sacrilegiously styled holy images ; for some are foolish

[1] Jonas, 332–342.   [2] *Ib.* 368.

enough to attribute sanctity to images devoid of soul.[1]
If converts from the worship of demons are required to
venerate the images, they will think that they have not
abandoned idols but changed their form.[2] The preservation of ancient representations like the Paneas group
are due to affectionate recollection and not any religious
sentiment.[3] The sensible gives a false impression, as St.
Augustine shows (*de ver. relig.*, 25, 33, 34, 55), which is the
danger that is involved in the use of pictures.[4] Human
creation expresses the minimum and not the maximum of
man. The veneration of the living man would be preferable to that of his representation.[5] The picture may be
contemplated as a mere lifeless picture and the eye may
be fed by the sight of it. Veneration of God is paid by the
mind alone.[6] A canon of the Council of Elvira shows that
the ancients had pictures, but their purpose was historical,
not for worship.[7] Nor will it serve to say that it is the
saints and not their pictures that are venerated, for that is
derogatory to Christ, who has an honour no man or angel
can claim.[8]

Hincmar, archbishop of Rheims (845–882), celebrated
for his predestinarian controversy with Gottschalk, also
issued a brief statement on the image question. This work
of Hincmar has not survived. The exact occasion and
date of it cannot therefore be determined. But it was after
the affair of Claudius, and the relation of Hincmar to the
Emperor, indicates that it represented the official Frankish
view. It was partly metrical,[9] and presumably therefore
for popular instruction. It maintained the moderate
position of Jonas, for it spoke of the Greek Iconoclasts and
image-worshippers as two extremes of error and referred
with approval to the *Libri Carolini*.[10]

Considerably earlier (circa 840/842) the moderate

---

[1] Agobard, *op cit.*, 212c.
[2] *Ib.* 215a. Puto quod videretur eis non tam idola reliquisse quam simu-
lacra mutasse. Again, it is the representations of the saints and not of Christ
that are in evidence.
[3] *Ib.* 215b.   [4] *Ib.* 220a.
[5] *Ib.* 222d.   [6] *Ib.* 225b.
[7] *Ib.* 226a.   [8] *Ib.* 226d.
[9] Scripsit etiam librum flagitantibus cœpiscopis fratribus suis qualiter
imagines salvatoris vel sanctorum ipsius venerandæ sint cum epilogo quodam
metrice digesto. Flod., *Hist. Eccl. Remens.*, III, 29.
[10] Hinc. Rem., *contra Hincm. Laud.*, 20.

position had been stated from the point of view of the scholar and ecclesiologist by the Benedictine monk Walafrid Strabo, subsequently abbot of Reichenau.[1] His view is the same as those already noticed, the *via media* between image-worship and Iconoclasm.[2] The examples of Moses (in the cherubim) and Solomon (in the animal representations in the Temple) show that the commandments do not refer to such pictures and images as are not intended to receive the worship due to God, such as those made to reveal a mystery (*e.g.* in the building of the ark and the temple), or to commemorate incidents or to stimulate the love of the spectators (*e.g.* the pictures of Christ and his saints). To condemn pictures simply because some give them mis-guided worship is no wiser than to condemn God for making the works of Nature which some worship.[3] Iconoclasm Walafrid designates a " so-called heresy," [4] the Greeks he considers have been refuted by the Emperor Lewis in synod.[5] Claudius of Turin, like his name, halts in the way of truth.[6] Had he trampled on the Emperor's image on a coin he would soon have awakened the Emperor's resentment. Decent and reasonable honour is not to be refused to the images, for if we destroy pictures we ought logically to destroy churches on the ground that God dwelleth not in temples made with hands.[7] Pictures are the letters of the illiterate.[8] Images and pictures therefore are to be retained with the proviso that they are not to be venerated in a way that is contrary to the Faith or that leads to the material superseding the spiritual.[9]

The Western image controversy was an episode of the Carolingian age.

(i) The Frankish attitude was partly accidental, the result of Charles's jealousy of the Greeks. It was main-tained under royal influence. Jonas, Agobard, Walafrid Strabo, even Claudius, were protégés of the Crown.

---

[1] In his *De exordiis et incrementis quarumdam in observationibus ecclesiasticis rerum*. He was born circa 809, and was at one time tutor to the son of Lewis the Pious.

[2] Earum (sc. imaginum) varietas nec quodam cultu immoderato colenda est ut quibusdam stultis videtur nec iterum speciositas ita est quodam despectu calcanda ut quidam vanitatis assertores existimant. *Op. cit.*, p. 482.

[3] *Ib.*   [4] Supradictam ut dixerunt hæresim. *Ib.*

[5] P. 483. The synod of Paris.

[6] *Ib.* Claudius from the root claud-.   [7] *Ib.*

[8] *Ib.* p. 484. Pictura est quædam litteratura illiterato.   [9] *Ib.*

272   *A History of the Iconoclastic Controversy*

(ii) Partly it was racial and temperamental. The Franks and North-Western Europe generally had not inherited the Græco-Roman civilisation with its artistic bent. Its affection for things was fixed on relics rather than on pictorial representation.

(iii) Western Europe passed through no such Christological crisis as the East had faced. The image question in the East was a Christological side issue. The representation of Christ scarcely entered into the Western discussion. In Italy alone did the Eastern idea hold its ground, because much of Italy was more akin to the East than to the West.

But even the Pope took singularly little notice of the Frankish attitude. Claudius carried out his campaign in Turin while the Pope remained silent. Everything points to one conclusion, that, outside of the spheres in which the Christological controversy had been fought to an issue, pictures and images were objects doctrinally insignificant.

When the learning of the Carolingian age faded, pictures and images increased, and a superstitious reverence gathered round them. Rarely were these representations of our Lord. The Virgin and the saints were provided with local cults, often in succession to ancient pagan gods, and their images were endowed with powers often again inherited from pagan predecessors. A system of helpers and intercessors thus grew up, partly connected with external objects like images, and it was at this system that the Reformation struck. It would be a mistake, however, to trace any direct connection either in fact or in spirit between the Iconoclasm of the eighth and ninth centuries and the Reformation. The Reformation was a campaign not only against images but against the thing suggested by the images. The image was to the Reformer a symbol of a more offensive object behind. The Greek Iconoclast was primarily concerned with the picture of Christ. He attacked the image not as a symbol of Christ but as a false symbol of Christ, a false symbol because inducing a wrong idea of what Christ was. Representations of saints were only a side issue in the Greek controversy. Their argument was : Christ ought not to be depicted, a fortiori the saints ought not to be depicted. Western Europe was more nearly in the situation of the sixteenth century. Representations of saints were the more real issue to them. But they did not depreciate the veneration of images of the saints because they desired to destroy a cult of the saints. It is here that the compromise of the Frankish attitude is logically assailable. With the exception of Claudius all the Franks were satisfied with this common-sense compromise which made no attempt to come down to first principles. They never passed beyond the sentimental view that pictures are instructive to the illiterate. They ignored the inevitable development. Granted the existence of pictures of the saints and the doctrine of the helping power of the saints either by intercessions or directly, a mutual association of the two must soon arise. It would be too large an assumption to represent Claudius as conscious of this. But he was logically consistent in making the repudiation of the intercession of the saints part of his theology. Coupled with his advanced Augustinianism this view of Claudius gives him a claim which must be denied to the rest of the Iconoclasts of having at least curious affinities with the sixteenth-century reformers. But of the whole controversy in Western Europe the most that can be said is that it was an illuminating exhibition of the independence of thought and intellectual life of the infant Frankish church. But the Frankish movement left little, if any, permanent mark on Christendom.

APPENDIX

The Iconoclasts and the Paulicians

It has been argued by F. C. Conybeare that a connection existed between Iconoclasm and the Paulicians. He even goes so far as to call the Paulicians the extreme left wing of the Iconoclasts.[1] There do not seem to be any real grounds for connecting the two movements. The exact character of Paulicianism remains obscure. It was clearly an anti-ecclesiastical movement, and preserved elements from Marcion, Manichæanism, and even from primitive Adoptianism.[2] We are concerned only to examine its alleged relationship with Iconoclasm.

1. Doctrinal resemblances.

(a) The Paulicians repudiated the use of images.

" Your father the evil one, who gave you this law, namely to baptise unbelievers [i.e. infants], to worship images, to make silver and gold into the form of an image . . . [some words erased] . . . and to adore the same, to pry into the sins of men and women, to explore the same and grant remission. . . ."[3]

" Concerning the mediation of our Lord Jesus Christ and not of any other holy ones either of the dead or of stones or of crosses and images.[4]

" Some have . . . followed after dead things and in especial after images, stones, crosses, waters, trees, fountains . . . as they admit and worship them, so they offer incense and candles and present victims, all of which are contrary to the Godhead." [5]

(b) The Virgin.

" After the birth they [i.e. evangelists] call her a wife and utterly deny her virginity." [6]

Christ denied any particular blessedness to his mother in Luke xi. 27.[7]

---

[1] Conybeare, Key of Truth, p. cvi.
[2] Conybeare makes the last the dominant characteristic of the Paulicians. The Paulician manual Key of Truth (ed. Conybeare, Oxford, 1898) clearly demonstrates the existence of Adoptianism in the Paulician theology, but Conybeare over-emphasises it.
[3] Key of Truth, p. 86.   [4] Ib. p. 115.
[5] Ib. p. 115.   [6] Ib. p. 113.   [7] Ib.

275

(c) Monks.

The monastic habit is described as one of the disguises of Satan.[1]

In these three points, it is true, there is a resemblance to the position of some of the Iconoclasts. But the resemblance is remarkably incomplete. With images the Paulicians forbade the cross, to which the Iconoclasts were curiously attached. Constantine Copronymus alone rejected the orthodox view of the Virgin, and not even Copronymus attacked monks as such. Paulicianism rejected the whole ecclesiastical system. To none of its really characteristic doctrines does Iconoclasm show any affinities. It is true that Conybeare finds in the incident that happened at the baptism of Constantine a symbolical declaration that like the Paulicians he rejected the doctrine of infant baptism. But there is not the slightest evidence that he did so. Conybeare's unsupported explanation is too fantastic to be seriously entertained. Iconoclasm further knows nothing of Adoptianist Christology. It is indeed at the opposite extreme, Monophysite. There are no signs among the Iconoclasts of the Paulician single order of ministry nor of their sacramental and anti-ecclesiastical doctrine. It is hardly, therefore, too much to say that a doctrinal connection between the Paulicians and Iconoclasm is practically non-existent.

2. Facts and incidents that might imply a connection.

(i) Paulicianism was an Armenian sect. The Iconoclastic emperors came from the Eastern frontier of the Empire. This fact alone would mean nothing.

(ii) The third leader of the Paulicians, Gegnæsius, was summoned to Constantinople by Leo the Isaurian in 717 on the occasion of a schism in the sect, was examined by the Patriarch Germanus, whom he satisfied by equivocal answers, and obtained a safe conduct home.[2] None of the chroniclers of the Isaurian period record the incident. So that no importance attached to it, nor does it seem likely that Leo was able to find in Gegnæsius encouragement for the views on images that he had not yet formulated, if he had even conceived them.

(iii) Once or twice the chroniclers apply the name Paulician to the Iconoclasts. George the Monk calls Constantine Copronymus a Paulician. But the context shows that the name is simply an epithet of abuse. " He was not a Christian (God forbid) but a Paulician, or to speak more truly and fitly an idolater, a worshipper of devils. "[3] Theophanes gives the same title to

[1] *Key of Truth*, chh. viii and ix. Other persons including bishops and apostles are also so described.
[2] Photius, contr. Manich., I, 54, 56.
[3] Georg. Mon., II, p. 751.

the leaders of the revolt against Michael Rhangabe. "They appeared to be Christians but were really Paulicians."[1] The meaning of such passages is rather that the Iconoclasts were not Paulicians. The word is an epithet thrown at any heterodox person as was Manichæan both at this time and throughout the Middle Ages.

(iv) In 754 Constantine transplanted to Thrace Syrians and Armenians from Theodosiopolis and Melitene. "By these," says Theophanes, "the sect of the Paulicians was augmented."[2] We have seen that the character of these people is more correctly interpreted by George the Monk as Monophysites. The emperor Nicephorus was, according to Theophanes,[3] a warm friend of the Manichæans, "now called Paulicians." But Nicephorus, as we have seen, was not an Iconoclast. Elsewhere[4] Theophanes describes the Paulicians and Athingani as Iconoclasts, which they were, but the inference cannot be drawn, nor is it implied by Theophanes, that all Iconoclasts were Paulicians. The erroneous inference is due to "Iconoclast" being used in two senses. The Paulicians were Iconoclasts in the sense that among their tenets was rejection of the use of sacred pictures. They were not Iconoclasts in the sense of having any direct association with the heresy technically called Iconoclasm. The utmost that can be said confidently is that many Iconoclasts expelled from the Church joined the Paulicians. This would be the case in Asia and is indeed stated by the Armenian writer John of Oznun (circa 730).[5]

We may conclude therefore that Iconoclasm and Paulicianism had some common elements, but there is no inter-dependence between them. Paulicianism flourished mostly outside the frontiers of the Empire, but in the course of the Iconoclastic struggle it came into notice. Among the troops recruited on the Eastern frontier there would be Paulicians. Orthodox partisans found the name a useful term of abuse to apply to the Iconoclasts, especially once it was recognised that the Paulicians were in some way the heirs of the Manichæans.[6] The consequence was that at the final triumph of orthodoxy Theodora entered on a campaign against Paulicianism. George the Monk says that with the Iconoclasts were expelled the Manichæans their authors.[7] A campaign was carried out against them in Asia.[8]

[1] Theoph., 1005a.   [2] *Ib.* 865a ; Georg. Mon., II, p. 752.
[3] Theoph., 983a.   [4] *Ib.* 996a.
[5] *Key of Truth*, pp. lvii, lviii. Niceph.. *Antirrh.*, III, 502b, agrees that Iconoclasts joined the Manichæans (*i.e.* Paulicians).
[6] Cf. Niceph., *loc. cit.*   [7] Georg., II, p. 802.
[8] Cont. Theoph., 180c, who connects the campaign with a revolt of Carbeas, an officer of the Dux of the Anatolic theme, who professed Paulicianism. But Bury (*East. Rom. Emp.*, p. 277) shows that on the evidence of

Paulicianism found through Iconoclasm an appeal to some minds within the Empire, but we cannot press the connection further. The latest example within the Iconoclastic period is Zelix, the secretary of the Empress Theodora, who recanted after being implicated in a private heresy which appears to have been more Paulician than Iconoclastic, for it rejected the cross and designated Christ a creature.[1] We shall, therefore, conclude that the relationship between Iconoclasm and the Paulicians was never more than casual and accidental.

Act. XLII Martyr. Amor., γ 29, the affair of Carbeas should be placed in the reign of Theophilus or even in that of Leo V. While this does not deny Theodora's campaign, it is further evidence of the sporadic contact between Paulicianism and the army on the Eastern frontier.

[1] See Bonwetsch in R.E., XV, 53 ; Krumbacher, *Byz. Litt.*, p. 987.

TABLE OF RULERS

	EMPERORS	PATRIARCHS	WESTERN KINGS	POPES
715		Germanus (deposed)		Gregory II
717	Leo III the Isaurian			
729		Anastasius		
731				Gregory III
740	Constantine V Copronymus			
741				Zacharias
752			Pippin	Stephen (died 3 days after election)
753		Constantine II (deposed)		Stephen II or III
757				Paul I
765		Nicetas		
767				Constantine (Anti-pope)
768			Charles and Carlomann	Stephen III or IV
771			Charles (alone)	
772				Hadrian I
775	Leo IV the Khazar			
780	Constantine VI	Paul IV		
784		Tarasius		
795				Leo III
797	Irene			
800			Charles Emperor	
802	Nicephorus I			
806		Nicephorus (exiled)		
811	[Stauracius]			
811	Michael I Rhangabe			
813	Leo V the Armenian			
814			Lewis the Pious	
815		Theodotus		
816				Stephen IV or V
817				Pascal I

TABLE OF RULERS—*continued*

	EMPERORS	PATRIARCHS	WESTERN KINGS	POPES
820	Michael II the Stammerer			
821		Antony		
824				Eugenius
827				Valentinus
827				Gregory IV
829	Theophilus			
832		John VII (deposed)		
842	Michael III the Drunkard			
843		Methodius		
844				Sergius II

INDEX

Agobard (bishop of Lyons), 269
Alcuin, 229
Anastasius (Patriarch of Constantinople), 34, 42
Antony (Patriarch of Constantinople), 163, 202
Arianism, 135, 190, 263
Art, Christian, 18 *sqq.*
  miraculous elements in, 22, 29, 101
  iconoclastic developments, of, 63, 64, 220

Cæsaro-papism, 3, 10, 28, 33, 89, 124, 179, 203
Caroline Books, 225, 228 *sqq.*
Charles (Frankish King and Emperor), 83, 223 *sqq.*, 271
Christ, figures and pictures of, 21, 31, 65, 144
Christology. *See under* Monophysitism, etc.
Chronology, 12, 18 n., 33 n., 59, 202 n., 207 n.
Claudius of Turin, 226, 263 *sqq.*
Constantine V Copronymus (Emperor), 35, 39 *sqq.*, 69, 78, 111, 157, 210, 217, 274, 275
Constantine VI (Emperor), 86, 151
Constantine (Patriarch of Constantinople), 52, 60, 65
Councils of the Church :
  Bethlehem, 218
  Eighth General, 217
  Frankfort, 250
  Gentilly, 81
  Iconoclastic of 753..45 *sqq.*, 79
  Iconoclastic of 815..47, 171 *sqq.*, 184
  Nicæa, Second of (Seventh General), 16, 44, 92 *sqq.*, 223
  Paris, 230, 252, 257
  Quinisext, 20, 142
  Roman, 75, 77, 82

Dungal, 264, 266 *sqq.*

Eastern Church, Orthodox, 6, 11, 186, 218

Ecloga, 7, 17, 35
Epigrams, 129, 196, 210
Eucharist, the, 127, 181
Eugenius II (Pope), 204

Franks, 79 *sqq.*, 203, 222 *sqq.*, 271

George of Cyprus, 35, 53, 142
Germanus (Patriarch of Constantinople), 25, 29, 32, 41, 53, 112
Gregory II (Pope), 36, 48, 74, 115
Gregory III (Pope), 77

Hadrian I (Pope), 91, 224, 228 *sqq.*
Hagiology, 8 n., 14, 32 n., 160, 206
Heraclius (Emperor), 6
Hincmar of Rheims, 270

Iconoclasm :
  Asiatic character of, 34, 109
  authority for, 130 *sqq.*, 190, 193, 237 *sqq.*, 257
  effects of, 219, 273
  final collapse of, 215
  in West, 73 *sqq.*, 222 *sqq.*, 262 *sqq.*
  irrational character of, 4
  martyrs and persecution under, 53, 66, 174 *sqq.*, 210
  outbreak of, 18, 25
  resistance of monks to, 54, 63, 69, 174
  theology of, 111 *sqq.*, 184 *sqq.*
  treatment of Church buildings, 64, 106, 248
Image Worship :
  authority for, 83, 99, 131 *sqq.*, 164, 190, 194, 226 *sqq.*, 237 *sqq.*, 257
  character of, 116, 226
  restoration of, 215
Irene (Empress), 86, 151, 162, 224
Italy, 73 *sqq.*, 205, 263

John of Damascus, St., 14, 33, 35, 48, 53, 111, 116
John the Grammarian (Patriarch of Constantinople), 8, 163, 169, 188, 205, 207, 213

281   U

THE END